Penguin Education

Capital and Growth

Edited by G. C. Harcourt and N. F. Laing

Penguin Modern Economics Readings

General Editor
B. J. McCormick

Advisory Board
K. J. W. Alexander
R. W. Clower
G. R. Fisher
P. Robson
J. Spraos
H. Townsend

Capital and Growth

Selected Readings

Edited by G. C. Harcourt and N. F. Laing

Penguin Books

Penguin Books Ltd, Harmondsworth,
Middlesex, England
Penguin Books Inc., 7110 Ambassador Road,
Baltimore, Md 21207, U.S.A.
Penguin Books Australia Ltd,
Ringwood, Victoria, Australia

First published 1971
This selection copyright © G. C. Harcourt and N. F. Laing, 1971
Introduction and notes copyright © G. C. Harcourt and
N. F. Laing, 1971

Made and printed in Great Britain by
Richard Clay (The Chaucer Press) Ltd,
Bungay, Suffolk
Set in Monotype Times

Contents

Introduction[1]

Part I

Measuring the immeasurable[2]

Capital theory is notorious for the controversies with which it is
associated. They arise from two sources, ideology and difficulty,
so that both passions and understanding are involved (see
Solow, 1963b, pp. 9–13). The present selection of Readings is a
necessary (but not a sufficient) background to the latest outburst,
the brawls between Cambridge, England, and Cambridge, Massa-
chusetts, which have their origin in a famous article by Joan
Robinson which was written in 1953 (see Reading 1, pages 47–64).
(For a brawl by brawl description, see Harcourt, 1969.) We shall
for convenience, but loosely and dangerously, refer to the two
groups as the neo-Keynesians and the neo-neo-classicals respectively. The context of the debates is the reawakened interest in the
post-war period in the problems of economic growth and income
distribution over time, coupled with the clash of rival ideologies
as to how these problems are best tackled in both developing and
developed economies. Capital theory became relevant when the

1. This volume of Readings is jointly edited. We do, however, depart from
Marshall to this extent, that responsibility for errors, confusions and libels
in Part I of the Introduction is taken by G. C. Harcourt. Those in Part II
are the responsibility of N. F. Laing. The editors have widely divergent
views on the issues that are discussed in this volume – G.C.H. is proud to
wear the all-red colours of the neo-Keynesian club, while N.F.L. sports
with distinction those of the neo-neo-classicals. Nevertheless, like Malthus
and Ricardo (in this aspect alone, we modestly hasten to add), we remain
good friends. Many of the issues are both controversial and still unsettled.
We thought it best, therefore, to present two views in the Introduction,
despite some inevitable overlap, and to select Readings that were representative of both sides of the various issues. We leave the reader to make
up his own mind, on the basis of the evidence presented, which team to
support.

2. I am most grateful to my co-editor and to John Dixon, Masao Fuku-
oka, John Vaizey and R. H. Wallace for their comments on this and the
other sections of Part I of the Introduction.

problem of the choice of technique, and the explanation of distributive shares and of productivity change over time, both theoretically and empirically, were discussed. As there is already a selection of Readings on the theory of economic growth in the Penguin Modern Economics series (see Sen, 1970), the selections in this book are weighted heavily in favour of capital theory.

The opening rounds of the debate were concerned with an old problem, the search for a unit in which to measure (aggregate) social capital. The desired unit had to be independent of distribution and relative prices, so that it could be used, 'without arguing in a circle', in an explanation of production and distributive shares and prices set within the context of the neo-classical theoretical fiction of a stationary state (see Robinson, 1971; Wicksell, 1934). To both sides this has come to be thought of as a search for a will-o'-the-wisp, but for different reasons. To the neo-neo-classicals, the search, *as conducted by the other side*, represents a return to an old confusion, that between explanations based on prior cause and effect as opposed to those associated with systems of mutual determination of equilibrium values (see Reading 3, page 113). To the neo-Keynesians, the search bogs down in the impossibility of finding (outside the confines of a one, all-purpose commodity model) a unit which would serve two purposes *simultaneously*, one of which was to measure *physical* capital goods in order that their contribution to the production of national (or industrial) output might be assessed, usually by formal expression in an aggregate production function (in the sense of the relationship between aggregate output per head and aggregate capital per man). The other was to serve as a measure of the *value* of the capital *property* owned by the capitalist class, the ownership of which confers on the capitalists, if not the right, then the ability to take a share of the surplus created by the production process. (Both sides, therefore, feel that they have exposed the Achilles heel of the other.)

It was to a discussion of these puzzles that Joan Robinson's article was addressed. In her book, *The Accumulation of Capital* (1956), these puzzles are associated with her discussion of the choice of techniques, a problem that she regards as of secondary importance, though not of difficulty, in the context of growth. The main propositions of her book are established by use of a model in which there is only one technique available at any moment of time, an approach which is currently gaining wider acceptance (see Atkinson and Stiglitz, 1969). It should be noted that both prior to and alongside the developments here described, though unknown to many, Sraffa was writing a fundamental work of criticism of neo-classical analysis (see Reading 4, pages 125–30). *Production of Commodities by Means of Commodities* was published in 1960 but its central propositions were established in the mid-twenties. Joan Robinson, in particular, acknowledges her indebtedness to the hints of what was to come contained in Sraffa's introduction to *The Works and Correspondence of David Ricardo* (Sraffa with Dobb, 1950–55).

Drawing on Wicksell (1934), Joan Robinson proposed to measure capital in terms of dated labour time[3] (or 'real capital', as she dubbed it), a measure that, within the confines of a stationary state, solved the first problem in the sense of allowing capital to be related to output, but not the second. When capital is so measured, distributive prices and shares cannot be obtained by partially differentiating output with respect to the relevant factor supplies (in order to find prices) and then multiplying the given supplies by the marginal products (in order to give shares). Moreover, it is *intentionally* not a measure which is independent of distribution and prices. Champernowne's reaction (see Reading 2, pages 65–100) was to accept Joan Robinson's logic but to pine for the traditional neo-classical solutions. He worked within the same confines as Joan Robinson and the neo-classicals whom she was discussing, i.e. a stationary state (or a steady state) in which there is perfect competition; full employment; constant-returns-to-scale; sometimes, sometimes not, discrete technologies; and static, realized expectations concerning the future courses of factor and product prices. He provided the required dual purpose unit in a chain-index measure of capital. This measure allowed the impact of changes in the equilibrium values of the rates of profits and wages on the measurement of capital values in terms of commodities to be removed from the unit in which capital was measured when used in a production function. The values of the

3. i.e. inputs of labour weighted by exogenous rates of profits, suitably compounded to reflect the stages of production when the inputs occur (see Harcourt, 1969, p. 371).

capital per head associated with successive pairs of techniques were measured at common sets of rates of profits, r, and wages, w; the resulting ratios of values were chained, i.e. spliced, onto one another, so allowing reference back to a common base, even when r and w took on different values. This device permitted aggregate capital to serve the two purposes outlined above; but it should be noted that either w or r had to be known from elsewhere than within the production system itself. In order to avoid a multi-valued production function, in the sense of the same level of output being associated with two (or more) values of capital and r – a possibility due solely to the technical characteristics of production – Champernowne discovered, fully discussed (see Reading 2, pages 72, 75–7, 90–94) and then, by assumption and for convenience, dismissed from the analysis, the phenomenon which subsequently became known as *double-switching*, the possibility that the *same* technique may be the most profitable at two or more values of r, even though others are the more so at values in between.

Solow (1955–6), in commenting on Joan Robinson's article, provided some very stringent conditions whereby heterogeneous capital goods *could* be aggregated into a single index. However, he suggested that, in general, this aggregation was not on (rigorously) once we left the one, all-purpose commodity world of Ramsey (see 1928) and J. B. Clark (see 1889). In this world, the *same* physical commodity served three purposes: as a flow, it could be either consumed or saved (equals invested); as a stock, it was capital – and it could, of course, be measured in terms of its own physical unit; it could also be moulded, costlessly, painlessly and timelessly, into any form desired, i.e. it was malleable, so making possible the full employment of capital and labour at any moment of time and over time, even when technical progress was occurring.

It was this model which Swan used in the famous article (1956) which preceded his even more famous appendix (see Reading 3, pages 101–24), the latter being designed to keep off 'the index-number birds and Joan Robinson herself'. The strict logic of his growth model requires that capital be malleable. He justified the assumption, first, by his famous analogy of capital as Meccano sets that allow instant cross-section and time series aggregation and, secondly, by invoking Champernowne's chain-index method.

The latter, he showed, was admirably suited to the neo-classical procedure of concentrating on *points* of equilibrium when these were to be extended (approximately, not rigorously) into curves, hoping that the ensuing rupture of equilibrium would not detract too much from the stories that were told (see Reading 2, pages 65–100). Joan Robinson, however, would regard this as the illegitimate procedure of applying theorems associated with comparisons of different equilibrium situations in the entirely different contexts of process, change – and disequilibrium. Sraffa, incidentally, and in one short paragraph, thoughtfully bracketed (see Reading 4, page 130), knocks over, once and for all, the possibility of measuring capital in a unit which is independent of distribution and prices. He shows, by means of the concept of dated labour, that the relative prices of two commodities will change when r and w change even though there has been no change in their technical methods of production. 'The reversals in the direction of the movement of relative prices in the face of unchanged methods of production, cannot be reconciled with *any* notion of capital as a measurable quantity independent of distribution and prices' (see Reading 4, page 130).

Productivity growth, technical progress and fossils

The equality of factor prices with marginal products as a result of assuming perfect competition, static expectations, constant-returns-to-scale and malleability are the key assumptions which underpin the early post-war econometric studies of the relative contributions of technical progress and capital accumulation (via deepening, i.e. increases in capital per man) to the growth of productivity. These assumptions also underlie the concept of the constant elasticity of substitution (CES) production function which served this among other purposes. We reprint as Reading 5 (pages 133–55), excerpts from the 1961 paper by Arrow, Chenery, Minhas and Solow on the CES production function, which is one of the two most influential papers in this field. (The other is Solow's 1957 paper on technical change and the aggregate production function, which is reprinted in the volume on *Growth Economics* – Sen, 1970.)

Solow argued, *solely for econometric convenience*, that we should view actual statistics *as if* they were observations taken from a one, all-purpose commodity world in which, however, the cross-section, well-behaved relationship between output per man (Y/L) and capital per man (K/L) drifts up neutrally over time due to disembodied technical change, i.e. factor amounts are unaffected but their productivities at each given K/L ratio are raised in like proportions as time goes by. The annual rate of neutral technical change may then be estimated from knowledge of the rates of growth of productivity and capital deepening (the latter weighted by the share of capital in income, itself interpretable as the relevant exponent of the aggregate production function). Deflating the observations on Y/L by the estimates of neutral technical progress brings into view the underlying production function, now stripped of the contribution of technical change (which in this context is a hold-all for everything but the contribution of deepening), so that the contribution of deepening to productivity growth may also be estimated. It turns out that technical progress explains much and capital accumulation little, principally because of the relevant orders of magnitude involved in most capitalist economies (except Japan). Thus productivity grows at 2 to 4 per cent per annum and capital's share in income is of the order of 25 to 40 per cent, which gives 'deepening' large amounts of lead in its saddlebag even before the race commences.

Arrow *et al.* were after different game. An empirical association in the form of straight-line regressions had been found between the logarithms of productivity and those of the money-wage rates in the *same* industries of *different* countries. These were treated *as if* they were observations taken from production functions which spanned national boundaries, each point being chosen by profit-maximizing, static expectations, perfect competitors reacting to the pulls of the different relative factor prices in each country. With these assumptions it was shown that the slopes of the regression line were estimates of the elasticities of substitution of capital for labour of the underlying 'as if' production functions. Their values were found usually to be less than one but greater than zero, so casting doubt on the applicability of two famous growth models – the fixed coefficients (zero elasticity of substitution) case of (vulgar) versions of Harrod–Domar, and the unitary value case of Cobb–Douglas.

Concurrent with these developments was the work on embodied technical change and vintage models. The pioneers in this area were Salter (1959, 1960,[4] 1965) in the UK and Johansen (1959, 1961) in Norway. The essential point of the approach is that substitution possibilities should be confined to *ex ante* investment decisions and removed from *ex post* production ones. Capital may be substituted for labour when one aspect of the investment decision – what sort to undertake – is decided upon. Businessmen are viewed as faced with a series of possible investment–labour ratios (I/L) – the latest 'best practice' techniques – formally presented as the isoquant of a unit of output (which, due to technical advances, drifts in towards the origin over time). Given the market structures, their expectations and relative factor prices, businessmen choose those techniques which may be expected to minimize costs and maximize profits. Once installed, though, the possibility of substitution is greatly reduced, in the limit, disappears altogether, and the bulk of production is done by the existing vintages ('fossils') that make up the capital stocks. Vintage machines are kept in use as long as they continue to earn positive quasi-rents, even though these may be most disappointing in relation to the hopes abounding when they were first installed. Scrapping is determined by the zero quasi-rent point. (Product wages, i.e. the wages paid by businessmen measured in terms of their products, are assumed to rise over time and earlier vintages are assumed to have higher labour requirements per unit of output than later ones.) The *volume* of investment is determined by market supply and demand forces which establish the equilibrium outputs and prices of final products. The prices so established promise only a normal rate of profits on the *latest* vintages. Any production which cannot be catered for by existing profitable machines must therefore be done by the newly installed ones. Provided that technical change does not occur faster than the time needed to establish these equilibrium outputs and prices, period by period, they may be regarded as the trend values of actually observed outputs and prices, values which come from a historical process of accumulation and scrapping in which *gross investment* is the vehicle by which technical change is embodied in

4. Originally his Cambridge, England, Ph.D. dissertation of 1955.

capital stocks and productivity growth is brought about (see Salter, 1965, for an excellent exposition of this process).

Increasingly, in growth theory and econometric studies alike, embodied technical progress has tended to replace disembodied, a view which, moreover, does away with the need to measure an aggregate capital stock. The new theory is associated with putty–clay models – before decisions are made we play with putty, once made, putty is baked into clay and malleability is over (or greatly reduced). Excellent examples of this approach are Bardhan (1969), Bliss (1968), Kaldor and Mirrlees (1962), Solow (1962a, 1963a)[5] and Reading 16 by Nuti (see pages 314–39). With the exception of the Kaldor–Mirrlees model, though, essentially neo-classical marginalist procedures are used. However, in the more recent examples, static expectations have been dropped in favour of expectations of rising product wages, an assumption that drives a wedge between the *simple* equivalence of marginal products and factor prices (see Bardhan, 1969; Bliss, 1968; Harcourt, 1968).

On the econometric front, while many attempts have been made to use vintage models to estimate changes in productivity and the contribution of technical progress to them – Solow (1960, 1962b, 1963a) are typical examples – emphasis has shifted towards the 'proper' measurement of the services of factor inputs and the concept of *total* factor productivity. This has reached the limit (some might say, a giddy one) in the papers of Jorgenson and Griliches (Griliches and Jorgenson, 1966; Jorgenson and Griliches, 1967) in which they advance the (refutable) hypothesis that *if* the services of inputs are properly measured and *if* neo-classical commodity and factor market equilibrium conditions may be supposed to prevail, changes in total factor productivity, as measured by the difference between changes in a quantum index of outputs and those of a similar index of inputs, should be zero. Thus from having been the star, technical progress has now been written out of the script and the traditional neo-classical forces of factor substitution again get star billing. Aloof from the high fliers, Lydall (1969) has provided an eminently sensible economic statistician's approach to the problem, one which keeps an eye on the errors of magnitude involved when certain con-

5. Solow (1962a and 1963a) span theory and econometric specification.

venient assumptions are made rather than on rigorous justifi-cations of dubious theoretical procedures.

The rate of return on investment

Another avenue of escape from the capital measurement puzzle, both in theory and in empirical work, has been the attempt, principally by Solow (but see also Dewey, 1965; Hirshleifer, 1958) to make Irving Fisher's rate of return on investment the central concept of capital theory, i.e. to make the approach, at least in a technocratic sense, a theory of the rate of interest rather than of capital. (As Solow candidly ignores the problem of uncertainty he may speak interchangeably of 'the rate of interest' and 'the rate of profits', a procedure which will no longer do when un-certainty re-enters; see Robinson, 1971.) This way, he thought, lay clarity and fruitfulness, as opposed to controversy and con-fusion along the other. Solow's views are set out in his de Vries Lectures, the first of which we reprint in part as Reading 6, and in his contribution to the Dobb *Festschrift* (Solow, 1967), in which he tried to link the rate of profits in capitalist society to the rate of return on investment.

Solow is concerned essentially with the practical and vital question: what is the pay-off to society in the future of a little more saving (equals investment) now? He develops a series of rates of return measures – for one period, for several, for infinity – that are designed to answer the question. His one-period measure will serve to illustrate the approach. Suppose that society decides technocratically to follow an (efficient) consumption stream of: $C_0 - h$, $C_1 + k$, $C_2, \ldots$ over the next three periods instead of one of: C_0, C_1, $C_2, \ldots$. Then $(k/h) - 1$ is a natural definition of a one-period rate of return. Solow's contribution is to use this and allied measures in contexts where technical progress occurs, and to derive measures of them for a variety of theoretical economies, ranging from simple neo-classical to Worswick's (1959) version of Joan Robinson's one-technique model of accumulation, and for two real ones, the USA and West Germany. Unfortunately, in order to obtain the latter, capital *has* to be measured empirically and so his middlebrow statistics as opposed to his highbrow theory are not free of a concept of aggregate capital – a point which Joan Robinson certainly does *not* overlook in her review article which we reprint as Reading 7 (see pages 168–79). She also examines in Reading 7 the role of effective demand in the determination of distributive shares, a puzzle which is vanquished from neo-neo-classical analysis (and from some neo-Keynesian ones, especially in Kaldor's worlds) either for convenience (see Reading 2, pages 65–100), or by an all-wise government (see Meade, 1961; Swan, 1956), or by belief in the (*long-run*) efficacy of market forces (see possibly, Hicks, 1960, and any neo-Samuelson and neo-Solow). (Solow and Stiglitz have since provided an excellent analysis of the effective demand puzzles raised by Joan Robinson, an analysis that starts with the view that the real wage rate is a *goods* market clearing price to neo-Keynesians and a *labour* market clearing price to neo-neo-classicals; see Solow and Stiglitz, 1968.)

Get with it: double-switch and capital-reverse

Both sides in the debate have examined heterogeneous capital models in which, within any one activity, factor proportions are given and fixed so that aggregate proportions may be changed (meaningfully) only by going over from one technique with its activities to another with its, as a result either of the pull of changing relative factor prices or of changes in the composition of demand.[6] The object of these exercises varies as between the two sides. To the neo-Keynesians they represent an attack on the marginal method of analysis, an attack lead in spirit by Sraffa (see Reading 4) who subtitled his book *Prelude to a Critique of Economic Theory*, by which he meant marginalist neo-classical theory. If the subsequent critique held, the outcome presumably would be a return to classical modes of analysis wherein the theory of value dealt with the formation of relative prices *once* distribution puzzles had been solved elsewhere, not in time but in context, so that in order to close the system the value of either the real wage or the rate of profits is provided from outside the production system (but not via relative demands). The neo-classical view, on the other hand, is that distributive prices, like commodity prices, are determined by the forces of supply and demand, and

6. When input–output coefficients vary as between the activities of a *given* technique, aggregate factor proportions in value terms may change when r and w change.

the theory of value (now modern microeconomics) encompassed the *lot*, so banishing from attention or relevance institutions and social classes, and opening the door for algebra and rigour.

A magnificent exposition of Sraffa's viewpoint is contained in Mrs Bharadwaj's review (see Reading 8, pages 183–95) of Sraffa's book (see Reading 4). The significance for theories of growth of the differences in the two theories of value is challengingly analysed by Nell (Reading 9, pages 196–210). Nell's discussion stresses the distinction between, on the one hand, the neo-classical view of the production system as a one-way flow from factors of production to final outputs with intermediate goods (with which, in reality, the action is) lost from view and, on the other, the classical view whereby commodities are produced by commodities in a circular process, so that intermediate goods are restored to the centre of the stage, and capitalists and labour share in (fight over) the resulting surplus or net product.

The neo-neo-classicals argue that while rigorous analysis, using modern programming techniques and all the ploys of modern microeconomic analysis, is essential for highbrow capital theory, yet certain fundamental truths may be imparted by way of simple parables based on simple, one-commodity, all-purpose (jelly) models deriving from J. B. Clark (see the opening paragraphs of Reading 10, pages 213–15). These truths would also serve to provide a partial justification for econometric studies which proceed *as if* observed statistics may be viewed as coming from such worlds. The latter is the object of Samuelson's famous paper on the surrogate (as if) production function (see Reading 10). In it he christened a tool, namely, the factor-price frontier (FpF), the use of which runs through all this literature and which had been used before (but not named) by Sraffa (see Reading 4) and Champernowne (see Reading 2).

Factor-price frontiers (FpFs) can apply to a single technique (or stationary economy) which contains two or more activities, i.e. given methods of producing commodities, some or all of which constitute the net product, after their using up in production has been accounted for; in which case, they (FpFs) show the highest r that could be paid (and under the stress of competition *will* be paid) given the value of w (and vice versa). Or it may refer to the *envelope* which is formed by the FpFs of a series of possible techniques (possible islands of stationary-state equilibria; see Solow, 1963a) and which shows the highest r of any of the techniques associated with a given value of w. The FpF for a single technique and the FpF envelope for several are shown in Figures 1 and 2.

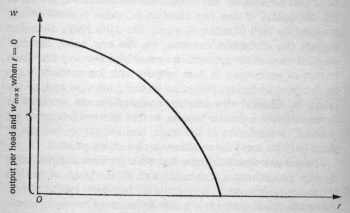

Figure 1 FpF for a single technique[7]

Samuelson was concerned to show that it would be possible to get a one-to-one correspondence between the jelly world of parable and the heterogeneous capital goods world of 'reality' via the FpF envelope, provided that the right brand of jelly were used. Moreover, the distribution of income, for any given pair of r and w, would be measured by the simple Marshallian elasticity at the relevant point on the envelope, with factors being treated *as if* they were paid prices equal to the marginal products of the well-behaved, constant-returns-to-scale, jelly production function. Lower rates of profits would be associated with higher values of capital per head, output per head, capital–output ratios and sustainable steady states of consumption per head. A measure of capital could be obtained from knowledge of labour supplies and the slope of the envelope alone. To obtain these results, Samuelson assumed that within each technique (though not

7. FpFs may be any shape; usually (but not inevitably, see Reading 16, page 321) they slope downwards.

between), capital–labour ratios were identical in each activity. This gave each technique a straight-line FpF which, as the double-switching (and capital-reversing) debates subsequently showed, ensures that these above results are obtained – but only at the expense of never really leaving the jelly worlds of parable *within the confines of which nobody would ever deny that they held anyway.*

The double-switching and capital-reversing debates are *technically* about two propositions:

Double-switching. What happens if the same technique is the most profitable at two or more rates of profits so that it rates more than one (non-consecutive) place on the envelope, i.e. it comes back (as does technique *c* in Figure 2), even though others have been more profitable in between, e.g. technique *b* in Figure 2?

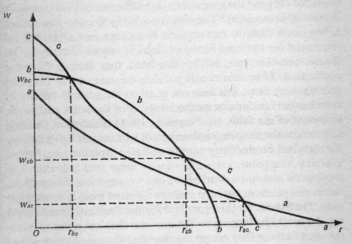

Figure 2 FpF envelope for several techniques

Capital-reversing. What happens if, when there is a change from one technique to another as a result of considering a lower value of *r*, instead of going to a higher value of capital, greater output per head technique, we go instead to a lower value of capital, lower output per head technique (as occurs when we switch from *c* to *b* in Figure 2)?

Both of these events may occur in either discrete or continuous technologies once individual FpFs are *not* straight lines. (Samuelson's 'summing up' in Reading 11 provides a very neat demonstration of why double-switching and capital-reversing may occur once there are truly heterogeneous capital goods and non-uniform inputs of labour into production over 'horizontal' time. The latter may be converted to as many intermediate stages of production as there are 'periods' of time and it is the differential impact of given changes in the value of r on the values of these processes that is responsible for the two phenomena.)

These results, which Levhari (1965) tried to show could not occur in an economy (interpreted as an integrated technology) though they could in an industry, are now unassailable (see, for example, Garegnani, 1970; Reading 12, pages 251–60; Reading 13, pages 261–86; and the symposium in the November 1966 *Quarterly Journal of Economics*).[8] They are regarded by the neo-Keynesians as the death blow to neo-classical economics and signal the re-emergence (or the need for it) of classical modes of analysis. To the neo-neo-classicals, on the other hand, they destroy the wider applications of certain simple parables to some rather (*ex post*) uninteresting cases, but bear not at all on the general validity of neo-classical maximizing methodology. (For the latest and purest statement of the faith, see Ferguson, 1969.) Bhaduri in Reading 12 provides the simplest explanation of why curved FpFs destroy the marginal productivity parable and also explains why, from a Marxian viewpoint, one unit cannot serve two purposes – a production one and a distribution one – once prices diverge from values and relations between men are divorced from technological ones. The articles by Garegnani (1970) and Pasinetti (Reading 13) are the most challenging to the neo-neo-classical point of view, not least because they *accept* the view that the existence or not of an aggregate production function, whether at an economy or industry level, has nothing to do, necessarily, with the validity or not of the marginal productivity theory of distribution. (These two questions have sometimes been treated as synonymous. The results of the present debate *do* destroy the validity of a rigorous

8. Pasinetti was the first to provide a counter example to Levhari's theorem, originally in his paper to the 1965 Rome Congress of the Econometric Society.

concept of an aggregate production function, especially one implying that r equals the marginal product of capital, in a world of heterogeneous capital goods.) Garegnani and Pasinetti, however, are after bigger game. To them, the results destroy the concept of a demand curve for capital (aggregate or industrial) in the sense of a unique, inverse relationship between rates of profits and values of capital. Such a demand curve implies that higher values of capital are associated with more capital-intensive and productive methods of production, so that the marginal product of 'capital' declines with an increase in 'capital', is a true scarcity price and is independent of the rate of profits itself, and so may play a part in the determination of the value of the latter. Both authors tackle this one: Garegnani within the contexts of the works of Marshall, Böhm-Bawerk, Wicksell – and Samuelson; Pasinetti within the context of the reappraisal of Irving Fisher's work.

Pasinetti's contribution is to show that Fisher's second concept of the rate of return over cost [9] – the marginal returns in perpetuity as related to the sacrifice now needed to change from one technique to another – was meant to serve in a heterogeneous capital model as a surrogate for a physical rate of return and marginal product of capital in a one-commodity world. It performed this function – or appeared to have done so – because 'an unobtrusive postulate' had been slipped into the analysis (alongside subsidiary ones of malleability and continuous substitution possibilities) *whereby, in effect, capital-reversing and double-switching were ruled out*. Remove this postulate, *for which there is no* a priori *or empirical justification*, and with it there goes one of the main props of the traditional neo-classical demand-and-supply approach to distributive questions. Such is the case, answerable, possibly, only by the logical point that in equilibrium and, thus, with *given* prices, profit-maximizing, static expectations price-takers in situations of perfect competition *must* pay factors their

9. Pasinetti argues that Fisher's first concept which, in effect, identifies the rate of return on investment with a switch point rate of profits, is purely definitional and, as such, is 'of no help at all . . . being compatible with any explanation, i.e. any theory, of the rate of profit(s)' (see pages 266–8). It should be noted that it is Pasinetti, not Fisher, who identifies the two concepts of the rate of return.

marginal products, *suitably defined*, in linear or any other models, and variables may then be measured in terms of 'an equilibrium dollar's worth' (as Swan shows in Reading 3). The trouble is – as Swan also shows – that while this is true of a *point*, it is not true of a *curve*, in the sense that a *different* equilibrium dollar's worth will be associated with each point.[10]

It's class that counts: the rate of profits in capitalist society

The inability in neo-Keynesian eyes of neo-classical analysis to explain adequately – or at all – distributive shares and prices has led to the analysis, especially by Kaldor, Pasinetti and Joan Robinson, of factors outside the production system (and *not* concerned in the traditional manner with *relative* demands), namely, those associated with the Keynesian forces of saving and investment; in particular, in the long run, the rate of growth of the economy (g) and the saving propensity of the capitalist class (s_c). The starting point of the subsequent controversy (as opposed to the analysis) is Pasinetti's (1962) article which is reprinted in Sen (1970). Prior to this there is the analysis in Kaldor's famous (1937) article (a vintage that Solow, 1963b, p. 9, prefers to the more recent one), von Neumann's equally famous (1945–6) model of an expanding economy in which $r = g$, and Kaldor's post-war papers on a Keynesian theory of distribution (1955–6) and the rate of growth under inflation (1959a and b). Kalecki's (1939) work has also influenced greatly the analysis of distributive *shares*.[11]

Pasinetti shows that *if* we are in golden-age, full-employment,

10. In her review article (Robinson, 1970) of Ferguson (1969), Joan Robinson returns to this point; she argues that neither the marginal product of labour nor that of capital *can* be defined, either in the short run or in the long run, *unless* capital is jelly, i.e. completely malleable, so that short-run utilization functions are identical with long-run 'pseudo' production functions. (It is only in this world that any economic sense may be made of the statement, 'other factors remaining constant', in the definitions of marginal products.) That is to say, Joan Robinson rejects entirely 'as if' parables in both theory and applied work.

11. It is clear from the dates at which these papers were published that this account of how the strands of the arguments fit together is more an *ex post*, hindsight one than a literal description of how the participants necessarily saw the points at issue when they made their contributions.

long-run equilibrium – why, we need not ask – and if we consider a two-class society in which the workers, *because* they save, get two types of income, wages and interest (equal profits) on their savings, which are lent to the 'pure' capitalists who get profits only, then $r = (g/s_c)$, where g is the rate of growth compounded of the rate of growth of the labour force and Harrod neutral technical progress. This is a remarkable result because the rate of profits is independent of both the workers' saving habits (s_w) and the production function. Certain conditions must hold for this to be so, notably that $s_w < I/Y_f < s_c$, a condition that applies to Kaldor's theory of distributive shares as well.

Meade (see Meade 1963; Meade and Hahn, 1965; and Reading 14, pages 289–94) and, later, Samuelson and Modigliani (1966a and b) have examined what happens outside this range, deducing a dual result whereby $Y_f/K = g/s_w$ and the rate of profits *does* depend on the production function (in long-run, steady-state equilibrium, *if* such an equilibrium exists). In Reading 14 Meade beautifully and persuasively sorts out all these issues within the compass of a single simple diagram. Samuelson and Modigliani (together with, it must be said, Kaldor's reply – see Reading 15, pages 295–313) provide both the high jinks and the fireworks. Kaldor not only goes for neo-neo-classical methodology with no holds barred but also provides a neo-Pasinetti theorem which brings in the capitalists' borrowing function and that 'with it' statistic, the valuation ratio, and removes some of the limitations of Pasinetti's original approach. There is some doubt as to whether orders of magnitude taken from actual economies are of relevance to these disputes. Nevertheless, both sides indulge in 'explicit realism' when it suits them (don't we all?) and it does seem that the Pasinetti condition holds for the relevant ranges of the actual orders of magnitude. Thus the dual case, while a fascinating analysis of the existence and local and global stability of a world of workers' socialism, ushered in by a bloodless revolution, is of little relevance for a discussion of what determines r in a capitalist economy.[12]

12. Pasinetti's result depends upon all classes receiving the same return on their savings. Laing (1969) analyses the plausible case where the workers get less.

Golden Rules, economist-style [13]

To conclude, we note two strands of analysis which lead off from the areas covered above. The first is the debate about the reality and/or relevance of the assumption of maximizing behaviour in neo-classical methodology, about which Kaldor has some stringent things to say in Reading 15, and which Solow also touches on in his (1968) contribution to the IEA volume on income distribution along with his neat reconciliations of differing views on distribution (which do, however, involve more than just trivial changes in assumptions and algebra).

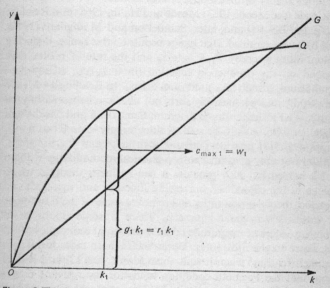

Figure 3 The Golden Rule of Accumulation (by T. C. Koopmans, as told to the Pope)

The other strand concerns the Golden Rule of Accumulation or neo-neo-classical theorem whereby the choice of the method of the production which maximizes consumption per head, c_{max}, is analysed, given the full-employment rate of growth of the econ-

13. A fuller discussion of these and related issues will be found in **Part II** of the Introduction.

omy; and it is shown that the choice implies that $r = g$. The interesting result that emerges in the present context is that the relationship between c_{max} and g is the exact *dual* of that between w and r on the FpF envelopes of either neo-classical or heterogeneous capital good models. This has been shown most simply (for the neo-classical case) by Koopmans (1965), and we reproduce his diagram as Figure 3. On the vertical axis we measure

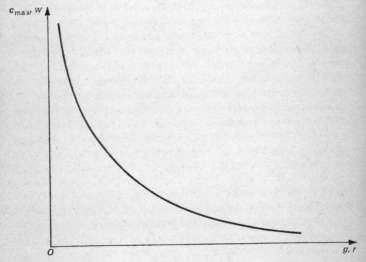

Figure 4 'and the two shall be as one': FpF and $c_{max} - g$

output per head (y), on the horizontal axis capital per head (k), in a jelly world with a well-behaved production function, OQ. OG has a slope of g_1, the given rate of growth. Vertical distances between OG and Ok are amounts of investment per head, gk. When OG is parallel to OQ (at Ok_1), consumption per head is maximized and $r_1(= \partial y / \partial k_1) = g_1$. Moreover, with $r_1 = g_1$, $g_1 k_1 = r_1 k_1$, i.e. profits per head, so $c_{max\ 1} = w_1$. Now consider other possible given values of g and swivel OG upwards as g rises; it is clear that c_{max} falls and r rises so that we may show, interchangeably, the FpF and the c_{max}, g relationship as the downward sloping line in Figure 4.

Nuti's contribution (see Reading 16, pages 314–39) – a great one, not least because it analyses a *real* puzzle – is to examine the implications of this dual result for technologies which require time both to set up and to produce. He invokes putty–clay (but with some new twists), allows double-switching to occur and places the techniques, first, in a textbook capitalist economy and, secondly, in two brands of socialism, one decentralized, the other centralized. He analyses what happens when r, which guides investment decisions in the first two but not in the third, diverges from g and what may be done about it.

Thus we started with real puzzles, those to do with growth, accumulation and distribution, detoured into the realms of high theory – and high polemics – and fittingly we exit on a real note. For if economic theory, no matter how beautiful and pure its abstract logic may be, does not deal with real puzzles and real people it quickly ceases to have a life of its own and withers and dies. We hope enough warm blood has flowed through the arteries of this introduction – and our selected Readings – to allow it, and them, long lives.

Part II[14]

A neo-classical view of the recent controversies in capital theory

Joan Robinson has contended (see Reading 1) that since capital cannot be measured without a knowledge of the rate of interest, a production function with aggregate capital as an input cannot be regarded as an independent determinant of the equilibrium rate of interest without circularity. Contemporary neo-classical economists have been largely content to show the correctness of their own analyses (see Samuelson's opening remarks in Reading 10, as an example of this) and her contention has gone unchallenged. The main object of what follows is to give a neo-classical analysis of the determination of the equilibrium rate of interest in stationary-state conditions, drawing attention to the role of the aggregate production function in which capital is measured at constant prices. The analysis will be presented in terms of the intertemporal production function. The nineteenth-century history and the meaning of this concept will be discussed briefly

14. Grateful acknowledgement is made to John Dixon, G. C. Harcourt, H. G. Johnson and P. Wagstaff for their comments on an earlier draft.

first. A number of other controversial matters in capital theory are touched on in the course of the exposition. The discussion serves as a stepping stone to an important result, originally proved by Koopmans (1957, pp. 115–21), that in equilibrium the marginal product of aggregate capital, measured at prices which equal the relevant marginal rates of substitution, equals the true rate of interest given by the marginal rates of substitution. The criticism of the neo-classical rate of interest theory based on the phenomenon of the 'double-switching' of techniques is considered next. Conditions are given for double-switching to be avoided in the economy as a whole even though the conditions which make double-switching possible in each sector are satisfied. In the concluding section optimum growth theory is discussed briefly.

The history of the intertemporal production function. Jevons, in 1872, was the first of the neo-classicals to employ an intertemporal production function, that is, a production function in which each input and output is distinguished by the time at which it occurs. The idea of an intertemporal production function synthesized two strands of classical (especially Ricardian) thought – its value theory, which treated capital as the embodiment of earlier labour inputs, and its production theory, which allowed for changes in factor proportions in agriculture and employed the concept of the marginal product of the variable factor, labour-plus-capital. The division of the product between the rent of land, on the one hand, and wages and profits, on the other, was determined by the principle that the variable factor, labour-plus-capital, must earn its marginal product. The division of the marginal product between wages and profits was determined by the principle that profits are a surplus over wages, the wage rate being equal to the conventional minimum needed for the subsistence of labour in the long run. The rate of profit is determined in the agricultural sector where, Ricardo held, output and input are in the same units.

There were important developments in capital theory between the time of Ricardo and the first neo-classicals. N. Senior and J. Rae deserve special mention for their recognition of the contribution to production of the roundaboutness of a productive method. Longfield and von Thünen applied the marginal principle to capital and labour separately. These developments are discussed by Schumpeter (1954). But the dominant school, at least in England, remained the Ricardian in the hands of, for example, J. S. Mill.

The form of intertemporal production function used by Jevons was a single primary input/final output cycle or stream with the duration of the process a variable, subject to choice. The longer the process the more the investment which is required and the smaller eventually is the incremental return. Jevons established the profit-maximizing condition as equality of the marginal product of investment with the rate of interest. But to establish the relation between the *stock* of capital and the *flow* of product with a given labour force, it was necessary to postulate the existence of a stationary state. In the stationary state there is employed at any one time a set of identical input–output streams, each one at a different stage so that they mature and yield their output in turn, giving a constant flow of output. Economies in this condition necessarily abstract from the conditions of change in the real world. But it was only on the basis of some such abstraction that capital theory could be pushed forward in the desired way. Jevons was unable to make this step and it fell to Böhm-Bawerk working in the Austrian tradition of by-passing intermediate goods, to take it. He was interested in measuring capital by the average period of production, which need not detain us here. He was followed by Wicksell who also framed his analysis so as to focus on the choice of the duration of a productive process. It is a different contribution of his which is important in the present context. He assumed that a labour input of any date, past as well as present, can contribute separately to production – that is, if all inputs other than that one are held constant, increasing it increases output. He saw that an intertemporal production function in which this occurs makes interest possible because of the difference between the marginal product of 'saved-up' compared with 'current' labour – that this is what is meant by the productiveness of time (see Wicksell, 1934, p. 154). The ratio of the two marginal products is an own rate of interest – the rate at which a commodity exchanges for itself one period later. This is represented geometrically by the slope of an equi-product curve with labour of different dates the inputs which substitute for each other in a movement along the curve.

Wicksell gave great emphasis to this latter contribution and stated explicitly that Jevons's view that the whole of capital was fundamentally free capital (that, in the course of wearing out and being renewed, it could take a different form) was 'too one-sided a view of the matter' (ibid., p. 145). However, he also emphasized that a theory of the rate of interest required that capital be regarded as an aggregate of value, not measured by the cost of production of capital goods as Walras had supposed it should be, since that would involve circularity (part of the costs would be due to capital), but traced back to its original primary inputs – 'a single coherent mass of saved-up land and labour' (ibid., p. 150). Wicksell's contribution should, therefore, be regarded as belonging to a phase of transition in economic thought; he had not shaken off the idea, which perhaps has its roots in the classical wage fund doctrine, that capital can be regarded as a homogeneous aggregate, but he had grasped the significance of the intertemporal substitution of inputs and was fully aware of the heterogeneous nature of capital goods.

Wicksell's difficulty was to reconcile the heterogeneity of capital goods with the existence of a single rate of interest 'in equilibrium' (ibid., p. 149). He made the reconciliation by reducing different sorts of capital to comparable value terms. But *own* rates of interest need not be equal in equilibrium except in a stationary state. The rates of return on different investments must be equal *when expressed in terms of the same commodity* but the own rates of interest in terms of different commodities may, in general, differ. It is only in a stationary state that there is a single rate of interest and the 'reconciliation' is then achieved by assumption.

Properties of the intertemporal production function. The neo-classical economists of the Austrian school framed their assumptions so as to focus attention on the choice of the duration of a roundabout production process. When, following Wicksell, the intertemporal production function is generalized to allow for substitution of the different dated inputs for each other, transformation of the different dated outputs into each other and transformation of inputs into outputs,[15] this choice must be interpreted as determining the number of dimensions in which a process can be represented, there being a dimension for each (dated) input and each (dated) output. A process or intertemporal technique is represented by a point in these dimensions and a change in the coordinates of the point along the production function in any pair of dimensions, all other inputs and outputs being held constant, represents the substitution and transformation possibilities.

The idea of a finite intertemporal production process can be interpreted quite generally to embrace the use of durable (but not infinitely durable) machinery as well as such natural processes as growing trees or maturing wine. The process can be interpreted to cover many generations of machinery, each generation, as well as the process as a whole, having an optimum life. The problems of joint products implied by the durability of machines (raised by Sraffa, 1960, p. 63) do not arise with an intertemporal production function since simultaneous account is taken of outputs and inputs. (Sraffa's problem was to reduce a machine of a particular age purely to dated labour.) If the machines at any stage are traced to the earlier inputs and outputs which led up to them, an infinite sequence is obtained. However, the series must become a diminishing one and can be approximated to by a finite sequence. The approximation is equivalent to allowing that in a stationary state there is some labour which produces capital goods unaided by capital goods. But the amount of such labour can be made as small as desired by tracing the sequence further back. Sraffa has pointed out (see Reading 4, page 126) that the approximation is only valid if labour earns a finite wage. With this exception (which does not seem to be a serious one) the approximation which is being adopted means that the neo-classical circulating capital model (i.e. the model in which the intertemporal production function has a finite time span) embraces all forms of capital goods other than those which last for ever; capital goods with this characteristic are like land and new ones could not be produced in a stationary state.

Technical progress could be assumed to occur during the

15. This generalization was put forward by Hicks (1946, ch. 15).

course of an intertemporal production process, becoming embodied in new machines and influencing the scrapping of old machines. (The difficult thing to explain from this point of view is disembodied technical progress!) When the production functions of different time spans are compared, technical progress shows itself by the shift inwards of equi-product curves and outwards of their counterparts, equi-input curves. Technical progress is neutral if, for all given input and output patterns, the inputs are reduced in the same proportion. This is neutral in the Hicks sense from a formal point of view but it is also neutral in the Harrod sense in being labour-augmenting. (For the definition and a discussion of Hicks- and Harrod-neutrality see Hahn and Matthews, 1964, pp. 825–32.)

Continuous technical progress would, of course, introduce a growth element into what would otherwise be a stationary state. The stationary-state analysis which follows can, as modern economists have shown, readily be adapted to allow for this, and for growth of the primary factor supplies, provided that the technical progress is neutral. It is clear that although incorporating these two sources of growth brings the analysis much nearer the real world, it remains essentially a piece of abstract capital (and now growth) theory.

The assumptions behind the intertemporal production function are very similar to those of a heterogeneous capital goods model. The two approaches offer different ways of looking at the nature of capital and give different insights. However, there appears to be one appreciable advantage of the former approach – that it leaves the form of the intermediate (i.e. capital) goods free to change when substitution is being allowed for (as in a comparison of stationary states) and when technical progress is present. The units in which primary inputs and final outputs are measured must not change but this abstraction is shared by both approaches. A model which specifies the nature of capital goods appears to be indispensable in international trade theory. One has to be prepared to adopt different approaches to deal with different problems, as Solow has pointed out (1963b, pp.14–16).

The stationary-state analysis. In a stationary state with labour inputs of different periods combining to produce different final outputs, conditions for the efficient allocation of labour may be laid down. It can readily be shown that they require that the marginal rates of substitution of labour of all periods for labour of the following period must be equal and that, similarly, the marginal rates of transformation of the final output of all periods into the final output of the following period must be equal at the same rate. This rate is the rate of interest which would make the technique optimal for a competitive producer and could be called the technique's scarcity rate of interest. With convexity of the production function (treating outputs as negative inputs) and continuous substitution possibilities, each efficient technique must have a different scarcity rate of interest.

We are now in a position to analyse, by means of a comparison of stationary states, the determination of the equilibrium rate of interest – that rate of interest which equates saving and investment. Pigou (1935) was first in bringing together the demand and supply sides of the stationary state. A one-product case is dealt with first.

The conditions of a stationary state are achieved quite arbitrarily by assuming that a stationary state has always existed and is expected to continue to exist. It is as though stationariness is imposed on people's choices. This is tantamount to assuming perfect foresight, which is perhaps the main source of abstraction in the analysis. The approach being adopted is essentially the same as that used by Joan Robinson in dealing with steady-state growth. We are making the stationary state a golden age with zero growth rate.

The mechanisms whereby full employment is achieved are those of static, perfectly flexible price, perfect competition models. The demand for labour with the optimum technique increases if supernormal profits are made and decreases if losses are made, while the wage rate (in real terms) falls if there is an excess supply, or rises if there is an excess demand, for labour. These two mechanisms imply that labour must be fully employed at a wage equal to its current marginal product.

The choice of intertemporal technique at any rate of interest implies that a certain quantity of labour at each stage of production of the technique is invested or disinvested. Investment takes place in any period if more is paid to labour in terms of final product than is currently produced with that technique. The aggregate gross investment demand is the sum, in any one period, of the gross investments (at the stages in which there is gross investment) of all the input–output streams. (Consumption loans are abstracted from.) The gross investment is financed by borrowing from people (consumers) doing gross saving, and the borrowings are repaid by the *surpluses* made when disinvestment takes place.

The gross investment demand is derived from the optimum choice of technique at each rate of interest and can be expressed either in terms of labour or in terms of the payment in final product for this labour. With *both* methods the amount of investment at any stage of a given technique depends upon the level of the real-wage rate, which varies with the rate of interest and choice of technique. But both measures of investment are equally real.

At any rate of interest the optimum choice of technique determines the level and distribution of income. Gross savings are then determined by the (intertemporal) consumer preferences and the rate of interest. (The interdependence of demand and supply – the determination of income by the choice of technique – reflects the general equilibrium nature of the analysis and is a strength rather than a fault of this approach.) Savings, like investment, can be expressed either in terms of final output or in terms of labour and, as for investment, both ways of expressing savings must be affected by the real-wage rate.

The equilibrium rate of interest is determined by the intersection of the gross savings and investment schedules, that is, by the interaction of the demand and supply for loans. The mechanism is one in which the supply conditions are equivalent to the factor endowments of a static model and the demand conditions are derived on marginal productivity principles – in which, in short, the rate of interest is a scarcity rent.

The analysis which has just been given in terms of saving and investment could be reworked in terms of the demand and supply for a stock of capital without in any way altering the principles involved. Each technique requires that a certain stock of capital, which can be valued at the scarcity prices of that technique, be employed – i.e. demanded – and, likewise, consumer preferences imply that consumers prefer to hold a certain stock of capital at each technique and rate of interest. The stock of capital demanded can be regarded either as embodying past inputs net of past outputs or as embodying the potential for future outputs net of future inputs. The stock of capital (potentially) supplied can be regarded either as the accumulation of past saving or as the potential for future consumption. Whichever point of view is adopted the aggregation requires the use of the rate of interest and real wage rate which define the stationary state. These prices vary as between the different stationary states. Hence the relation between the value of capital demanded and output as between different stationary states cannot be thought of as the cross-section of a production function from which the demand for capital schedule is derived. Changes in the amount of capital reflect revaluations due to the change in prices as well as changes in quantity. The 'marginal product' of capital measured at varying prices generally differs from the rate of interest in equilibrium. This was pointed out by Böhm-Bawerk in criticism of von Thünen's analysis (see Lutz, 1966).

Joan Robinson has objected to the use of a relation between capital measured at constant prices and output. If the constant prices are those which prevail in equilibrium, the marginal product of capital in equilibrium does equal the rate of interest (see below). But there is the problem of circularity; the equilibrium prices must be known to start with.

But a different interpretation can be put on the relation between capital measured at constant prices and output as between different stationary states – that it is the relation in terms of which the choice of technique is made by entrepreneurs *within each stationary state* when the constant prices are those of that stationary state. The marginal product of capital for the technique chosen in each stationary state equals the rate of interest which defines that stationary state. In the stationary state for which the supply of capital equals the demand, the marginal product of capital equals the equilibrium rate of interest. This way of presenting the matter seems to avoid any circularity; the capital-to-output relations at all prices are relevant and the equilibrium relation is determined by the fact that it satisfies the condition that savings and investment are equal.

Koopmans was the first to show that in equilibrium the marginal product of capital measured at prices equal to the relevant marginal rates of substitution equals the rate of interest given by the marginal rates of substitution. He employed a description of technology in terms of intermediate goods which is in some ways more general than that used above and which required the use of difficult mathematics. The writer arrived at the same result for the technology described above (Laing, 1965). His proof is chosen as Reading 17 because of its simplicity.

So far the assumption of gradual substitution possibilities has been made. It has had the consequence of giving a one-to-one relation between rates of interest and techniques. But it should be noted that once the intertemporal production function has more than two dated primary inputs or two dated final outputs there is no presumption (because of the assumption of convexity of the production function) that a rise in the rate of interest gives a substitution of later for earlier primary inputs or of earlier for later final outputs. The substitution may go the 'wrong' way in all pairs of periods so that the technique becomes unambiguously *more* capital-intensive even though the rate of interest has risen[16] (see 2nd edn of Laing, 1965). What gradual substitutability does mean is that 'double-switching' of discrete techniques, as illustrated by Samuelson (see Reading 11), is impossible. The case used by Samuelson of two techniques each using at least three inputs has a counterpart in the case of two techniques with at least three outputs – which is also, of course, ruled out by the existence of gradual substitutability.

Another assumption which has been made, that of a single final output, is also relevant to the possibility of double-switching. The substitution by consumers of final outputs which use the same inputs but, in different proportions, in effect allows the inputs to substitute for each other in the economy as a whole. If the intertemporal production function for each final product is expressed as a relation between final output flow and dated primary inputs, a 'factor indifference curve' (Laing, 1963) which

16. It is, in effect, this conclusion, rather than the double-switching which may occur when techniques are not gradually substitutable, which has been held to be particularly damaging to the orthodox neo-classical results (see, for example, Reading 13).

shows the alternative combinations of dated primary inputs which produce the same (flow) level of consumer satisfaction can be constructed. If there is a sufficient number of final products (as many as there are dated primary inputs) which are gradually substitutable in the consumer preference system, the factor indifference curve exhibits gradual substitutability so long as all the final products are being produced – even though there are only two discrete techniques in the production of each final product. In the economy as a whole there is then a one-to-one relation between rates of interest and preferred factor proportions. (The analysis of the stationary state using factor indifference curves has not been presented but the statement is plausible.) Again there is no presumption on the basis of the convexity of the factor indifference curve that a fall in the rate of interest gives a substitution of later for earlier inputs.

A sufficient condition for the avoidance of double-switching in the economy as a whole (as explained by the foregoing analysis) is that each final product should not be required as an input in the production of other final products. It would be surprising if this assumption could not be weakened without destroying the conclusion. Even if this is not so, the sort of commodity for which the case is proved is of considerable relevance in practice. These results have not been noted in the literature. They were first suggested by the writer in 1967.

Optimum growth theory. The conditions for maximum efficiency in the allocation of resources in a static economy (that is, in a single period) have a precise counterpart in a growing economy with resources and a technology which are, in the widest sense, given. Maximum efficiency in a growing economy requires that it be impossible to produce more of any final output in any period without reducing the production of some other final output in that period or of any final output in any other period. An outstanding exposition of this aspect of optimum growth theory was given by Dorfman, Samuelson and Solow (see Reading 18). If the conditions of a stationary state are also assumed to hold, the sort of restriction on the choice of technique which was referred to in the previous section is obtained. The other conditions for maximum efficiency in a static economy also have their counterparts in a growing economy but they appear to have attracted little attention.

The choice among alternative efficient intertemporal resource allocations also has a static counterpart. The problem was first posed by Irving Fisher (1907) in an essentially static (and micro) form – with given intertemporal consumption preferences and production possibilities. The first analysis of this choice in the setting of a growth model was by Ramsey (1928); this paper is reprinted in Sen (1970). The literature on this topic has burgeoned in recent years but, while it gives fresh insights into growth relationships, its failure to allow for uncertainty means that it remains no more than an interesting abstraction.

There are many ways in which the presence of time in a growth model constrains the relationships in the model and so poses problems not met in static analysis. But there are two problems for optimum growth theory which are conceptually new – they have no conceivable meaning in a static context. One is the infinity of future time with its implication that a terminal stock of capital should remain after any finite time and that a finite analysis is not, therefore, self-contained. Malinvaud (1953) has solved the mathematical problem of infinite time in a path-breaking paper.

The other problem (fortunately of a less exalted nature) is the choice of the capital-intensity which maximizes the *per capita* flow of final products as between different steady growth states. The problem is that whereas the resources which must be devoted to replacing and expanding the capital stock increase in proportion to the capital–labour ratio, output increases less than in proportion. An early diagrammatic exposition of this problem by Pearce (1962) goes straight to the heart of the matter. Pearce was concerned to show that even if the optimal steady growth path is feasible, steady growth need not be optimal.

The condition for maximization of *per capita* final output was discovered by a number of people mostly within a year or two of each other in the late 1950s and early 1960s. It was quickly pointed out by Samuelson (1962) that this result is 'a special case of' the solution to the problem of the choice of the capital-intensity to maximize the growth rate when labour is in perfectly elastic supply. Von Neumann solved this problem in a paper published in 1938 (see von Neumann, 1945–6) and is generally credited with being the father of optimum growth theory. (An outstanding exposition of his analysis by Hahn and Matthews, 1964, explains its relation to the consumption maximization condition.) The people who have credited von Neumann with this discovery seem to have overlooked their Wicksell! The following two passages are taken respectively from pages 152 and 153 of his *Lectures on Political Economy* (1934). Wicksell is discussing a technology in which capital is used up in one period and is produced in the previous period by labour unassisted by capital. The context is a stationary state. (The problem can be visualized in terms of (a) a schedule in L_t and L_{t-1} dimensions, $\bar{L} = L_t + L_{t-1}$, showing the alternative combinations of the two orders of labour, current labour and invested labour, available in different stationary states ($\bar{L}$ is the total labour supply in each period); and (b) a production function in these dimensions (with the final output occurring in period t) representing technology. Clearly final output is maximized at a point of tangency of the former schedule with an equi-product curve of the production function.) This is what Wicksell had to say:

As soon as capital has once been formed, then *just as much labour and land will go to provide each year's production and consumption as was originally employed in the non-capitalistic state*. But since a part of these resources has been saved from the preceding year, the total product will, as a rule, be considerably greater than before – at any rate up to a certain limit; and it will be greater in proportion as the part of the resources of labour and land thus employed in a saved-up form is increased.

Now experience shows that the replacement of a certain quantity of current labour and land by an equal quantity of stored-up resources of a similar kind tends in many cases to increase productivity, and since we assume that the quantity saved is only sufficient for use in these cases (and not even for all of them) it follows that the *marginal* productivity of the saved resources of labour and land is greater than that of the current resources – at any rate up to a certain point, not yet actually reached.

Wicksell has here given, on the assumptions of his model, the condition for final output to be maximized, namely, equality of the marginal product of last year's (saved) with that of this year's (current) labour. The model is very special but there is no mistaking the problem and its solution.

Modern writers have widened the assumptions about technology and introduced growth. Perhaps the most notable widening has been to get away from the assumption of a steady state. This was achieved by Phelps (1967, pp. 31–54). Phelps proves, with the help of Koopmans and Cass, that a path which does not eventually approach the consumption-maximizing path is intertemporally inefficient. The proof is generalized to non-steady-state conditions, confirming the intuition that the possibility of the capital stock being excessive is not dependent on the steady-state assumption. Nevertheless, as Phelps points out, the practical relevance of this result is the limit which it sets to the desirable amount of *permanent* capital deepening. Hence it meets the difficulty of uncertainty which we saw optimum savings theory also runs into. It is true that whereas the latter is an attempt to work out a step-by-step programme for getting to the consumption-maximizing condition, the former involves merely a proposition about the direction in which it lies. But even this is an act of faith. It must be added that uncertainty implies another difficulty – that consumption is not the sole end of economic activity. Fei (1965) is one author to have emphasized this.

The condition for consumption maximizing is a proposition about continuing growth. It is not relevant to allocation over a finite time except in so far as its place is taken by the whole set of conditions for production to be efficient. Where there is a problem of maximizing a terminal capital stock it has been discovered that the von Neumann growth path has the property of attracting towards it growth paths which do not start or finish on it. This interesting idea has given rise to a large but technical literature so we have omitted it in this selection.

References

ATKINSON, A. B., and STIGLITZ, J. E. (1969), 'A new view of technological change', *Econ. J.*, vol. 79, pp. 573–8.

BARDHAN, P. K. (1969), 'Equilibrium growth in a model with economic obsolescence of machines', *Q. J. Econ.*, vol. 83, pp. 312–23.

BLISS, C. J. (1968), 'On putty–clay', *Rev. econ. Stud.*, vol. 35, pp. 105–32.

CLARK, J. B. (1889), 'Possibility of a scientific law of wages', *Pubns AEA*, vol. 4, no. 1, pp. 39–63.

DEWEY, D. (1965), *Modern Capital Theory*, Columbia University Press.

FEI, J. C. H. (1965), 'Per capita consumption and growth', *Q. J. Econ.*, vol. 79, pp. 52–72.

FERGUSON, C. E. (1969), *The Neo-Classical Theory of Production and Distribution*, Cambridge University Press.

FISHER, I. (1907), *The Rate of Interest*, Macmillan Co.

GAREGNANI, P. (1970), 'Heterogeneous capital, the production function and the theory of distribution', *Rev. econ. Stud.*, vol. 37, pp. 407–36.

GRAAF, J. DE V. (1957), *Theoretical Welfare Economics*, Cambridge University Press.

GRILICHES, Z. and JORGENSON, D. W. (1966), 'Sources of measured productivity change: capital input', *Amer. econ. Rev., Pap. Proc.*, vol. 56, pp. 50–61.

HAHN, F. H., and MATTHEWS, R. C. O. (1964), 'The theory of economic growth: a survey', *Econ. J.*, vol. 74, pp. 779–902.

HARCOURT, G. C. (1968), 'Investment-decision criteria, investment incentives and the choice of technique', *Econ. J.*, vol. 78, pp. 77–95.

HARCOURT, G. C. (1969), 'Some Cambridge controversies in the theory of capital', *J. econ. Lit.*, vol. 7, pp. 369–405.

HICKS, J. R. (1946), *Value and Capital*, Oxford University Press, 2nd edn.

HICKS, J. R. (1960), 'Thoughts on the theory of capital – the Corfu Conference', *Oxf. econ. Pap.*, vol. 12, pp. 123–32.

HIRSHLEIFER, J. (1958), 'On the theory of optimal investment decision', *J. polit. Econ.*, vol. 66, pp. 329–52.

JOHANSEN, L. (1959), 'Substitution versus fixed production coefficients in the theory of economic growth: a synthesis', *Econometrica*, vol. 27, pp. 157–76.

JOHANSEN, L. (1961), 'A method for separating the effects of capital accumulation and shifts in production functions upon growth in labour productivity', *Econ. J.*, vol. 71, pp. 775–82.

JORGENSON, D. W., and GRILICHES, Z. (1967), 'The explanation of productivity change', *Rev. econ. Stud.*, vol. 34, pp. 249–83.

KALDOR, N. (1937), 'Annual survey of economic theory: the recent controversy on the theory of capital', *Econometrica*, vol. 5, pp. 201–33.

KALDOR, N. (1955–6), 'Alternative theories of distribution', *Rev. econ. Stud.*, vol. 23, pp. 83–100.

KALDOR, N. (1959a), 'Economic growth and the problem of inflation – part I', *Economica*, vol. 26, pp. 212–26.

KALDOR, N. (1959b), 'Economic growth and the problem of inflation – part II,' *Economica*, vol. 26, pp. 287–98.

KALDOR, N., and MIRRLEES, J. A. (1962), 'A new model of economic growth', *Rev. econ. Stud.*, vol. 29, pp. 174–92.

KALECKI, M. (1939), *Essays in the Theory of Economic Fluctuations*, Allen & Unwin.

KOOPMANS, T. C. (1957), *Three Essays in the State of Economic Science*, McGraw-Hill.

KOOPMANS, T. C. (1965), 'On the concept of optimal economic growth', in *Pontificiae Academiae Scientiarum Scripta Varia*, North-Holland Publishing Co., pp. 236–9.

LAING, N. F. (1963), 'A diagrammatic approach to general equilibrium analysis', *Rev. econ. Stud.*, vol. 30, pp. 43–55

LAING, N. F. (1965), *Trade, Growth and Distribution. A Study in the Theory of the Long Run*, privately published, University of Adelaide; 2nd edn 1969.

LAING, N. F. (1969), 'Two notes on Pasinetti's theorem', *Econ. Rec.*, vol. 45, pp. 373–85.

LEVHARI, D. (1965), 'A non-substitution theorem and switching of techniques', *Q. J. Econ.*, vol. 79, pp. 98–105.

LUTZ, F. A. (1966), *The Theory of Interest*, Reidel, Dordrecht.

LYDALL, H. F. (1969), 'On measuring technical progress', *Austral. econ. Pap.*, vol. 8, pp. 1–12.

MALINVAUD, E. (1953), 'Capital accumulation and efficient allocation of resources', *Econometrica*, vol. 21, pp. 233–68.

MEADE, J. E. (1961), *A Neo-Classical Theory of Economic Growth*, Allen & Unwin.

MEADE, J. E. (1963), 'The rate of profit in a growing economy', *Econ. J.*, vol. 73, pp. 665–74.

MEADE, J. E., and HAHN, F. H. (1965), 'The rate of profit in a growing economy', *Econ. J.*, vol. 75, pp. 445–8.

PASINETTI, L. L. (1962), 'Rate of profit and income distribution in relation to the rate of economic growth', *Rev. econ. Stud.*, vol. 29, pp. 267–79.

PEARCE, I. F. (1962), 'The end of the Golden Age in Solovia: a further fable for growthmen hoping to be "one-up" on Oika', *Amer. econ. Rev.*, vol. 52, pp. 1088–97.

PHELPS, E. S. (1967), *Golden Rules of Economic Growth*, North-Holland Publishing Co.

PIGOU, A. C. (1935), *The Economics of Stationary States*, Macmillan.

RAMSEY, F. P. (1928), 'A mathematical theory of saving', *Econ. J.*, vol. 38, pp. 543–59.

ROBINSON, J. (1956), *The Accumulation of Capital*, Macmillan.

ROBINSON, J. (1970), 'Capital theory up to date', *Canad. J. Econ.*, vol. 3, pp. 309–17.

ROBINSON, J. (1971), *Economic Heresies: Some Old-Fashioned Questions in Economic Theory*, Basic Books.

SALTER, W. E. G. (1959), 'The production function and the durability of capital', *Econ. Rec.*, vol. 35, pp. 47–66.

SALTER, W. E. G. (1960), *Productivity and Technical Change*, Cambridge University Press.

SALTER, W. E. G. (1965), 'Productivity growth and accumulation as historical processes', in E. A. G. Robinson (ed.), *Problems in Economic Development*, Macmillan, pp. 266–91.

SAMUELSON, P. A. (1962), 'Comment', *Rev. econ. Stud.*, vol. 29, pp. 251–4.

SAMUELSON, P. A., and MODIGLIANI, F. (1966a), 'The Pasinetti paradox in neo-classical and more general models', *Rev. econ. Stud.*, vol. 33, pp. 269–301.

SAMUELSON, P. A., and MODIGLIANI, F. (1966b), 'Reply to Pasinetti and Robinson', *Rev. econ. Stud.*, vol. 33, pp. 321–30.

SCHUMPETER, J. A. (1954), *History of Economic Analysis*, Allen & Unwin.

SCITOVSKY, T. (1942), 'A reconsideration of the theory of tariffs', *Rev. econ. Stud.*, vol. 9, pp. 89–110.

SEN, A. K. (ed.) (1970), *Growth Economics*, Penguin.

SOLOW, R. M. (1955–6), 'The production function and the theory of capital', *Rev. econ. Stud.*, vol. 23, pp. 101–8.

SOLOW, R. M. (1957), 'Technical change and the aggregate production function', *Rev. Econ. Stat.*, vol. 39, pp. 312–20.

SOLOW, R. M. (1960), 'Investment and technical progress', in K. J. Arrow, S. Karlin and P. Suppes (eds.), *Mathematical Methods in the Social Sciences, 1959*, Stanford University Press, pp. 89–104.

SOLOW, R. M. (1962a), 'Substitution and fixed proportions in the theory of capital', *Rev. econ. Stud.*, vol. 29, pp. 207–18.

SOLOW, R. M. (1962b), 'Technical progress, capital formation and economic growth', *Amer. econ. Rev.*, *Pap. Proc.*, vol. 52, pp. 76–86.

SOLOW, R. M. (1963a), 'Heterogeneous capital and smooth production functions: an experimental study', *Econometrica*, vol. 31, pp. 623–45.

SOLOW, R. M. (1963b), *Capital Theory and the Rate of Return*, North-Holland Publishing Co. [See Reading 6.]

SOLOW, R. M. (1967), 'The interest rate and transition between techniques', in C. H. Feinstein (ed.), *Socialism, Capitalism and Economic Growth. Essays Presented to Maurice Dobb*, Cambridge University Press, pp. 30–39.

SOLOW, R. M. (1968), 'Distribution in the long and short run', in J. Marchal and B. Ducros (eds.), *The Distribution of National Income*, Macmillan, pp. 449–75.

SOLOW, R. M., and STIGLITZ, J. E. (1968), 'Output, employment and wages in the short run', *Q. J. Econ.*, vol. 82, pp. 537–60.

SRAFFA, P. (ed.), with DOBB, M. H. (1950–55), *The Works and Correspondence of David Ricardo*, 10 vols., Cambridge University Press.

SRAFFA, P. (1960), *Production of Commodities by Means of Commodities. Prelude to a Critique of Economic Theory*, Cambridge University Press. [See Reading 4.]

SWAN, T. W. (1956), 'Economic growth and capital accumulation', *Econ. Rec.*, vol. 32, pp. 334–61. [See Reading 3.]

VON NEUMANN, J. (1945–6), 'A model of general economic equilibrium', *Rev. econ. Stud.*, vol. 13, pp. 1–9.

WICKSELL, J. G. K. (1934), *Lectures on Political Economy*, trans. from 3rd edn by E. Classen, Routledge & Kegan Paul.

WORSWICK, G. D. N. (1959), 'Mrs Robinson on simple accumulation: a comment with algebra', *Oxf. econ. Pap.*, vol. 11, pp. 125–41.

Part One
Capital as a Unit Independent of Distribution and Prices

The search for a unit in which to measure aggregate (or social) capital in order that it may be used in an aggregate production function as an ingredient in the explanation of distributive shares and prices is an old puzzle which gained new prominence in Joan Robinson's article (Reading 1). As we have seen, Joan Robinson suggested that capital be measured in terms of labour time, i.e. as real capital, a unit which is not, however, independent of the rate of profits. Champernowne (Reading 2) criticized this unit of measurement and suggested in its place a chain-index measure. Swan (Reading 3) examines in detail both the substance of Joan Robinson's critique and the rationale of neo-classical procedures in this context. He also uses Champernowne's chain-index measure to rework some puzzles that were tackled initially by Wicksell (1934) and which had been discussed anew, now within the contexts of growth, distribution and the choice of techniques, in *The Accumulation of Capital* (Robinson, 1956). Reading 4 is an extract of the arguments which lead up to Sraffa's view that it is not possible to conceive of 'capital as a measurable quantity independent of distribution and prices'.

References

ROBINSON, J. (1956), *The Accumulation of Capital*, Macmillan.
WICKSELL, J. G. K. (1934), *Lectures on Political Economy*, trans. from 3rd edn by E. Classen, Routledge & Kegan Paul.

1 Joan Robinson

The Production Function and the Theory of Capital

Joan Robinson, 'The production function and the theory of capital',
in *Collected Economic Papers*, vol. 2, Blackwell, 1965, pp. 114–31.
First published in *Review of Economic Studies*, vol. 21, 1953–4,
pp. 81–106.

Introduction

The dominance in neo-classical economic teaching of the concept
of a production function, in which the relative prices of the factors
of production are exhibited as a function of the ratio in which
they are employed in a given state of technical knowledge, has
had an enervating effect upon the development of the subject,
for by concentrating upon the question of the proportions of
factors it has distracted attention from the more difficult but
more rewarding questions of the influences governing the supplies
of the factors and of the causes and consequences of changes in
technical knowledge.

Moreover, the production function has been a powerful instrument of miseducation. The student of economic theory is taught
to write $O = f(L, C)$ where L is a quantity of labour, C a quantity
of capital and O a rate of output of commodities.[1] He is instructed
to assume all workers alike, and to measure L in man-hours of
labour; he is told something about the index-number problem
involved in choosing a unit of output; and then he is hurried on
to the next question, in the hope that he will forget to ask in what
units C is measured. Before ever he does ask, he has become a
professor, and so sloppy habits of thought are handed on from
one generation to the next.

The question is certainly not an easy one to answer. The
capital in existence at any moment may be treated simply as 'part
of the environment in which labour works' (Keynes, 1936).
We then have a production function in terms of labour alone.
This is the right procedure for the short period within which the

1. Throughout this essay we shall be abstracting from land as a factor of
production, so we will not bother the student with it.

supply of concrete capital goods does not alter, but outside the short period it is a very weak line to take, for it means that we cannot distinguish a change in the stock of capital (which can be made over the long run by accumulation) from a change in the weather (an act of God).

We may look upon a stock of capital as the specific list of all the goods in existence at any moment (including work-in-progress in the pipe-lines of production). But this again is of no use outside the strict bounds of the short period, for any change in the ratio of capital to labour involves a reorganization of methods of production and requires a change in the shapes, sizes and specifications of many or all the goods appearing in the original list.[2]

As soon as we leave the short period, however, a host of difficulties appear. Should capital be valued according to its future earning power or its past costs?

When we know the future expected rate of output associated with a certain capital good, and expected future prices and costs, then, if we are given a rate of interest, we can value the capital good as a discounted stream of future profit which it will earn. But to do so, we have to begin by taking the rate of interest as given, whereas the main purpose of the production function is to show how wages and the rate of interest (regarded as the wages of capital) are determined by technical conditions and the factor ratio.

Are we then to value capital goods by their cost of production? Clearly money cost of production is neither here nor there unless we can specify the purchasing power of money, but we may cost the capital goods in terms of wage units; that is, in effect, to measure their cost in terms of a unit of standard labour.

To treat capital as a quantity of labour time expended in the past is congenial to the production-function point of view, for it corresponds to the essential nature of capital regarded as a factor of production. Investment consists, in essence, in employing labour now in a way which will yield its fruits in the future while saving is making current products available for the workers to consume in the meantime; and the productiveness of capital consists in the fact that a unit of labour that was expended at a

2. In Professor Robertson's example, when a tenth man joins nine who are digging a hole, nine more expensive spades are turned into nine cheaper spades and a bucket to fetch beer (Robertson, 1931, p. 47).

certain time in the past is more valuable today than a unit expended today, because its fruits are already ripe.

But here we encounter a fundamental difficulty which lies at the root of the whole problem of capital. A unit of labour is never expended in a pure form. All work is done with the assistance of goods of some kind or another. When Adam delved and Eve span there were evidently a spade and a spindle already in existence. The cost of capital includes the cost of capital goods, and since they must be constructed before they can be used, part of the cost of capital is interest over the period of time between the moment when work was done in constructing capital goods and the time when they are producing a stream of output. This is not just a consequence of capitalism, for equally in a socialist society a unit of labour, expended today, which will yield a product in five years' time, is not the same thing as a unit which will yield a product tomorrow.

Finally, even if it were possible to measure capital simply in terms of labour time, we still should not have answered the question: of what units is C composed? When we are discussing accumulation, it is natural to think of capital as measured in terms of product. The process of accumulation consists in refraining from consuming current output in order to add to the stock of wealth. But when we consider what addition to productive resources a given amount of accumulation makes, we must measure capital in labour units, for the addition to the stock of productive equipment made by adding an increment of capital depends upon how much work is done in constructing it, not upon the cost, in terms of final product, of an hour's labour. Thus, as we move from one point on a production function to another, measuring capital in terms of product, we have to know the product-wage rate in order to see the effect upon production of changing the ratio of capital to labour. Or if we measure in labour units, we have to know the product-wage in order to see how much accumulation would be required to produce a given increment of capital. But the wage rate alters with the ratio of the factors; one symbol, C, cannot stand both for a quantity of product and a quantity of labour time.

All the same, the problem which the production function professes to analyse, although it has been too much puffed up by the attention paid to it, is a genuine problem. Today, in country Alpha, a length of roadway is being cleared by a few men with bulldozers; in Beta a road (of near enough the same quality) is being made by some hundreds of men with picks and ox-carts. In Gamma thousands of men are working with wooden shovels and little baskets to remove the soil. When all possible allowances have been made for differences in national character and climate, and for differences in the state of knowledge, it seems pretty clear that the main reason for this state of affairs is that capital in some sense is more plentiful in Alpha than in Gamma. Looked at from the point of view of an individual capitalist, it would not pay to use Alpha methods in Gamma (even if unlimited finance were available) at the rate of interest which is ruling, and looked at from the point of view of society, it would need a prodigious effort of accumulation to raise all the labour available in Gamma even to the Beta level of technique. The problem is a real one. We cannot abandon the production function without an effort to rescue the element of common sense that has been entangled in it.

The quantity of capital

'Capital' is not what capital is called, it is what its name is called. The capital goods in existence at a moment of time are all the goods in existence at that moment. It is not all the things in existence. It includes neither a rubbish heap nor Mont Blanc. The characteristic by which 'goods' are specified is that they have value; that is, purchasing power over each other. Thus, in country Alpha an empty petrol tin is not a 'good', whereas in Gamma, where old tins are a source of valuable industrial raw material, it is.

The list of goods is quite specific. It is so many actual particular objects, called blast furnaces, overcoats, etc., etc. Goods grouped under the same name differ from each other in details of their physical specifications and these must not be overlooked. Differences in their ages are also important. A blast furnace twenty years old is not equivalent to a brand new one of the same specification in other respects, nor is an egg twenty days old equivalent to a brand new one. There is another relevant characteristic of the goods. An overcoat requires one body to wear it, and an egg one mouth to eat it. Without one body, or one mouth, they are useless, and two bodies or mouths (at a given moment of time) cannot share in using them. But a blast furnace can be used by a certain range of numbers of bodies to turn iron ore into iron. Therefore the description of a blast furnace includes an account of its rate of output as a function of the number of bodies operating it. (When long-period equilibrium prevails, the number of bodies actually working each piece of equipment is the number which is technically most appropriate to it.)

There is another aspect of the goods which is quite different. Of two overcoats, completely similar in all the above respects, one is on the body of Mrs Jones, who is purring with inward delight at her fine appearance. Another is on the body of Mrs Snooks, who is grizzling because, her husband's income being what it is, she is obliged to buy mass-produced clothes. In what follows we shall not discuss this aspect of goods at all. We take it that an overcoat (Mark IV) is an overcoat (Mark IV), and no nonsense.

Now, this enormous who's who of individual goods is not a thing that we can handle at all easily. To express it as a *quantity* of goods we have to evaluate the items of which it is composed. We can evaluate the goods in terms of the real cost of producing them – that is, the work and the formerly existing goods required to make them, or in terms of their value expressed in some unit of purchasing power; or we can evaluate them according to their productivity – that is, what the stock of goods will become in the future if work is done in conjunction with it.

In a position of equilibrium all three evaluations yield equivalent results; there is a quantity which can be translated from one number to another by changing the unit. This is the definition of equilibrium. It entails that there have been no events over the relevant period of past time which have disturbed the relation between the various valuations of a given stock of goods, and that the human beings in the situation are expecting the future to be just like the past – entirely devoid of such disturbing events. Then the rate of profit ruling today is the rate which was expected to rule today when the decision to invest in any capital good now extant was made, and the expected future receipts, capitalized at the current rate of profit, are equal to the cost of the capital goods which are expected to produce them.

When an unexpected event occurs, the three ways of evaluating the stock of goods part company and no amount of juggling with units will bring them together again.

We are accustomed to talk of the rate of profit on capital earned by a business as though profits and capital were both sums of money. Capital when it consists of as yet uninvested finance is a sum of money, and the net receipts of a business are sums of money. But the two never co-exist in time. While the capital is a sum of money, the profits are not yet being earned. When the profits (quasi-rents) are being earned, the capital has ceased to be money and become a plant. All sorts of things may happen which cause the value of the plant to diverge from its original cost. When an event has occurred, say a fall in prices, which was not foreseen when investment in the plant was made, how do we regard the capital represented by the plant?

The man of deeds, who has decisions to make, is considering how future prospects have altered. He is concerned with new finance or accrued amortization funds, which he must decide how to use. He cannot do anything about the plant (unless the situation is so desperate that he decides to scrap it). He is not particularly interested (except when he has to make out a case before a Royal Commission) in how the man of words, who is measuring capital, chooses to value the plant.[3]

The man of words has a wide choice of possible methods of evaluation, but none of them is very satisfactory. First, capital may be conceived of as consisting either in the cost or in the value of the plant. If cost is the measure, should money cost actually incurred be reckoned? It is only of historical interest, for the purchasing power of money has since changed. Is the money cost to be deflated? Then by what index? Or is capital to be measured at current replacement cost? The situation may be such that no one in his senses would build a plant like this one if he were to build now. Replacement cost may be purely academic. But even if the plant is, in fact, due to be replaced by a replica of itself at some future date, we still have to ask what proportion of the value of a brand new plant is represented by this elderly plant? And the

3. 'A man of words but not of deeds
   Is like a garden full of weeds.'
This is sadly true of the theory of capital.

answer to that question involves future earnings, not cost alone.

If the capital is to be measured by value, how decide what the present value of the plant is? The price at which it could be sold as an integral whole has not much significance, as the market for such transactions is narrow. To take its price on the Stock Exchange (if it is quoted) is to go before a tribunal whose credentials are dubious. If the capital-measurer makes his own judgement, he takes what he regards as likely to be the future earnings of the plant and discounts them at what he regards as the right rate of interest for the purpose, thus triumphantly showing that the most probable rate of profit on the capital invested in the plant is equal to the most appropriate rate of interest.

All these puzzles arise because there is a gap in time between investing money capital and receiving money profits, and in that gap events may occur which alter the value of money.

To abstract from uncertainty means to postulate that no such events occur, so that the *ex ante* expectations which govern the actions of the man of deeds are never out of gear with the *ex post* experience which governs the pronouncements of the man of words, and to say that equilibrium obtains is to say that no such events have occurred for some time, or are thought liable to occur in the future.

The ambiguity of the conception of a quantity of capital is connected with a profound methodological error, which makes the major part of neo-classical doctrine spurious.

The neo-classical economist thinks of a position of equilibrium as a position towards which an economy is tending to move as time goes by. But it is impossible for a system to *get into* a position of equilibrium, for the very nature of equilibrium is that the system is already in it, and has been in it for a certain length of past time.

Time is unlike space in two very striking respects. In space, bodies moving from A to B may pass bodies moving from B to A, but in time the strictest possible rule of one-way traffic is always in force. And in space the distance from A to B is of the same order of magnitude (whatever allowance you like to make for the Trade Winds) as the distance from B to A; but in time the distance from today to tomorrow is twenty-four hours, while the distance from today to yesterday is infinite, as the poets have often remarked.

Therefore a space metaphor applied to time is a very tricky knife to handle, and the concept of equilibrium often cuts the arm that wields it.

When an event has occurred we are thrown back upon the who's who of goods in existence, and the 'quantity of capital' ceases to have any other meaning. Then only that part of the theory of value which treats of the short period, in which the physical stock of capital equipment is given, has any application.

Long-period equilibrium

One notion of equilibrium is that it is reached (with a constant labour force) when the stock of capital and the rate of profit are such that there is no motive for further accumulation. This is associated with the idea of an ultimate thorough-going stationary state (Pigou, 1935), in which the rate of profit is equal to the 'supply price of waiting'. In this situation an accidental increase in the stock of capital above the equilibrium quantity would depress the rate of profit below this supply price, and cause the additional capital to be consumed; while any reduction would raise the rate of profit, and cause the deficiency to be made good. Equilibrium prevails when the stock of capital is such that the rate of profit is equal to the supply price of that quantity of capital.

But this notion is a very treacherous one. Why should the supply price of waiting be assumed positive? In Adam Smith's forest there was no property in capital and no profit (the means of production, wild deer and beavers, were plentiful and un-appropriated). But there might still be waiting and interest. Suppose that some hunters wish to consume more than their kill, and others wish to carry consuming power into the future. Then the latter could lend to the former today, out of today's catch, against a promise of repayment in the future. The rate of interest (excess of repayment over original loan) would settle at the level which equated supply and demand for loans. Whether it was positive or negative would depend upon whether spendthrifts or prudent family men happened to predominate in the community. There is no *a priori* presumption in favour of a positive rate. Thus, the rate of interest cannot be accounted for as the 'cost of waiting'.

The reason why there is always a demand for loans at a positive rate of interest, in an economy where there is property in the means of production and means of production are scarce, is that finance expended now can be used to employ labour in productive processes which will yield a surplus in the future over costs of production. Interest is positive because profits are positive (though at the same time the cost and difficulty of obtaining finance play a part in keeping productive equipment scarce, and so contribute to maintaining the level of profits).

Where the 'supply price of waiting' is very low or negative, the ultimate stationary equilibrium cannot be reached until the rate of profit has fallen equally low, capital has ceased to be scarce and capitalism has ceased to be capitalism. Therefore this type of equilibrium is not worth discussing.

The other way of approaching the question is simply to postulate that the stock of capital in existence at any moment is the amount that has been accumulated up to date, and that the reason why it is not larger is that it takes time to grow. At any moment, on this view, there is a certain stock of capital in existence. If the rate of profit and the desire to own more wealth are such as to induce accumulation, the stock of capital is growing and, provided that labour is available or population growing, the system may be in process of expanding without any disturbance to the conditions of equilibrium. (If two snapshots were taken of the economy at two different dates, the stock of capital, the amount of employment and the rate of output would all be larger, in the second photograph, by a certain percentage, but there would be no other difference.) If the stock of capital is being kept constant over time, that is merely a special case in which the rate of accumulation happens to be zero. (The two snapshots would then be indistinguishable.)

In the internal structure of the economy conditions of long-period equilibrium may then be assumed to prevail. Each type of product sells at its normal long-run supply price. For any one type of commodity, profit, at the rate ruling in the system as a whole, on the cost of capital equipment engaged in producing it, is part of the long-run supply price of the commodity, for no commodity will continue to be produced unless capital invested for the purpose of producing it yields at least the same rate of profit as the rest. (It is assumed that capitalists are free to move from one line of production to another.) Thus the 'costs of production' which determine supply price consist of wages and profits. In this context the notion of a quantity of capital presents no difficulty for, to any one capitalist, capital is a quantity of value, or generalized purchasing power, and, in a given equilibrium situation, a unit of any commodity can be used as a measure of purchasing power.

Since the system is in equilibrium in all its parts, the ruling rate of profit is being obtained on capital which is being used to produce capital goods, and enters into their 'cost of production'. Profit on that part of the cost of capital represented by this profit is then a component of the 'cost of production' of final output. A capitalist who buys a machine ready made pays a price for it which includes profit to the capitalist who sells it. The profit a capitalist who has the machine built in his own workshops will expect to receive, from sales of the final output, includes profit on the interest (at a notional rate equal to the ruling rate of profit) on the cost of having the machine built reckoned over the period of construction. For when he builds the machine himself he has a longer waiting period between starting to invest and receiving the first profit. If he could not earn profit on the notional interest cost, he would prefer to make an investment where there was a shorter waiting period, so that he could receive actual profit earlier. The actual profit he could plough into investment, thus acquiring (over the same waiting period) the same quantity of capital as in the case where he builds the machine for himself. (He would also have the advantage that he could change his mind and consume the profit, whereas in the first case he is committed to the whole scheme of investment once he begins.) Thus, investments with a long gestation period will not be made unless they are expected to yield a profit on the element of capital cost represented by compound interest over the gestation period (if there were uncertainty, they would have to be expected to yield more, to compensate for the greater rigidity of the investment plan).

We need not go back to Adam to search for the first pure unit of labour that contributed to the construction of existing equipment. The capital goods in being today have mutually contributed to producing each other, and each is assumed to have received the appropriate amount of profit for doing so.

So much for the supply price of an item of new equipment. How are we to reckon the supply price of part-worn equipment? Investment in new equipment is not made unless its gross earnings (excess of output over wages bill in terms of output) are expected to be sufficient to amortize the investment over its working life, allowing for interest at the ruling rate on accrued amortization funds, as well as providing profit at the ruling rate. The supply price of an equipment which has been working for a certain time may be regarded as its initial cost accumulated up to date at compound interest, *minus* its gross earnings also accumulated from the dates at which they accrued up to the present, for this corresponds to the expectations which induced capitalists in the past to make the investment concerned.

Since initial cost is incurred at the beginning, and earnings accrue over time, the element of interest on cost in the above calculation exceeds the element of interest on earnings. Thus when an equipment has yielded a quarter of its expected total earnings, its supply price, in this sense, is somewhat more than three-quarters of its initial cost; half-way through, somewhat more than half its initial cost, and so forth, the difference at any moment being larger the higher the rate of interest. Over its life the accumulated interest on its earnings, so to say, catches up upon the accumulated interest on its cost, so that at the end of its life it is fully paid off and its supply price (abstracting from scrap value) has fallen to zero.

The value of an equipment depends upon its expected future earnings. It may be regarded as future earnings discounted back to the present at a rate corresponding to the ruling rate of interest. In equilibrium conditions the supply price (in the above sense) and the value of an equipment are equal at all stages of its life.[4]

4. The equalization of the value of two annuities at any point of time entails their equalization at any other point of time. If the cost of a new machine is equal, at the moment when it is brand new, to the discounted value of its expected gross earnings, it follows that, at any later point of time, the accumulated value of the original cost and gross earnings up to date will, if expectations have been proved correct up to date and are unaffected for the future, be equal to the present value of the remaining gross earnings expected over the future. cf. Wicksell (1934, p. 276).

Equilibrium requires that the stock of items of equipment operated by all the capitalists producing a particular commodity is continuously being maintained. This entails that the age composition of the stock of equipment is such that the amortization funds provided by the stock as a whole are being continuously spent on replacements. When the stock of equipment is in balance there is no need to inquire whether a particular worker is occupied in producing final output or in replacing plant. The whole of a given labour force is producing a stream of final output and at the same time maintaining the stock of equipment for future production. Nor is it necessary to inquire what book-keeping methods are used in reckoning amortization quotas. These affect the relations between individual capitalists, but cancel out for the group as a whole.

In equilibrium the age composition of the stock of equipment is stable, but the total stock may be in course of expanding. The average age of the plants making up a balanced stock of stable age composition varies with the length of life of individual plants. If the total stock is remaining constant over time, the average age is equal to half the length of life. If the stock has been growing, the proportion of younger plants is greater and average age is less than half the life span. (There is an exact analogy with the age composition of a stable population.)

The amount of capital embodied in a stock of equipment is the sum of the supply prices (reckoned as above) of the plants of which it is composed, and the ratio of the amount of capital to the sum of the costs of the plants when each was brand new is higher the greater the rate of interest.[5]

5. The order of magnitude of the influence of the rate of interest is shown by the formula provided in the Mathematical Addendum by D. G. Champernowne and R. F. Kahn (see appendix to Robinson, 1956). For this formula it is necessary to assume (a) that the total stock of capital is constant over time, (b) that earnings are at an even rate over the life of the plant. C is the capital value of an investment, K the initial outlay, r the rate of interest and T the period over which the asset earns. For values of rT less than 2 we use the approximation $C/K = \frac{1}{2}(1 + \frac{1}{2}rT)$.

On this basis, when the rate of interest is, for example, 6 per cent, a machine of ten years' life costing £100 when new must earn £13·3 per annum surplus over the current outlay on working it (including current repairs). The yield will then be 6 per cent on a capital value of £55.

A group of ten such machines of ages zero to nine years has a pattern of

Equilibrium requires that the rate of profit ruling today was expected to be ruling today when investment in any plant now extant was made, and the expectation of future profits obtaining today was expected to obtain today. Thus the value of capital in existence today is equal to its supply price calculated in this manner. The heavy weight which this method of valuing capital puts upon the assumptions of equilibrium emphasizes the impossibility of valuing capital in an uncertain world. In a world where unexpected events occur which alter values, the points of view of the man of deeds, making investment decisions about the future, and of the man of words making observations about the past, are irreconcilable, and all we can do is botch up some conventional method of measuring capital that will satisfy neither of them.

Wages and profits

The neo-classical system is based on the postulate that, in the long run, the rate of real wages tends to be such that all available labour is employed. In spite of the atrocities that have been committed in its name there is obviously a solid core of sense in this proposition. To return to our road builders, employment per unit of output is much higher in Gamma than in Alpha, and it seems obvious that this is connected with the fact that real wages there are much lower – that the plethora of labour keeps real wages down, and so helps to get itself employed. Let us try to see what this means.

The basic data of the system are: the labour force, the amount of capital and the state of technical knowledge, expressed as the

---

values, at any moment, which corresponds to the pattern over time of a single machine. It requires an annual outlay on renewals of £100 permanently to maintain the stock of machines. They represent a capital value of £550 and yield a return of £33 per annum.

If the rate of interest were 10 per cent, rT would be equal to 1 and the capital value (abstracting from a higher initial cost of machines due to the higher interest rate) would be £583; the earnings of each machine would then have to be £15·8 to yield the required rate of profit.

If the length of life of machines was twenty years, and the rate of interest 5 per cent, capital value would again be £583, and each machine would have to yield £7·9 per annum (£5 for amortization and £2·9 for interest); at 10 per cent, rT would be equal to 2; the capital value would then be £666, and each machine would have to yield £11·7 per annum.

hierarchy, ranged according to degrees of mechanization, of the possible techniques of production. In order to satisfy the neo-classical postulate of full employment, the given amount of capital must employ the given amount of labour.

At any given wage rate, the interplay of competition between capitalists, each seeking to maximize his own profits, is assumed to ensure that the technique will be chosen that maximizes the rate of profit. Thus, the technique is a function of the wage rate. The outfit of productive equipment in existence is determined by the technique and the total amount of capital. A given outfit of equipment offers a given amount of employment. Thus, we have the amount of employment as a function of the wage rate. We can then state the neo-classical postulate: the wage rate is assumed to be such that the technique of production is such that the given quantity of capital employs the given labour force. It is necessary to postulate that the amount of real wages (which is not the same thing as the wage bill but is governed by it) in relation to the cost of subsistence is at least sufficient to maintain the given labour force in being.

The condition that the given amount of capital employs the given amount of labour thus entails a particular rate of profit. But the value of the stock of concrete capital goods is affected by this rate of profit and the amount of 'capital' that we started with cannot be defined independently of it.

What becomes of the neo-classical doctrine if we read it the other way round: that the rate of profit tends to be such as to permit all the capital that comes into existence to be employed? Suppose that the wage rate has been established at a level which yields some conventional minimum real wage, and that, the technique having been chosen which maximizes the rate of profit, the quantity of capital in existence does not employ all available labour, so that there is a reserve of unemployment. Accumulation can then proceed at a constant factor ratio and constant rate of profit until all available labour is employed. If population is increasing at least as fast as capital is accumulating, full employment is never attained, and the expansion of the economy can continue indefinitely (we have postulated that there is no scarcity of land, including all non-produced means of production).

So far the argument is dismally simple. What are we supposed to imagine to happen when there is full employment in the long-period sense, that is, when there is sufficient plant in existence to employ all available labour? One line of argument is to suppose that the capitalists who are accumulating act in a blindly individualistic manner, so that a scramble for labour sets in; the money-wage rate is bid up, and prices rise in an indefinite spiral. (It is of no use to bring the financial mechanism into the argument, for if the supply of the medium of exchange is limited, the interest rate is driven up; but what the situation requires is a fall in the rate of interest, to encourage the use of more mechanized techniques.)

Or we may postulate that the capitalists, while fully competitive in selling, observe a convention against bidding for labour – each confines himself to employing a certain share of the constant labour force. Then anyone who wishes to increase the amount of capital that he operates shifts to a more mechanized technique. Those who first make the change may be supposed to compete for wider markets and so to reduce prices relatively to money wages. A higher degree of mechanization then becomes eligible, and the switch to more mechanized techniques proceeds at a sufficient rate to absorb new capital as it accrues. Alternatively, we might imagine that an excessive number of plants of the less mechanized type are actually built, and that their redundancy, relatively to labour to man them, reduces profit margins, so that the wage rate rises and induces mechanization. (Whichever line we follow the argument is necessarily highly artificial, for in reality the state of trade is the dominant influence on investment. The situation which promotes the mechanization of production is full employment and full order books, that is to say, a scarcity of labour relatively to effective demand, but the equilibrium assumptions do not permit us to say anything about effective demand.)

Somehow or other, accumulation may be conceived to push down the rate of profit, and raise the factor ratio.

But the very notion of accumulation proceeding under equilibrium conditions at changing factor ratios bristles with difficulties. The rate at which the factor ratio rises is not governed in any simple way by the pace at which accumulation goes on – it depends upon the extent to which the rising wage rate causes capital to be absorbed by the Wicksell effect. Moreover, the effect of a given change in the factor ratio depends upon the speed at which it is made, relatively to the length of life of plant. If capital per man is rising rapidly some capitalists' plants appropriate to a variety of degrees of mechanization will be operating side by side.

Even if we can find a way through these complications, there remains the formidable problem of how to treat expectations when the rate of profit is altering. An unforeseen fall in the rate of profit ruptures the conditions of equilibrium. Capitalists who are operating on borrowed funds can no longer earn the interest they have contracted to pay, and those operating their own capital find themselves in possession of a type of plant that they would not have built if they had known what the rate of profit was going to be.

On the other hand, if we postulate that accumulation goes on in the expectation of a gradually falling rate of profit, the whole basis of the analysis becomes immensely complicated. We can no longer argue in terms of a single interest rate. There is a complex of rates for loans of different lengths, the rates for shorter terms standing above the rates for longer terms. Moreover, the pace at which the rate of profit falls as the factor ratio rises is dictated by technical conditions. Over its early reaches the factor-ratio curve may be supposed to be steep, with the rate of profit falling slowly. Then it passes over a hump, with a rapid fall in the rate of profit, and flattens out again with a lower but more slowly falling rate of profit. To be correct, the expectations of the capitalists cannot merely be based on past experience but require a highly sophisticated degree of foresight.

Thus, the assumptions of equilibrium become entangled in self-contradictions if they are applied to the problem of accumulation going on through time with a changing factor ratio. To discuss accumulation we must look through the eyes of the man of deeds, taking decisions about the future, while to account for what has been accumulated we must look back over the accidents of past history. The two points of view meet only in the who's who of goods in existence today, which is never in an equilibrium relationship with the situation that obtains today.

In short, the comparison between equilibrium positions with different factor ratios cannot be used to analyse changes in the factor ratio taking place through time, and it is impossible to discuss changes (as opposed to differences) in neo-classical terms.

The production function, it seems, has a very limited relevance to actual problems, and after all these labours we can add little to the platitudes with which we began: in country Gamma, where the road builders use wooden shovels, if more capital had been accumulated in the past, relatively to labour available for employment, the level of real wages would probably have been higher and the technique of production more mechanized, and, given the amount of capital accumulated, the more mechanized the technique of production, the smaller the amount of employment would have been.

Postscript

I have included here only the negative part of this article as the constructive parts are better done in my book, *The Accumulation of Capital* (1956). The trouble which I was trying to expose arose from burdening the concept of a production function with inappropriate tasks. The notion of a range of possible techniques, co-existing in time in the form of blue prints, amongst which choices are made by firms or investment planners when new productive capacity is being set up, is useful and has a genuine operational meaning (though it is very difficult to apply in the complicated situations that arise in reality). In that context, it is appropriate to measure the investible resources about to be committed in terms of value. The difficulties that present themselves arise out of the uncertainty of the future and can be imagined to disappear in conditions of perfect tranquillity.

When presented with the task of determining the distribution of the product of industry between labour and capital, the neo-classical production function comes to grief (even in the most perfect tranquillity) on the failure to distinguish between 'capital' in the sense of means of production with particular technical characteristics and 'capital' in the sense of a command over finance.

When presented with the task of analysing a process of accumulation, the production function comes to grief on the failure to distinguish between comparisons of equilibrium positions and movements from one to another.

The remarks about equilibrium on page 53 above seemed very queer to Sir Dennis Robertson (1957, p. 95), and, indeed, they are not well worded. My point was this: a state of equilibrium is one in which each individual is satisfied that he could not do better for himself by changing his behaviour. Applied to long-lived capital equipment, this means that the stock in existence today is in all respects what it would have been if those concerned had known, at relevant dates in the past, what expectations about the future they would be holding today. But periods affected by different decisions overlap and the relevant past stretches back indefinitely. Thus, an economy can be following an equilibrium path today only if it has been following it for some time already. A thorough-going stationary state is a limiting case in which nothing changes except the date as the economy moves along its equilibrium path.

Elsewhere I have tried to show how the neo-classical production function can be rescued if we bring the Keynesian conditions to its aid (Robinson, 1959). The equilibrium path of accumulation and distribution of income can then be traced out. But there is still lacking any plausible account of a mechanism to keep the economy in equilibrium.

References

KEYNES, J. M. (1936), *The General Theory of Employment, Interest and Money*, Macmillan.
PIGOU, A. C. (1935), *The Economics of Stationary States*, Macmillan.
ROBERTSON, D. H. (1931), *Economic Fragments*, King.
ROBERTSON, D. H. (1957), *Lectures on Economic Principles*, vol. 1, Staples Press.
ROBINSON, J. (1956), *The Accumulation of Capital*, Macmillan.
ROBINSON, J. (1959), 'Accumulation and the production function', *Econ. J.*, vol. 69, pp. 433–42.
WICKSELL, J. G. K. (1934), *Lectures on Political Economy*, vol. 1, trans. from 3rd edn by E. Classen, Routledge & Kegan Paul.

2 D. G. Champernowne

The Production Function and the Theory of Capital: A Comment[1]

D. G. Champernowne, 'The production function and the theory of capital: a comment', *Review of Economic Studies*, vol. 21, 1953–4, pp. 112–35.

Introduction

In her note on the production function,[2] Joan Robinson (1953–4) has drawn attention to the difficulties inherent in any attempt to measure the quantity of capital in a community by a single number, and of the consequent dangers in teaching pupils to regard output as a function of the amounts of labour and capital employed. In an effort to avoid in time 'sloppy habits of thought', she has adopted the position that 'when we consider what addition to productive resources a given amount of accumulation makes, we must measure capital in labour units' and hence determined a method of measuring the quantity of capital under the equilibrium conditions of a simplified model: this threw light on the manner in which the factor ratio (quantity of capital available per employed person) affected the choice of productive technique, the rate of interest and the real-wage rate, and hence the distribution of product between capital and labour. For brevity we shall refer to the labour units of quantity of capital which Joan Robinson uses, as JR units.

The present comments will be directed towards the following points.

1. If we propose to regard output as a function of the quantities of labour and capital employed, it is not very convenient to measure capital in JR units because, if we do: (a) The same

1. I have been greatly helped in the writing of this article by criticism from Professors Robinson, Kahn and Johnson, and by instruction from Professor Kaldor. I need only add the customary rider that none of them bears any responsibility for the shortcomings of the article.
2. See Reading 1 [*Eds.*].

physical stock of capital equipment and working capital, producing the same flow of consumption goods, can appear under two equilibrium conditions, differing only in respect of the rate of interest and rate of real wages, as two different amounts of capital. (b) The wage rate of labour and the reward per unit of capital will, in general, differ under perfect competition from the partial derivatives of output with respect to the quantities of labour and capital employed. (c) Output per head may be negatively correlated with quantity of capital per head measured in JR units, despite the assumption of a given state of technical knowledge. This can lead to the paradoxical result that a reduction of the capital per head (in JR units) is required to increase productivity.

2. If we abandon JR units of capital and employ instead a straightforward chain index of quantity of capital, then we can again obtain, in principle, a production function $O = f(L, C)$ with the property that the social product O is distributed into shares $L(\partial f/\partial L)$ for labour and $C(\partial f/\partial C)$ for capital.

3. A clear and rigorous deduction of these results requires a careful statement of the assumptions underlying the model and the explicit exclusion of certain exceptional cases. The exceptional cases themselves are of some interest as indicating situations where the production function is no longer single-valued and in which some of Joan Robinson's conclusions are falsified.

4. The use of the chain index for measuring capital facilitates the discussion of the case where a 'continuous spectrum' of techniques is available. The distribution of O into $L(\partial f/\partial L)$ and $C(\partial f/\partial C)$ still holds in this case.

5. The remaining sections of the article are concerned with the effects of relaxing the three simplifying conventions: (a) only stationary states are to be considered and compared; (b) there are no technical advances; (c) labour and capital are the only two factors employed.

6. An appendix giving particular arithmetical and algebraic examples throws light on the working of the general model.

Choice of units for measuring quantity of capital

In her introduction, Joan Robinson complains that the student of economic theory is taught to regard output as a function of the amounts of labour and capital but is not taught in what units the quantity of capital is to be measured. Her own answer is that under the simplified conditions which she assumes, the quantity of capital should be measured in units of labour and should be equated to the labour input which it costs, compounded at the ruling rate of interest; if the capital has already been used to produce output, an appropriate deduction from its cost should be made on this account.

There is nothing inconsistent in this method, but it is not the only possible method and it is inconvenient if we wish to regard output as a function of the quantities of labour and capital. Suppose, for example, that as described in Joan Robinson's section 'Technique of production', there exists a hierarchy of techniques, which may become profitable at various stages of capital development. To each such technique there will correspond a range of interest rates at which it can be fully competitive (given appropriate wage rates) compared to all other techniques. It is thus possible to conceive two stationary states, each using one and the same technique, with identical amounts and composition of capital equipment, with identical labour input and product output: yet, although both are in equilibrium, they may have differing real wage rates, and two different interest rates, each within the range over which the technique can be fully competitive. For purposes such that output is to be regarded as technically determined by the amounts of labour and capital employed, it would be convenient to regard the quantities of capital employed in these two stationary states as the same, because the capital stock, the labour input and the output stream are identical in the two states. Yet because the rate of interest differs in the two states, the quantities of capital as measured by J R units must differ also.

Conversely, it is easy to see that two equilibrium stationary states may exist with different techniques with the same labour input, but with different interest rates, and different outputs, which will appear, with J R units, to have equal amounts of capital as well as of labour. Thus, whilst, on the one hand, the same physical capital can be measured as two different amounts of capital yet, on the other hand, the same amounts of labour and capital may result in different outputs. The function giving output in terms of the factor inputs fails to be single-valued.

These difficulties arise from the index-number problem involved in measuring the quantity of capital. They result simply from the fact that mere difference in interest rates, without necessarily corresponding to any difference in the productive possibilities or physical characteristics of the stocks of capital available in two stationary states, can yet affect their cost measured in JR units. Hence, comparing the amounts of capital in a sequence of stationary states, we shall obtain a set of numbers reflecting differences of interest rates as well as differences relevant to productive potential. There is a close analogy to an attempt to compare quantities of production by an index giving their money values in a sequence of stationary states with slightly different price systems.

It may be asked whether these inconveniences disappear when we consider not a sequence of discrete equipments but a continuous spectrum, with the appropriate rate of interest altering continuously as we pass down the spectrum. The answer is that the most glaring inconveniences do disappear, but the basic weakness of the method remains: differences in interest rates which are irrelevant to the production possibilities (although not to the profit possibilities) of two sets of capital equipment still are allowed to affect the comparison of their amounts of capital when measured in JR units. That the distortion that this involves may be so great as to contradict common sense is suggested by the following extreme example. Suppose that there is a continuous spectrum of basic equipments E_u, with u a continuous variable. If now instead of discussing stationary states, we think of a very slow progress with constant employment, but changing type of equipment providing an increasing output, we should not go very far wrong by supposing wages and interest rates to move through the stationary state values appropriate to the various types of equipment.

Suppose that constant replacement of worn-out equipment by types providing more output per head involves the withholding of some labour from producing consumption goods, then this situation is such as is normally described as one with positive net investment, and we can legitimately require that any proposed system of measurement may show the quantity of capital to be increasing.

The following simple example is discussed in some detail on pages 94–6. Each basic equipment E_u costs the work of 100 men spread evenly over one year; when complete, the equipment E_u needs $100u$ men to work it and produces a uniform output flow at the rate of $100(1+11u)^{1/11}$ units per annum: at the end of one year the equipment wears out. It is shown that if 1 per cent of the labour force is withheld from other activity and devoted to replacing worn-out equipments by a (larger) number of equipments needing less men to operate them in relation to those required to build them, then as u steadily decreases and the number of equipments increases, the rate of interest will fall, real wages will rise and the output of food will rise. If in this example we use the chain-index method described on page 71–4, and in Appendix 1, each equipment can be regarded as 100 units of capital, and the total quantity of capital will increase at a rate of K per cent per annum where K is the proportion that the annual net income bears to the value of all capital.

Now consider how this process appears when JR units are used for the measurement of capital. It is shown in the Appendix that an equipment of type E_u will at the time of its use contain approximately $1000u/\log(1+10u)$ JR units of capital. If the total number of men employed is $100N$ then the total number of equipments of type E_u is approximately $N/(1+u)$, so that the total number of units of capital is, approximately

$$1000N_u/(1+u)\log(1+10u).$$

Numerical calculation shows that if $u = 2 \cdot 326$ initially and capital accumulation proceeds as described above, u will fall from $2 \cdot 326$ towards zero, and the quantity of capital measured in JR units will simultaneously *fall* from about $219N$ down to $100N$. Thus, in this example, a process of capital accumulation carried out by labour withheld from making consumption goods, and financed out of saving, appears when JR units are used as a steady *decrease* in the quantity of capital. This is an extreme example of the negative bias induced in measurement of net investment when

JR units are used, and this bias is due to including a negative element reflecting a fall in the rate of interest.

Thus our warning against the incautious use of JR units is based not merely on considerations of convenience, but also on the danger that as soon as we draw approximate conclusions from a comparison of stationary states about a process of very slow investment, their use may cause what plainly is *positive* net investment in the customary sense of these words to appear as *negative* net investment.

Another inconvenience arising from the use of JR units is that if the marginal productivity of labour is obtained by partial differentiation of the production function, it will in general be found to differ from the equilibrium wage of labour, when JR units of capital are used, despite whatever heroic assumptions of perfect competition may be adopted. This symptom again suggests that 'keeping the amount of capital constant' in JR units does not correspond to what is usually understood by keeping the amount of capital constant.

A natural method by which to construct an index of quantity of capital in a historical sequence would be to form a chain index, increasing the index at each step by the proportion in which the cost of the capital at current wage and interest rates at the end of the step exceeded the cost of capital at the beginning of the step, calculated at the same wage and interest rates. By shortening the steps, the distortion due to choosing wage and interest rates at the *end* of each step could be made as small as we pleased.

The same method can be used to construct an index of quantity of capital in a sequence of stationary states, and provided these are arranged in an order so that the difference between one and the next is always a small step, the distortion due to the method can again be reduced to negligible proportions. The method has the advantage that changes of cost merely due to changes in the interest rate do not affect this measure of the quantity of capital.

The technique of constructing the index number is further explained in the following section and in Appendix 1. It will suffice to say here, that to a statistician accustomed to the problem of sorting out quantities from price changes, this measure of quantity of capital would probably seem the most satisfactory one (at any rate for comparison of states fairly close together in the sequence), and that the use of this measure removes the more glaring difficulties in the way of regarding aggregate output as a function of the amounts of labour and capital employed. In particular, we shall show on pages 74–5 that the rewards per unit of the factors are once again given by the partial derivatives of the aggregate production function if stationary-state conditions with perfect competition are assumed.

A development of the theory of capital using these units needs a careful statement of the simplifying assumptions underlying the model. This is attempted in the following section, which describes a 'discrete' model closely similar to that discussed by Joan Robinson.

Simplifying assumptions for discontinuous model

In line with Joan Robinson, we shall assume:

1. The output of consumption goods is homogeneous. We shall refer to these goods as food.

2. Food may be produced in a constant stream by any of a number of techniques, each of which employs a distinctive outfit of equipment and a constant stream of labour, part of which may be devoted to maintaining or replacing the equipment.

3. Equipment is already complete at the moment when the food stream begins to flow, having been built up by a varying stream of labour during the past.

4. For each technique constant returns prevail, in the sense that the equipment outfit and the labour stream are infinitely divisible; that when each is multiplied by any number λ, so also is the food output stream; and that the outputs and inputs of the sum of two or more different equipment outfits are the sum of their individual outputs and inputs.

5. At any level of food-wages of labour, the rate of interest will settle at the highest level which any employer can pay without making losses.

6. The conditions of the stationary state hold, in the sense that

everyone believes that prices, wage rates of labour and interest rates will remain fixed for ever and

either this is true

or we retain this as a convention in calculating our rates of interest in assumption 5.

It follows that at any given food-wage rate of labour V, there will be a rate of profit R_{vs} associated with each equipment E_s, which an employer can earn on its capital value if he builds E_s and uses it for producing food. By assumption 5, if the rate of food-wages of labour is V, competition will drive the rate of interest to the level $R(V) = \max_s R_{vs}$ of the greatest of the R_{vs}. We may call this the competitive rate of interest at V, and when food-wages are at V, only that (those) equipment(s) E_s for which $R_{vs} = R(V)$ will be built for use. We may call this (these) equipment(s) 'competitive at V'.

There may be equipments which are not competitive at any V: these we shall call ineffective equipments; equipments which for some V are competitive will be called effective equipments.

In order to avoid giving special attention to possible exceptional cases, we shall introduce the following further assumptions.

7. There exists a finite set of 'basic' equipments $E_1, E_2,..., E_n$, such that any effective set of equipments is composed of one or more of these basic equipments.

It follows from assumptions 4 and 7 that any equipment competitive at V is composed only of those basic equipments which are competitive at V.

8. There is never more than one food-wage rate at which two given basic equipments are both competitive.

9. Every set of values of V for which a basic equipment is competitive is a closed connected set.

From among our basic equipments select those each of which are competitive at more than one food-wage rate, and hence over a closed range of rates. It follows from assumption 8 that these ranges do not overlap and from 5 that between them they cover the whole range of V from O to V_{max}, the level at which the competitive interest rate is zero. Hence the ranges of V fall into a natural order and we may number our selected basic equipments accordingly $E_1, E_2, \ldots, E_m$, letting E_1 be that which is competitive at zero food-wage and E_m that which is competitive at V_{max}.

We may denote by V_1 that V at which E_1 and E_2 are both competitive, and in general by V_s that rate at which E_s and E_{s+1} are both competitive. We may denote by R_s the competitive rate of interest at V_s, namely $R(V_s)$.

We may describe any adjacent pair of equipments E_s and E_{s+1} as consecutive equipments.

At this point we part company with Joan Robinson and introduce a definition about quantity of capital which conflicts with any use of JR units.

Definition. The ratio of the quantities of capital in any two equipments which are both competitive at the same rate of interest (and food-wage rate)[3] is equal to the ratio of their costs calculated at that rate of interest (and food-wage rate).

Since this definition applies to every pair of consecutive equipments, it determines the amount of capital in every one of the selected basic equipments, save for an arbitrary multiplying constant. It does this without contradiction, since the assumptions ensure that none of them is competitive at the same rate of interest as is any other except the two adjacent to it in the sequence: moreover, any consecutive pair E_s and E_{s+1} compete at a unique rate of interest R_s. The definition also covers without ambiguity those basic equipments which are competitive at only one interest rate. To extend the measure to mixed equipments composed of more than one basic equipment we adopt the following definition.

Definition. The quantity of capital in any mixed equipment is the total of the quantities in the basic equipments of which it is composed.

We refer to this method of comparing the amounts of capital in different effective equipments as the chain-index method, because of the obvious analogy with a chain index of quantities.

3. The reference to the food-wage rate is not essential to the definition, but is included in order to facilitate the extension of the definition to the case with many factors employed.

The extension of the definition to the case where basic equipments form a continuous spectrum, instead of a sequence, is discussed in Appendix 1.

The equality of marginal product and reward

Let E and E' be any two equipments both competitive at the rate of interest $R(V)$. Let employer A employ quantities Y of E and Y' of E', but employer B use quantities $Y+y$ of E and $Y'-y$ of E'. Then the cost at food-wage rate V and interest rate $R(V)$, of the total equipment of each employer is the same. Hence the interest paid by each employer is the same. Hence, interest rates being at the competitive level $R(V)$ proper to V, the difference in the two wage bills must equal the difference between the values of the two product flows, since under competition profits of each employer are zero. It follows that the extra product of the employer employing the more labour is just sufficient to pay the wages of that labour at the competitive rate, or in technical language the competitive wage of labour equals the marginal product of labour, the quantity of capital being held constant.

This may be expressed algebraically as

$$w_x = \frac{\partial}{\partial x} f(x, z),\qquad\qquad 1$$

where w_x is the food-wage of labour, x is the amount of labour employed, z is the quantity of capital, $f(x, z)$ is the flow of product from these quantities of factors.

Now by our assumption 4 of constant returns,

$$f(\lambda x, \lambda z) = \lambda f(x, z)$$

for all real λ and hence

$$x \frac{\partial f}{\partial x} + z \frac{\partial f}{\partial z} \equiv f.\qquad\qquad 2$$

Also under competition, by assumption 5,

$$x w_x + z w_z = f,\qquad\qquad 3$$

where w_z is the food reward under competition of each unit of capital.

Hence $zw_z \equiv f - xw_x \equiv f - x\dfrac{\partial f}{\partial x} \equiv z\dfrac{\partial f}{\partial z}.$

Hence $w_z \equiv \dfrac{\partial f}{\partial z},$

or in other words, the reward of each unit of capital is equal in value to its marginal social product.

Our method has thus the added convenience that it provides a means of expressing capital as a quantity and yet enabling us still to say that under perfect competition the two factors, labour and capital, are each paid according to their marginal productivity to society.

Possible anomalies in the two-factor model

It may seem intuitively obvious that the function $f(x, z)$ expressing output as a function of labour and capital must be single-valued. But our assumptions are not sufficient to ensure this.

Let $f(1, z) = \varphi(z)$ then by our assumption of constant returns $f(x, z) = x\,\varphi(z/x)$ so that a knowledge of $\varphi(z)$ is sufficient for a knowledge of $f(x, z)$.

Contrary to intuitive expectation, our assumptions do not ensure that a graph of $\varphi(z)$ is a single-valued curve sloping upwards to the right. For example, a graph of the form shown in Figure 1 is quite possible.

The further assumption that is needed in order to eliminate this possibility is that of two equipments E_{s-1} and E_s (both competitive at R_{s-1}), E_s (that competitive at the lower range of interest) will have the higher productivity, i.e. the higher ratio of food output to labour input. Under this assumption a gradual fall in the rate of interest would entail increases both in productivity and in the quantity of capital per head. But although this may fit in well with our preconceived notions, there is no logical justification for the assumption. It is logically possible that over certain ranges of the rate of interest, a fall in interest rates and rise in food-wages will be accompanied by a *fall* in output per head and a *fall* in the quantity of capital per head.

Suppose now, that instead of comparing stationary states, we are considering a sequence of states in time. If we conceive of the rise in food-wages and the accompanying fall in the rate of interest as being caused by a steady process of net investment, with all labour employed, it is interesting to consider what would happen next when a further rise in real wages and fall in the rate of interest would make competitive only equipment with lower productivity and employing *more* men per unit quantity, and thus

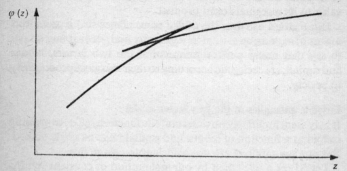

Figure 1

requiring negative net investment. Presumably, the only way that investment could remain positive without a prolonged interval of disinvestment would be for food-wages to leap up and the rate of interest to leap down to levels where capital equipment even more productive than that in existence became competitive.

The fall in the rate of interest would be sufficient despite offsetting factors to cause a sudden increase in the (demand) value of existing capital equipment bringing windfall gains to its owners: on the other hand, the rise in wages would be sufficient, despite offsetting factors, to raise the replacement cost of existing equipment even more than its (demand) value, so that no more of it would be produced. During the switch to the new type of equipment it would no longer be true that the factor rewards were equal to the values of their marginal products. A fuller discussion of this case is given in Appendix 2.

A related inadequacy of our model arises in connection with our assumption 9. This rules out the possibility that an equipment may be competitive over *two* ranges of the rate of interest, although not competitive over an intermediate range. This assumption is necessary in order to get neat results, and intuition suggests that the excluded case is unrealistic, but it is shown in the Appendix by simple numerical examples that there is no logical justification for the assumption: it is as easy to imagine a world featuring the excluded case as one free of it. If we drop assumption 9 we admit again the possibility of two stationary states each using the same items of equipment and labour force, yet being shown as using different quantities of capital, merely on account of having different rates of interest and of food-wages.

Accumulation and technical progress

The model which we have so far discussed suffers from three serious limitations.

1. It is confined to stationary states.
2. A given state of technical knowledge is assumed.
3. Labour and capital are the only two factors of production.

The concluding sections of the article will be concerned with the extension of the theory to the case where more than two factors are employed, but before advancing to this, it is worthwhile to consider what interest our results may have in spite of the two other limitations 1 and 2.

Joan Robinson has pointed out that a rigorous discussion of the theory under conditions of steady increase in capital per head would be excessively complicated. However, the interest of a comparison of a sequence of stationary states is due to the presumption that this will give us a first approximation to a comparison of successive positions in a slow process of steady accumulation. This presumption is far stronger when we are considering a spectrum of basic equipments E_u, with u a continuous variable, than when the basic equipments form a discrete series E_s with $s = 1, 2, 3, ..., n$.

Provided that R, the rate of interest, is now regarded as the short-term rate, and employment is assumed constant, it is reasonable to expect that where the rate of net investment is of the first order of small quantities, then by using the stationary state analysis to provide snapshots of stages in a process of growth we shall incur errors only of the second order of small quantities. The result suggested by the above theory is that we may then regard output as determined by a function of the amounts of labour and capital employed, where capital itself is increasing at a rate equal to the net rate of saving measured in our units of capital. The rewards of the two factors at any stage may be found by the usual marginal rule: in particular, the investment will increase or decrease the relative share of capital according as the elasticity of substitution of capital for labour is greater or less than unity. On the other hand, it is worth noting that the *mere* knowledge of the production function, although it enables us to obtain the reward per unit of capital at each point, cannot of itself enable us to calculate the rate of interest at any point without further information.

It is reassuring to find that the orthodox analysis fits in so well with the new presentation, once a convenient method has been found for measuring the quantity of capital. But this does not mean that the new presentation adds nothing to the old. It shows that the form of the production function cannot be properly known until the whole history of the advancing economy is known: for it is only then that the quantity of capital can be appropriately measured. This capital must be a balanced outfit as regards age distribution, and must include capital equipment under construction sufficient to enable the balanced outfit to be maintained. Similarly, the labour employed must include labour engaged in replacing and maintaining capital equipment. The appropriate definition of output is net output, i.e. output excluding maintenance and replacement of capital equipment: similarly, the appropriate concepts of saving and investment are net concepts, giving the excess of net output over consumption output, so that investment is equal in value to the rate of increase in the quantity of capital, as well as to the rate of saving. There is room for argument whether this concept of saving is the one that may most reasonably be regarded as a function of income, but this argument is quite distinct from any of the topics discussed in this article. It is, however, relevant to the question of the rate at which the accumulation of capital is likely to continue in any given model: this question we shall not pursue here.

In real life, the introduction of more productive capital equipment takes place most often because of advances in technical knowledge. Such investment lies outside the scope of the model so far discussed. The production function itself depends upon the state of technical knowledge, and the results we have obtained depend on the assumption that nobody expects technical advances to be made. New technical discoveries would involve a change in the whole production function and an entirely new theory is required to investigate the effects of this.

The difficulty of tracing the effects of technical advance in a model like ours lies in the need to decide which capital equipment after the change can be provided without further saving, and with constant employment, to replace the existing equipment as it wears out. The difficulty of this decision is due to the difference in the times required to build up different types of equipment.

These difficulties may be side-tracked by assuming the simple conditions of the model discussed on page 69 and again on pages 94–6. Here each equipment costs the labour of 100 men spread over one year: it needs $100u$ men to operate it and produces $100\varphi(u)$ tins of food over one year, at the end of which it wears out. It is easily shown that in this case the wage of labour is the slope of the curve relating $\varphi(u)$ to u, and the relative share of labour is $1+(1/u)$ times the slope of the curve, relating $\log \varphi(u)$ to $\log u$. Retaining the simplifying assumptions, we may represent a technical advance by a transference from the curve $\varphi(u)$ to some higher curve $\psi(u)$; moreover, in virtue of our special assumptions, the effect of the advance will be a move from a point on the $\varphi(u)$ curve to a point on the $\psi(u)$ with u unchanged. The new wage will be given by the slope of the $\psi(u)$ curve at this point and the new relative share of labour will be $1+(1/u)$ times the slope at the corresponding point of the curve relating $\log \psi(u)$ to $\log u$.

Roughly speaking, we may regard capital saving inventions as having the effect

$$\psi(\theta u) \equiv \theta \, \varphi(u) \qquad \theta > 1;$$

and inventions which economize labour in the using of equipment as having the effect

$$\psi(\theta u) \equiv \varphi(u) \qquad \theta < 1;$$

and inventions which economize labour equally in the building of equipment and in the use of equipment as having the effect

$$\psi(u) \equiv \theta \, \varphi(u) \qquad \theta > 1.$$

If for further simplicity we supposed $\varphi(u)$ to have been such that the relative share of labour was insensitive to changes in the factor ratio, this would be supposing that the slope of the curve relating log $\varphi(u)$ to log u, was approximately proportionate to $1+(1/u)$. It could then be shown that the effects of the three types of technical advance would be: (a) to increase wages but decrease labour's relative share; (b) to increase wages and increase labour's relative share; (c) to increase wages but leave the relative shares unchanged.

These results could most easily be obtained by considering the effects at given u, on the slope of the curve relating log $\varphi(u)$ to log u, of a uniform shift of the curve: (a) at forty-five degrees upwards and to the right; (b) to the left; (c) upwards.

These results, whilst being suggestive and of some interest in their context, depend on the extra set of simplifying assumptions built into the model for this purpose: these assumptions exclude any differences in the construction periods of different types of equipment. We shall not attempt to analyse the effects of technical advance when this assumption is relaxed.

The remainder of the article will be concerned with the removal of our other simplifying assumption that only two factors, labour and capital, are employed.

Extension of theory to case where three factors are employed

It is possible to extend the above theory to the case where several homogeneous factors are employed with equipment, if we limit attention to the production function for the economy as a whole, and if the amounts employed of the homogeneous factors in the economy as a whole are fixed or in fixed proportions. In this case, we may define a composite factor, composed of the homogeneous factors, combined in the given fixed proportions, and regard output in the economy as a whole as a function of the amounts employed of the composite factor and of capital. It is possible to measure capital in such a manner that in any stationary-state equilibrium, units of capital and units of the composite factor will be rewarded according to their marginal productivity.

The extension of the earlier theory is not quite so straightforward as might be supposed owing to the fact that the relative cost of two outfits of equipment will no longer depend only on the rate of interest, but also on the relative wage rates of the various homogeneous factors. This complication is sufficiently serious to wreck any attempt to regard output as a function of the quantity of capital and the amounts of the homogeneous factors, *each* homogeneous factor being paid according to its marginal product.

The possibilities and limitations of the extended theory may be adequately illustrated by a consideration of the case where there are two homogeneous factors, labour and land.

We first amend our assumptions 1 to 6 (see pages 71–2) by inserting the words 'and land' after 'labour' whenever it occurs.

We now note, as a consequence of our assumptions, that at any pair (V, W) of food-wage rates of labour and land there will be a rate of interest $R_{\lambda, vw}$ which an employer can just afford on its capital cost if he builds E_{λ} and uses it for producing food. By assumption 5 if the food-wages of labour and land are (V, W), competition will drive the rate of interest to the level

$$R(V, W) = \max_{\lambda} R_{\lambda, vw} \qquad\qquad 5$$

of the greatest of the $R_{\lambda, vw}$. We may call this the competitive rate of interest at (V, W). When food-wages of labour and land are at (V, W) only that (those) equipment(s) E_{λ} will be built for which $R_{\lambda, vw} = R(V, W)$; we may call these equipments 'competitive at (V, W)'.

Equipments competitive at some (V, W) will be called effective; the others will be called ineffective.

We now introduce assumption 7 unmodified. It follows from this assumption that any equipment competitive at (V, W) is composed of basic equipments effective at (V, W).

We modify assumption 8 to the form:

8. There is no closed region of finite area, of the plane of (V, W) throughout which two basic equipments are both competitive.

9. Every set of the values of (V, W) for which a basic equipment is competitive is a closed connected set.

It is helpful at this stage to consider Figure 2, showing which basic equipments are competitive at various wage rates (V, W).

Each cell of the diagram represents a region of (V, W) in which one particular basic equipment is competitive (the cells have for simplicity been drawn as hexagonal with straight sides, but, in general, the sides will be curved and the number of vertices may vary from cell to cell). If we imagine R rate of interest to be

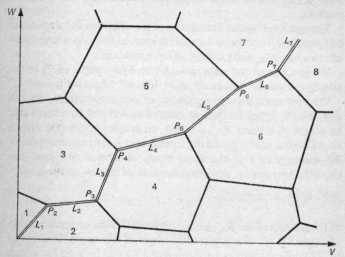

Figure 2

measured along a third axis, then we may regard the diagram as showing a lot of intersecting surfaces, only that with the highest R, appearing above each point (V, W). Where rents are high and wages low, the competitive equipment is likely to employ a high proportion of labour to land and vice versa: hence, if we divide the basic equipments into those with more men per acre, and those with less men per acre than the density laid down for the economy as a whole, the two types are likely to be separated on our diagram by a critical boundary such as that shown by the double line, those employing many men per acre lying above it.

It is clear that the only pairs of wage rates which will allow a stationary state employing the required number of men per acre will be those corresponding to points on the critical boundary which we have just described. For only when (V, W) is any such point will it be possible to combine a basic equipment employing less than the required number of men per acre with one employing more than it, and thus to employ the correct number of men per acre in the economy as a whole.

Having found the critical boundary we may number off the basic equipments whose cells have edges along the boundary, odd numbers lying to one side and even numbers to the other side of it. To each consecutive pair will correspond cells with a common edge along the critical boundary, and from such a pair we may construct a composite equipment employing the correct number of men per acre. Let the composite equipment composed of basic equipments E_s and E_{s+1} be called F_s, then the points (V, W) at which F_s is competitive form that segment of the critical boundary which joins the cells of E_s and E_{s+1}: call this segment L_s. Finally, let the point where L_{s-1} meets L_s be called P_s: then at the wage rates (V, W) represented by P_s, both composite equipments F_{s-1} and F_s are competitive, and so is any combination of them.

From this point, the theory proceeds as in the case of two factors only. The composite equipments $F_1, \ldots, F_{m-1}$ now take the place of the basic equipments $E_1, E_2, \ldots, E_m$ of the two-factor theory. Analogously to that theory, we compare the quantities of capital in two consecutive composite equipments, by costing them at the factor wages (V, W) at which both are competitive, and at the rate of interest which is competitive at that rate. The composite equipments all employ the same number of men per acre, so we may measure men and land in terms of a composite factor embodying men and land in that proportion. When this is done output may be expressed as a function of quantity of capital and quantity of composite factor, and it follows by the same argument as before that in each stationary state, units of capital and units of the composite factor will each be paid according to their marginal productivity.

This extended theory is, however, limited by the fact that quantity of capital has been defined only for composite equipments and not for basic equipments. In any stationary state which does not employ land and labour in the specified proportions, the quantity of capital remains undefined. Hence, we cannot speak of the marginal productivity of labour, the quantities of land and capital being kept constant. Any attempt to define quantity of capital to cover these situations, and to develop a function relating output $f(x, y, z)$ to the quantities of labour, land and capital will fail to satisfy the hoped-for equations,

$$w_x \equiv \frac{\partial f}{\partial x}, \qquad w_y \equiv \frac{\partial f}{\partial y}, \qquad w_z \equiv \frac{\partial f}{\partial z}, \qquad\qquad 6$$

where w_x, w_y, w_z denote the wage rates of the three factors.

This failure springs from the fact that the ratio of the costs of two consecutive basic equipments E_s and E_{s+1} will *not* in general be the same at the wage rates and competitive interest rates corresponding to the two points P_s and P_{s+1}, at *both* of which the two basic equipments are competitive. This divergence is associated with changes in the relative wage rates of labour and land and to the fact that the two basic equipments embody different proportions of land and labour.

It is a matter of interest that the quantities of capital can still be compared as between the *odd*-numbered basic equipments – namely those employing *more* than the required number of men per acre. To compare the quantities of capital in basic equipment E_{2s-1} and E_{2s+1} we simply compare their costs in the only situation in which both are competitive, namely at the wage rates and interest rates proper to P_{2s}; similarly, we may compare the quantities of capital in even-numbered basic equipments (those using *less* than the required number of men per acre). But we cannot satisfactorily compare the amount of capital in basic equipments using more than the required number of men per acre with that in those using less. To loosen the style let us call these two types of capital labour-using and land-using.

We can regard output as a function of four variables, namely the amounts of labour x, land y, labour-using capital z_1 and land-using capital z_2, provided we confine attention to those stationary states in which wage rates and interest rates are at such levels that it would be *possible* to produce without loss, using the required number of men per acre. This may still allow considerable variation of the number of men employed per acre, as it includes the possibility of using either only land-using equipment or only labour-using equipment. Although there are four factors, there are from a technical point of view only three degrees of freedom in varying them, so that only a three-dimensional subset in the region (x, y, z_1, z_2) represents combinations of factors which are technically possible. When, therefore, we represent output as a function $O \equiv f(x, y, z_1, z_2)$ of technically possible combinations of the four factors, we cannot in general give meaning to the partial derivatives, and so we cannot say that each factor is rewarded according to its marginal product.

But an analogous proposition can be established, namely, that if $(\Delta x, \Delta y, \Delta z_1, \Delta z_2)$ represents any technically possible small variation in the amounts of the four factors, then

$$\Delta f \equiv W_x \, \Delta x + W_y \, \Delta y + W_{z_1} \, \Delta z_1 + W_{z_2} \, \Delta z_2; \qquad 7$$

where W_x, W_y, W_{z_1}, W_{z_2} are the wage rates of the four factors before the change. This proposition asserts that any combination of factors which has a productivity at the margin receives a wage rate equal to that marginal product. This proposition will apply for example to appropriate combinations of any pair of the four factors.

The need for measuring capital by the two variables z_1 and z_2 arises from the fact that the wage rates of labour-using capital and land-using capital will be in different ratio to one another in different stationary states.

Extension of theory to the case where several factors are employed

Even in the case where only land, labour and equipment were employed, a rigorous statement of the simplifying assumptions needed for clear-cut results has not been achieved. Many of our assumptions were packed into the drawing of Figure 2, where we placed the numbered cells neatly along a corridor without thorough supporting discussion.

This topological device does not spring so readily to hand when we extend the discussion to the case where several factors are employed, and one can only suggest by analogy what results should be obtainable from a proper enlargement of the simplifying assumptions to that case.

If the quantities employed (or their proportions) of the homogeneous factors are fixed for the economy as a whole, we should still be able to express output as a function of the quantities employed of (a) a single composite factor, (b) capital, and in such a way that both the composite factor and capital would, in each permissible stationary state, be rewarded according to its marginal product.

But if we wish to construct a function of output to cover cases where the quantities of homogeneous factors employed are *not* in the required proportions, we should have to represent capital by as many variables as there are homogeneous factors. In this case, marginal adjustments to the quantities of factors would in general involve combinations of them. It should be possible to prove that in each of certain permissible stationary states any such combination of factors would receive a wage rate equal to its marginal productivity.

Appendix 1. The chain-index method of measuring capital

On page 73 a definition was given which determined the amounts of capital in each of a discrete series of selected basic equipments. This definition may be reformulated as follows: the unit of capital is so defined that where $C(s, R, V)$ denotes the cost per unit of capital, of equipment type E_s at interest rate R and wage rate V, then, for all s, V,

$$C(s, R_s, V) = C(s+1, R_s, V),$$

where R_s denotes that rate of interest at which both the consecutive equipments E_s and E_{s+1} are competitive.

When we consider a continuous spectrum of equipments E_u with u a continuous variable, we may adapt this definition as follows: let $C(u, R, V)$ denote the cost per unit of capital of equipment of type E_u at rate of interest R and wage rate V, the units of capital must be such that, for all u and V,

$$\left[\frac{\partial}{\partial u} C(u, R, V) \right]_{R = R_u} = 0,$$

where R_u is the rate of interest at which E_u is competitive.

Appendix 2. Numerical examples
Simplified two-factor model with a finite sequence of basic equipments

Suppose that there are N basic equipments E_1, E_2,..., E_N. Let x_s be the number of men required to operate and maintain E_s

and let O_s be the annual food output produced by E_s. Let the cost of E_s consist of the expenditure of X_s man-years of labour during a short interval of time at T_s years before the food flow begins. If we define date of completion of the machine to be that at which the food flow begins, then the food cost of E_s at the date of completion is given by:

$$C_s = VX_s e^{RT_s}, \qquad\qquad 8$$

where R is the rate of interest and V the food-wage rate.

Suppose that each E_s can be maintained permanently. The highest interest rate R_{vs} which can be afforded with E_s at wage rate V is given by

$$O_s = V(x_s + R_{vs} X_s e^{R_{vs} T_s}). \qquad\qquad 9$$

Numerical example involving no anomalies. Suppose that there are four basic equipments and that their technical coefficients x_s, O_s, T_s, X_s are those given in the following table.

s	x_s	O_s	T_s	X_s
1	4	10	0	20
2	3	9	1	17·193
3	2	7	2	14·920
4	1	4	4	10·054

The values of R_{vs} calculated for formula 2 are shown for each equipment, for food-wages in the range one to four tons of food per annum, in Figure 3. The competitive interest rate at each food-wage is shown by the envelope of the four curves. It can be seen from the diagram that for food-wages up to and including 1·25 tons of food per annum, equipment 1 is competitive; in the range 1·25 to 1·837 tons of food per annum, inclusive, equipment 2 is competitive; in the range 1·837 to 2·481 tons of food per annum, inclusive, equipment 3 is competitive; and in the range 2·481 to 4 tons of food per annum, inclusive, equipment 4 is competitive. At food-wages exceeding 4 tons per annum, the wage bill would exceed the maximum national income technically possible.

We may distinguish two possible kinds of stationary state:

1. Pure – employing only one basic type of equipment. The food-wage rate may be at any level at which that basic equipment is

competitive, and the rate of interest will be at the corresponding competitive level.

2. Mixed – employing some combination of a consecutive pair of equipments at the food-wage level at which both are competitive, and at the competitive level of the rate of interest.

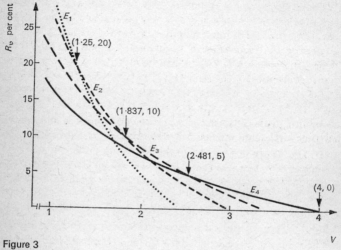

Figure 3

In our model, just three mixed types of stationary state are possible:

1. Employing a combination of E_1 and E_2 at a wage of 1·25 tons of food per annum and interest rate 20 per cent per annum.

2. Employing a combination of E_2 and E_3 at a wage of 1·837 tons of food per annum and interest rate 10 per cent per annum.

3. Employing a combination of E_3 and E_4 at a wage of 2·481 tons of food per annum and interest rate 5 per cent per annum.

To establish what quantity of capital is embodied in a unit of each of the four basic equipments we merely compare the costs in each consecutive pair at the rate of interest at which they compete. We find that at a rate of interest of 20 per cent the cost of items of equipments 1 and 2 are in ratio 20:21. At a rate of interest of 10 per cent, items of equipments of types 2 and 3 have costs in ratio 34·89:33·26. At a rate of interest of 5 per cent items of equipments of types 3 and 4 have costs in ratio 40·76:30·38. Accordingly, we take units of the four basic types of equipment to represent quantities of capital 20, 21, 20·16 and 14·96.

Food output may now be uniquely expressed in terms of the amounts x, z of labour and capital employed: we find it correctly given (in tons of food per annum) by

$$f(x, z) \equiv 1·250x + 0·25z \qquad \text{where } 5x \leqslant z \leqslant 7x,$$

$$f(x, z) \equiv 1·837x + 0·1661z \qquad \text{where } 7x \leqslant z \leqslant 10·08x,$$

$$f(x, z) \equiv 2·481x + 0·1011z \qquad \text{where } 10·08x \leqslant z \leqslant 14·96x. \qquad \mathbf{10}$$

The three forms of the equation correspond to the three mixed types of stationary state and they overlap at the two pure types with basic equipments 2 and 3.

In every stationary state of mixed type, labour is paid a wage equal to $\partial f/\partial x$, the coefficient of x in the production function; and each unit quantity of capital earns $\partial f/\partial z$, the coefficient of z. In the pure types with basic equipments 2 and 3, the appropriate equation to use in calculating marginal productivity differs according to whether an increase or decrease is considered. In these pure types the factors are rewarded at rates within the closed ranges terminating in their two marginal productivities. In the pure state, with only equipment type 1, the marginal productivities give an upper limit to wage rates and a lower limit to the reward of each unit of capital. In that with only type 4 they give a lower limit for wage rates and an upper limit for the reward of each unit of capital.

Figure 4, which shows $f(x, z)/x$ plotted against z/x, further illustrates the form of the production function in this example.

From our knowledge of $f(x, z)$ we can calculate how labour's relative share of output varies with the quantity of capital employed per head. This brings out clearly the phenomena which Joan Robinson describes in connection with the Wicksell effect and the Ricardo effect.

Increases in labour's share only 'take place' on the three occasions when the conditions are those of a pure stationary state;

all increases of capital per head from one stationary state to another within the same mixed class involve an increase in output which accrues wholly to the owners of capital.

Exceptional case. To illustrate the anomalies which may arise when food-wages and productivity vary inversely, consider the model represented by the following table, which superficially represents the normal example we have just discussed.

s	x_s	O_s	T_s	X_s
1	4	12	0	20
2	2	9	0	20
3	4	16	4	20·854
4	2	10	4	21·221

When we calculate the interest rates R_{vs} at which the four equipments can compete at various food-wage rates, we find E_1 competitive above 20 per cent, E_2 in the range 10 to 20 per cent, E_3 in the range 5 to 10 per cent and E_4 at 5 per cent. Following our earlier procedure, we should argue that three mixed types of

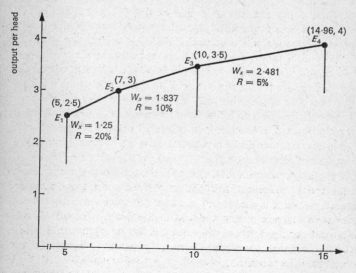

Figure 4

Capital as a Unit Independent of Distribution and Prices

stationary state are possible, E_1 and E_2; E_2 and E_3; E_3 and E_4; the three appropriate pairs of values of the food-wage and interest rate being 1·5, 20 per cent; 2·25, 10 per cent; and 3·034, 5 per cent.

In order to consider the production function, let us now assign a quantitative measure of capital as before. E_1 and E_2 may each count as 20 units; E_2 and E_3 compete at 10 per cent and the ratio of their costs is then 20:31·11, so E_3 must be taken as 31·11 units. E_4 and E_3 at all rates of interest have their costs in the ratio 21·221:20·854; applying this ratio to 31·11, we find that E_4 must represent 31·657 units of capital.

We may now draw up a table showing for each of the four equipments, O_s the food output, x_s the number of persons employed, z_s the quantity of capital, and hence capital per head z_s/x_s, and output per head O_s/z_s.

s	O_s	x_s	z_s	z_s/x	O_s/z_s
1	12	4	20	5	3
2	9	2	20	10	4·5
3	16	4	31·11	7·777	4
4	10	2	31·657	15·828	5

We could construct a diagram[4] showing the output per head as a function of capital per head in the various possible stationary states, the points for mixed types again being obtained by drawing straight lines to join the pair of points relating to the consecutive pair of equipments which are combined. We may also write down the production function $f(x, z)$ as

$$\left. \begin{aligned} f(x, z) &\equiv 1·5x + 0·3z & (5x \leqslant z \leqslant 10x), \\ f(x, z) &\equiv 2·25x + 0·225z & (7·777x \leqslant z \leqslant 10x), \\ f(x, z) &\equiv 3·034x + 0·124z & (7·777x \leqslant z \leqslant 15·828x). \end{aligned} \right\} \quad \mathbf{11}$$

These three forms corresponding to the three mixed types of stationary state: (E_1, E_2); (E_2, E_3); and (E_3, E_4).

This production function is triple-valued for those values of x and z such that $7·777x < z < 10x$. This is no paradox, since the function merely tells about various possible stationary states. The function preserves the property that each factor is paid a

4. This diagram is not shown, but its main features would be the same as those of Figure 1 on page 76.

wage equal to its marginal product: thus $W_x = \partial f/\partial x$ and $W_z = \partial f/\partial z$ in all the mixed-type stationary states.

This triple-valued feature of the production function cannot be attributed to our method of measuring the quantities of capital per head in E_2 and E_3, for any plausible method would ascribe more capital per head to E_2 than to E_3; for example, Joan Robinson's method would give as large or larger a margin in the factor ratio.

It may again be objected that no employer in his senses would use E_3 and E_4 in the combination with the same factor ratio as E_2, since he could obtain higher output per head by using E_2; the answer is that if wage rates were at 3·034 tons of food per annum, then E_3 and E_4 could compete at 5 per cent, but E_2 could not. *At this interest rate of 5 per cent*, unit quantity of E_2 would cost considerably more than unit quantity of E_3 or E_4, and so much so as more than to offset the advantage in productivity.

Although the production function is quite satisfactory for describing possible stationary states it is in this case definitely inconvenient for illustrating a time sequence. Suppose an economy, at constant employment, slowly, out of its saving, to have converted from E_1 to E_2 equipment. Wages have stood at 1·5 tons of food per annum and interest rates at 20 per cent. If, after the conversion, wages rise just above 2·25 tons of food and interest rates fall just below 10 per cent, E_3 will become the only competitive equipment, and E_2 will still be more nearly competitive than E_4. But any attempt to use E_3 must *lower* the national income and *decrease* the quantity of capital employed, on account of its lower productivity and lower factor ratio than E_2. The only way positive net investment and the rise in productivity can continue uninterrupted is for real wages to jump up to above 3·034 and interest rates fall below 5 per cent. If this is done, there will ensue a period of conversion from E_2 to E_4, and the economy will for a time be a mixture of E_2 and E_4. But such a mixture is certainly not possible in a stationary state, since there is no real wage rate and rate of interest at which E_2 and E_4 are both competitive.

In our particular example we have assumed that the equipments never need replacement, but the same features of a multi-valued production can arise without this simplifying device.

Suppose for the moment that the equipment needs renewal after a certain life, then if the rate of interest had been pushed down to the level at which E_4 is competitive, E_2 would fail by a considerable margin to be competitive. *All* E_2 would be replaced by E_4 as it fell due, and unless the life of E_2 was long, this would represent a tremendous demand on the investment industries – so that the capital per head could increase from 10 to 15·828 during one lifetime of an E_2 equipment. This would take us far from the conditions of slow and gradual accumulation, to which our model, with its expectation of constant conditions, had a limited relevance.

The outcome of this discussion is that, although our method of measuring quantity of capital provides us with a production function satisfactory for describing the family of stationary states, formidable difficulties arise when we consider a sequence of states in time in a developing economy, unless we rule out cases in which a lowering of interest rates can cause the introduction of techniques with a *lower* productivity than those used up till then. A numerical example has shown that these cases cannot be ruled out merely on logical grounds.

To illustrate the case where assumption 9 breaks down so that an equipment is competitive over each of two separated intervals of V, consider the position when, of our four equipments, only E_2 and E_3 have been invented. The condition that both E_2 and E_3 should be competitive at the interest rate R may be expressed

$$\frac{x_2 + Re^{T_2 R} X_2}{O_2} = \frac{x_3 + Re^{T_3 R} X_3}{O_3}, \qquad 12$$

so that substituting numerical values,

$$\frac{2 + 20R}{9} = \frac{4 + 20 \cdot 854 Re^{4R}}{16}.$$

Therefore $R(320 - 187 \cdot 686 e^{4R}) = 4.$ \qquad **13**

It may be verified that there are two positive solutions for R, namely $R = 0 \cdot 3$ and $R = 0 \cdot 0402$.

The corresponding food-wage rates are 2·25 and 3·21. We find that for wage rates below 2·25, E_2 is competitive; for wage rates between 2·25 and 3·21, E_3 is competitive; and for wage rates from 3·21 to 4·5, E_2 is competitive.

Moreover, since E_2 and E_3 are both competitive at $V, R = 2·25$, 10 per cent, and also at 3·21, 4·02 per cent, there are two possible bases for comparing the quantities of capital in E_2 and E_3. Counting E_3 as 31·11 units as before, the two possible methods ascribe to E_2 either 20 units or 25·4 units.

The formal solution is to regard E_2 as 20 units if it is used at a rate of interest of 10 per cent or over, and as 25·4 units if it is used at a rate of 4·02 per cent or less. This procedure has, however, little to recommend it, apart from its enabling one still to regard the factors as being rewarded according to their marginal productivity.

One final and somewhat fanciful remark may be made with reference to this example. Two mixed types of stationary state using E_2 and E_3 are possible, one at $V, R = 2·25$, 10 per cent and one at 3·21, 4·02 per cent. Both use the same equipment, but the question of which V, R, and hence what income-distribution between labour and capital is fixed, is left in this model for political forces to decide. It is interesting to speculate whether more complex situations retaining this feature are ever found in the real world.

Simplified two-factor model with continuous sequence of equipments

Consider a sequence of basic equipments E_u with u as a continuous variable. Suppose that to build any equipment E_u requires the work of 100 men spread over one year. Suppose that equipment E_u when completed requires $100u$ men to operate it and produces a flow of $100g(u)$ tons of food per annum, where $g(u)$ is a function of u. Suppose that the working life of each equipment E_u is one year, at the end of which it has no value.

At any rate of interest R and wage V, the cost of any equipment E_u is

$$K_R = 100\frac{e^R-1}{R} V \qquad\qquad 14$$

when new. By the formula for balanced equipment in the integrated case given in Champernowne and Kahn (1953–4, p. 109), it may be shown that the expression **14** also gives correctly the cost of the balanced set of equipment in equilibrium. Now this expression is the same for all u, and it follows (see Appendix 1) that we can regard each equipment E_u as containing 100 units of capital, consistently with the chain-index method.

We are now in a position to write down the production function, for we know that the balanced equipment E_u represents 100 units of capital, employs $100u$ men for production and 100 men for replacement and produces an output stream of $100g(u)$. Hence the production function must satisfy

$$f\{100(1+u), 100\} = 100g(u), \qquad\qquad\qquad 15$$

and since it must be homogeneous of degree one, it must be given in terms of the function $g(u)$ by

$$f(x, y) = y\, g\left(\frac{x-y}{y}\right) \qquad\qquad\qquad 16$$

for those values of x and y which give to $u = (x-y)/y$ a value such that E_u is effective.

By the marginal principle, the wages of labour and capital are

$$w_x = g'(u), \quad \text{the derivative of } g(u) \text{ where } u = \frac{x-y}{y}, \qquad 17$$
$$w_y = g(u) - (u+1)g'(u).$$

Finally, the rate of interest R_u at which E_u is competitive is given in virtue of **14**, by

$$g'(u)(u+e^{R_u}) = g(u) \quad \text{whence } R_u = \log\left[\frac{g(u)}{g'(u)} - u\right]. \qquad 18$$

Although each E_u contains the same amount of capital as measured by the chain index, they do not contain equal amounts of capital measured in JR units. The amount Q_u of capital in JR units in E_u is given by the condition **14** as

$$Q_u = 100\frac{e^{R_u}-1}{R_u},$$

which in virtue of **18** may also be written

$$Q_u = 100\frac{\{g(u)/g'(u)\}-u-1}{\log_e[\{g(u)/g'(u)\}-u]}. \qquad\qquad\qquad 19$$

It is possible for $Q_u/(1+u)$ to decrease with decreases in u, even in cases where a decrease in u clearly involves an increase in productivity and an increase in the proportion of the labour force devoted to replacing rather than operating equipment. That is to say, that a decrease in u involving what would ordinarily be understood as deepening or increased capital per head, will be shown as a reduction of the quantity per head of capital measured in JR units. As an example of this, consider the case where

$$g(u) = (1+11u)^{1/11}; \qquad\qquad 20$$

then production per head is

$$\frac{(1+11u)^{1/11}}{1+u} \qquad\qquad 21$$

which increases as u decreases, and the proportion $1/(1+u)$ of labour devoted to replacement increases. But the quantity of capital per head in JR units is by **19**:

$$\frac{Q(u)}{100(1+u)} = \frac{10u}{(1+u)\log(1+10u)}, \qquad\qquad 22$$

and numerical calculation shows that this *decreases* from 2·19 to 1·00 as u decreases in the range 2·326 to 0, and the rate of interest meanwhile falls from 3·19 to 0. But production per head *increases* from 0·405 to 1·000 and capital per head, measured by the chain index, from 0·307 to 1·000.

It is evident that a variety of other forms for the function $g(u)$ could be chosen so as to demonstrate similar paradoxical results of measuring capital in JR units.

Model involving three factors

In this model we shall allow five basic equipments E_1, E_2, E_3, E_4 and E_5. E_s will be supposed to cost at interest R, $X_s/(0\cdot6-R)$ units of labour, and $Y_s/(0\cdot6-R)$ units of land, as would happen, for example, if it had been built up by using $e^{-0\cdot6t}X_s$ units of labour and $e^{-0\cdot6t}Y_s$ units of land from the distant past $t = \infty$ up till $t = 0$. E_s will be supposed to employ x_s units of labour and y_s units of land permanently to produce a flow of O_s tons of food per annum.

The numerical values of these parameters are given in the following table.

s	x_s	y_s	O_s	X_s	Y_s
1	5	4	109·6	6	5
2	3	4	88	4	5
3	3	2	64	4	3
4	1	2	40	2	3
5	2	1	38	3	3

We shall suppose that in the economy as a whole the numbers of 'men' and 'acres of land' are equal. It will be seen that equipments 1, 3 and 5 are labour-using, whereas equipments 2 and 4 are land-using.

The values of $R_{s,vw}$ are given by such equations as the following,

$$\frac{R_{1,vw}}{0 \cdot 6 - R_{1,vw}}(6V + 5W) + 5V + 4W = 109 \cdot 6. \qquad 23$$

By calculating various loci in the VW plane of the type $R_{s,vw} = R_{s',vw}$ and by making a few auxiliary calculations we may construct the following diagram (Figure 5), which shows in which regions of the VW plane (i.e. for what factor-wage combinations) the various basic equipments are competitive.

An equipment employing one man per acre can be obtained by the appropriate blend of a labour-using (odd-numbered) equipment, with a land-using (even-numbered) equipment.

The only combinations of factor-rewards VW for which this is possible are at points along the zigzag corridor in the diagram which runs between consecutive pairs of the five equipments.

In the example only four of the pairs of equipments: (E_1, E_2); (E_2, E_3); (E_3, E_4); and (E_4, E_5) can be suitably married; let us call these married couples F_1, F_2, F_3 and F_4.

Then we can construct a table for F_1, F_2, F_3 and F_4 similar to the table above.

s	x_s	y_s	O_s	X_s	Y_s
1	8	8	197·6	10	10
2	6	6	152	8	8
3	4	4	104	6	6
4	3	3	78	5	6

The equipments F_1 and F_2 will be competitive only at the point where equipments E_1, E_2 and E_3 are all competitive: this point is the point P_2 in Figure 5, namely 7·2, 8, and the competitive rate of interest is 20 per cent. Similarly, F_2 and F_3 are both competitive at P_3, namely 10, 10, with competitive interest rate 10 per cent. Finally, F_3 and F_4 are both competitive at P_4, namely 12, 14, with competitive interest zero.

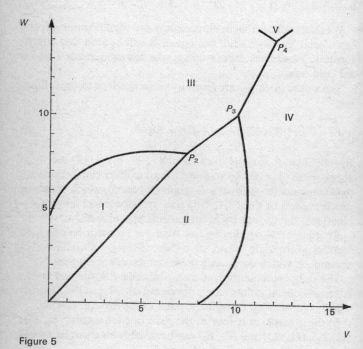

Figure 5

At P_2 and rate of interest 20 per cent, F_1 and F_2 have costs of 380 and 304 tons of food.

At P_3 and rate of interest 10 per cent, F_2 and F_3 have costs of 320 and 240 tons of food.

At P_4 and zero rate of interest F_3 and F_4 have costs of 260 and 240 tons of food.

Hence, counting F_1 as 38 units of capital, we must count

F_2 as 30·4 units of capital,

F_3 as 22·8 units of capital and

F_4 as 21·05 units of capital.

Counting one man with one acre as one unit of composite factor, and letting η and ζ represent the amounts employed of composite factor and capital, we can obtain the following production function for stationary states employing F_1, F_2, F_3, F_4 or pairs of them under competitive conditions.

$$f(\eta\zeta) = 15\cdot2\eta + 2\zeta \quad \text{for } 4\cdot25\eta \leqslant \zeta \leqslant 5\cdot07\eta,$$
$$f(\eta\zeta) = 20\eta + 1\cdot05\zeta \quad \text{for } 5\cdot07\eta \leqslant \zeta \leqslant 5\cdot72\eta,$$
$$f(\eta\zeta) = 26\eta \quad\quad\quad\ \text{for } 5\cdot72\eta \leqslant \zeta \leqslant 7\cdot1\eta,$$

and in the mixed-type stationary states the composite factor and capital will be paid at rates equal to the marginal productivities as calculated from the appropriate one of the above three equations.

Returning now to the problem of evaluating the quantities of capital in each of the five basic equipments, we note that E_1 and E_3 only compete at P_2 with $R = 20$ per cent; under these conditions their costs are 208 and 132 and E_2 and E_4 only compete at P_3 with $R = 10$ per cent; under these conditions their costs are 130 and 100 and E_3 and E_5 only compete at P_4 with $R = O$; under these conditions their costs are 150 and 130.

Hence, arbitrarily choosing E_1 and E_2 to represent 20 and 18 units of capital respectively, we find E_3, E_4 and E_5 represent 12·7, 10 and 11 units of capital respectively.

We may construct the following table.

s	x	y	z_1	z_2	O	y/x	z_1/x	z_2/x	O/x
1	5	4	20	0	109·6	0·8	4	0	21·92
2	3	4	0	18	88	1·33	0	6	29·33
3	3	2	12·7	0	64	0·67	4·23	0	21·33
4	1	2	0	10	40	2·0	0	10	40
5	2	1	11	0	38	0·5	5·5	0	19

It is now possible to express output as a function of three variables, x, z_1, z_2, representing the amounts used of labour, labour-using capital and land-using capital, it being assumed that the technically necessary amount of land is provided. The function is

$$f(x, z_1, z_2) = 32 \cdot 08x - 2 \cdot 54z_1 - 0 \cdot 64z_2$$

$$f(x, z_1, z_2) = 13 \cdot 333x + 1 \cdot 891z_1 + 2 \cdot 667z_2$$

$$f(x, z_1, z_2) = 28 \cdot 2x - 1 \cdot 67z_1 + 1 \cdot 18z_2$$

$$\left.\begin{array}{c} 24 - 4z_2/x \leqslant 6z_1/x \\ \leqslant 24 \cdot 8 - 4 \cdot 13z_2/x. \\ 24 \cdot 8 - 6z_1/x \leqslant 4 \cdot 13z_2/x \\ \leqslant 41 \cdot 7 - 10z_1/x. \\ 41 \cdot 3 - 4 \cdot 13z_2/x \\ \leqslant 10z_1/x \leqslant 58 \cdot 7 - \\ - 5 \cdot 87z_2/x. \end{array}\right\} \quad \mathbf{24}$$

Consider, for example, the second equation. This relates to mixed stationary states using basic equipments 2, 3 and 4. The partial derivatives are $13 \cdot 333$, $1 \cdot 891$ and $2 \cdot 667$.

$13 \cdot 333$ is the marginal productivity not merely of labour, but of labour plus the extra land needed to increase labour without altering the amount of either labour-using capital or land-using capital. It is, in fact, the marginal product of 'one man and one-third of an acre'. Similarly, $1 \cdot 079$ is the marginal product of 'one unit of labour-using capital and $0 \cdot 891$ acres', whereas $2 \cdot 667$ is the marginal product of 'one unit of land-using capital and one-sixth of an acre'. Under competition, the wages paid for these three combinations of factors will in these stationary states be paid at rates equal to $13 \cdot 333$, $1 \cdot 891$ and $2 \cdot 667$.

The reason that the marginal productivities of some of these factors can be negative is that the adoption of such factors involves using less land, so that it is worthwhile employing them although it lowers product flow, in order to save rent. Thus the factor combination with negative productivity is always one involving a negative amount of land.

It can be verified that in our example the combined wage rate of each factor combination is, in fact, equal to its marginal productivity as given by the appropriate regression coefficient in equations **24**.

References

CHAMPERNOWNE, D. G., and KAHN, R. F. (1953–4), 'The value of invested capital', *Rev. econ. Stud.*, vol. 21, pp. 107–11.
ROBINSON, J. (1953–4), 'The production function and the theory of capital', *Rev. econ. Stud.*, vol. 21, pp. 81–106. [See Reading 1.]

3 T. W. Swan

Notes on Capital[1]

Excerpt from T. W. Swan, 'Economic growth and capital accumulation', *Economic Record*, vol. 32, 1956, pp. 343–61.

Joan Robinson's puzzle

If we had to put up a scarecrow (as Joan Robinson calls it) to keep off the index-number birds and Joan Robinson herself, it would look something like this: labour and land are homogeneous man-hours and acres respectively; capital is made up of a large number of identical Meccano sets, which never wear out and can be put together, taken apart and reassembled with negligible cost or delay in a great variety of models so as to work with various combinations of labour and land, to produce various products and to incorporate the latest technical innovations illustrated in successive issues of the Instruction Book; output consists of goods (including Meccano sets) that are all produced and sold at constant price-ratios amongst themselves, no matter how the rates of wages, rents and profits may vary – i.e. they are all produced by similar (but continuously variable) combinations of labour, land and capital, with similar efficiency, and under similar competitive conditions; saving = investment = accumulation is the current output of Meccano sets, and can always be measured (by virtue of the constant price-ratios) at a constant value per Meccano set in terms of peanuts or any other consumption product forgone: etc. With assumptions of this kind, the basic model of the text could be rigorously established in a form that would deceive nobody.

1. These notes are concerned with certain difficulties in the idea of capital as a factor of production that were first seen by Wicksell and have now been greatly elaborated on by Joan Robinson (1953–4, 1955, 1956). See also Champernowne (1953–4), Champernowne and Kahn (1953–4) and Solow (1955–6). The criticism here ventured is in no sense a book review: it touches on only one aspect of a very important book.

Fortunately, economists have usually been willing to hope that even very complicated aggregates like output might somehow still contain, for some purposes, a rough kernel of meaning 'in an index-number sense' – a meaning not literally dependent upon the fantastic assumptions required to avoid all index-number ambiguities. Joan Robinson[2] has spoilt this game for us by insisting that the social capital, considered as a factor of production accumulated by saving, cannot be given *any* operative meaning – not even in the abstract conditions of a stationary state.

That there should be great difficulties in handling the concept of capital in a process of change is not surprising. A piece of durable equipment or a pipe-line of work-in-progress has dimensions in time that bind together sequences of inputs and outputs jointly demanded or jointly supplied at different dates.[3] The aggregation of capital into a single stock at a point of time is thus the correlative of an aggregation of the whole economic process,

2. The following passages are from Robinson (1953–4, pp. 81, 82):

'The student of economic theory is taught to write $O = f(L, C)$ where L is a quantity of labour, C a quantity of capital and O a rate of output of commodities. He is instructed to assume all workers alike, and to measure L in man-hours of labour; he is told something about the index-number problem involved in choosing a unit of output; and then he is hurried on to the next question, in the hope that he will forget to ask in what units C is measured. Before ever he does ask, he has become a professor, and so sloppy habits of thought are handed on from one generation to the next. . . .'

'When we are discussing accumulation, it is natural to think of capital as measured in terms of product. The process of accumulation consists in refraining from consuming current output in order to add to the stock of wealth. But when we consider what addition to productive resources a given amount of accumulation makes, we must measure capital in labour units, for the addition to the stock of productive equipment made by adding an increment of capital depends upon how much work is done in constructing it, not upon the cost, in terms of final product, of an hour's labour. Thus, as we move from one point on a production function to another, measuring capital in terms of product, we have to know the product-wage rate in order to see the effect upon production of changing the ratio of capital to labour. Or if we measure in labour units, we have to know the product-wage in order to see how much accumulation would be required to produce a given increment of capital. But the wage rate alters with the ratio of the factors: one symbol, C, cannot stand both for a quantity of product and a quantity of labour time.'

3. Like the wool and mutton of Marshall's sheep (Wicksell, 1934, p. 260).

not only in cross-section (which gives rise to the ordinary index-number problems), but also in time itself: in other words, the reduction of a very high-order system of lagged equations – in which each event, its past origins and its future consequences, could be properly dated and traced backward and forward in time – to a more manageable system with fewer lags. This second kind of aggregation introduces a further set of ambiguities, similar in principle to those of index numbers, but as yet hardly investigated.[4] Our scarecrow assumptions dodge both sets of ambiguities – the first because all price-ratios within output are held constant, the second because capital, in the form of Meccano sets, is both infinitely durable and instantaneously adaptable. This is an extreme of aggregation. From the idea of capital as a single stock there is in principle no sudden transition to 'the enormous who's who of all the goods in existence' (Robinson, 1953–4, pp. 83–5). Between the two extremes lies an ascending scale of nth-order dynamic systems, in which capital like everything else is more and more finely subdivided and dated, with ascending degrees of (potential) realism and (actual) complexity. In fact, most of us are left at ground-level, on ground that moves under our feet.

4. By what test should the (relative) success of a proposed scheme of aggregation be judged? Probably, by some measure of the degree of preservation of the dominant behaviour patterns which would be represented in the linear case by the larger roots of an appropriate high-order micro-system; surely not by the degree of 'realism' of the scarecrow assumptions necessary to give literal validity to the low-order macro-system. In the present context, we are saved the trouble of trying to apply the suggested criterion by the fact that no appropriate micro-sytem is available (no one has yet set *Value and Capital* in motion, except under assumptions almost as rigidly fantastic as our own scarecrow). The puzzle may actually be easier if there are strong non-linear features (floors, ceilings, thresholds, etc.), since these sometimes lead to a limited number of highly characteristic patterns of behaviour.

If the hands of a clock give a fair approximation to the even flow of time, in spite of the diminishing force exerted by the spring as it unwinds, our thanks are due to the discontinuous, non-linear mechanism of the escapement. This result is achieved at the price of an ambiguity – the finite intervals between ticks. Even the best clock is a mere scarecrow model of Time, and absurdly unrealistic from the viewpoint of the General Theory of Relativity. A bad clock that still ticks, or a good one wrongly set, may mean that its user mises the bus.

In a stationary state, all the complexities of dating disappear. Related inputs and outputs, investments and returns, events and expectations, may be generations removed, but what happens at any time is exactly repeated at any other time. No information is lost and no ambiguity created by aggregating all times into an eternal present; the shadows of past and future appear only in the form of profit steadily accruing at the ruling rate of interest on the time-consuming investment processes of which every moment has its share. Joan Robinson still insists that capital cannot be given a meaning conformable with those neo-classical exercises in comparative statics for which the stationary state is expressly designed. In particular, capital cannot be put into a production function from which, given the supplies of labour and land, under perfect-competition profit-maximization assumptions, the equilibrium rates of real wages, rent and profit may be deduced in the form of marginal productivities. If this scheme is unworkable in a stationary state, it can hardly be sensible to retain it in a dynamic model (like that of our text).

From the various accounts given by Joan Robinson it is not easy to pick out the 'basic fallacy' of the marginal productivity scheme. In the passage already quoted (see footnote 2) she makes the novel suggestion that the production function itself works only if the stock of capital is measured by its value in wage units, in which case it becomes useless for explaining the equilibrium factor-rewards. But it soon appears that, whatever may be the defects of the neo-classical production function, one geared to what Champernowne calls JR units can produce only mental and diagrammatic contortions. (Are there perhaps signs in *The Accumulation of Capital* of the reluctant beginnings of regret for this aberration?)

Frequently Joan Robinson seems to be explaining the factor-rewards by a widow's cruse type of distribution theory.[5] At first sight, it is not altogether clear whether she puts this forward as

5. The widow's cruse theory of distribution is set out by Kaldor (1955–6, pp. 94 ff.) who calls it the Keynesian theory. Briefly the theory says that, given the ratio of investment to income, and given the propensities to save out of profits and wages respectively, the distribution of income between profits and wages must be such as to make the saving ratio equal the invest-ment ratio. For examples see Robinson (1956, pp. 48, 75–83, 255, 271, 312, 331).

an independent explanation, or is merely exhibiting the other side of the double-entry national income accounts, which of course always balance in exact confirmation of the theory.[6] Before long, the reader begins to understand that this profoundly arithmetical organon is not a rival economic calculus, but a subsidiary device that applies, as it were, only in blank spots

6. Consider the following example of widow's cruse reasoning (Robinson, 1956, p. 312):

'The relation of the rate of profit to the marginal product of investment is seen in its simplest form in the imagined state of bliss, where the highest technique known is already in operation throughout the economy and population is constant. The marginal product of investment is then zero. If there is no consumption out of profit (and no saving out of wages or rents) the rate of profit also is zero, and the wages and rent bill absorbs the whole annual output.

'But if there is consumption out of profits (and no saving out of rent or wages) the rate of profit remains positive, for the prices of commodities (in relation to money wages and rents) are such that their total selling value exceeds their total costs by the amount of expenditure out of profits. The total of real wages then falls short of total output by the amount of consumption of rentiers, that is, of purchase of commodities out of profit and rent incomes.'

It is possible to clarify the two cases distinguished in these paragraphs. In a state of bliss with constant population investment is zero. Since, therefore, the amount saved has to be zero, any positive profit-saving propensity, whether unity or less, certainly precludes a positive amount of profits; so the second paragraph must refer only to a zero profit-saving propensity, as in effect its two sentences twice affirm (profits = selling value − (wages + rents) = consumption out of profits). Keeping the assumption of no saving out of wages or rents, the meaning of Joan Robinson's two cases may now be rendered as follows:

(a) If the capitalists save some part of any profits they may get, they get no profit, *either* because the rate of profit on capital employed is zero *or* because their saving propensity 'multiplies' output itself down to zero (bliss becomes Nirvana).

(b) If the capitalists consume the whole of any profits they may get, their profits equal the amount they consume, which is positive if they get any profits to consume. (The reason for this ham and eggs dictum is supplied by Kaldor, 1955–6, p. 95.)

The marginal productivity theory, on the other hand, infers that in a state of bliss the rate of profit is zero: capital has become a free good, and full employment output is blissfully consistent with zero profits. The true contribution of Keynesian theory is to point out that in these circumstances any positive saving propensity *out of wages or rents* is inconsistent with full employment output.

on the map of economic calculation.[7] In Joan Robinson's world, the blanks are enlarged into great zones marked out by frontier-lines of technical discontinuity. Typically, all products are consumed in fixed proportions and capable of being produced by a single discontinuous 'hierarchy of techniques'; each technique has its own fixed factor-proportions which are rigidly unadaptable; techniques displace each other in profitability across iso-cost 'frontiers' defined by well-separated critical sets of factor-rewards; any frontier applies uniformly and simultaneously to every industry throughout the economy.[8] Only at the frontier between two techniques is economic calculation, or the Principle of Substitution, fully effective. Within each zone (i.e. within the limits of the critical sets of factor-rewards along its frontiers) almost anything may happen.

The paradoxes and fabulous histories that enliven *The Accumulation of Capital* have their licence in these extremes of discontinuity. They are not the consequence of any special feature of Joan Robinson's view of capital or of the marginal calculus. When eventually she considers a primitive agricultural economy in which continuous factor substitution is for once allowed,[9] her theory runs familiarly in terms of discounted products, following Wicksell. Again, when she indulges in some pronouncements concerning the nature of the factor of production and their marginal products, the substance of her thoughts is recognizable as that of the so-called Austrian view of the role of capital and time in production, more especially in the form which it was given by Wicksell (Robinson, 1956, pp. 310–11; cf. Wicksell, 1934, p. 150).

To find the kernel of Joan Robinson's meaning, it is best to

7. Just as the multiplier theory (to which the widow's cruse is closely related) applies when aggregate economic calculation is suspended by Keynesian unemployment.

8. Note how 'realistic' it seems to allow for technical discontinuities (one thinks of coke-ovens, blast furnaces, etc.). The end-result in Joan Robinson's model is that the opportunities for substitution are limited in any situation to a single, universal choice between two techniques; and this restriction becomes the dominant feature of the economy as a whole. The 'neo-classical vice of implicit theorizing' has here its counterpart in the vice of *explicit realism*.

9. 'This . . . is purely a repetition of our former argument in a simpler setting' (Robinson, 1956, pp. 291–2).

go back to Wicksell,[10] to whose ideas she pays repeated and generous tribute. Pages 111 to 119 of this appendix examine the problem from Wicksell's viewpoint. But first look again at the early Joan Robinson polemic against the neo-classical scheme (quoted on page 102), and consider four comments:

1. The value of a stock of capital 'in terms of product' is no more plausible than its value in J R units as an input to be fed into a production function. If capital is to be treated, from a productive viewpoint, on all fours with labour and land, it must somehow be measured 'in terms of its own technical unit',[11] in spite of the obvious difficulties. (In our scarecrow model it is the *number* of Meccano sets, along with the number of man-hours and acres, that directly determines the volume of output – not their value in terms of anything, although it happens that in our model the value of a Meccano set in terms of product is constant.)

Joan Robinson is correct in so far as she is complaining that the neo-classical tradition contains no indication of how a 'technical unit' for capital may be devised.

2. On the other hand, there is an ambiguity in her view that capital 'measured in terms of product' goes naturally with a

10. If I were advising a student on a method of approach to *The Accumulation of Capital*, I would recommend the following preparations: (a) reread the whole of Wicksell (1934); (b) concentrate in particular on a full understanding of the discontinuous 'exception' described by Wicksell in the last complete paragraph of his page 177 – this sets the stage for Joan Robinson's book; (c) read Bensusan-Butt (1954a and b) for an analysis which in several respects anticipates Joan Robinson, but in terms of a much simpler, and also more flexible, model.

11. Wicksell (1934, p. 149). Wicksell rejected the possibility of employing such a unit, partly because he could see no way of combining the different kinds of 'tools, machinery, and materials, etc.' in a 'unified treatment' (though he did not shrink from treating labour, land and product as if each were homogeneous), and partly because he believed at the time that the Walrasian solution of the pricing of newly produced capital goods involved 'arguing in a circle'. This latter problem, he thought, would still have to be solved before the 'yield' of particular capital goods could be linked up with the rate of interest. Later (1934, p. 226) he seems to have realized that this criticism was mistaken. The circularity that worried Wicksell (the fact that the rate of interest enters as a cost in the production of capital goods themselves) is merely another aspect of the mutual interdependence of all variables in the Walrasian system. For a similar example, see page 119.

discussion of accumulation because 'accumulation consists in refraining from consuming current output in order to add to the stock of wealth'. What is the addition to the stock of wealth that is made by current accumulation? It is not the *change in the value* of the stock, measured in terms of product, but rather the *value of the change*, measured in terms of product, i.e. the (real) value of the current output not consumed, and so added to the stock. Only the latter element corresponds with the idea of accumulation, unless current output, income, saving and investment are defined to include current revaluations of the pre-existing stock of capital goods – which is not the conventional usage.[12]

Joan Robinson apparently takes it for granted that the value of the capital stock in terms of product is the same thing as the cumulated value (the time-integral) of investment and saving in terms of product. The two measures may in fact diverge very widely, if there is any change in relative values between 'capital goods' and 'product': in the first measure, every such change is reflected in an immediate revaluation of the whole capital stock; in the second, the capital stock is recorded as a 'perpetual inventory' accumulated by saving at original cost in terms of product. The first measure is certainly Wicksell's. The second is the neo-classical tradition – or rather the tradition of all the economists from Adam Smith to Keynes who have thought of current output as being divided between consumption on the one hand and additions to the capital stock (saving, investment, accumulation) on the other. In a stationary equilibrium, the two measures coincide: but they part company even for infinitesimal variations at the margin of a stationary state, if those variations involve any change in relative values between 'capital goods' and 'product'.

3. A measure of the capital stock in its own technical unit – if

12. The value changes that accrue as 'depreciation' are of course allowed for in the conventional definitions, but we are here concerned with quite a different issue. The relevant distinction is often made explicit in national income statistics in the form of an *inventory revaluation adjustment*. This adjustment is made only in respect of inventories, since revaluations of other capital assets are not included in the figures in the first place.

that were feasible, as with Meccano sets – is of course not the same thing as either of the two measures 'in terms of product'. When capital is measured in Meccano sets, its marginal productivity – the rate of increase of product with respect to the number of Meccano sets employed – does not correspond in equilibrium with the ruling rate of profit (the rate of interest), but with that rate multiplied by the value of a Meccano set in terms of product.[13] At the same time, the rate of increase in the number of Meccano sets is the current rate of saving divided by the value of a Meccano set. Thus for the purpose of any marginal calculation in which the value of a Meccano set enters as a constant, capital may be measured in terms of product (as the accumulation of saving), and its marginal productivity will then correspond with the rate of profit.

This is the *rationale* of the neo-classical procedure. Two elements of calculation are involved, and in both the value of a Meccano set is correctly taken as constant: (a) a maximization process in which all prices, including the price of Meccano sets, are treated in perfect competition as constant parameters, and (b) a marginal increment of accumulation – the translation of a small amount of product by saving into additional Meccano sets – in which the 'error' in measuring the capital stock arising from an associated marginal change in the value of a Meccano set is confined to the marginal addition being made to the capital stock, and so is of 'the second order of smalls'. (The revaluation of the pre-existing stock, which occurs in the measure of capital in terms of product that Joan Robinson has in mind, is of a very different order.)

As soon as this point is accepted, it follows that the neo-classical procedure does not, after all, depend on the existence of a 'technical unit' of capital – the Meccano set – the value of which is in any case cancelled out. For marginal variations about the stationary equilibrium position – i.e. for all the purposes of the neo-classical theory – the natural unit of capital is simply 'an

13. To the profit-maximizing, cost-minimizing entrepreneur, the cost of the annual services of a Meccano set, comparable with the real wage in terms of product which is the cost of the annual services of a unit of labour, is the annual interest bill on the price of a Meccano set in terms of product.

equilibrium dollar's worth' regardless of the physical variety of capital goods, and regardless of marginal value changes or marginal adaptations of capital towards different physical forms.[14]

4. The foregoing argument is evidently quite symmetrical with respect to every factor and indeed every product: at the margin of a stationary state, capital, labour, land and output can each be measured in terms of 'an equilibrium dollar's worth'. From the 'tangency' and 'convexity' conditions prevailing at the equilibrium point – by virtue of the first- and second-order conditions of the economic maximization process – all valid theorems (as Samuelson might say) can then be deduced. In the given unit, aggregation is itself quite superficial: the equalities and inequalities that hold for the aggregates at the equilibrium point hold uniformly in terms of 'an equilibrium dollar's worth' of every possible subdivision of factor and product right down to the level of the individual firm. That is why the neo-classical theory often appears to be both aggregative and exact.

However, this achievement involves an inherent limitation, against which Joan Robinson has all along been tilting. The theory tells us something about the properties of an equilibrium point, but it gives no information in finite terms about one point in relation to any other point.[15] For instance, it does not enable us to 'draw' the hypothetical isoquants of a production function combining (say) capital and labour. All we know, from the neo-classical or any similar theory, is certain curvature properties that must hold at any point that is capable of being an equilibrium point. Assuming one such point, we are entitled to draw an invisibly small segment of a curve with the known properties – a grin without a cat. Yet why should we expect a theory to produce even a hypothetical cat? The trouble is that if we were supplied with all the hypotheses or empirical data in the world, we should still be puzzled to draw the rest of the curve,

14. This is essentially the familiar principle which Samuelson calls the Wong–Viner–Harrod envelope theorem (Samuelson, 1948, pp. 34, 66, 243, 1953–4, p. 5). See also Marshall (rebuking J. A. Hobson) (Marshall, 1890 – see p. 409 of 1920 edn).

15. In a footnote Joan Robinson (1956, p. 414) says something rather like this.

because we should want each point on it to be a potential equilibrium point, whereas our unit – 'an equilibrium dollar's worth' – is defined only for a single equilibrium point and changes its character at any point separated by a finite distance from the first. It may do no harm to sketch in a metaphorical curve, provided the argument touches only a single equilibrium point and its immediate neighbourhood. On these terms, 'comparative statics' is a misnomer: not different situations, but only 'virtual' displacements at the margin of one situation, can be considered.

For structural comparisons 'in the large' (e.g. as between two stationary states with different factor endowments), either the variables must be measurable in naturally homogeneous technical units (like Meccano sets and man-hours), or else some artificial means must be found to co-ordinate measurements made at different points. For the latter purpose, Champernowne (1953–4, p. 112) has proposed the use of a *chain index*, an approach which is entirely in keeping with the true character of aggregative analysis. Champernowne's chain index, as presented, looks like a rather *ad hoc* and specialized device to cope with Joan Robinson's difficulties. The next part of these notes is intended to show how a chain index of capital emerges naturally from the analysis of a simple problem considered by Wicksell.

The Wicksell effect

Joan Robinson finds extraordinary significance in Wicksell's demonstration that an increase in the social capital is partly 'absorbed by increased wages (and rent), so that only the residue . . . is really effective as far as a rise in production is concerned' (Wicksell, 1934, p. 268). 'The amount of employment offered by a given value of capital depends upon the real-wage rate. At a lower wage rate there is a smaller value of a given type of machine' (Robinson, 1956, p. 391). To its discoverer, the *Wicksell effect* seemed mainly important as an obstacle to the acceptance of 'von Thünen's thesis', the marginal productivity theory of interest. To Joan Robinson, 'this point of Wicksell's is the key to the whole theory of accumulation and of the determination of wages and profits' (Robinson, 1956, p. 396).

To identify the Wicksell effect we may rework very briefly his 'point-input, point-output' case.[16] For Wicksell's grape-juice we substitute labour, imagining a productive process in which the application of an amount of labour N at a point of time results after a 'period of production' t in a final output Q which is greater the longer the period of production allowed. Other variables are the real wage rate w, the value of capital in the form of goods-in-process K (both w and K measured in terms of product), and the competitive rate of interest or profit r. Interest is instantaneously compounded; e is the base of natural logarithms. Wicksell's main equations then appear as follows

$$Q = Nf(t). \tag{1}$$

$$w = \frac{Q}{N}e^{-rt}. \tag{2}$$

$$r = \frac{f'(t)}{f(t)}. \tag{3}$$

$$K = Nw \int_0^t e^{rx}\,dx = Nw\frac{e^{rt}-1}{r}. \tag{4a}$$

$$K = \frac{Q-Nw}{r}. \tag{4b}$$

Equation 1 is the production function, showing output per unit of labour as an increasing function $f(t)$ of the period of production. Equations 2 and 3 flow from 1 under perfect-competition profit-maximization assumptions: the wage rate is the discounted product per unit of labour, and the interest rate the (relative) 'marginal productivity of waiting'. Equation 4a evaluates K from the cost side as the wages bill continuously invested in production and cumulated at compound interest over the period t; while 4b, using 1 and 2, shows that K is also the capitalized value of total profits $Q - Nw$. Using the second-order maximiza-

16. See Wicksell (1934, pp. 172–81, esp. pp. 178–80). In the following reformulation, nothing material is changed. The reader is referred to Wicksell for further explanations. Where our symbols differ from his, the equivalents are: $Q/N = W$, $N_w = V_0$, $r = \rho$. Wicksell's 'one hectolitre of grape-juice', which does not appear explicitly, is our N, but the change is only formal. Our numbering of the equations is not the same as Wicksell's. For the mathematics of this case, see Allen (1938, pp. 248, 362, 403).

tion condition upon $f(t)$, Wicksell proved that in equilibrium (for given N) increasing K necessarily means increasing w, decreasing r and increasing t. In Joan Robinson's language, increasing t represents a higher 'degree of mechanization', made profitable as w increases – the *Ricardesque effect*.

Differentiating **1** and **4a** or **4b** while holding N constant, Wicksell next derived a formula for the rate of increase of Q with respect to K. This formula can be expressed in four distinct ways:

$$\frac{dQ}{dK} = r - K\left[\frac{r}{w}\frac{dw}{dK} + \left(\frac{rt}{1-e^{-rt}}-1\right)\frac{dr}{dK}\right], \tag{5a}$$

$$= r + \left(K\frac{dr}{dK} + N\frac{dw}{dK}\right), \tag{5b}$$

$$= r + (K-Nwt)\frac{dr}{dK}, \tag{5c}$$

$$= r - \left(\frac{K-Nwt}{wt}\right)\frac{dw}{dK}. \tag{5d}$$

The second term in these expressions is always negative – i.e. the 'marginal productivity of capital' in this sense is always less than the rate of interest, part of the increase in K having been 'unproductively absorbed'. This is the Wicksell effect. Our four versions suggest that it is somewhat misleading to ascribe the 'absorption' simply to increased wages. **5a** shows the Wicksell effect from the viewpoint of the *cost* of the capital stock (**4a**), as the consequence of a higher wage rate only partly offset by a lower interest rate. **5b**, from the viewpoint of *capitalized profits* (**4b**), shows it as the consequence of a lower interest rate only partly offset by a higher wage rate. **5c** and **5d** use the relation between r and w given in **2** to attribute the whole Wicksell effect on the one hand to a lower interest rate, and on the other hand to a higher wage rate. The multiplicity of explanations shows how treacherous is the idea of causation amongst interdependent variables.

Yet the different versions of the Wicksell effect have one common feature which is itself a complete explanation. To see this, we first write out the logarithmic total differential of **4a** and **4b**, giving four alternative expressions for a (proportional) change in the value of capital to parallel the four versions of **5**:

$$\frac{dK}{K} = \left[\frac{dN}{N} + \frac{rt}{1-e^{-rt}}\frac{dt}{t}\right] + \left[\frac{dw}{w} + \left(\frac{rt}{1-e^{-rt}} - 1\right)\frac{dr}{r}\right], \qquad \textbf{6a}$$

$$= \left(\frac{Q}{Kr}\frac{dQ}{Q} - \frac{Nw}{Kr}\frac{dN}{N}\right) - \left(\frac{Nw}{Kr}\frac{dw}{w} + \frac{dr}{r}\right), \qquad \textbf{6b}$$

$$= \left(\quad_{,,}\qquad_{,,}\quad\right) - \left(\frac{K-Nwt}{K}\frac{dr}{r}\right), \qquad \textbf{6c}$$

$$= \left(\quad_{,,}\qquad_{,,}\quad\right) + \left(\frac{K-Nwt}{Krt}\frac{dw}{w}\right). \qquad \textbf{6d}$$

Here the terms are grouped by brackets into two columns. The first column shows the component of a change in the value of capital due to 'productive' features (more labour, a longer period of production, greater output). The second column shows the component due to 'financial' features (changes in the wage and interest rates). It is easy to verify that the different versions in each column are vertically equivalent: i.e. the 'productive' component and the 'financial' component of a change in K are respectively the same, whether considered (a) in terms of cost or (b) in terms of capitalization, and in the case of the 'financial' element whether ascribed (c) to an interest change or (d) to a wage change. Let us make this distinction explicit by defining two synthetic variables, k and p, with the following properties at a certain equilibrium point:

$$kp = K, \qquad\qquad\qquad 7$$

$$\frac{dk}{k} = \frac{dN}{N} + \frac{1-e^{-rt}}{rt}\frac{dt}{t}, \qquad\qquad \textbf{8a}$$

$$\frac{dp}{p} = \frac{dw}{w} + \left(\frac{rt}{1-e^{-rt}} - 1\right)\frac{dr}{r}. \qquad\qquad \textbf{8b}$$

In these definitions, K is broken into two components which may be interpreted as a 'quantity' k, and a 'price' (in terms of product) p; dk/k is identified with the first column of **6**, and dp/p with the second column. The stated properties cannot hold generally, because the product of the integrals of **8a** and **8b** is not, in general,

K. Nevertheless the definitions involve no contradiction if they are restricted to a particular set of equilibrium values of *w*, *r* and *t* – namely, those prevailing at the equilibrium point for which in any particular case the differentials in **5** or **6** are also calculated. We shall return in a moment to the question of integrating **8a** and **8b** so as to define *k* and *p* for other points.

Next we can put

$$dK = K\left(\frac{dk}{k}+\frac{dp}{p}\right) = p\,dk + k\,dp$$

in **5a**, and arrange the result as follows:

$$\frac{dQ}{p\,dk} = r + \frac{kr}{dk}\left[\frac{dp}{p} - \frac{dw}{w} - \left(\frac{rt}{1-e^{-rt}}-1\right)\frac{dr}{r}\right]. \qquad \textbf{5a}'$$

According to the definition of *dp/p* in **8b**, the second term – which previously showed the Wicksell effect – is now identically zero: when the increment of capital is taken as *K dk/k*, or *p dk* ('the value of the change'), its marginal productivity corresponds with the rate of interest. The same result can of course be obtained by a similar substitution in the other three versions of **5**. Here is the common feature of all four versions of the Wicksell effect, that the effect disappears when the marginal change in capital is measured so as to exclude *K dp/p*, or *k dp*, which is the revaluation of the capital stock resulting from an associated marginal change in wage and interest rates. *The Wicksell effect is nothing but an inventory revaluation.*

The wage rate, previously given by **2** as the average product of labour discounted over the period of production, may now also be derived as the marginal productivity of labour. Differentiating **1**, using **3** and substituting for *dt* from **8a**, we obtain

$$\frac{dQ}{Q} = e^{-rt}\frac{dN}{N} + (1-e^{-rt})\frac{dk}{k}. \qquad \textbf{9}$$

By **1**, **2** and **4b**, the two coefficients in **9** are the proportional shares of wages and profits in output, *Nw/Q* and *Kr/Q*, respectively. Therefore:

$$dQ = w\,dN + rp\,dk. \qquad \textbf{10}$$

Accordingly, when the quantity of capital k is held constant,

$w = dQ/dN$.

The component $p\,dk$ is the value at ruling prices (in terms of product) of an increment of capital goods, and so corresponds with the usual idea of investment, saving, or accumulation. It may be convenient to call $dQ/p\,dk(=r)$ the *marginal efficiency of investment*, reserving the term *marginal productivity of capital* for $dQ/dk(=rp)$. In relation to our earlier discussion, dk is an increment of capital measured 'in terms of its own technical unit' (like Meccano sets), while $p\,dk$ is an increment measured in terms of 'an equilibrium dollar's worth'.

But we are now a step forward. The definitions of k and p in **7** and **8** can be recognized in their essential character as the differential definitions of *chain indexes* of quantity and price, by which Divisia provided 'an elegant logical justification' of Marshall's original invention of the chain index.[17] Thus although **8a** and **8b** cannot usually be integrated to give exact measures of k and p, such that $kp = K$ at every point, they can in principle be integrated numerically in successive small 'links' (correcting the weights as each link is added) so as to form a consistent pair of chain indexes of the 'quantity' and 'price' of capital. With these indexes approximate structural comparisons 'in the large' between different equilibrium situations may be made. The index k enters with N in the production function, while the index p measures for each point of the production function the amount of accumulation in terms of product necessary to achieve a given addition to k – in effect, converting 'an equilibrium dollar's worth' at one point into its productive equivalent at another point.

This operation can most easily be visualized by considering a special case in which **8a** and **8b** lend themselves to exact integration – namely, the case in which the function $f(t)$ is of constant elasticity, and may be written $f(t) = t^{\alpha}$. Then by **3** $rt = \alpha$. The proportional share of profits in output is also now a con-

17. See Frisch (1936, pp. 7–8). The elementary index-number formula used to construct each link of the chain will vary, as Frisch points out, 'according as we choose the approximation principle for the steps of the numerical integration'.

stant, which it is convenient to write $1 - e^{-rt} = \beta$. Therefore **8a** and **8b** become

$$\frac{dk}{k} = \frac{dN}{N} + \frac{\alpha}{\beta}\frac{dt}{t}, \qquad \textbf{8a}'$$

$$\frac{dp}{p} = \frac{dw}{w} + \left(\frac{\alpha}{\beta} - 1\right)\frac{dr}{r}, \qquad \textbf{8b}'$$

and in this form they give immediately the integrals

$$k = C_1\, N t^{\alpha/\beta}, \qquad \textbf{a}'$$

$$p = C_2\, w r^{\alpha/\beta - 1}, \qquad \textbf{b}'$$

where C_1 and C_2 are constants of integration.[18] The production function **1** may now be expressed in terms of N and k, and its partial derivatives with respect to these factors of production will appear as w and rp:

$$Q = N^{1-\beta} k^{\beta}, \qquad \textbf{1}'$$

$$w = (1-\beta)\frac{Q}{N}, \qquad \textbf{2}'$$

$$rp = \beta\frac{Q}{K}. \qquad \textbf{3}'$$

Given the definitions of k and p in **a**′ and **b**′, the new system is in all respects the equivalent of Wicksell's, as the reader may readily confirm by substitution. Although the wage rate w and the yield (or quasi-rent) of a unit of capital rp are derived from the new production function as the marginal productivities of labour and capital, it seems at first sight that in order to discover r we must know p, and vice versa. However, in **b**′ there is another relation between w, r and p, which enables r and p to be separately determined once the values of w and rp are given at any point of the production function.[19]

18. In order that k and p may satisfy **7** and **4**, C_1 and C_2 must satisfy
$C_1 C_2 = (e^{\alpha} - 1)a^{-\alpha/\beta}$
It is convenient to choose units so that $C_1 = 1$. This choice accounts for the absence from **1**′ below of any explicit constant of integration.

19. In this special case where the production function is such that the proportional share of each factor in output is constant, there is obviously

When the elasticity of $f(t)$ is not constant, this exact formulation in terms of k and p is no longer possible 'in the large'. Nevertheless the chain indexes of k and p are available as approximate measures, and they will play in principle the same role as k and p in the special case just considered.[20]

But why bother to show that with the help of chain indexes the neo-classical scheme can approximately mimic the solution of a highly artificial problem already obtained in an exact form by Wicksell? One answer is that Wicksell's analysis is exact only when K – the *value* of capital in terms of product – is taken as an independent variable. To consider the effect of a given amount of *accumulation* – the foregone consumption of a given amount of product – Wicksell, too, would have been driven to approximations and index numbers. Another answer is that the elements which appear in our definitions of the indexes k and p are merely particular illustrations, drawn from Wicksell's model, of the 'productive' and the 'financial' attributes of capital goods that have to be distinguished in measuring their 'quantity' and 'price': index-number measurements may still be appropriate when capital does not take those particular forms which enabled Wicksell to specify its productive effect directly in terms of a period of time.

Wicksell himself thought of the period of production or period of investment as no more than a notional index of the time aspect of capital – 'a mathematical concept, without direct physical or psychic significance', but which 'should, nevertheless, be retained as a concise general principle, reflecting the essence of productive capital' (Wicksell, 1934, p. 184). If Joan Robinson will allow Wicksell in this spirit to draw a production function

no difficulty in extending the above analysis to cover any number of different factors of production. As far as I can see, the chain-index approach in the general case also extends to any number of factors, provided that continuous adjustments in factor proportions are assumed to be possible. Champernowne (1953–4, pp. 121–5, 132–5) shows that the chain index in general breaks down for more than two factors when techniques are discontinuous.

20. Of course a chain index is not necessarily a 'better' approximation than some other kind of index number. For the present purpose, however, the chain index in its Divisia formulation is very convenient in that it shows a consistent way of making approximate measurements 'in the large', while keeping the advantage of theoretical exactness 'in the small'.

involving N, t and (indirectly) K, she ought not to object if others prefer to draw one involving N, k and (indirectly) p: for there is, as we have seen, a method by which one scheme may be translated into the other.

Åkerman's problem

By the same method, Gustaf Åkerman's problem of durable capital equipment – as analysed by Wicksell in a celebrated essay[21] – can also be solved in accordance with the marginal productivity theory. Wicksell's analysis was mainly intended to refute Åkerman's claim that this could be done.

In the model which Wicksell developed for the purpose, capital consists of axes which can be made more or less durable by putting more or less labour into their manufacture; the optimum life of an axe, n years, is chosen to maximize profits; the stock of axes in the stationary equilibrium is a 'balanced equipment' with a uniform age distribution from 0 to n years; M labourers out of the total labour force A are occupied in replacing the nth part of the stock that wears out each year, while $A - M$ 'free labourers' co-operate with the stock of axes to produce a (net) output π. K is the value of the stock of axes (in terms of product), l the wage rate and ρ the rate of interest.[22]

K is evaluated by Wicksell in equation **15** (p. 283). With one substitution from equation **4** (p. 276), **15** becomes:

$$K = Mnl\left(\frac{1}{1-e^{-\rho n}} - \frac{1}{\rho n}\right). \qquad \textbf{15.1}$$

Here Mnl is the replacement cost of the whole stock of axes, while the bracketed expression can be recognized as the Champernowne–Kahn formula for the value of a 'balanced

21. First published in Swedish in 1923, then republished in Wicksell (1934, pp. 274–99). Until the Joan Robinson and Kahn and Champernowne papers of 1953–4, this essay seems to have been the only analysis available in English of the specific questions posed for (long-run) capital theory by durable, depreciable, capital equipment.

22. Wicksell's notation is preserved. In this case no attempt will be made to reformulate Wicksell's model. Assuming that the interested reader will look up the original, we give the essentials of the argument with a minimum of incidental explanation.

equipment' as a proportion of its replacement cost.[23] Differentiating **15.1** as it stands, and then making a substitution from Wicksell's equation **9** (p. 278), we obtain the logarithmic total differential of K

$$\frac{dK}{K} = \left[\frac{dM}{M} + \frac{(1-v)\{v+\varphi(v)\}}{v+\varphi(v)-1}\frac{dn}{n}\right] +$$

$$+ \left[\frac{dl}{l} + \left(\frac{1-v}{v+\varphi(v)-1} - v\right)\frac{d\rho}{\rho}\right]. \quad \textbf{15.2}$$

The proportional change in the value of capital is split by the square brackets into a 'productive' and a 'financial' component, just as in **6a** on page 114. Again we identify dk/k with the first component, and dp/p with the second. This time the distinction is easier to visualize. The 'technical unit' of capital in which k is measured is in effect a *standard axe* (of given durability and age), while p is the value of such an axe, calculated at current wage and interest rates. This follows simply from the fact that the second component of **15.2** is the differential of **15.1** with respect to l and ρ, calculated as of constant M and n. In the present model the definition of a 'standard axe' creates no index-number problems: Wicksell's constant elasticity formulae mean that the coefficients in **15.2** are constants, so that k and p can be obtained by direct integration as indexes with correct and constant weights

23. Wicksell's derivation of **15** is explained by Allen (1938, p. 405). The Champernowne–Kahn formula is derived by Champernowne and Kahn in four different ways (Champernowne and Kahn, 1953–4, pp. 107–11). Joan Robinson reports in her preface that C. A. Blyth has derived it independently.

The underlying principle can be seen in graphical terms. The cost or value of a 'machine' is equal to its future gross earnings discounted to the present moment. Given the prospective earnings at each point of its life, and given the rate of interest at which they are to be discounted, a curve showing the machine's value as a function of its age will fall from its starting point at age 0 (replacement cost) down to zero at age n years when it falls to pieces. The average value of the machine *per year of life* is the area under the curve divided by n. A 'balanced equipment' of such machines is of uniform age distribution from 0 to n, and so repeats in cross-section the life-history of a single machine. The average value *per machine* in a 'balanced equipment' is, therefore, also the area under the curve divided by n. In the particular case when the earnings of a machine are at a constant rate throughout its life, the Champernowne–Kahn formula gives the ratio of this average value to the original value at age 0.

at every point. Moreover, M is a constant proportion of the total labour force A (Wicksell, 1934, p. 287), and is therefore determined when A is taken as an independent variable.

The rest follows as on pages 111 to 119 – the Wicksell effect disappears, the production function[24] can be written in terms of A and k, etc. In fact, with an appropriate revision or reinterpretation of the various constants, our earlier equations $\mathbf{a}'$, $\mathbf{b}'$, $\mathbf{1}'$, $\mathbf{2}'$ and $\mathbf{3}'$ will now serve as an exact representation in neoclassical form of Wicksell's analysis of Åkerman's problem.

The Wicksell effect in reverse

One new feature emerges. In the model of pages 111–19 increasing K (or k) always means increasing p: the wage rate rises and the interest rate falls, but the net effect is necessarily a rise in the value of a unit of capital in terms of product. Thus the Wicksell effect is an apparent absorption of capital. However, in the model of pages 111–19 it turns out that the two components of **15.2** may very well be of opposite sign. So long as the 'convexity' conditions for profit maximization are satisfied, a higher wage rate and a lower interest rate must still accompany increasing K (or k), but the interest effect on p may now outweigh the wage effect.[25] The value of a 'standard axe' may fall. *In this event the Wicksell effect goes into reverse.*

When Wicksell calculated $d\pi/dK$ he found again that by this

24. With k defined as above, it can be shown that the production function given by Wicksell in equation 17 *bis* (p. 287) is corrrectly reproduced by the integral of the following expression:

$$\frac{d\pi}{\pi} = \left[(1-\beta)\frac{v+\varphi(v)-1}{v+\varphi(v)} \right]\frac{dA}{A} + \beta\frac{v+\varphi(v)-1}{v+\varphi(v)}\frac{dk}{k}.$$

By Wicksell's assumptions, the coefficients are constants.

25. Here we are looking at capital from the viewpoint of cost, as in **6a**. It is possible as before to express dp/p in terms of either the wage rate or the interest rate alone. For instance, corresponding with **6c**, the second component of **15.2** may be written:

$$\frac{dp}{p} = -\left[v+\beta(1-v)-\frac{1-v}{v+\varphi(v)-1} \right]\frac{d\rho}{\rho}.$$

The second-order maximization conditions imply that β and v are each less than unity, and that the denominator of the third term is positive. But the sign of the sum within the brackets (which in **6c** is always positive) depends on the relative magnitudes of β and v; it can be negative if β is small and v neither very near unity nor very near zero.

measure Åkerman's and von Thünen's thesis was 'not verified', but he found also that in his new model $d\pi/dK$ might actually exceed the rate of interest, i.e. he discovered the Wicksell effect in reverse. This phenomenon left Wicksell very puzzled and caused him to admit that his previous explanation, in terms of the absorption of capital in increased wages, was '*not* general'.[26]

Once it is realized that the Wicksell effect merely reflects a revaluation of the capital stock, it is no longer puzzling that it may go in either direction. When wages rise and interest falls, whether the value of a 'standard axe' goes up or down in terms of product may be expected to turn (broadly speaking) on a comparison of the relative importance of the two factors for the axe, on the one hand, and for the product, on the other. In general, there is no presumption either way. But in Wicksell's previous models, before his analysis of Åkerman's problem, the product typically emerged only at the last and most 'capitalistic' stage of production. In such models (as on pages 111–19) a higher wage rate and a lower interest rate must depress the final product, and elevate the goods-in-process at the earlier stages, in relative value. Hence Wicksell's surprise on finding himself at the age of seventy-two in a new world of durable capital equipment, in which this rule no longer applies.

What is more puzzling is why Joan Robinson thirty years later should write as if she and Wicksell were both back in the old world where capital was goods-in-process. Her rule that 'at a lower wage rate there is a smaller value of a given type of machine' need not hold even for Wicksell's hand-made axe, far less for a typical machine, itself a capitalistic product.[27] The

26. Wicksell (1934, pp. 292–3). It is interesting to note that Wicksell in these pages experimented with the possibility of adjusting his measure of the increase in capital, by deducting the effect of the rise in the wage rate, precisely as we have done in defining dk/k and dp/p. He failed to reach the same conclusion only because he did not allow for the lower interest rate as well as for the higher wage rate.

27. The influence of interest on the value of an axe is confined in **15.1** and **15.2** to the Champernowne–Kahn term of **15.1**, i.e. to the effect of the interest rate on the value of a 'balanced equipment' of axes as a proportion of its replacement cost. The latter consists of labour cost alone. If axes were themselves made with the co-operation of capital, their replacement cost would also contain an interest element, and it would be much easier for the reverse Wicksell effect to occur.

revaluation of a given machine in an opposite direction to the wage rate (in the same direction as the interest rate) is a reverse Wicksell effect, but there is nothing perverse about it,[28] and in general it is just as likely to happen as its obverse, the original Wicksell effect.

Most puzzling of all is how the possibility of a shift in relative value between capital good and product *in an unpredictable direction* can become in Joan Robinson's hands 'the key to the whole theory of accumulation and of the determination of wages and profits'.

References

ALLEN, R. G. D. (1938), *Mathematical Analysis for Economists*, Macmillan.

BENSUSAN-BUTT, D. M. (1954a), 'Some elementary theory about accumulation', *Oxf. econ. Pap.*, vol. 6, pp. 306–27.

BENSUSAN-BUTT, D. M. (1954b), 'A model of trade and accumulation', *Amer. econ. Rev.*, vol. 44, pp. 511–29.

CHAMPERNOWNE, D. G. (1953–4), 'The production function and the theory of capital: a comment', *Rev. econ. Stud.*, vol. 21, pp. 112–35. [See Reading 2.]

CHAMPERNOWNE, D. G., and KAHN, R. F. (1953–4), 'The value of invested capital', *Rev. econ. Stud.*, vol. 21, pp. 107–11.

FRISCH, R. (1936), 'Annual survey of general economic theory: the problem of index numbers', *Econometrica*, vol. 4, pp. 225–39.

KALDOR, N. (1955–6), 'Alternative theories of distribution', *Rev. econ. Stud.*, vol. 23, pp. 94–100.

MARSHALL, A. (1890), *Principles of Economics*, Macmillan, 8th edn, 1920.

ROBINSON, J. (1953–4), 'The production function and the theory of capital', *Rev. econ. Stud.*, vol. 21, pp. 81–106. [See Reading 1.]

ROBINSON, J. (1955), 'The production function', *Econ. J.*, vol. 65, pp. 67–71.

ROBINSON, J. (1956), *The Accumulation of Capital*, Macmillan.

28. The perverse case discussed by Joan Robinson, in which a higher wage rate and a lower interest rate make a *less* mechanized technique relatively profitable, has nothing to do with the direction of the Wicksell effect, though one might easily get the impression that Joan Robinson thinks it does (Robinson, 1953–4, pp. 95–6, 106; 1956, pp. 109–10, 147–8, 418). The perversity arises essentially from a failure over a certain range of the second-order ('convexity') conditions for profit maximization, as indeed Wicksell pointed out in his analysis of Åkerman's problem (1934, pp. 294–7, esp. p. 295n). Only in his earlier goods-in-process model would a reverse Wicksell effect imply the failure of those conditions, and so perversity.

SAMUELSON, P. A. (1948), *The Foundations of Economic Analysis*, Harvard University Press.

SAMUELSON, P. A. (1953–4), 'Prices of factors and goods in general equilibrium', *Rev. econ. Stud.*, vol. 21, pp. 1–14.

SOLOW, R. M. (1955–6), 'The production function and the theory of capital', *Rev. econ. Stud.*, vol. 23, pp. 101–8.

WICKSELL, K. (1934), *Lectures on Political Economy*, vol. 1, trans. from 3rd edn by E. Classen, Routledge & Kegan Paul.

4 P. Sraffa

Reduction to Dated Quantities of Labour

Excerpt from P. Sraffa, 'Reduction to dated quantities of labour', in *Production of Commodities by Means of Commodities. Prelude to a Critique of Economic Theory*, Cambridge University Press, 1960, pp. 34–8.

1. In this chapter prices are considered from their cost-of-production aspect, and the way in which they 'resolve themselves' into wages and profits is examined. Had it not been for the necessity of following one line of argument at a time, the subject would have been introduced earlier in the discussion. Indeed, although not properly introduced, it has been anticipated in allusions to the quantity of labour which 'directly and indirectly' enters a product.

2. We shall call 'reduction to dated quantities of labour' (or 'reduction' for short) an operation by which in the equation of a commodity the different means of production used are replaced with a series of quantities of labour, each with its appropriate 'date'.

Take the equation which represents the production of commodity a (and where the wage and prices are expressed in terms of the Standard commodity):

$$(A_a p_a + B_a p_b + \ldots + K_a p_k)(1+r) + L_a w = A p_a.$$

We begin by replacing the commodities forming the means of production of A with *their own* means of production and quantities of labour; that is to say, we replace them with the commodities and labour which, as appears from their own respective equations, must be employed to produce those means of production; and they, having been expended a year earlier [see § 9, p. 10, of original], will be multiplied by a profit factor at a compound rate for the appropriate period, namely the means of production by $(1+r)^2$ and the labour by $1+r$. (It may be noted that A_a, the quantity of commodity a itself which is used in the production of A, is to be treated like any other means of production, that is to say, replaced by its own means of production and labour.)

We next proceed to replace *these latter* means of production with their own means of production and labour, and to these will be applied a profit factor for one more year, or, to the means of production $(1+r)^3$ and to the labour $(1+r)^2$.

We can carry this operation on as far as we like and if next to the direct labour L_a we place the successive aggregate quantities of labour which we collect at each step and which we shall call respectively $L_{a_1}, L_{a_2}, ..., L_{a_n}, ...$, we shall obtain the 'reduction equation' for the product in the form of an infinite series.

$$L_a w + L_{a_1} w(1+r) + ... + L_{a_n} w(1+r)^n + ... = A p_a.$$

How far the reduction need be pushed in order to obtain a given degree of approximation depends on the level of the rate of profits: the nearer the latter is to its maximum, the further must the reduction be carried. Beside the labour terms there will always be a 'commodity residue' consisting of minute fractions of every basic product; but it is always possible, by carrying the reduction sufficiently far, to render the residue so small as to have, at any prefixed rate of profits short of R, a negligible effect on price. It is only at $r = R$ that the residue becomes all-important as the sole determinant of the price of the product.

3. As the rate of profits rises, the value of each of the labour terms is pulled in opposite directions by the rate of profits and by the wage, and it moves up or down as the one or the other prevails. The relative weight of these two factors varies of course at different levels of distribution; and, besides, it varies differently in the case of terms of different 'date', as we shall presently see.

We have seen [see § 30, p. 22, of original] that, if the wage is expressed in terms of the Standard net product, when the rate of profits r changes, the wage w moves as

$$w = 1 - \frac{r}{R},$$

where R is the maximum rate of profits.

Substituting this expression for the wage in each term of the reduction-equation the general form of any nth labour term becomes

$$L_{a_n}\left(1-\frac{r}{R}\right)(1+r)^n.$$

Consider now the values assumed by this expression as r moves from 0 to its maximum R.

At $r = 0$ the value of a labour term depends exclusively on its size, irrespective of date.

With the rise of the rate of profits, terms divide into two groups: those that correspond to labour done in a more recent past, which begin at once to fall in value and fall steadily throughout; and

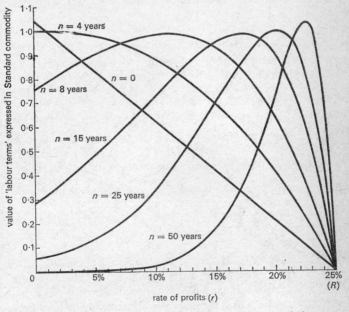

Figure 1 Variations in value of 'reduction terms' of different periods $[L_n w(1+r)^n]$ relative to the Standard commodity as the rate of profit varies between 0 and R (assumed to be 25 per cent).

The quantities of labour (L_n) in the various 'terms', which have been chosen so as to keep the curves within the page, are as follows: $L_0 = 1\cdot04$, $L_4 = 1$, $L_8 = 0\cdot76$, $L_{15} = 0\cdot29$, $L_{25} = 0\cdot0525$, $L_{50} = 0\cdot0004$

those representing labour more remote in time, which at first rise and then, as each of them reaches its maximum value, turn and begin the downward movement. In the end, at $r = R$, the wage vanishes and with it vanishes the value of each labour term.

This is best shown by a selection of curves, representing terms of widely different dates, n, and different quantities of labour, such as is given in Figure 1. In this example R is supposed to be 25 per cent.

It is as if the rate of profits, in its movement from 0 to R, generated a wave along the row of labour terms the crest of which was formed by successive terms, as one after the other they reached their maximum value. At any value of the rate of profits the term which reaches its maximum has the 'date'

$$n = \frac{1}{R-r}.$$

And, conversely, the rate of profits at which any term of date n is at its maximum is

$$r = R - \frac{1}{n}.$$

Accordingly, all the terms for which $n \leqslant 1/R$ have their maximum at $r = 0$ and thus form the group of 'recent dates' mentioned above as falling in value throughout the increase of r.

4. The labour terms can be regarded as the constituent elements of the price of a commodity, the combination of which in various proportions may, with the variation of the rate of profits, give rise to complicated patterns of price movement with several ups and downs.

The simplest case is that of the 'balanced commodity' [see § 21, p. 15, of original] or of its equivalent, the Standard commodity taken as an aggregate: its reduction would result in a perfectly regular series, the quantity of labour in any term being equal to $1+R$ times the quantity in the term immediately preceding it in date.

As an example of the more complicated type we may suppose two products which differ in three of their labour terms (chosen from those represented in Figure 1), while being identical in all the others. One of them, a, has an excess of twenty units of labour applied eight years before, whereas the excess of the other, b, consists of nineteen units employed in the current year and one unit bestowed twenty-five years earlier. (They are thus not unlike the familiar instances, respectively, of the wine aged in the cellar and of the old oak made into a chest.) The difference between their Standard prices at various rates of profits, namely

$$p_a - p_b = 20w(1+r)^8 - \{19w + w(1+r)^{25}\},$$

is represented in Figure 2.

The price of 'old wine' rises relative to the 'oak chest' as the rate of profits moves from 0 to 9 per cent, then it falls between 9 per cent and 22 per cent, to rise again from 22 per cent to 25 per cent.

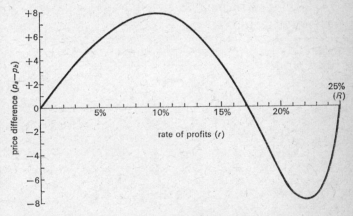

Figure 2 Difference, at various rates of profits, between the prices of two commodities, which are produced by equal quantities of labour equally distributed over time, with the exception that (a) a unit of commodity A requires in addition twenty units of labour eight years before its production is completed; (b) a unit of commodity B requires in addition one unit of labour twenty-five years before its production is completed and nineteen units in the last year.

The equation of the curve is

$$p_a - p_b = 20w(1+r)^8 - \{19w + w(1+r)^{25}\},$$

where $w = 1 - \dfrac{r}{25\%}$.

(The reduction to dated labour terms has some bearing on the attempts that have been made to find in the 'period of production' an independent measure of the quantity of capital which could be used, without arguing in a circle, for the determination of prices and of the shares in distribution. But the case just considered seems conclusive in showing the impossibility of aggregating the 'periods' belonging to the several quantities of labour into a single magnitude which could be regarded as representing the quantity of capital. The reversals in the direction of the movement of relative prices, in the face of unchanged methods of production, cannot be reconciled with *any* notion of capital as a measurable quantity independent of distribution and prices.)

Part Two
An Econometric Application of the Concept of an Aggregate Neo-Classical Production Function

The article by Arrow, Chenery, Minhas and Solow, an excerpt of which is reprinted here as Reading 5, is an outstanding example of the attempts to interpret empirical findings in terms of the neo-classical theory of production and distribution. It introduced to a wide audience the concept of the constant elasticity of substitution (CES) production function and is the forerunner of many subsequent applications of this concept in empirical work. Arrow *et al.* in fact assume that technical progress is disembodied, i.e. affects the productivity of all factors, *including that of capital goods already existing*, that capital may be treated 'as if' it were malleable and that profit-maximizing businessmen have static expectations concerning the future courses of factor and product prices. Much of the work that follows their pioneering article is concerned with the introduction of embodied technical change through vintage models and with the implications of the assumption of more sophisticated expectations by businessmen concerning the future course of prices. There is not, unfortunately, the space to reprint examples of these approaches here but the reader is referred to the references cited in the appropriate section of the Further Reading list.

5 K. J. Arrow, H. B. Chenery, B. S. Minhas and R. M. Solow

Capital–Labour Substitution and Economic Efficiency[1]

Excerpts from K. J. Arrow, H. B. Chenery, B. S. Minhas and
R. M. Solow, 'Capital–labor substitution and economic efficiency',
Review of Economics and Statistics, vol. 43, 1961, pp. 225–34, 246–8.

In many branches of economic theory, it is necessary to make some assumption about the extent to which capital and labor are substitutable for each other. In the absence of empirical generalizations about this phenomenon, theorists have chosen simple hypotheses which have become widely accepted through frequent repetition. Two competing alternatives hold the field at present. the Walras–Leontief–Harrod–Domar assumption of constant input coefficients;[2] and the Cobb–Douglas function, which implies a unitary elasticity of substitution between labor and capital. From a mathematical point of view, zero and one are perhaps the most convenient alternatives for this elasticity. Economic analysis based on these assumptions, however, often leads to conclusions that are unduly restrictive.

The crucial nature of the substitution assumption can be illustrated in various fields of economic theory:

1. The unstable balance of the Harrod–Domar model of growth depends in a critical way on the assumption of zero substitution between labor and capital, as Solow (1956), Swan (1956) and others have shown.

1. This study grows out of the research program of the Stanford Project for Quantitative Research in Economic Development. It is one in a series of analyses based on international comparisons of the economic structure. Hendrik Houthakker contributed substantially to the formulation of both the statistical and theoretical analyses. Arrow's participation was aided by Contract 251(33), Task N4047–004, Office of Naval Research.
2. It is only fair to note that the general equilibrium theories of Walras and Leontief never assume fixed proportions for gross aggregates like capital and labor.

2. The effects of varying factor endowments on international trade hinge on the shape of particular production functions. In this case, either zero or unitary elasticities of substitution in *all* sectors of the economy lead to Samuelson's strong assumption as to the invariability of the ranking of factor proportions. Variations in elasticity among sectors imply reversals of factor intensities at different factor prices with quite different consequences for trade and factor returns.

3. In analysing the relative shares of income received by the factors of production, it is tempting to assume unit elasticity of substitution to agree with the supposed constancy of the labor share in the United States. Recent work has called into question both the observed constancy and the necessity of the assumption (see Kravis, 1959; Swan, 1956).

Turning to empirical evidence, we find every indication of varying degrees of substitutability in different types of production. Technological alternatives are numerous and flexible in some sectors, limited in others; and uniform substitutability is most unlikely. The difference in elasticities is confirmed by direct observation of capital–labor proportions, which show much more variation among countries in some sectors than in others.

The starting point for the present study was the empirical observation that the value added per unit of labor used within a given industry varies across countries with the wage rate. Evidence of this relationship for twenty-four manufacturing industries in a sample of nineteen countries is given in section I. A regression of the labor productivity on the wage rate shows a highly significant correlation in all industries and also a considerable variation in the regression coefficients.

These empirical findings led to attempts to derive a mathematical function having the properties of (a) homogeneity, (b) constant elasticity of substitution between capital and labor, and (c) the possibility of different elasticities for different industries. In section II it is shown that there is one general production function having these properties; it includes the Leontief and Cobb–Douglas functions as special cases.[3] The function contains

3. This function and its properties were arrived at independently by Solow and Arrow.

three parameters, which are identified as the substitution parameter, the distribution parameter and the efficiency parameter. [. . .]

I. Variation in labor inputs with labor cost

International comparisons are probably the best available source
of information on the effect of varying factor costs on factor
inputs. The observed range of variation in the relative costs of
labor and capital is of the order of 30:1, which is much greater
than that observed in a single country over any period for which
data are available. The observations on factor inputs refer to a
specific industry or set of technological operations rather than
to the different industries conventionally employed in cross-
section studies within a single country. Finally, taking observations that are close together in time, one can assume access to
approximately the same body of technological knowledge;
while not strictly true, this hypothesis is more valid than the same
assumption applied to time-series analysis.

Data

The substantial number of industrial censuses in the postwar
period that use comparable industrial classifications makes it
possible to exploit some of these potential advantages of inter-
country analysis. The sample used, the data collected and the
relationships explored are determined primarily by the nature of
the census materials.

Countries in the sample. The sample consists of countries having
the requisite wage and output data in a reasonable number of
industries. The countries, average wage rates and number of
industries available for each are shown in Table 1. The data
pertain to different years between 1949 and 1955.

Industries. Data were collected for all industries at the three-digit
level of the United Nations International Standard Industrial
Classification having sufficient observations (at least ten). The
twenty-four industries analysed are listed in Table 2 and defined
in the ISIC. There is, of course, considerable variation in the
composition of output within a given industrial category among
countries at different income levels, which cannot be allowed for
here.

Table 1 Countries in the Sample

	Country	Year of census	Average wage* (current dollars)	Number of industries used
1	United States	1954	3841	24
2	Canada	1954	3226	23
3	New Zealand	1955–6	1980	22
4	Australia	1955–6	1926	24
5	Denmark	1954	1455	24
6	Norway	1954	1393	22
7	Puerto Rico	1952	1182	17
8	United Kingdom	1951	1059	24
9	Colombia	1953	924	24
10	Ireland	1953	900	15
11	Mexico	1951	524	21
12	Argentina	1950	519	24
13	Japan	1953	476	23
14	El Salvador	1951	445	16
15	Brazil	1949	436	10
16	S. Rhodesia	1952	384	6
17	Ceylon	1952	261	11
18	India	1953	241	17
19	Iraq	1954	213	2

* Unweighted average of wages in industries in sample.

Labor inputs and costs. Labor inputs are measured in man-years per $1000 of value added. They include production workers, salaried employees and working proprietors. Labor costs are measured by the average annual wage payment, computed as the total wage bill divided by the number of employees. The data on wage payments for different countries include varying proportions of non-wage benefits, and we made no allowance for such variations. The data on employment are not corrected for intercountry differences in the number of hours worked per year or the age and sex composition of the labor force. [...]

Exchange rates. All conversions from local currency values into US dollars were at official exchange rates or at free market rates where multiple exchange rates prevailed. No allowance was

Table 2 Results of Regression Analysis

ISIC no.	Industry	Regression equations		Standard error Sb	Coeff. of deter. $\bar{R}^2$	Test of significance on b	
		Log a	b			Degrees of freedom	Confidence level for b different from 1 %
202	Dairy products	0·419	0·721	0·073	0·921	14	99%
203	Fruit and vegetable canning	0·355	0·855	0·075	0·910	12	90
205	Grain and mill products	0·429	0·909	0·096	0·855	14	*
206	Bakery products	0·304	0·900	0·065	0·927	14	80
207	Sugar	0·431	0·781	0·115	0·790	11	90
220	Tobacco	0·564	0·753	0·151	0·629	13	80
231	Textile – spinning and weaving	0·296	0·809	0·068	0·892	16	98
232	Knitting mills	0·270	0·785	0·064	0·915	13	99
250	Lumber and wood	0·279	0·860	0·066	0·910	16	95
260	Furniture	0·226	0·894	0·042	0·952	14	95
271	Pulp and paper	0·478	0·965	0·101	0·858	14	*
280	Printing and publishing	0·284	0·868	0·056	0·940	14	95
291	Leather finishing	0·292	0·857	0·062	0·921	12	95
311	Basic chemicals	0·460	0·831	0·070	0·898	14	95
312	Fats and oils	0·515	0·839	0·090	0·869	12	90
319	Miscellaneous chemicals	0·483	0·895	0·059	0·933	14	90
331	Clay products	0·273	0·919	0·098	0·878	11	*
332	Glass	0·285	0·999	0·084	0·921	11	*
333	Ceramics	0·210	0·901	0·044	0·974	10	95
334	Cement	0·560	0·920	0·149	0·770	10	*
341	Iron and steel	0·363	0·811	0·051	0·936	11	99
342	Non-ferrous metals	0·370	1·011	0·120	0·886	8	*
350	Metal products	0·301	0·902	0·088	0·897	11	*
370	Electric machinery	0·344	0·870	0·118	0·804	12	*

* Not significant at 80 per cent or higher levels of confidence.

made for the variation in the purchasing power of the dollar between different census years. [. . .]

Regression analysis

The variables available for statistical analysis are as follows:

V = value added in thousands of US dollars
L = labor input in man-years
W = money-wage rate (total labor cost divided by L) in dollars per man-year.

As an aid in formulating the regression analysis, we make the following preliminary assumptions, the validity of which will be examined in section III [not included here].

1. Prices of products and material inputs do not vary systematically with the wage level.
2. Overvaluation or undervaluation of exchange rates is not related to the wage level.
3. Variation in average plant size does not affect the factor inputs.
4. The same technological alternatives are available to all countries.

On these assumptions, we can treat $1000 of value added as a unit of physical output in each industry. We also assume a single production function for all countries, which implies that there will be a determinate relation between the labor input per unit of value added and the wage rate. Before exploring the possible forms of this function in detail, we tested two simple relations among the three variables statistically:

$$\frac{V}{L} = c + dW + \eta, \qquad \textbf{1a}$$

$$\log \frac{V}{L} = \log a + b \log W + \varepsilon. \qquad \textbf{1b}$$

Both functions give good fits to the observations, the logarithmic form being somewhat better. The results of the latter regression are shown in Table 2.[4] It is apparent from the small standard errors of b and the high coefficient of determination

4. Independently of this study, Minasian (1961) has fitted equation **1b** to US interstate data for a number of industries.

$\bar{R}^2$ that the fit is relatively good. In twenty out of twenty-four industries, over 85 per cent of the variation in labor productivity is explained by variation in wage rates alone.[5]

Implied properties of the production function

The regression analysis provides an important basis for the derivation of a more general production function: the finding that a linear logarithmic function provides a good fit to the observations of wages and labor inputs. The theoretical analysis of the next section will therefore start from this assumption.

It is shown in section II that under the assumptions made here the coefficient b is equal to the elasticity of substitution between labor and capital. It is therefore of interest to determine the number of industries in which the elasticity is significantly different from 0 or 1, the values most commonly assumed for it. Results of a t test of the second hypothesis are given in Table 2. In all cases, the value of b is significantly different from zero at a 90 per cent level of confidence. In fourteen out of twenty-four industries it is significantly different from 1 at 90 per cent or higher levels of confidence. We therefore reject these hypotheses as inadequate descriptions of the possibilities for combining labor and capital, and we proceed to derive a production function that allows for a different elasticity in each industry.

II. A new class of production functions

Section I presents observations on the relation between V/L and w within each of several industries at a single point of time. It is a natural first step to give an account of the results in terms of profit-maximizing responses to given factor prices. Under the assumptions of constant-returns-to-scale and competitive labor markets, the standard theory of production shows how any particular production function entails a particular relation between V/L and w. We shall show that the reverse implication also holds: that a particular relation between V/L and w determines the corresponding production function up to one arbitrary constant.

5. For the economy as a whole, the level of wages depends on the level of labor productivity, but for a given industry the labor input per unit of output is adjusted to the prevailing wage level in the country with relatively small deviations due to the relative profitability of the given industry.

Output per unit of labor, real wages and the production function under constant returns

If the production function in a particular industry is written $V = F(K, L)$, and assumed to be homogeneous of degree one, then $V/L = F(K/L, 1)$; and if we put $V/L = y$, $K/L = x$, we can say $y = f(x)$. In these terms the marginal products of capital and labor are $f'(x)$ and $f(x) - x f'(x)$ respectively. Let w be the wage rate with output as *numéraire*. If the labor and product markets are competitive then

$$w = f(x) - x f'(x) \qquad\qquad 2$$

which can be inverted to give a functional relation between x and w, and thence, since $y = f(x)$, a monotone increasing relation between y and w. Conversely, suppose we begin (as we do) with such an observed relation between y and w, say $y = \varphi(w)$. Then from **1** we see that

$$y = \varphi\left(y - x \frac{dy}{dx}\right) \qquad\qquad 3$$

which is a differential equation for $y(x)$. It will have a solution

$$y = f(x; A) \qquad\qquad 4a$$

where A is a constant of integration. Returning to the original variables we get the one-parameter family of production functions

$$V = L f\left(\frac{K}{L}; A\right). \qquad\qquad 4b$$

Of course for **4** to do duty as a production function it should have positive marginal productivities for both inputs and be subject to the usual diminishing returns when factor-proportions vary. An elementary calculation shows that these conditions are equivalent to requiring that $f'(x) > 0$ and $f''(x) < 0$. The latter condition is also sufficient to permit the inversion of **2**. Geometrically these conditions state that output per unit of labor is an increasing function of the input of capital per unit of labor, convex from above, just as the curve is normally drawn. In addition one would desire that $f(x) > 0$ for $x > 0$. All these requirements should hold for at least some value of A.

This way of generating production functions brings to light a connection with the elasticity of substitution which does not seem to have been noticed in the literature, although closely related results were obtained by Hicks and others (see Allen, 1938, p. 373). The slight difference has to do with the treatment of product price. Let s stand for the marginal rate of substitution between K and L (the ratio of the marginal product of L to that of K). Then the elasticity of substitution σ is defined simply as the elasticity of K/L with respect to s, along an isoquant. For constant-returns-to-scale it turns out,[6] in our notation,

$$\sigma = -\frac{f'(f - xf')}{xf''}. \qquad \qquad 5$$

Now consider the relation between y and w as determined implicitly by 2. Differentiating with respect to w we obtain

$$1 = f'\frac{dx}{dy}\frac{dy}{dw} - xf''\frac{dx}{dy}\frac{dy}{dw} - f'\frac{dx}{dy}\frac{dy}{dw},$$

and since $\dfrac{dx}{dy} = \dfrac{1}{f'}$,

$$\frac{dy}{dw} = -\frac{f'}{xf''}.$$

Thus the elasticity of y with respect to w is, from 2,

$$\frac{w}{y}\frac{dy}{dw} = -\frac{f'(f - xf')}{xf''} = \sigma. \qquad \qquad 6$$

That is to say, if the relation between V/L and w arises from profit maximization along a constant-returns-to-scale production function, the elasticity of the resulting curve is simply the elasticity of substitution. Information about σ can be obtained, under these assumptions, from observation of the joint variation of output per unit of labor and the real wage.

We may also observe another simple and interesting relation associated with production functions homogeneous of degree one. As has been seen the marginal productivity of capital is a decreasing function of x, the capital–labor ratio, while the marginal productivity of labor is of course an increasing function. Hence, for competitive markets, the gross rental (r), measured

6. On all this see Allen (1938, pp. 340–43).

with output as *numéraire*, is a decreasing function of the wage rate. More specifically, we may differentiate the relations $r = f'(x)$ and **2** to yield,

$$\frac{dr}{dx} = f''(x) \; ;$$

$$\frac{dw}{dx} = f' - xf'' - f' = -xf''$$

so that $\dfrac{dr}{dw} = \dfrac{dr/dx}{dw/dx} = -\dfrac{1}{x} = -\dfrac{L}{K}$,

whence the elasticity of the rate of return with respect to the wage rate is,

$$\frac{w}{r}\frac{dr}{dw} = -\frac{wL}{rK}, \qquad\qquad\qquad 7$$

i.e. the ratio of labor's share to capital's share in value added.

Rationalizing the data of section I

We found in section I that in general a linear relationship between the logarithms of V/L and w, i.e.

$$\log y = \log a + b \log w \qquad\qquad\qquad 8$$

gives a good fit. Along such a curve, the elasticity of y with respect to w is constant and equal to b. We are forewarned that the implied production function will have a constant elasticity of substitution equal to b, so that in deducing it we provide a substantial generalization of the Cobb–Douglas function. Indeed the Cobb–Douglas family is the special case $b = 1$ in **8**. Our empirical results imply that elasticities of substitution tend to be less than one, which contrasts strongly with the Cobb–Douglas view of the world. We will return subsequently to the distributional and other implications of this conclusion.

The differential equation **3** becomes

$$\log y = \log a + b \log\left[y - x\frac{dy}{dx} \right]. \qquad\qquad 9$$

Taking antilogarithms and solving for dy/dx, we find

$$\frac{dy}{dx} = \frac{a^{1/b}\,y - y^{1/b}}{a^{1/b}\,x} = \frac{y(1 - \alpha y^\rho)}{x}$$

where we have set $\alpha = a^{-1/b}$ and $\rho = (1/b)-1$ for convenience. The equation

$$\frac{dx}{x} = \frac{dy}{y(1-\alpha y^\rho)}$$

has a partial-fractions expansion:

$$\frac{dx}{x} = \frac{dy}{y} + \frac{\alpha y^{\rho-1}\, dy}{1-\alpha y^\rho}$$

which can be integrated to yield

$$\log x = \log y - \frac{1}{\rho}\log(1-\alpha y^\rho) + \frac{1}{\rho}\log\beta$$

or $x^\rho = \dfrac{\beta y^\rho}{1-\alpha y^\rho}$

which in turn can be solved for y^ρ, and then y, to give

$$y = x(\beta + \alpha x^\rho)^{-1/\rho} = (\beta x^{-\rho} + \alpha)^{-1/\rho}. \qquad \textbf{10}$$

Written out in full the production function is

$$V = L(\beta K^{-\rho} L^\rho + \alpha)^{-1/\rho}$$
$$= (\beta K^{-\rho} + \alpha L^{-\rho})^{-1/\rho}. \qquad \textbf{11}$$

As for our requirements on the shape of the production function, it is clear that $y > 0$ for $x > 0$ as long as $\alpha > 0$ and $\beta > 0$. Differentiation of **10** shows that the only requirement for positive marginal productivities is $\beta > 0$. A second differentiation yields one further condition for diminishing returns, namely $\rho + 1 > 0$ which is equivalent to $b > 0$ and in accordance with our empirical results.

The family of production functions described by **10** or **11** comprises all those which exhibit a constant elasticity of substitution for all values of K/L. To be precise, the elasticity of substitution $\sigma = 1/(1+\rho) = b$. For this reason we will call **10** or **11** a constant elasticity of substitution production function (abbreviated to CES).[7] Admissible values of ρ run from -1 to ∞, which permits σ to range from $+\infty$ to 0. Since our empirical

7. We note that Trevor Swan has independently deduced the constant elasticity of substitution property of **11**. The function itself was used by Solow (1956, p. 77) as an illustration.

values of b are almost all significantly less than one, they imply positive values of ρ and elasticities of substitution in different industries generally less than unity.

Properties of the CES production function

We can write **10** and **11** more symmetrically by setting $\alpha+\beta=\gamma^{-\rho}$ and $\beta\gamma^\rho = \delta$, in which notation they become

$$y = \gamma\{\delta x^{-\rho}+(1-\delta)\}^{-1/\rho}, \tag{12}$$
$$V = \gamma\{\delta K^{-\rho}+(1-\delta)L^{-\rho}\}^{-1/\rho}. \tag{13}$$

A change in the parameter γ changes the output for any given set of inputs in the same proportion. It will therefore be referred to as the (neutral) *efficiency parameter*. The parameter ρ, as has just been seen, is a transform of the elasticity of substitution and will be termed the *substitution parameter*. It will be seen below (equation **23**) that for any given value of σ (equivalently, for any given value of ρ), the functional distribution of income is determined by δ, the *distribution parameter*.

Apart from the efficiency parameter (which can be made equal to one by appropriate choice of output units), **13** is a class of function known in the mathematical literature as a 'mean value of order $-\rho$'.[8]

The lowest admissible value for ρ is -1; this implies an infinite elasticity of substitution and therefore straight-line isoquants. One verifies this by putting $\rho = -1$ in **13**.

For values of ρ between -1 and 0 we have elasticities of substitution greater than unity. From **12** we see that $y \to \infty$ as $x \to \infty$, and $y \to \gamma(1-\delta)^{-1/\rho}$ as $x \to 0$. That is to say, output per unit of labor becomes indefinitely large as the ratio of capital to labor increases; but as the capital–labor ratio approaches zero, the average product of labor approaches a positive lower limit.

The case $\rho = 0$ yields an elasticity of substitution of unity and should, therefore, lead back to the Cobb–Douglas function. This is not obvious from **13**, since as $\rho \to 0$ the right-hand side is an indeterminate form of the type 1^∞. But in fact the limit *is* the Cobb–Douglas function. This can be seen (a) by direct application of L'Hôpital's Rule to **13**; (b) by integration of **9** with

8. See Hardy, Littlewood and Pólya (1934, p. 13). It may also be shown that the function **13** is the most general function which can be computed on a suitable slide rule.

$b = 1$; or (c) by appealing to the purely mathematical theorem that the mean value of order zero is the geometric mean (Hardy, Littlewood and Pólya, 1934, p. 15, theorem 3). Thus the limiting form of **13** at $\rho = 0$ is indeed $V = \gamma K^{\delta} L^{1-\delta}$.[9]

For $0 < \rho < \infty$, which is the empirically interesting case, we have $\sigma < 1$. The behavior is quite different from the case $-1 < \rho < 0$. As $x \to \infty$, $y \to \gamma(1-\delta)^{-1/\rho}$; as $x \to 0$, $y \to 0$. That is, as a fixed dose of labor is saturated with capital, the output per unit of labor reaches an upper limit. And as a fixed dose of capital is saturated with labor, the productivity of labor tends to zero.

Whenever $\rho > -1$, the isoquants have the right curvature ($\rho = -1$ is the case of straight-line isoquants, and $\rho < -1$ is ruled out precisely because the isoquants have the wrong curvature). The cases $\rho < 0$ and $\rho \geqslant 0$ are different; when $\rho < 0$, the isoquants intersect the K and L axes, while when $\rho \geqslant 0$, the isoquants only approach the axes asymptotically. [. . .]

Our survey of possible values of ρ concludes with two final remarks. The case $\rho = 1$, $\sigma = \frac{1}{2}$ is seen to be the ordinary harmonic mean. And as $\rho \to \infty$, the elasticity of substitution tends to zero and we approach the case of fixed proportions. We may prove this by making the appropriate limiting process on **13**. And once again the general theory of mean values assures us that as a mean value of order $-\infty$ we have (Hardy, Littlewood and Pólya, 1934, p. 15, theorem 4)

$$\lim_{\rho \to \infty} \gamma \{\delta K^{-\rho} + (1-\delta) L^{-\rho}\}^{-1/\rho}$$
$$= \gamma \min (K, L) = \min \left(\frac{K}{\gamma^{-1}}, \frac{L}{\gamma^{-1}} \right). \quad \textbf{14}$$

This represents a system of right-angled isoquants with corners lying on a 45° line from the origin. But it is clearly more general than that, since the location of the corners can be changed simply by measuring K and L in different units.

So far we have simply provided one possible rationalization of the data of section I. We turn next to some of the testable implications of the model, and in so doing we consider the possibility of lifting or at least testing the hypothesis of constant-returns-to-scale. [. . .]

9. This special case reinforces our singling-out of δ as a distribution parameter.

Testable implications of the model

Returns to scale. So far we have assumed the existence of constant returns to scale. This is more than just convenience; it is at least suggested by the existence of a relationship between V/L and w, independent of the stock of capital. Indeed, homogeneity of degree one (together with competition in the labor and product markets) entails the existence of such a relationship. Clearly, not all production functions admit of a relationship between V/L and $w = \partial V/\partial L$; the class which does so, however, is somewhat broader than the homogeneous functions of degree one. We have the following precise result: if the labor and product markets are competitive, and if profit-maximizing behavior along a production function $V = F(K, L)$ leads to a functional relationship between w and V/L, then

$$F(K, L) = H\{C(K), L\}$$

where H is homogeneous of degree one in C and L, and C is an increasing function of K.

In proof, since $w = \partial V/\partial L$, we can write this functional relation as:

$$\frac{\partial V}{\partial L} = h\left(\frac{V}{L}\right).$$

Since this holds independent of K we may hold K constant and proceed as with an ordinary differential equation. Introducing $y = V/L$, we have

$$L\,\frac{\partial y}{\partial L} + y = \frac{\partial V}{\partial L}$$

and therefore

$$\frac{\partial y}{\partial L} = \frac{h(y) - y}{L}.$$

Since K is fixed we may write this

$$\frac{dy}{h(y) - y} = \frac{dL}{L}$$

and integrate to get

$$L = C\,g(y)$$

15

where $g(y) = \exp \int \dfrac{dy}{h(y) - y};$

and C, the constant of integration must be taken as a function of K. (We also assume $h(y) < y$; that is, the average productivity of labor exceeds its marginal productivity.) Upon inversion of **15** we have y as a function of $L/C(K)$ alone, say $y = G\{L/C(K)\}$ and therefore

$$V = LG\left[\frac{L}{C(K)}\right] = H\{C(K), L\} \qquad \textbf{16}$$

as asserted, where H is homogeneous of degree one in its arguments. If K is to have positive marginal productivity, C must be an increasing function of K, since $g(y)$ is decreasing.

Thus under our assumptions production exhibits constant-returns-to-scale, not necessarily in K and L, but in $C(K)$ and L. We have constant-returns-to-scale if C is proportional to K. But $C(K)$ can be given an interpretation in any case. Let P represent all non-labor income, whether returns to capital or not. Then by Euler's Theorem, $P = C\partial H/\partial C$.

And $\quad \dfrac{\partial V}{\partial K} = \dfrac{\partial H}{\partial C}\dfrac{dC}{dK}.$

Hence $\quad \dfrac{C}{C'} = \dfrac{P}{\partial V/\partial K} \qquad \textbf{17}$

so that C/C' represents the 'present value' of the stream of profits, discounted by the marginal productivity of capital.

The argument leading to **16** provides us with an empirical test of the hypothesis of constant-returns-to-scale. As we have noted, the latter is equivalent to $C(K)/K$ being constant. But from **15**,

$$\frac{C}{K} = \frac{L}{K}\frac{1}{g(y)} = \frac{1}{x\,g(y)}. \qquad \textbf{18}$$

So a stringent test of the hypothesis is that $x\,g(y)$ be constant within any industry and over all countries for which we have data on capital. The stringency of the test comes from the fact that it relies on data (namely K) which have not been used in the previous analysis. If the test is passed, then not only have we validated the assumption of constant returns, but also **15** and with it our whole approach to the production function.

When $h(y)$ is obtained by solving for w in **8**, the integration needed to determine $g(y)$ is a repetition of the argument leading to **10**.

Then, $\quad \dfrac{1}{x\,g(y)} = \dfrac{\beta^{VP}}{K}(1-\alpha y^\rho)^{-1/\rho}.$

Since β is a constant, a test of constancy of returns to scale is obtained by the condition that

$$c = \left(\frac{V}{K}\right)(1-\alpha y^\rho)^{-1/\rho} \qquad\qquad 19$$

is a constant.

Capital and the rate of return. It should not be overlooked that up to the previous paragraph our production functions have appeared only as rationalizations of the observed relation between y and w under assumptions about competition. We can not be sure that they do in fact describe production relations (i.e. holding among V, L and K), and it is indeed intrinsically impossible to know this without data on K, or equivalently on the rate of return. Should such data be available, however, we can perform some further very strong tests of the whole approach.

Suppose we have observations on K for a particular industry across several countries. Then we know x as well as y and we can test directly whether our deduced production function **3** or **4** does in fact hold for some value of A. If it does, then this provides an estimate of A and a stringent external check on the validity of our approach.

This is merely a rephrasing of our test for constant returns, to emphasize that it really goes somewhat further; if the hypothesis of constant-returns-to-scale is accepted, so is the validity of the implied production function.

Neutral variations in efficiency. From the argument leading to **10** and **11**, it is seen that the parameters α and ρ are derived directly from our empirical estimates of a and b in section I. But β is a constant of integration and can be determined only from observed data including measurements of K or x. Now the test quantity c in **19** depends on α and ρ, but not on β, on the assumption that β is constant across countries. Failure of data to pass the stringent test based on **19** may be read as suggesting that β varies across countries while α and ρ are the same. From **11**, this is equivalent to the statement that the efficiency of use of capital varies from country to country, but not the efficiency of use of labor.

A more symmetrical (and more plausible) possibility is that international differences in efficiency affect both inputs equally. This amounts to assuming in **13** that the efficiency parameter γ varies from country to country while δ and ρ remain constant. Since $\beta/\alpha = \delta/(1-\delta)$, we can put this by saying that β and α vary proportionately. We can provide a test of this hypothesis.

From the definition of the elasticity of substitution and its constancy and the competitive equivalence of factor-price ratios and marginal rates of substitution, it follows that w/r is proportional to $(K/L)^{1/\sigma} = (K/L)^{(1+\rho)}$. It is easy enough to calculate the constant of proportionality directly; we have

$$\frac{w}{r} = \frac{1-\delta}{\delta}\left(\frac{K}{L}\right)^{1+\rho} \tag{20}$$

and

$$\frac{\beta}{\alpha} = \frac{\delta}{1-\delta} = \frac{r}{w}\left(\frac{K}{L}\right)^{1+\rho}. \tag{21}$$

Thus for countries from which we have data on r and K, and given our estimate of ρ for an industry, we may compare the values of the right-hand side of **21**. If they are constant or nearly so, we conclude that there are neutral variations in efficiency from country to country, and we are able simultaneously to estimate δ. Then from δ and ρ we can use **12** to estimate the efficiency parameter γ in each country involved, for this particular industry.

Factor intensity and the CES production function. From **20** we see that:

$$x = \frac{K}{L} = \left(\frac{\delta}{1-\delta}\frac{w}{r}\right)^{\sigma}. \tag{20a}$$

Now imagine two industries each with a CES production function although with different parameters, and buying labor and capital in the same competitive market. Then

$$\frac{x_1}{x_2} = \left(\frac{\delta_1}{1-\delta_1}\right)^{\sigma_1}\left(\frac{\delta_2}{1-\delta_2}\right)^{-\sigma_2}\left(\frac{w}{r}\right)^{\sigma_1-\sigma_2} = J\left(\frac{w}{r}\right)^{\sigma_1-\sigma_2}. \tag{22}$$

If $\sigma_1 = \sigma_2$ (i.e. $\rho_1 = \rho_2$), then this relative factor-intensity ratio is independent of the factor-price ratio. That is, industry one, say, is more capital intensive than industry two, at all possible price ratios. This is the case both for the Cobb–Douglas function ($\sigma_1 = \sigma_2 = 1$) and the fixed-proportions case ($\sigma_1 = \sigma_2 = 0$). But once $\sigma_1 \neq \sigma_2$, this factor-intensity property disappears and it is impossible to characterize one industry as more capital intensive than the other independently of factor prices. For **22** says quite clearly that there is always a critical value of w/r at which the factor-intensity ratio x_1/x_2 flips over from being greater than unity to being less. There is only one such critical value at which the industries change places with respect to relative capital intensity. The nature of the switch is in accord with common sense: as wages increase relative to capital costs, ultimately the industry with the greater elasticity of substitution becomes more capital intensive. Such switches in relative factor intensity should be observable if one compares countries with very different factor-price structures, which we have done for Japan and the United States [see section IV of the original article].

The relative factor-intensity ratio plays an important role in discussions of the tendency of international trade in commodities to equalize factor prices in different countries (and for that matter, in the more general problem of the relation between factor prices and commodity prices in any general equilibrium system).

Time series and technological change. The CES production function is intrinsically difficult to fit directly to observations on output and inputs because of the non-linear way in which the parameter ρ enters. But, provided technical change is neutral or uniform, we may use the convenient factor-price properties of the function to analyse time series and to estimate the magnitude of technical progress.

A uniform technical change is a shift in the production function leaving invariant the marginal rate of substitution at each K/L ratio. From **13** and **20**, uniform technical progress affects only the efficiency parameter γ, and not the substitution or distribution parameters, ρ or σ.

One notes from **20** that

$$\frac{wL}{rK} = \frac{1-\delta}{\delta}\left(\frac{K}{L}\right)^{\rho} \qquad\qquad 23$$

which is independent of γ. Hence if historical shifts in a CES function are neutral, **23** should hold over time, and its validity provides a test of the hypothesis of neutrality.

Suppose we have observations on x and on w/r at two points on the production function, say two countries or two points of time in the same country. Then, from **20a**,

$$\frac{x_1}{x_2} = \left[\frac{(w/r)_1}{(w/r)_2}\right]^{\sigma}. \qquad\qquad 24$$

Thus an estimate of σ may be made. Note further that, since γ does not enter into **20a**, the estimate is valid even if the efficiency parameter has changed between the two observations, provided the distribution and substitution parameters have not, that is, provided that technological change is neutral.[10]

If the hypothesis of neutrality is acceptable, we may try to trace the shifts in the efficiency parameter over time. One way to do this is to go back to **8**. From $V/L = aw^b$ and the definitions of the parameters α, σ, δ and γ, one calculates first that

$$\frac{wL}{V} = \left(\frac{1}{a}\right)w^{1-b} = \alpha^{\sigma}w^{1-\sigma}$$

$$= (1-\delta)^{\sigma}\gamma^{\sigma-1}w^{1-\sigma}. \qquad\qquad 25$$

Two possibilities now present themselves. For given values of the parameters σ and δ, one can use **25** to compute the implied time path of γ. Or alternatively one may assume a constant geometric rate of technological change, so that $\gamma(t) = \gamma_0 10^{\lambda t}$, and fit

$$\log\left(\frac{wL}{V}\right) = \{\sigma\log(1-\delta)+(\sigma-1)\log\gamma_0\}+$$
$$+(1-\sigma)\log w + \lambda(\sigma-1)t \qquad 26$$

to estimate σ and λ.

10. This method of estimating the elasticity of substitution has been used by Kravis (1959, pp. 940–41).

Variation in commodity prices among countries. The accepted explanation of the variation in commodity prices among countries is based on differences in capital intensity and factor costs. In our production function the capital intensity depends both on σ and δ (instead of only on δ, as in the Cobb–Douglas function), and we also allow for differences in efficiency among sectors. The corresponding explanation of price differences is therefore more complex.

The price of a commodity in our model is defined as the direct labor and capital cost per unit of value added:

$$P = Wl + Rk = Wl\left(1 + \frac{R}{W}x\right),$$

where W and R are wages and return on capital in money terms (rather than using output as *numéraire*), $l = L/V = 1/y$, and $k = K/V$.

Substituting from **12** for the labor coefficient gives:

$$P = \frac{W}{\gamma}\{\delta x^{-\rho} + (1-\delta)\}^{1/\rho}\left(\frac{r}{W}x + 1\right) \qquad \textbf{27}$$

in which the price of a commodity depends on factor costs and capital intensity. For a given production function, the ratio of prices in countries A and B can be stated as a function of the factor prices only by using **20a** to eliminate x:

$$\frac{P_A}{P_B} = \frac{W_A}{W_B}\frac{\gamma_B}{\gamma_A}\left[\frac{(\delta/1-\delta)^\sigma (w_A/r_A)^{\sigma-1} + 1}{(\delta/1-\delta)^\sigma (w_B/r_B)^{\sigma-1} + 1}\right]^{1/(1-\sigma)}. \qquad \textbf{28}$$

[. . .][11]

Conclusion

This article has touched on a wide range of subjects: the pure theory of production, the functional distribution of income, technological progress, international differences in efficiency, the sources of comparative advantage. In part this broad scope reflects, as our introduction suggests, the fundamental economic significance of the degree of substitutability of capital and labor.

11. Sections III, IV and V of the original article, 'Tests of the CES production function', 'Factor substitution and the economic structure' and 'Substitution and technological change', respectively, have been omitted [*Eds.*].

In part it points to a wide variety of unsettled questions which are left for future research and better data. (In part, no doubt, it is simply due to the large number of authors of the paper!) Since our work does not lend itself to detailed summary, we content ourselves with a brief *reprise* of some of our findings, some speculation about others and some suggestions for future research.

Findings

We have produced some evidence that the elasticity of substitution between capital and labor in manufacturing may typically be less than unity. There are weaker indications that in primary production this conclusion is reversed. Although our original evidence comes from an analysis of the relationship between wages and value added per unit of labor, we have interpreted it by introducing a new class of production functions, more flexible and (we think) more realistic than the standard ones.

Although we began our empirical work on the naïve hypothesis that observations within a given industry but for different countries at about the same time can be taken as coming from a common production function, we find subsequently that this hypothesis cannot be maintained. But we get reasonably good results when we replace it by the weaker, but still meaningful, assumption that international differences in efficiency are approximately neutral in their incidence on capital and labor. A closer analysis of international differences in efficiency leads us to suggest that this factor may have much to do with the pattern of comparative advantage in international trade.

Finally, our formulation contributes something to the much-discussed question of functional shares. If, on the average, elasticities of substitution are less than unity, the share of the rapidly growing factor, capital, in national product should fall. This is what has actually occurred. But in the CES production function it is possible that increases in real wages be offset by neutral technological progress in their effect on relative shares.

Speculation

In his original work on what has since come to be known as the 'Leontief scarce-factor paradox', Professor Leontief (1953) advanced tentatively the hypothesis that the United States exports relatively labor-intensive goods not because labor is relatively abundant when measured conventionally, but because the efficiency of American labor is something like three times the efficiency of overseas labor. In our notation, this amounts to the suggestion that international differences in efficiency take the form of variations in β/α or, equivalently, of δ. We have proposed instead the hypothesis that β/α is constant across countries, while differences in efficiency are neutral. But we have also found some slight indications, in comparing Japan and the United States, that the American advantage in efficiency tends to be least in capital-intensive industries. This pattern, if it were verified, would seem to lead to an alternative interpretation of the Leontief phenomenon. But it also opens wide the question of why this association between differential efficiency and capital intensity should occur. Some possible explanations were mentioned in section IV-C [of the original article], but the reader can think of others. We may be missing something important by excluding third factors, or external effects or the importance of gross investment itself as a carrier of advanced technology into a sector.

Another active area of economic research where our results may have some interest is the theory of economic growth. A paper by Pitchford (1960) considers the introduction of a CES production function into a macroeconomic model of economic growth and concludes that at least in some cases this amendment restores to the saving rate some influence on the ultimate rate of growth. Even more interesting are the possible implications for disaggregated general equilibrium models. Given systematic intersectoral differences in the elasticity of substitution and in income elasticities of demand, the possibility arises that the process of economic development itself might shift the over-all elasticity of substitution.

Unsettled questions

Our general reference under this heading is *passim*. To begin with, as usable capital data for more countries and more industries become available, all of our results become subject to check for validity and generality. In particular, our speculations about the causes of varying efficiency are based primarily on comparisons between Japan and the United States. A more extensive study might easily controvert them.

Another loose end has to do with the question of returns to scale. We note that the stringent test for constant returns to scale and constancy of all parameters clearly has to be rejected. But it would be useful to explore the possibility of increasing returns to scale on a broader front. In view of equation **16** is there some choice of the function $C(K)$ which would yield a test on increasing returns? What light might this throw on the international comparisons, especially in connection with the less developed ecomies?

Finally, the whole question of further disaggregation calls out for exploration. We have in mind here not so much a finer industrial breakdown as a finer input breakdown. Can our labor and capital inputs be usefully subdivided? How about natural resource and purchased material inputs?

References

ALLEN, R. G. D. (1938), *Mathematical Analysis for Economists*, Macmillan.

HARDY, G. H., LITTLEWOOD, J. E., and PÓLYA, G. (1934), *Inequalities*, Cambridge University Press.

KRAVIS, I. B. (1959), 'Relative income shares in fact and theory', *Amer. econ. Rev.*, vol. 49, pp. 917–49.

LEONTIEF, W. W. (1953), 'Domestic production and foreign trade: the American capital position re-examined', *Proc. Amer. Phil. Soc.*, vol. 97, pp. 331–49.

MINASIAN, J. B. (1961), 'Elasticities of substitution and constant-output demand curves for labor', *J. polit. Econ.*, vol. 69, pp. 261–70.

PITCHFORD, J. D. (1960), 'Growth and the elasticity of factor substitution', *Econ. Rec.*, vol. 36, pp. 491–500.

SOLOW, R. M. (1956), 'A contribution to the theory of economic growth', *Q. J. Econ.*, vol. 65, pp. 65–94.

SWAN, T. W. (1956), 'Economic growth and capital accumulation', *Econ. Rec.*, vol. 32, pp. 334–61. [See Reading 3.]

Part Three
The Rate of Return on Investment

One of Irving Fisher's major contributions to economic theory was to discuss some of the issues of capital theory in terms of his concept of 'the rate of return on sacrifice'. Solow attempted to rehabilitate this concept in his de Vries Lectures both in order to try to escape from capital measurement puzzles and to answer, theoretically and empirically, the important question: what is the pay-off to society in the future of a little more saving now? We reprint an excerpt from his first lecture (Reading 6) in which he explains why he feels that an approach to capital theoretic puzzles via the concept of the rate of return on investment rather than by one of capital is likely to be more fruitful both in theory and in empirical work. In her review article of Solow's book, which is reprinted here as Reading 7, Joan Robinson argues that Solow's version of the rate of return on investment does not in fact succeed in replacing (or doing without) the concept of aggregate capital, gives her view of the role of the concept of the rate of return and criticizes the economic theory and econometric methodology which is specifically associated with Solow's work on aggregate production functions.

6 R. M. Solow

Capital and the Rate of Return

Excerpt from R. M. Solow, *Capital Theory and the Rate of Return*,
North-Holland Publishing Co., 1963, pp. 16–28.

The rate of return on investment

Thinking about saving and investment from this technocratic
point of view has convinced me that the central concept in capital
theory should be *the rate of return on investment*. In short, we
really want a theory of interest rates, not a theory of capital.
I do not believe that this shift of emphasis makes the theory of
capital easy; but I do believe that concentrating on the rate of
return leads to clarity of thought, while concentrating on 'time',
or 'capital', or the 'marginal productivity of capital' or the
'capital–output ratio' has led to confusion. It seems to me that
almost any important planning question we wish to ask about
the saving-investment process has an unambiguous if perhaps
approximate answer in terms of rates of return, whereas the
answers sometimes given in terms of marginal products of capital
and capital–output ratios are sometimes right, sometimes wrong
and often misleading. I suppose that my point of view could
be described as a modern amalgamation of Wicksell and Irving
Fisher.

I must emphasize that I am not now identifying the rate of
return on investment with the rate of profit or the observed market rate of interest or any form of income receipt in a capitalist
economy. That can perhaps sometimes be done, but it is in any
case part of the descriptive theory. My technocratic notion of the
rate of return on investment must be entirely independent of the
institutional arrangements of the economy. I had better suggest
such a definition in fairly general terms; later I shall show how
the general definition works in the context of particular models.

Imagine an economy which produces a single consumer good
(which may be a fixed-weight bundle of various elementary

consumer goods) according to any reasonably well-behaved technology. There may be any number of primary factors of production, from natural resource deposits to labor of different quality and skill characteristics. I assume that production makes use of physical capital goods which are themselves produced – buildings, machines, inventories; in addition, the production of the consumer good and some or all of the capital goods may involve delay periods of various lengths, fixed or variable. One could hardly ask for more freedom in describing the techniques of production. Now imagine any arbitrary planned allocation of resources in this economy for the current year. By an allocation of resources I mean a complete specification of productive activities for the period: how much of the consumer good is to be produced, with what resources, capital goods and labor services; how much of what kinds of capital goods are to be produced, and with what inputs. All I ask of this arbitrary allocation is that it be efficient in the usual sense that, with the labor, resources and capital goods available, it would not be possible to produce a bundle of capital and consumer goods providing more of some useful things without providing less of others. Efficiency implies, among other things, that there is no 'non-structural' unemployment of labor or other primary resources or of productive capacity.

The planning authority in this economy could, and should, at least contemplate neighboring efficient resource allocations which produce a little less of the consumer good, i.e. which involve a little more saving, than the planned one. Because all the allocations considered are efficient, those which produce less consumption must also produce more of at least some kinds of capital goods. To be specific, consider all allocations which yield, say, h units less of current consumption than the planned allocation (where h is a small number). Now the planning authority must think ahead. If it adopts the planned allocation for the current period, the society will be left with certain supplies of primary factors and stocks of capital goods in the next period, and thus with a collection of possible allocations for the next period. Let the planning authority decide which one it will in fact choose from the collection. Call C_0 the planned consumption for the current period and C_1 the planned consumption for the next period. At the end of the next period the economy will possess certain productive capacities and potentials for periods 2, 3 and later.

Now return to those possible current allocations which yield $C_0 - h$ in current consumption and which leave, presumably, generally more capacity available for the next period. For each of these alternative current allocations, select a next-period allocation which would send the economy on into period 2 with the same productive capacities and potentials as the planned current and next allocations (or with *equivalent* capacities and potentials, in the sense that any stream of consumption producible by one stock of capital and resources is producible by the other). Suppose that such a next-period allocation yields next-period consumption of $C_1 + k$. Presumably k will be positive, since the alternative allocation yields more current saving and therefore more next-period capacity than the planned allocation; in any case k cannot be negative for all alternative allocations, unless the economy is already over-saturated with capital goods. Finally, among all the alternative current and next-period allocations allowing $C_0 - h$ consumption in the current period and equivalent potentials for period 2 and later, find the one which yields the largest k, the largest gain in next-period consumption over the planned pair of allocations. Thus by sacrificing h units of consumption in the present, society can earn an extra consumption of k units next period and suffer no ill effects thereafter. In such a case I would, of course, define the one-period rate of return on investment as $(k-h)/h = k/h - 1$. This is perfectly natural usage. If by saving an extra \$1.00 of consumption this year society can enjoy at most \$1.10 of consumption next year without endangering its later prospects, then one would certainly want to say that society has earned 10 per cent on its investment.

Before I go further, let me make two fairly obvious remarks. First, the technocratic planning authority could just as well contemplate an increase in current consumption which would have to be paid for by a decrease in next-period consumption, in order to leave more distant future prospects undamaged. In that case h and k would both be negative and the one-period rate of return could be calculated exactly as before. If the technology is very smooth, then the rates of return for increases and decreases in saving will be approximately the same, and will draw closer together as h gets smaller. But even in quite well-behaved technologies of the not-so-smooth linear-programming type, the upward and downward rates of return can differ even for very small h. If the technology exhibits constant-returns-to-scale and enough diminishing returns, the rate of return for decreases in saving will exceed that for increases in saving, if they differ at all.

Second, my restriction to a consumption bundle of unchanging composition is only an expository simplification. If there are many consumption goods, then the planned current allocation, since it is efficient, implies certain marginal rates of transformation among them. (If the allocation is Pareto-optimal with respect to the preferences of citizens or technocrats then these rates of transformation will coincide with marginal rates of substitution in consumption.) For small changes in saving, it is adequate to calculate the rate of return at the margin in terms of any one consumer good or subtractions and additions of small bundles of consumer goods of arbitrary composition. This is so for the same reason that, in static production theory, when costs are being minimized, marginal labor costs equal marginal material costs equal marginal equipment costs equal marginal costs no matter how a small increment in output is obtained. In non-smooth technologies the situation will not be so simple.

The concept discussed so far is clearly a one-period or short-run rate of return; it is as if the economy could deposit consumption goods in a bank account and draw them out, with interest, at the end of the year. The rate of return, as I have defined it, is the rate of interest paid by the bank on one-year deposits – only the bank is really the complete collection of capital-using production processes in the economy. (In a technology with corners and jumps, the interest earned on an extra deposit may differ from the interest lost on an extra withdrawal, and the difference may not be small. There is nothing ambiguous in such a situation, but it is more complicated to describe. One should not slay the theoretical messenger for bringing the bad news that the world is complicated.)

There is a case for saying that these one-period rates of return are the fundamental ones because, in a highly developed and complex growing economy, saving-investment decisions come up for reconsideration every period and can easily be changed or even undone; so that even a long and complicated investment program can probably be duplicated by a series of cleverly chosen short-term programs. Nevertheless, the planning authority may, sometimes by choice, sometimes by technological necessity, compare the consumption stream yielded by the planned allocation with alternatives stretching over more than two periods. The choice of time profiles for enjoying the fruits of a current increment to saving is uncomfortably wide. For some of them it is easy to define a rate of return to the initial act of saving-investment. If the alternative is to save an extra h units of consumption now, hold consumption next period at the same level C_1 as in the planned allocation, consume all that is possible in the period after – $C_2' = C_2 + k$ – under the constraint that C_3, $C_4, \ldots$ must ever after be at their levels in the trial planned allocation, then the average rate of return per period on this two-year investment is defined by $k/h = (1 + r_{t2})^2$. Quite similarly, if the authority should decide to save now, go back to planned consumption levels for $n-1$ periods, and then splurge everything in the n'th period (subject to the same guarantee about subsequent periods), and if C_n were the originally planned n'th period consumption and C_n' the most that can be consumed under the alternative plans, then the average n-period rate of return must be the solution of $(C_n' - C_n)/(C_0 - C_0') = (1 + r_{tn})^n$. As usual, I am assuming $C_0 - C_0'$ to be small.

There is one other easy case – in principle at least. The planning authority could choose to sacrifice an extra h units of consumption and then so arrange things as to add a constant amount to each period's previously planned consumption, in perpetuity. Thus we have $C_0' = C_0 - h$, $C_1' = C_1 + p$, $C_2 = C_2 + p$, etc. If p is the largest such perpetual increment to consumption that can be maintained, it is natural to describe p/h as the average rate of return in perpetuity. I will work out such a calculation for a particular model later.

More complicated time profiles are more difficult to summarize in a single rate of return per period. It is tempting to take an arbitrary stream of algebraic increments to the originally planned consumption stream, some positive, some negative, and find the rate of interest that equates its present value to the current saving making it possible; this is in effect simply a marginal efficiency of investment or internal rate of return. It is, of course, open to the difficulty that if there are negative as well as positive changes in planned consumption, then there may be more than one marginal efficiency of investment for a single alternative consumption program. It is open to the much more serious objection that it often leads to incorrect decisions. The best procedure is to get along without internal rates. The short-run, technologically defined rates of return are the basic material and all that is necessary can be constructed from them. They need not be averaged into some over-all figure.

This difficulty with complicated multi-period consumption programs gets even deeper when one considers economies in which technological progress is occurring, as I shall do in the next lecture [not included here]. Even without technological change, the nature of the problem is illustrated by the fact that as I have defined it even the one-period rate of return on investment depends (perhaps sensitively, perhaps not) on the level of consumption for this period and the next period as they appear in the original plan. *A fortiori*, for longer periods the stream of returns from a marginal act of saving-investment now will depend on what had been planned for the future anyway. This dependence merely reflects the fact that I am considering small variations around some pre-existing situation, as is always done in static economics (and that restriction is not strictly necessary except for shadow-price interpretations). But since time plays a role in my problem, I must specify the base situation, from which possible displacements occur, in full detail.

This is a problem of execution, not of principle, and I do not think it either surprising or terribly important. In the first place, it clearly does not signify that the planning problem has no solution. The abstract technocrat or planner need never worry about helpful little constructs like the rate of return on investment. He need 'only' consider all possible future time profiles for the economy emanating from the current state of affairs, eliminate the obviously inefficient ones and choose the best (the most preferred) out of the ones remaining. There is no reason on earth to expect this procedure in full generality to reduce to the business of calculating a bunch of rates of return and a bunch of rates of time preference and comparing the two bunches. But the middlebrow economist may want to have some such routine because a simplified model yielding an approximate result may be good enough for him. (As to the thin line between simplified and over-simplified models, I can do no better than quote the English philosopher J. L. Austin: ' . . . we must at all costs avoid over-simplification, which one might be tempted to call the occupational disease of philosophers if it were not their occupation'.)

This is the role the special notion of the stationary state played in nineteenth-century capital theory. It provided a simple and convenient class of base situations from which one could easily calculate possible displacements: either from one stationary state to a neighboring one, or from a stationary state to a slight deviation and then back to the same stationary state. In the modern mood we are more likely to take as our base situations the class of states of balanced growth at the natural rate of growth, and go through the same routine of considering small displacements. My guess is that for most of the problems likely to confront the general economist, some natural comparison will present itself. I have already mentioned the likelihood that in a complex modern economy the one-period return is likely to be specially important because decisions regenerate themselves fairly quickly. These two advantages taken together suggest to me that for many macroeconomic problems in capital theory it is enough to look at, say, the one-year rate of return on investment, the rate of return in perpetuity and perhaps a ten-year rate of return in between.

I have been suggesting that the rate of return on acts of saving and investment is a good organizing concept for middlebrow capital theory. One of the advantages of looking at capital theory this way is that one automatically dodges most or all of the real or imaginary 'problems' that have beset this branch of economics for so long. In particular, to calculate the rate of return in my sense requires no measurement of the stock of 'capital'. What is more, a careful person will see that the whole process can be described without even mentioning the word 'capital'. If there are concrete capital goods, or inventories or delay periods, these will all, of course, affect the rate at which bundles of current consumption goods can be transformed into bundles of future consumption goods. But unless it is a natural thing to do under the technological circumstances, there is no need to identify or measure a stock of generalized capital. If the economy throws up market prices or if the process of analysis yields some kind of efficiency prices, then there is no harm in adding up various value sums which may correspond to the market (or other) value of the stock of capital goods. But such value sums are not 'capital' in the sense of something that belongs in a production function and has a marginal product. Similarly, it may turn out in theory that the rate of return on investment is equal to the rate of interest, defined as the ratio of the value of certain flows of goods to the value of the stock of capital goods. But then again, it may not. In any case all of this begins to belong to the descriptive theory of capital. I am content with the point that the problem of measuring 'capital' simply does not arise in my way of looking at the theory.

It is also said sometimes, that neo-classical capital theory must rest on such obviously absurd assumptions as that capital goods are 'malleable' in the sense that one kind of machine can be instantaneously and costlessly transformed into any other kind or that specific capital goods can be substituted smoothly for labor and other inputs in the production of homogeneous output. The idea is that 'malleability' is necessary in order that there be something called 'capital' to calculate the marginal productivity of, and 'smooth substitutability' is necessary in order to calculate the marginal productivity of 'it'. I think you can see that both of these contentions are wrong. Extreme assumptions like malleability and smooth substitutability make neo-classical capital theory easier (whether they give badly distorted conclusions is hard to say); but they are not essential to it. To the extent that neo-classical capital theory can be built around the rate of return concept – including the accompanying efficiency-price theory and the possible identification with market prices and interest rates – it can accommodate fixity of form and proportions both.

The kernel of useful truth in the John Bates Clark picture of capital as a kind of jelly that transforms itself over time is that indeed, over time, something like this does happen as capital goods wear out and are replaced by different capital goods. The rigorous counterpart of this process is this: when capital goods are highly specific there may be sudden jumps in one-period rates of return relating to the present and near future. But as one looks further and further into the future the substitution possibilities become smoother and smoother and rates of return narrow down.

These are negative advantages of thinking in terms of the rate of return. I think there are positive advantages too. For rational planning at the microeconomic level, whether within a business firm or a government agency concerned with particular investment projects, admittedly there is no substitute for detailed knowledge of technical and economic interrelations. But at a more macroeconomic stage there appears to be no substitute for summary statistics. It seems to me that the needs of high-order decision making, about such things as the over-all rate of consumption and the choice among broad areas of investment, are best served by information cast in the form of rates of return. The only way one can make sense of the capital–output ratios or incremental capital–output ratios or other such numbers that occasionally crop up, is to suppose that they are meant as crude approximations to one or another of the social rates of return on investment. If that is so, there are many reasons to believe that they are very crude approximations indeed, and economists have a responsibility to do better. One only has to ask whether rational saving-investment decisions can be independent of the durability of the structures and equipment involved or of the complementary inputs of labor and materials required. In all cases when the answer is no – that is, in all cases – the rate of return is a useful indicator of the choices facing society, while capital–output ratios are not.

7 Joan Robinson

Solow on the Rate of Return

Joan Robinson, 'Solow on the rate of return', in
Collected Economic Papers, vol. 3, Blackwell, 1965, pp. 36–47.
First published in Economic Journal, vol. 74, 1964, pp. 410–17.

The three lectures delivered by Professor Solow (1963) at the
F. de Vries Foundation[1] are full of sharp observations and interesting asides. The main theme is the reinterpretation and
defence of the concept of marginal productivity, which provides
an occasion to try to advance towards a better understanding of
the latter-day neo-classics.

He opens boldly by asserting that everyone except Joan Robinson
agrees about capital theory. However, there is one point on which
I agree with him – that the notion of factor allocation in conditions
of perfect competition makes sense in a normative theory for a
planned economy rather than in a descriptive theory for a capitalist economy, and that the notion of the marginal productivity of
investment makes sense in the context of socialist planning. I have
tried to start students thinking along these lines.

For the planner who takes over at a particular moment in
history there are in existence certain concrete means of production, and 'a given state of knowledge' that includes all the techniques that have been in use anywhere in the world since 1760.
The cost to society of a slightly greater amount of investment this
year can be expressed in terms of the consumption that has to be
forgone. For instance, if there is an excess of available labour over
the employment offered by equipment for producing consumable
commodities, which is the typical state of affairs in under-
developed economies, the cost to society of labour employed in
investment is zero. The benefit to society of a little more rather
than a little less investment this year is derived from the additional
means of production that it creates. Professor Solow measures

1. See Reading 6 for an excerpt from the first of these lectures [Eds.].

this benefit by the amount of extra consumption that could take place next year without reducing future growth below the amount that would have been achieved if the extra investment had not taken place. This seems to be somewhat arbitrary. The purpose of investment is to increase productive capacity. Why work out what would happen if it were disinvested again next year? It would be very troublesome to make the calculation. The planner, who must be concerned with long-lived installations, has to think in terms of alternative paths to be followed over the next twenty years or so, and even a small change in the amount of investment decided upon this year may require extensive changes in the physical specifications of the plan over a long future as well as for this year. And so does the consumption to be permitted next year. However, Professor Solow admits that his is only one possible measure of the marginal productivity of investment from the point of view of society, and I have argued that it can, in principle, be measured; if everyone else is of the same opinion, so much the better.

The difficulty is to connect this line of thought to the neo-classical theory of distribution. We may postulate that, in the planned economy, consumable income is distributed as wages, and that all production can be divided into outputs of consumable commodities and capital equipment (abstracting from armaments, social services, etc., and from investment in working capital). Then, labour in the two sectors being alike, the real wage bears the same proportion to the average output per man employed in producing commodities that employment in that sector bears to total employment. (When 20 per cent of labour is otherwise employed the wage is 80 per cent of the average output of a man in the commodity sector.) It has nothing whatever to do with the marginal product of labour. This is most sharply seen in the extreme cases, where the marginal product of labour in the commodity sector is zero because all plant is already working to capacity, and where it is equal to average productivity, because there is idle plant of not less than average quality. (This might occur where the planner has taken over an economy which was formerly saving less than he now decrees.)

How can this be reconciled with the neo-classical micro-economic proposition that in conditions of perfect competition (abstracting from interest on working capital) the marginal product of labour equals the real wage? Logic is the same for everyone. There cannot be a special kind of neo-classical logic. When Professor Solow and I make the same assumptions we ought to come to the same conclusions, errors and omissions excepted.

Let us take his assumptions. All output consists of a homogeneous physical substance; let us call it butter for short. There is a proper neo-classical production function with butter as output and labour and butter as input. With a given heap of butter in existence, there is a definite marginal product, at full employment of the labour available, being the output of butter lost when one man-year of labour is withdrawn. This is, evidently, independent of the consumption of butter. The wage, however, depends upon the proportion of the year's output of butter that is to be added to stock.

Now consider a capitalist economy with the same labour force, the same quantity of butter in existence and investment plans which will cause the same quantity of butter to be added to stock, as in the planned economy. First take a case where the level of investment is rather low, so that in the planned economy the wage rate would exceed the marginal product of labour. If, in the capitalist economy, the wage was equal to the full-employment marginal product, the wage bill in terms of butter and the amount of butter put to stock would not exhaust full-employment output. Full employment could be realized only if the capitalists consumed a sufficient amount of butter.

If workers save some of their wages, consumption of unearned income has to be all the greater.

Perhaps it is helpful to introduce a money price of butter into the argument. The wage rate is fixed in terms of money, and butter is sold for consumption. If the only purchasers are the wage-earners the total gross profit on the sale of butter for consumption cannot exceed the wage bill for the butter added to stock. With butter selling at this price the value of the marginal product of labour at full employment is less than the wage. *A fortiori* it is less than the wage *plus* interest on the wage fund, which is the marginal cost of employing an additional man with a given quantity of butter. Therefore employment must be sufficiently less than full to ensure that the higher physical product per man, together with the larger gross profit per unit of butter sold, raises the value of the marginal product to equality with the marginal cost of labour to an employer. Alternatively, capitalists may spend a sufficient proportion of their profits on consumption of butter to secure full employment.

When the rate of investment is so high that, in the planned economy, the wage would be less than the marginal product at full employment there would be excess demand for labour in the capitalist economy. In money terms the wage rate would be bid up by employers eager to get hands until some action was taken to check the inflation. Either investment must be checked or there must be a levy on wage-earners to reduce consumption.

Given the propensities to consume of capitalists and workers, when the rate of investment is such as to secure full employment without excess demand for labour, the marginal product of labour at full employment is equal to the wage plus interest on the wage fund.

Once the real-wage rate is known, with given technical conditions we know the share of gross profits in the value of output. In the butter economy we can calculate the rate of profit on capital (after slipping in a proviso that the value of a stock of butter is independent of its age). But Professor Solow agrees with me about the difficulty of giving a meaning to the value of capital, and therefore to the rate of profit, outside the butter economy, in a short-period situation with an arbitrarily given stock of means of production.

The expected rate of profit on new investment (which may be supposed to influence decisions of capitalists) depends upon what they expect to happen to prices and wages in the future. If they project the present prices of various products (abandoning the butter assumption) they will see different rates of profit on different investments, and presumably each investor will go in for the lines within his sphere of competence that promise the highest rate. Over the long run there is a tendency in Marshall's sense, for the rate of profit towards equality in different lines. But this arises because each individual capitalist wants to get the best return on his individual investment. There does not seem to be any reason for the planner to act so. He may have worked out the marginal productivity of investment in some sense, but he does not care about the expected rate of profit, while the capitalists are interested in the rate of profit and do not care about marginal productivity.

In the next lecture the scene changes. The economy gets into long-period equilibrium, with a constant rate of profit. This must mean that all products are selling at normal prices, in the sense that gross margins cover depreciation and profit at the ruling rate on the value of equipment and working capital involved in production. At any moment, with given technical conditions, the real-wage rate is then determined. Technical progress is going on and full employment is being preserved. To simplify, let us suppose that employment is constant. Output is then growing at the rate (g) at which output per head is rising – the 'natural' rate of growth in Harrod's sense.

Now that we are in equilibrium I do not see why we should not talk about the value of capital. When the share of net profit in the value of net output (reckoned in terms of commodities) and the rate of profit are both constant the value of capital is growing at the rate g. If K is the value of capital and I a year's net investment, $I/K = g$. When all wages are consumed, $I = sP$, where P is net profit and s the proportion of net profits saved. Then P/K, the rate of profit, is equal to g/s.

These are merely accounting identities, but it is useful to keep them in mind.

For Professor Solow, however, 'capital' is something physical. The discussion of technical progress is not easy to follow because, in spite of all his good resolutions, he frequently refers to the quantity of 'capital' without saying what it is a quantity of.

In the case of purely disembodied progress, which affects old plants, not merely the blue-prints for new ones, presumably 'capital' means a stock of equipment. When employment is constant and equipment is being kept intact, disembodied technical progress is raising the output of commodities at the rate g. Since the rate of profit is constant, the real-wage rate must be rising at g. Once more it simplifies matters to bring money wages into the argument. Let us postulate that the money price of commodities is constant. Then the money-wage rate is rising at

g; the reproduction cost, and therefore the money value, of the stock of physically unchanged equipment is rising at the same rate.

A kind of technical progress can be conceived in which physical equipment per unit of output remains constant, while output per man both in producing equipment and in producing commodities rises at a steady rate. (Cloth per loom remains constant, but the number of looms that a weaver can mind is rising at the rate g, and so is the number of looms produced per man employed in the investment sector.) This seems to be the picture that Professor Solow has in mind when he discusses embodied technical progress. He mentions, but does not elaborate, the case of truly embodied progress, where improvements are made in the design of equipment, which is, therefore, continuously changing in physical form. In golden-age conditions, with a constant rate of growth and a constant rate of profit on capital (which entails that real wages are rising at the rate g), all three kinds of technical progress come to much the same thing.

In Professor Solow's scheme there is also a production function. What does this mean? Presumably we are invited to consider a number of economies, all being presented with the same series of technical possibilities as time goes by, each with a different rate of profit. An economy with a lower rate of profit has a higher real-wage rate at any moment of time and, measuring equipment in units of productive capacity, a larger stock of equipment.

The locus of points corresponding to the positions of these various economies at any moment is not, strictly speaking, a production function. It is similar to Professor Samuelson's so-called 'surrogate production function' and my 'real-capital-ratio curve', which show the possible positions of stationary long-period equilibrium compatible with one 'state of technical knowledge' in the sense of the book of blue-prints exhibiting the technology known at one moment in history. But there is a new book of blue-prints every year, the same for all the economies, and the locus of possible equilibrium points corresponding to each new book has the same shape all the time.

This seems to be an extremely implausible concept and quite unnecessary to the development of the analysis. Professor Solow has evidently introduced it out of piety to neo-classical traditions.

He tells us that his production function is Cobb–Douglas, but he does not say what the 'capital' which has a unit of elasticity of substitution with labour consists of. In each economy, with a different rate of profit, the pattern of relative prices of different products must be quite different (unless a fresh lot of fudge or butter is introduced into the assumptions) and the physical specifications of equipment are different (even in the looms-to-weaver kind of technical progress, looms at a later date that can be minded by fewer weavers are in some way different from earlier ones). Does the Cobb–Douglas nature of his production function mean that in all the economies, by a queer fluke, the share of wages in net value of output is the same? And if so, why is it interesting? Or does it mean that there is some idiosyncrasy in the technical conditions (in terms, say, of the number of man-years of work required, in each economy, to provide a man with the latest equipment for producing commodities) which makes 'labour embodied' in the stock of equipment proportional to output in the various economies? Or what?

There is also a short-period relation between employment and output, which we may call a *utilization function*, to distinguish it from a production function. It shows product per man falling as more labour is applied to given plant. In each economy, therefore, there is an intensive and an extensive margin, the marginal physical product of labour on the best plant in existence in each line at any moment being equal (under perfect competition) to the average product of the oldest, the value of both being equal to the wage, or rather to the wage plus interest on the requisite wage fund. This short-period utilization function has the same shape in each economy, and retains its shape as productive capacity grows. It, also, is said to be Cobb–Douglas, which presumably means that, in perfect competition with the value of the marginal product of labour in each line equal to the marginal cost of labour to an employer, the share of the wage bill in the total value of output is the same at each level of utilization.

All this seems to be a perfectly unnecessary piece of piety that complicates the argument without enriching it.

Let us concentrate on any one economy, chugging along with a constant rate of profit. From a highly fashionable proposition in neo-neo-classical economics, we know that, when the rate of profit is higher than the rate of growth, consumption exceeds the wage bill. Suppose that a planner took over an economy in this condition and decided to impose a greater rate of saving upon it for a time, so as to reach a position with a higher level of consumption, at some date in the future, than would have been reached on the former path, while continuing from then on to realize the former growth rate. (The growth rate that can be permanently maintained is the 'natural' rate given by autonomous technical progress.) The planner cuts down consumption and transfers some workers permanently from the commodity sector to the investment sector. It takes a period equal to the length of life of plant for the extra investment to build up a balanced stock of productive capacity at the higher level. During this period, with the larger output of the newest type of plant, more old plant than formerly has to be scrapped to release labour to man it. Average output per head in the commodity sector is rising at a faster rate than that given by technical progress. There is no need to bring the mysterious production function into the argument. Output per head rises because the proportion of the newest type of equipment in the total stock is increasing. When a balanced position is reached again the length of service life of equipment has been reduced, all plant older than the new maximum age has been scrapped and the economy has settled down to steady growth once more, having made a step up above the old path.

In such a case we could reckon the cost of making the change in terms of consumption forgone during the transition from the old path to a higher one, and so arrive at the marginal productivity of investment from the point of view of society.

This is not how Professor Solow looks at it. He considers the effect of making a little more investment in one year only, and allowing additional consumption thereafter to carry the economy back to its old path.

To see what this involves we may take a simplified example. Technical progress is fully embodied – at each round of gross investment there is a new blue-print for superior plant that raises the output of commodities per worker employed. Suppose that ten vintages of plant co-exist in the commodity sector, each manned by a cohort of 100 teams of men. One plant employs one team throughout its life. Taking a year as the gestation period for plant, each vintage is used for ten years. At the end of that time the real wage has risen to absorb its whole output and it is scrapped. Now, when plant of vintage V_{10} is being constructed, the capitalists, by consuming less than usual, release resources to have 101, instead of the usual 100, plants built. Thereafter they return to building 100 a year. To man the extra plant, a team must be taken from vintage V_1 which is entering its last year of life. Next year only ninety-nine teams are released when the remaining V_1 plants are scrapped. A team has to be taken from V_2 to man the hundredth V_{11} plant, and so on until V_{10} enters the last year of its life. One team is then transferred to V_{19}. At the end of the year the remaining 100 teams are released and go to V_{20}. The normal position is then restored.

Now, the additional output, over and above what would have been available without the extra V_{10} plant, in the first year consists of the output of one V_{10} team minus the output of one V_1 team. The V_1 output was scarcely more than the real wage of a team at the rate then ruling. Thus the additional output this year is equal to the quasi-rent on a V_{10} plant in the first year of its life. Next year the additional output is the output of a V_{10} team minus the output of a V_2 team, which is approximately this year's wage. It is thus equal to the quasi-rent on a V_{10} plant in the second year of its life. And so forth. The additional output, over the ten years, is equal to the series of quasi-rents of a plant, which yields the normal rate of profit on its initial cost. Thus (assuming that the economy was flexible enough to permit one extra plant to be built without additional cost) the extra consumption is equal to the rate of profit on the extra investment.

The argument is certainly ingenious, but what is it supposed to prove? There is a suggestion that Professor Solow thinks that it proves that the rate of profit must be higher when the pace of technical progress is faster. This is evidently not correct. A higher g (other things equal) requires a larger proportion of gross investment to output, but this may be offset by correspondingly greater thriftiness of the capitalists, that is by a larger proportion of profits being saved, so that the rate of profit is no higher in a high-g economy than in a low-g economy. In the low-g economy the difference in productivity between one vintage of plant and the next is lower than in the high-g economy, but the greater consumption out of profits depresses the real wage and makes the life of plant longer. Thus the difference between the output of the latest and the oldest plant at any moment is no less than in the high-g economy.

The rate of profit is constant because the rate of accumulation (which is here equal to g) and the excess of consumption over the wage bill are such as to keep it so. Professor Solow has managed to find a marginal something that is equal to it, and so has satisfied his piety in the manner of those modern parsons who say that they believe in the Virgin Birth, but only in a Pickwickian sense.

In the third lecture Professor Solow sets out to find, from actual statistics, the production function which piety obliges him to say that he believes to exist. However, it turns out that the production function is in terms of labour and the 'effective stock of capital'. This effective stock of capital is the actual plant in existence weighted by its productivity. Thus as output per head gradually rises with technical progress, whether embodied or not, the effective stock of capital grows.

Now, Professor Solow purports to be able to divide the rate of growth of output per head between the contribution due to technical progress and a contribution due to the increase in 'capital'. He works out what increase in 'capital' would have produced the observed increase in output per head if there had been no technical progress. Here is a mystery indeed.

The clue seems to lie in the short-period utilization function. With given plant in existence, in perfectly competitive conditions, a reduction in employment leads to a rise in output per head. The marginal physical product of labour in each line of activity rises, for the least efficient plant is put out of action and the intensity of cultivation of more efficient plant reduced. (If there were no short-period diminishing returns there could not have been perfect competition in the first place.) It seems that having postulated a short-period utilization function of a particular form, Professor Solow concludes that a comparable rise in output per head would take place if the ratio of 'capital' to labour were increased by investment, with constant employment. To adapt Sir Dennis Robertson's example, nine men with nine spades are digging a hole; dismiss eight; then we are to deduce from the productivity of one man with all nine spades what his productivity would be if he were working a bulldozer.

In his first lecture Professor Solow seemed to admit that it is impossible to describe the plant in existence at any moment as a quantity of capital. It is a specific stock of equipment of various kinds, built in various past phases of technical development. How can we deduce from actual outputs with different amounts of employment (which might be discovered over the course of short-period fluctuations) what productivity would have been if there had been no technical progress in the past, or what plant would be added to the stock if investment now took place without technical progress in the future?

It seems as though Professor Solow has, after all, never really emerged from his butter economy, where future and past melt into one. If everyone except me is perfectly happy to stop there I wish them joy.

The upshot of the statistical investigation appears to be that the rate of profit is about the same in the United States as in Germany, and in both much above the rate of growth. This indicates that the length of life of obsolescent plant is above the optimum and that more investment, matched by more saving out of profits, would be a jolly good thing. With this we can all agree.

Postscript

The reference to interest on the wage fund on page 170 has been added to the original text. Trying to meet Professor Solow on his own ground, I made a concession which is not really feasible. The orthodox micro-theory of perfect competition is that the individual employer, in short-period conditions with a given stock of equipment, offers employment to such a number of men as to equate the marginal cost of labour to him to its marginal product for him. Prime costs other than wages (for raw materials, power, etc.) are eliminated by postulating complete vertical integration, and user-cost of plant is ignored. Even then it is not true that the marginal cost of labour is merely the wage. The marginal product of a certain number of men must make it worthwhile to employ that number; it must compensate for the interest, as well as the wage, which would be saved by employing somewhat fewer.

In any case, of course, this line of thought is not applicable to modern manufacturing industry, where prices are formed by adding a margin to prime cost. The short-period marginal product of an additional man-week of employment with given plant (abstracting from materials, etc.) is equal to the wage plus the gross margin.

All this may appear to be mere logic chopping, but it points to the source of the trouble. The neo-classical theory of distribution is derived from a model in which land and labour are the only factors and no capital equipment is used. But if there is a wage, there must be an employer. When wages are paid in arrears, out of the harvest, the workers are lending to the landowners, and their income represents wages plus interest on their subsistence over the period of production. When wages are paid in advance, the cost of labour to the landowner includes interest. Either way, the marginal product of labour exceeds the wage by an amount equal to interest on the required wage fund. As Marshall pointed out, the only correct statement of the orthodox theory is the circular one: in equilibrium conditions of perfect competition the marginal *net* product of labour to the individual employer is equal to the wage.

In the original version of this paper, I did not mention interest on working capital as it is not relevant to the main point. When we accept all Solow's assumptions, it is still possible to say only that the marginal product of labour is determined by the short-period technical conditions (shown in the utilization function) and the state of effective demand. Unless effective demand happens to be just right, the marginal product will not be at the level which corresponds to full employment. This could be said perfectly well without assuming the butter, and, with the butter, we can say no more.

Reference

SOLOW, R. M. (1963), *Capital Theory and the Rate of Return*, North-Holland Publishing Co. [See Reading 6.]

Part Four
Prelude to a Critique of (Marginalist) Economic Theory

Sraffa subtitled his *Production of Commodities by Means of Commodities* (1960), *Prelude to a Critique of Economic Theory*, by which he meant neo-classical marginalist theory. What the nature of the critique would be is not made explicit by Sraffa, but a number of the reviewers of his book attempted to repair the omission with their own interpretations. We reprint here as Reading 8, one of the most perceptive of these – the review article by Mrs Bharadwaj. In Reading 9 Nell attempts to draw out the implications for the theory of growth of Sraffa's view of the theory of value – a view which contrasts strongly with that of the traditional neo-classical theory of value. Nell suggests that many puzzles which have occurred in growth theory either disappear or are tractable if the theory of value used in the analysis stresses the interdependence of the economic system through the production of commodities by means of commodities rather than the neo-classical distinction between factors of production, on the one hand, and final products, on the other.

Reference

SRAFFA, P. (1960), *Production of Commodities by Means of Commodities. Prelude to a Critique of Economic Theory*, Cambridge University Press. [See Reading 4.]

8 Krishna R. Bharadwaj

Value through Exogenous Distribution

Excerpts from Krishna R. Bharadwaj, 'Value through exogenous distribution', *Economic Weekly* (Bombay), 24 August 1963, pp. 1450–54.

Economic theory has its fair share of conundrums. Discarded as mere 'chimeras' by the more pragmatic and empirically oriented economists, these puzzles continue to fascinate those with a flair for abstraction and challenge their speculative ingenuity. Of these, the 'chimera of absolute value', long fallen into oblivion after the unsuccessful efforts, notably by Ricardo and Marx, to discover an invariant yardstick to measure value, has now been revived in Piero Sraffa's excellently expounded book *Production of Commodities by Means of Commodities*.

Sraffa resolves the Ricardian Riddle within a framework of analysis, wherein neither the output composition nor the proportions in which means of production are combined change. Thus, both the framework of investigation as also the central problem to which Sraffa particularly addresses himself are, in spirit, classical.

Those of us accustomed to economic analysis always running in terms of variations of factor-proportions or output-combinations would be struck by the extremely rigid framework within which Sraffa's analysis is conducted. Indeed, it is a unique accomplishment of his work that within this restricted economic domain is created a nucleus of deeply significant ideas which presumably have wide-sweeping consequences.

Sraffa begins with a simple model of production for subsistence where the total product is just sufficient to sustain the workers and to serve as means of production.[1] In such an economy,

---

1. See Sraffa (1960). What follows is largely an exposition of some of Sraffa's ideas contained in this book. Page numbers in the text refer to this source.

without surplus, there is a unique set of exchange values which restores the original distribution of products among industries, thus ensuring the possibility of the continuation of the cycle of production, period after period. Technology is all important in determining relative prices. In fact, these prices are embedded in the technology itself.

With the extension of this model to production with surplus, the problem of distribution appears on the scene. Uniformity of the rate of profit and the rate of wages in all industries is assumed. As the surplus has to be distributed proportionately to the means of production advanced in each industry – and this cannot be done unless the heterogeneous means of production are aggregated with the help of prices – and as prices cannot be determined before knowing the uniform rate of surplus, both prices and the rate of surplus will have to be determined simultaneously. When wage rate is fixed and consists 'of the necessary subsistence of the workers, thus entering the system on the same footing as the fuel for the engines or the feed of the cattle' (p. 9), technology acts as the price determinant even in this case of production with surplus. In fact, at this point, Sraffa's system resembles that of von Neumann (1945–6). However, Sraffa goes a step further in that he relaxes the condition of a fixed wage and treats it as a variable. Distribution in Sraffa's system is not endogenously generated through production relations.[2] In conjunction with prices, production relations determine only the net surplus that is to be distributed.[3] No theory of distribution is offered in the book. His wage rate is a variable which could be conceived to vary with the same ease as the profit rate. Wage is assumed to be paid *post factum*, so that profits and wages are surplus-sharing entities.

System of equations

With wage introduced as a variable, the system of equations turns out as follows:

2. This is a significant departure from the widely prevalent practice of obtaining distributive shares from the production function applying the marginal method.

3. Rather, prices and the rate of surplus are determined simultaneously given the production relations.

$$(A_a P_a + B_a P_b + \ldots + K_a P_k)(1+r) + L_a W = AP_a$$
$$(A_b P_a + B_b P_b + \ldots + K_b P_k)(1+r) + L_b W = BP_b$$
$$(A_k P_a + B_k P_b + \ldots + K_k P_k)(1+r) + L_k W = KP_k,$$

where the system is assumed to be in a self-replacing state. $A_a, B_a, \ldots, K_a$ are the quantities of commodities $a, b, \ldots, k$ required to produce the quantity A of a; $A_b, B_b, \ldots, K_b$ are the quantities of commodities $a, b, \ldots, k$ required to produce the quantity B of b and so on; $L_a, L_b, \ldots, L_k$ are the annual quantities of labour employed in the industries producing $a, b, \ldots, k$ respectively. The unknowns of the system are the prices $P_a, P_b, \ldots, P_k$ of commodities $a, b, \ldots, k$ respectively, the wage rate w and the uniform profit rate r. An additional equation defining the national income in terms of which the k prices and the wage is expressed is introduced.

$$\{A - (A_a + A_b + \ldots + A_k)\} P_a + \{B - (B_a + B_b + \ldots + B_k)\}P_b + \ldots$$
$$\ldots + \{K - (K_a + K_b + \ldots + K_k)\}P_k = 1.$$

The system now moves with one degree of freedom. Given the wage rate or the profit rate, prices are determined simultaneously. To begin with, Sraffa assumes that the wage rate is given. We could assume perhaps that the wage rate is determined by mutual bargaining or by an external authority or by social convection. In the later portions where Sraffa prefers assuming the rate of profit as given, there is a vague reference that the rate of profit is 'susceptible of being determined from outside the system of production, in particular by the level of the money rates of interest' (p. 33). This transfers the burden merely from one peg to another as no explanation regarding how the level of the money rates of interest is determined appears anywhere in the book. In fact, there are 'prices' in the book without any mention of money.

Importance of distribution

Even though Sraffa is not interested in distribution *per se*, distribution happens to be the key factor in the mechanism which determines relative prices, subject to the given technical relations and the uniformity of the wage rate and the profit rate. Sraffa's theory of relative prices belongs to that group of theories of value determination wherein the horizontal division between classes receives the major emphasis (cf. Robinson, 1962a, ch. 1). Demand plays no essential role in the system. The basic proposition of these theories is that, in an economy where all means of production are produced within the system and where constant-returns-to-scale prevail, normal prices, corresponding to any pattern of distribution, are determined by technical relations. Neither demand conditions nor output composition play any part in the determination of these prices. Given Sraffa's framework of no changes in the scale of operation, the question regarding constancy or otherwise of returns-to-scale does not arise. However, not all means of production are produced within the system. Labour and, later, land appear as non-produced factors. The presence of non-produced means of production seems to disturb the determinacy of the technology-cum-distribution relative price schema, based purely on the distribution pattern, the technical relations and conditions regarding the uniformity of the profit and the wage rate. The Marshallian blades of scissors, it looks as though, could no more be ignored.[4] However, the fundamental dichotomy in the structure of commodities in the Sraffa system – the differentiation between the basics and the non-basics – seems to hold the clue. A basic good (in the system with no joint products) is defined as one which enters as an input in the production of all commodities directly or indirectly.[5] A non-basic good, defined by exclusion, may be produced by a basic good with or without non-basics, but does not itself enter as an input into a basic good. The analytical significance of this distinction is that the non-basics have no part in the determination of the system of prices, in the sense that price changes in it would not be transmitted to other commodities.[6] Any price

4. In fact, the 'marginalist' strand in Ricardian theory, it may be recalled, arises in the explanation of rent.

5. This definition is later modified in the joint-products case and the general formulation of the distinction appears as: 'In a system of k productive processes and k commodities (no matter whether produced singly or jointly) we say that a commodity or more generally a group of n linked commodities (where n must be smaller than k and may be equal to one) are non-basic if of the k rows (formed by the $2n$ quantities in which they appear in each process) not more than n rows are independent, the others being linear combinations of these' (p. 51).

6. This proposition is extended to the joint products case (pp. 54–5).

changes, in the case of the basics, on the other hand, influence the prices and the profits of all the other commodities. With wage treated now as a variable and as a surplus-sharing entity, labour becomes a non-basic of the system and so also land, the other non-produced means of production. Relative prices are thus influenced, given the distribution pattern, by the production structure of the basics, which are produced means of production.

The 'Standard commodity'

The problem of relative prices is intimately related to that of absolute value and Sraffa's sterling contribution lies in the ingenious concept of the Standard commodity – the invariant measure of value. The essence of the problem is that unless we have an absolute measure of value 'it is impossible to tell of any particular price fluctuation whether it arises from the peculiarities of the commodity which is being measured or from those of the measuring standard' (p. 18). The problem of valuation is thus of isolating the price movements of a product so as to observe the changes in its value as if in vacuum. Ricardo faced the same dilemma when the distributable total output was to be evaluated independently of changes in the distribution pattern. Corn was sought as a measure of absolute value as there could be a 'material rate' of surplus in it, in the sense that the same product appeared both as net output and as input. This notion, with its roots in the physiocratic doctrine of 'net product', was based on extremely over-simplified assumptions. Ricardo, dissatisfied with this measure, turned to the unit of labour time as an answer to his problem. Conscious of the limitations of this measure as well, he did not subscribe to it unreservedly. Sraffa's own interpretation regarding the logical foundation of the corn measure as an absolute value is the genesis of the Standard commodity. He wrote in his preface to *The Works and Correspondence of David Ricardo* (1951, p. xxxii): 'The advantage of Ricardo's method of approach is that, at the cost of considerable simplification, it makes possible an understanding of how the rate of profit is determined without the need of a method for reducing to a common standard a heterogeneous collection of commodities.'

In order to discover such a commodity, Sraffa analyses the effects of changes in the wage rate on the rate of profit and on the prices of individual commodities, on the assumption that production methods remain unchanged. With the whole national income going to wages (with profit rate reduced to zero) relative values are determined by the direct and indirect labour gone into the commodities, supporting thus the labour theory of value. When profits are assigned positive values, the simple labour theory of value is no longer valid and the key to the determination of relative price movements lies in the inequality of the proportions in which labour and means of production are employed in various industries. The relative price movements depend not only upon this labour-to-means-of-production proportion of the product but also upon the corresponding ratios for each of the means of production and, in turn, for their means of production. With any wage reduction given the uniformity assumption regarding the rate of profit in all industries, price changes are called in to redress the balance in each of the deficit industries (those with relatively low labour-to-means-of-production ratio) and the surplus industries (those with relatively higher labour-to-means-of-production proportion). The industry which enjoys the critical balancing proportion so that it is under no compulsion arising from the conditions of production itself to change in value consequent upon the changes in the pattern of distribution, has the unique distinction of acting as an invariant standard of value. Since the critical balancing proportion has to persist throughout the structure of direct and indirect inputs, it is evident that the balancing ratio (expressed as the value ratio of the net product to the means of production) would be equal to the rate of profit which corresponds to zero wage, or the maximum rate of profits, called R by Sraffa. In the actual system, the commodity satisfying this condition might be a composite commodity and Sraffa constructs such a commodity with the technical characteristic that it consists of the same commodities combined in the same proportion as the aggregate of their means of production. The logic of this proposition implies that only basic commodities will enter the Standard commodity. Sraffa proves that such a miniature system is embedded in an actual economy. [. . .]

Search for absolute measure of value

The discovery of the technical properties of the invariant standard is a tribute to Sraffa's deductive logic. He has skilfully made use of this in deriving significant propositions. The search for an absolute measure of value has long been a source of frustration, and yet even in theoretical economic structures, apart from operational and empirical ones, quantitative notions have played a significant role – not purely by way of illustration but as a basis for deducing substantive propositions.[7] So long as the search for absolute value was in the domain of prime, non-produced factors, the factor of demand with its root in impregnable psychological factors was bound to interfere in valuation. Also, there could be no 'material rate of profit' as a ratio of only two arithmetical quantities. Scepticism regarding the very possibility of finding out an absolute value measure, comparable to the measures in the physical world seems unavoidable. 'Weight and length, of course, are human conventions but once the convention is established, they do not change, for practical purposes, because they refer to the *physical, non-human* world' (Robinson, 1962b, pp. 31–2; Bharadwaj's italics). It is precisely in the physical non-human world of technology that Sraffa's Standard system is embedded. There was another difficulty with the one-factor theory of value, namely that it failed to allow for differential patterns of factor-combinations in different sectors of the economy, even under conditions of no technical change. Basic difficulties for a labour theory of value arose on two accounts – the theory of differential rent as also the problem of organic composition of capital.[8] Problems arose also due to the non-

7. It is interesting to recall in this connection Sraffa's observation at the Corfu conference: 'One should emphasize the distinction between two types of measurements. First, there was the one in which the statisticians were mainly interested. Second, there was measurement in theory. The statistician's measures were only approximate and provided a suitable field for work in solving index-number problems. The theoretical measures required absolute precision. Any imperfections in these theoretical measures were not merely upsetting, but knocked down the whole theoretical basis' (see Lutz and Hague, 1961, p. 305).

8. Samuelson builds a land theory of value with land as an absolute value measure, assuming homogeneous land and subsistence wages. This exercise is typical of an economic theory that treats all 'factors' symmetrically so that a 'land theory' is equally as plausible as a 'labour theory'.

homogeneity of these prime factors. Sraffa's Standard system steers clear of these difficulties since it is based on the very fact of interconnectedness in production which the single factor theory of absolute value is incapable of handling. In fact, the labour theory of value becomes a special case of the Sraffa system when the rate of profit is zero and the entire net product goes to wages. [. . .] Sraffa's standard of value allows more flexibility to vary distribution patterns without landing itself into a dilemma.

With the help of the Standard commodity Sraffa then establishes a proposition which is the pivoting point of many of the important deductions. If W is the proportion of the net product of the *Standard system* that goes to wages and R, the maximum rate of profits, the actual rate of profit will be determined by a straight-line proportionality relation $r = R(1 - W)$. This fundamental wage-profit frontier appears as in Figure 1.

This relation is not limited to the imaginary Standard system alone but can be extended to the actual economic system. The actual economic system contains the same basic equations but in different proportions. As such, *provided that the wage is expressed in terms of the Standard commodity*, the same rate of profits which prevails in the Standard commodity as a ratio between *quantities* of commodities, will appear as the ratio of aggregate *values* in the actual economic system. This relation forms the foundation of later deductions in both the theory of value and the theory of capital.

Employing an operation – called by Sraffa a reduction to dated quantities of labour – by which 'in the equation of a commodity the different means of production used are replaced with a series of quantities of labour, each with appropriate "date"', Sraffa resolves prices into an infinite series composed of terms containing wages and profits. Prices never resolve themselves completely into these factor shares but carry along a commodity residue which becomes all important when wages are zero, thus setting always a finite upper limit to the maximum rate of profits. Sraffa also establishes in the no-joint-products case that irrespective of the standard in which wage is measured, an increase in the wage rate, *ipso facto*, implies a decline in profits. However, in the case with joint products, this proposition does not hold generally. To a particular wage, given in *any* standard, there may correspond several alternative rates of profits. This shows the absolute necessity of measuring the wage in terms of the Standard commodity, if unequivocal conclusions regarding the movements

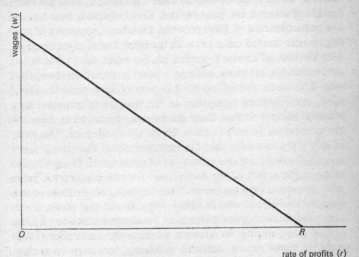

Figure 1 Relation between wages (as a proportion of the Standard net product) and the rate of profits

of the rate of profits given the wage rate are to be drawn. Measurement of the wage in terms of the Standard commodity gives us definite information regarding both the direction as well as the extent of change in the rate of profits, consequent upon a change in the wage rate. No other standard possesses this predictive value.

Measurement of capital

The most interesting use of the Standard commodity (and the wage–profit relation) arises in connection with the measurement of capital. Economists have long ceased to be complacent about the average period of production as a measure of capital. Sraffa's demonstration regarding the impossibility of measuring capital independently of distribution and prices is powerful and convincing. Resorting to the 'reduction to dated quantities of labour' and using the unique wage–profit relation, Sraffa proves the possibility of the reversals in the direction of price movements even when methods of production remain unchanged, when the rate of profits is altered. An alternative method of calculating 'correct' book value of capital after depreciation emerges from Sraffa's discussion on fixed capital. Fixed capital is now treated as a particular case of joint product. Durable instruments of production are treated on a par with the other means of production, with the annual intake recorded on the input side; what is left of the fixed capital (now, older by a year) is entered on the output side. This treatment of capital has now become quite familiar.[9] Also, every year of operation of the fixed asset is treated as a separate process so that there are as many processes as there are the number of years of active life of the fixed asset. The price of any given age of a durable instrument will thus result from solving the simultaneous equations of production. The difference between the prices of the instrument for two consecutive years gives the correct depreciation. This depreciation formula scores over the traditional one in many ways. In the first place, it can allow for any complex pattern of productive efficiency of the capital good during its lifetime whereas the conventional formula is based upon uniform efficiency, contrary to reality. Secondly, it can make allowance for variations of inputs in every production period so that changes in efficiency of other inputs are also permitted. Thirdly, it can be applied to the cases where the same machine is used in different productive operations with varying efficiency.

The quantity of capital which arises from the solution of the simultaneous equations is not distorted by variations in the measuring yardstick itself, since it is expressed in terms of the Standard commodity which is invariant with respect to changes in the distribution pattern. Efforts to reduce the durable instrument to dated quantities of labour are proved futile and so also the attempt to find in technology an average period of production, independent of prices and distribution. Measurement of capital under stationary-state conditions, where perfect tranquillity pre-

9. In his reference to literature (p. 95) Sraffa remarks that this method has fallen into oblivion after Marx. However, von Neumann's model makes use of such a concept.

vails, has not been much of a problem. Even with steady growth accompanied by confident expectations, the problem has an easy enough solution, if a constant rate of profit is assumed. Sraffa has now offered an answer to the problem in a more complicated situation where the profit rate is allowed to change but technical conditions are assumed to be unaltered. Measurement of capital under even more generalized conditions of changing distribution pattern coupled with changes in technology still eludes us.

Sraffa's contribution

Incidentally, the contribution of Sraffa's system as a fundamental analytical structure in the context of measurement of economic magnitudes may be noted here. The concept of stationary state, with its invariance of structure, offered itself as a convenient scale of reference to successive approximation; it provided a firm foundation on which to superimpose change. In Sraffa's system, we enjoy an additional degree of freedom – namely, the freedom to vary distribution pattern while retaining the focal point of reference – the Standard system. This is a step further towards a more realistic analytical foundation.

When Sraffa introduces multiple techniques and the process of switching over from one technique to another, complications arise, especially when a basic product is involved. The anchor of analysis – the Standard system – is itself in peril. With a new technique introduced, we move into a distinctly new economic system with its own maximum rate of profits. The analysis becomes rather involved. With his characteristic resourcefulness, Sraffa finds certain ways out. However, this portion of the book does indicate the complications we run into if the structure of the Standard system itself changes. There can be no smooth change in techniques without changing the entire configuration of relative prices. Furthermore, the changes are not only in terms of relative prices; but are more fundamental. They involve a comparison of two different economic worlds.[10]

10. Here, perhaps, is to be found another of the challenges to marginalism. In fact, the book, which is subtitled as *Prelude to a Critique of Economic Theory*, 'is designed to serve as a basis for a critique of that [marginal theory of value and distribution] theory' (preface).

Sraffa forewarns in his preface that no assumption regarding constancy-of-returns-to-scale is made. In fact, with no changes either in the scale of output or input proportions, this question is irrelevant.[11] However, when one thinks of incorporating growth into the system many questions relating to this assumption arise. This Standard commodity becomes vulnerable if we do not assume the linear homogeneity condition. Even in the simplest case where we assume that output proportions do not change, namely, of balanced expansion, the Standard system is bound to be vitiated if we make no assumption regarding the constancy-of-returns-to-scale. The technical relations will change with expansion in output throwing up a different Standard system with a different maximum rate of profits. The ideal analytical conditions for the same Standard commodity to continue its domination unruffled by change would be the von Neumann world of proportional expansion where constant-returns-to-scale prevail. So far as growth is concerned, a fusion of Sraffa's system with that of von Neumann appears to have promising potentialities.

Written in an unusually compact style and embellished with chiselled logic, the book bears the imprint of sustained reflection. Unmistakably, this is the work of a master written with authority and insight. Even though Sraffa regenerates the classical approach to economics, his researches are not of archaeological interest. We are told that his central propositions took shape as early as the late twenties, though published after a lapse of over three decades. However, time has dealt kindly with Sraffa's contribution. It is as relevant and sprightly today as it was when conceived.

11. Nevertheless, while reading the paragraphs relating to the construction of the Standard system (pp. 23–4) and more particularly the sub-systems (p. 89), one gets a feeling as though the assumption of constant-returns-to-scale is necessary. Such doubts could be easily warded off since the Standard commodity is purely an auxiliary construction having no physical existence in production relations. Similar is the case of the sub-systems which are used to derive the direct and indirect labour content of commodities (at zero profit rate).

References

LUTZ, F. A., and HAGUE, D. C. (eds.), (1961), *The Theory of Capital*, St Martin's Press.

ROBINSON, J. (1962a), *Essays in the Theory of Economic Growth*, Macmillan.

ROBINSON, J. (1962b), *Economic Philosophy*, C. A. Watts.

SAMUELSON, P. A. (1959), 'A modern treatment of Ricardian theory: part I', *Q. J. Econ.*, vol. 73, pp. 1–35.

SRAFFA, P. (ed.), with DOBB, M. H. (1951), *The Works and Correspondence of David Ricardo*, vol. 1, Cambridge University Press.

SRAFFA, P. (1960), *Production of Commodities by Means of Commodities. Prelude to a Critique of Economic Theory*, Cambridge University Press. [See Reading 4.]

VON NEUMANN, J. (1945–6), 'A model of general economic equilibrium', *Rev. econ. Stud.*, vol. 13, pp. 1–9.

9 E. J. Nell

Theories of Growth and Theories of Value

E. J. Nell, 'Theories of growth and theories of value',
Economic Development and Cultural Change, vol. 16, 1967, pp. 15–26.

Introduction

A number of recent treatments of growth, otherwise widely
divergent in approach, have found themselves confronted by
certain common problems.[1] For example, a series of questions
has arisen with respect to the concept of capital: how should it be
measured? Does it consist of one 'capital good' or of many
goods? Should materials and depreciation be included as part
of the capital upon which returns are calculated? Should the
wage bill likewise be included? Secondly, some closely related
questions concerning distribution have emerged, for the concept
of capital adopted in a model determines to a considerable extent
both what the model will say about the relation of the return to
capital to the wages of labor and how this relation will be affected
by growth. Consideration of relative shares leads naturally to a
third question concerned with the relation between the amounts
of the various factors advanced and the output produced. If this
relationship, the 'production function', is to be of any use in the
study of technical changes during growth, it must be disaggregated to exhibit the structure of production as a set of relationships between technologically specific inputs and outputs. But
in this case 'capital' will be composed of different specific goods
in different industries, with the result that the notion of a 'marginal physical product of capital' must be discarded as meaning-
less. This requires the development of some alternative theory of
distribution.

1. See Atsumi (1960), Dobb (1960), Hicks (1965), Kaldor (1960, 1961),
Kaldor and Mirrlees (1962), Lewis (1954, 1955), Little (1957), Mathur (1965)
Pasinetti (1962, 1963), Robinson (1960, 1962), Samuelson (1962), Sen (1968)
and Solow (1963). This list is meant to be representative rather than
exhaustive.

These problems are commonly believed to be inseparable from the consideration of growth, that is, to result from the fact that the models are designed to deal with an expanding economy. Yet this is not actually the case, as Walras, for example, knew. Even in a stationary economy, if there is net production, all the above difficulties about capital and the formation of a general rate of return arise (see Walras, 1954, p. 269). If inputs and outputs are broken down into their specific components, then capital in different industries will consist of different sets of goods, with the result that a marginal productivity theory cannot be employed. But if specific inputs are not shown, then the supply and demand equations for intermediate goods will not be stated explicitly (Walras, 1954, pp. 240–41). Moreover, when inputs are shown specifically a complication is introduced into the determination of prices. For it is customary to assume that prices are set so as to return at least a normal level of profit on the capital advanced. Yet when capital consists of a multiplicity of separate items, its quantity must be expressed in value terms, which can only be done when the prices of the individual items are known.

This suggests that some, at least, of these questions arise not so much from the fact that it is growth which is being examined as from the type of value theory which is assumed to underlie the growth model. Most models of growth are implicitly or explicitly set in the context of a Walrasian general equilibrium theory, which, as Wicksell (1954, p. 169) long ago pointed out, cannot easily accommodate a concept of capital – a fatal shortcoming in a theory which is expected to provide the foundations for growth theory. Fortunately, it is no longer necessary to rely on Walrasian theory; enough is known about the mathematical properties of linear production systems to place growth models in a Ricardian setting. The purpose of this paper will be to contrast Walrasian and Ricardian general equilibrium theories, and in doing so to suggest that providing a Ricardian value theory as the context for growth models eliminates the difficulties outlined above.

By a 'Walrasian theory of value' we mean a model[2] in which

2. Two well-known discussions of this type of value theory are Allen (1960, ch. 10) and Quandt (1958, ch. 5). A mathematically more advanced discussion is given in Debreu (1959).

there are a large number of consumers, variously endowed with property, and a large number of producers of each kind of good or service. Each consumer's preferences are described by a utility function, with positive first and negative second derivatives. Each producer's technical possibilities are described by a production function, also normally assumed to have positive first and (after a point) negative second derivatives. Consumers purchase final goods, maximizing their utility subject to the constraints of their incomes; they sell the services of factors, balancing disutility against expected return. Firms purchase factors, balancing expected productivity against cost, and sell final goods, setting quantities and prices so as to maximize their profits. Goods and services thus move in a circular flow: producers sell final goods to consumers, and with the proceeds from such sales they purchase factor services from consumers, which they combine into final products. With the proceeds from the sale of factor services consumers buy final products in accordance with their utilities. Competition ensures that demands and supplies will be equated in every market and that excessive profits will be eliminated. Briefly, marginal utility and marginal cost determine equilibrium in the final goods market; marginal disutility and marginal productivity do so in the factor market.

By contrast, in a 'Ricardian theory of value'[3] firms and consumers are not mentioned; only industries are shown or rather, only the techniques of production appear, each industry being defined by the technique it employs. These are taken as given and are assumed to be costly to change.[4] Given a set of techniques, including the amounts of labor needed for production at the unit level, the system will be termed 'productive' if and only if more of at least one good can be produced per period than is consumed in the aggregate in production, while at least as much is produced of every other good as is consumed. With given techniques productivity can be increased, for example, by cutting down on the labor time required per unit output. Prices are set so as to cover the technical costs of production, which are shown

3. The best example of a modern Ricardian model is Sraffa (1960).
4. Alternatively, it could be assumed that the time required to change to a new technique is greater than one period of production.

explicitly, and to return a uniform level of profit in all industries.[5] Final demand will determine the allocation of labor among the industries, but operating an industry at a higher or lower level of intensity will not affect prices, given the usual assumptions. Since the technical composition of each industry's input is shown explicitly, each industry's capital will be made up of different combinations of goods; hence, to set the level of normal or uniform profits, the prices of the inputs will have to be known. But since the outputs of some industries are the inputs of others, all prices and the rate of profit will have to be determined together. Yet the rate of profit cannot be determined until the share of profits is given. Once relative shares are fixed, however, prices, the wage rate and the profit rate can all be determined. Relative shares can be fixed, say, by collective bargaining. Given a wage rate, prices will be determined by the competitive condition that the rate of profit must be the same in every industry. To see the effect of changes in relative shares on prices, suppose the wage rate rises. At the given initial prices, labor-intensive industries will have to devote a greater than average share of their sales proceeds to paying their wage bill, leaving a less than average return on capital, while capital-intensive industries will find themselves in just the opposite position, with a greater than average return. To equalize the rate of profit, therefore, when the wage rises the prices of labor-intensive goods must rise, while those of capital-intensive goods must fall.

The contrast between Walrasian and Ricardian theories of value could hardly be sharper. The most obvious difference, and the one most frequently discussed, concerns substitution. In a Ricardian system the coefficients of production are fixed;

5. The modern Ricardian approach outlined here, while in important ways akin to a Leontief system, nevertheless must be sharply distinguished from the latter. A Leontief system represents production in the same way and is similarly concerned with technological interdependence and the role of intermediate goods. But a Ricardian system is principally concerned with the relation between prices, wages and profits under competitive conditions. Leontief systems never deal with a uniform rate of profit on capital nor with the effects of changes in distribution upon prices. Further, in so far as Leontief systems take account of fixed capital, they treat it as a necessary element in production and neglect its effects upon profits and prices. cf. Leontief (1953).

whereas in a Walrasian system continuous neoclassical production functions are assumed.[6] But this difference is both overworked and ultimately less important than others. For switches in technique are possible in Ricardian systems, and Walras in fact assumed fixed technical coefficients. More fundamental differences emerge when we look at the way the flow of transactions is presented. In Walrasian theory economic transactions are pictured as a circular flow of goods and services; in each market, whether for goods or for factors, the stream of goods moving in one direction is matched by a corresponding traffic traveling the opposite way. By contrast, modern Ricardian theory puts a good deal of emphasis on the fact that the payments to capital are dispositions of a surplus and do not involve any kind of exchange. There simply is no corresponding stream moving in the opposite direction. In Walrasian theory both prices and quantities are determined by supply and demand acting in conjunction; in Ricardian theory prices are determined wholly by the conditions of supply; demand is relevant only to the determination of quantities. In Walrasian theory intermediate products are eliminated as far as possible; in Ricardian theory such products are given pride of place. In a Walrasian system both supplies and demands are closely tied to individual decision-making units; in a Ricardian system no such units are assumed. A Ricardian system shows the interlocking of possibilities and necessities, rather than of motives, plans and information.

The significance of these contrasts for growth theory must now be shown explicitly. Since much of this significance arises from the Ricardian distinction between matters of technology and matters of appropriation – between features of the system which depend on techniques of production and features which depend on division of the product – it is important to begin by examining the Ricardian concept of what is to be divided, i.e. the net product, or 'surplus'.

In a Ricardian model the net output is a physical surplus of output over and above the amounts needed for replacement, to

6. It is worth remarking that part of the process of development has been the reduction in cost and difficulty of switching techniques; the difficulties in the way of the accomplishment (as well as the complexities involved in practice of switching techniques) should not simply be assumed away.

make good depreciation, and (in some models) for the maintenance and support of the working population in the customary style (see Sraffa, 1951; also Samuelson, 1957). We can represent net output more formally by means of a set of interdependent single-product industries, using only 'circulating' means of production:[7]

$$
\begin{array}{llll}
C_{11} & C_{12} & \dots & C_{1k} \to C_1 \\
C_{21} & C_{22} & \dots & C_{2k} \to C_2 \\
\vdots & \vdots & & \vdots \\
C_{k1} & C_{k2} & \dots & C_{kk} \to C_k.
\end{array}
$$

Each process will require the products of others, and at least one good must be used directly or indirectly by all processes. A composite consumption good supports labor, assumed fixed in amount. Normally some processes will produce goods that do not return to the system as inputs; these processes can be thought of as luxury industries. The surplus will be the vector, $(C_1 - \Sigma_i\, C_{i1}, C_2 - \Sigma_i\, C_{i2}, \dots, C_k - \Sigma_i\, C_{ik})$. The physical composition of the surplus can be varied (e.g. in response to demand) by reallocating labor (the 'fixed factor') among the industries. Such reallocation leaves prices, and value relationships generally, unaffected.

When the rate of profit and prices are added, the system generally becomes:[8]

$$
\begin{array}{l}
(1+R)(C_{11}\, p_1 + C_{12}\, p_2 + \dots + C_{1k}\, p_k) = C_1\, p_1 \\
(1+R)(C_{21}\, p_1 + C_{22}\, p_2 + \dots + C_{2k}\, p_k) = C_2\, p_2 \\
\vdots \quad\quad \vdots \quad\quad \vdots \quad\quad\quad\quad \vdots \\
(1+R)(C_{k1}\, p_1 + C_{k2}\, p_2 + \dots + C_{kk}\, p_k) = C_k\, p_k.
\end{array}
$$

Here the whole surplus goes to profit. When part of the surplus goes to labor, the wage can be shown as a uniform return paid

7. There are several ways of relaxing this assumption. If goods used in different industries are written off in the same number of periods, the columns showing the depreciation each period – which figures in circulating capital – can be multiplied by the write-off time. Alternatively, partly depreciated durable equipment can be treated as a joint product, produced along with the regular output.

8. When there is no surplus, call the matrix of inputs, C, and the matrix of outputs, P. Then for the price equation we have $Cp = Pp$ or $(C-P)p = 0$, a unique and positive solution of which is guaranteed by the fact that $|C-P| = 0$, given certain other restrictions on the matrices. For a full discussion see Gale (1960, ch. 8).

on the basic subsistence wage, and the rate of profit will fall in proportion to rises in the wage.

One reallocation can be defined in which the ratios of the net amounts of each good produced to the total amount of that good consumed in production will all be the same. This common ratio will be the maximum rate of profit, and also, of course, the maximum possible rate of growth. So this ratio can be interpreted as the ratio of the value of the surplus to the value of the total current or circulating input.[9]

A surplus can be put to many uses. It can be used for the public benefit in the form of common goods, for privately consumed luxuries, to fight wars or to support a lavish government. Or it can be reinvested productively, leading to growth. But in a private enterprise system, before one can say anything about the *allocation* of the surplus among these competing ends (or even about the influence of consumer preferences upon its composition), one must consider the logically prior question of its *distribution*. For in an economic system based on private property, everything produced belongs to someone, but the activity of production is carried out cooperatively by a number of different parties who, therefore, have competing claims. More specifically, the (value of the) net product must be divided among workers, managers, owners of capital and owners of land, though it is convenient for many purposes to lump the first two and last two together and treat the product as being divided between wages and profits. This division is accomplished through the competitive market at the same time that the exchanges necessary for reproduction take place. The market mechanism, therefore, is obliged to do two things at once. It must allocate goods to make reproduction possible, and it must distribute the full value of the product as wages and profits, which means, among other things, deciding how much shall go to each.

In general, this decision cannot be analysed in a static framework, for it both depends upon and affects growth. For example, when population growth equals or exceeds the rate of growth of capital, competition among laborers will force the wages down

9. For a proof that maximum rate of profits always exists, is unique and is associated with a unique set of positive prices see Sraffa (1960, chs. 4, 5). Also see Seton (1957).

toward the cost-of-living level, raising profits toward their maximum. When population growth is less than the rate of growth of capital, competition between employers will bid wages up, lowering profits. Such changes in distribution can be expected to affect savings, since workers and profit-takers will normally have different saving propensities. And changes in the rate of profit can be expected to affect decisions to invest.

This suggests a view of competitive price determination somewhat different from that which has become customary, for it means putting the conflict between labor and capital in the foreground, making relative prices depend on the outcome of this conflict.

In the system described above, the outputs of some industries served as the inputs of others. This makes it possible to trace chains of direct and indirect mutual dependence, which presents a further contrast with neoclassical thinking. For economic thought in the Walrasian tradition emphasizes the interdependence of markets, while neglecting the more fundamental technological interdependence of production. At first glance this may seem strange, since surely the analysis of one leads to the study of the other. But in a strictly neoclassical world this connection cannot be made so easily, for the factors influencing supply and those determining demand are assumed to be separate. In the neoclassical view of the economy, markets are connected not because the various products are consumed in the production of one another, but because, for example, an increase in the amount of any good purchased draws demand away from other markets; and similarly, an increase in the amount of any good produced draws factors away from the production of other goods. Production is regarded as a sort of one-way street, in which ultimate 'factors' are converted into 'final products' and all intermediate steps are ignored, as attention is concentrated, on the one hand, upon the conditions influencing the sale of final products and, on the other, upon the payments to the 'factors'. In a system of this kind production might be technologically interdependent,[10] but it is not necessary that it be

10. Walras, however, maintained that references to intermediate goods could be eliminated by 'reducing' them to equivalent expressions containing only primary factors. cf. Walras (1954, lesson 20).

so, for the scarcity of factors is a sufficient condition for the interdependence of markets.

It makes a good deal of difference in a growth model whether the interdependence emphasized is that of markets or of production. For if it is the former, the arguments of the production function will be factors which are specific not to technology but to the payment of income. Further, both supplies and demands will be tied to the decision-making units, the firm and the household. But the technological knowledge and the social conventions underlying production and consumption respectively are part of the common environment of all firms and households, and while for some purposes it may be important to emphasize the individual character of decisions to produce and consume, in the long term it may well be that this is less important than the influence of the common background. The introduction of irrelevant particulars concerning decision making is made possible only by sacrificing the consideration of relevant technological facts.

In classical (as in Marxian) economics, the focus of attention is the actual process of production. Such a concentration on technological interdependence leads to a different view of the role of the traditional 'factors of production'. These are now thought of as being kinds of income-bearing property, rather than actual productive agents. Of course, all income-bearing property is property in one form or another of means of production, but the point is that while 'capital' and 'labor' respectively receive profits (including interest and dividends) and wages, they do not, *as such*, enter into production. *Particular* goods – such as various raw materials, tools, fuel and power, and machines – and particular jobs requiring specific skills and training are involved in production, but the general categories 'capital' and 'labor' are not, being mere aggregates of the particular items. This is clear enough from the fact that to produce any specific good it is not enough to have a certain amount of capital; it must be embodied in the technologically appropriate plant and equipment, manned by an appropriately skilled labor force. But just the reverse is true in the receipt of income. Whatever the particular goods in which capital is embodied, in equilibrium the same amount of capital receives the same profit income (making due allowance for risk), and whatever the particular job, labor of the same degree of skill and training receives the same wage.

In other words, 'factors of production' are to be distinguished from 'inputs'. 'Inputs' are the goods considered technologically as items entering into a productive process; but 'factors of production' are collections of inputs held as income-bearing property. The fact that 'factors' are collections or aggregates of inputs held in a certain relationship means that neither 'capital' nor 'labor' can be measured independently of prices.[11]

In neoclassical thinking, the market for factors is normally regarded as analogous to the market for final products. But this revised view of the role of 'factors' implies a considerable difference between these 'markets'. In the markets for final and intermediate goods, value-equivalents are exchanged, i.e. objects differing in use value but equal in exchange value are traded either directly by barter or indirectly through some medium. But in the market for factors, income is paid out to those who have property rights in the productive process, in accordance with the nature and extent of their property. Of course, as the pattern of demand changes during development and as technological innovations change the pattern of production, both capital and labor will shift in response to differentials in earnings between industries. But such movement does not imply that any *exchange* takes place between the recipient of net income and the source of income. The only service the owner of capital renders to industry is the service of permitting it to be owned by him.[12] Labor

11. It is sometimes thought that a measure of the quantity of capital currently being invested can be got by considering the amount of consumption sacrificed. But this simply transfers the difficulties of measurement to consumption. An economy with a single consumption good is no more plausible than an economy with a single capital good. Also, the attempt to estimate the rate of return on investment by the ratio of later consumption to sacrificed current consumption runs into two difficulties. First, the growth rate need not equal the profit rate (i.e. the productivity of capital is a different matter from its profitability) and, second, the concern is for the return on capital in general, and not just on investment.

12. The owners of capital (the recipients of property income) are frequently said to sell the capital's 'service' to a firm, the factor price of the capital being the interest or dividend they receive in return. But this is just

receives wages in exchange for work, but the level of wages, which cannot fall below a basic cost of living, is determined by bargaining power and not, as in the case of ordinary commodities, by a relationship between cost of production and value of product. This can be seen from the fact that there is no inherent connection between changes in productivity and changes in the cost of living. In short, while the way the wage rate and the rate of return are made uniform is similar to the way prices are made uniform, the 'factor market' differs essentially from the markets for goods in that the payment of net income is not an exchange, despite the fact that the amount paid to a given factor will normally be determined through bargaining in a market.

There are also important differences between the various factor markets which are particularly relevant to distribution theory. For example, in the market for capital, savers compete with investors: the higher the rate of interest, the greater the earnings of savers and the lower the profits of investors. In such a competition one set of capitalists gains at the expense of another. Changes in this market will lead to a redistribution of profits among capitalists, but there is no direct effect upon relative shares. By contrast, the competition in the labor market directly involves relative shares, since what labor gains capital loses, and vice versa. Hence, given certain assumptions, it is possible to determine relative shares in this market alone.

The fact that in a Ricardian linear production model the payment of net income in the 'factor market' is not an exchange suggests that the concept of exchange, perhaps the most fundamental idea of economics, is defined differently in Walrasian and Ricardian models. Even in a context described by a Ricardian model, the laborers must choose between work and 'leisure', and the capitalist who puts his capital to work must thereby choose (at least implicitly) not to consume it (to 'wait'). But these rather strained 'choices' do not suffice to make the act of

a play on words, for the 'owners of capital' are also, *ipso facto*, the owners of the firm. They are therefore 'selling' this service to themselves. The 'firm' only appears to be different from the owners of its capital because of their limited liability; but important as this is, in this context it means merely that they can lose no more on a given project than they choose to put into it. Yet the project is still theirs.

receiving income an *exchange* in the sense appropriate to a Ricardian system. In order for a transaction to be an exchange (rather than, for example, a transfer payment) clearly defined, technologically useful goods or services must change hands; and for the exchange to be in equilibrium they must do so at a rate reflecting the relative production costs of the goods, given the competitive requirement that profit on capital be uniform. In other words, the Ricardian concept of exchange is irrevocably tied to the technological characteristics of the good involved; there is no exchange unless both items traded have a production equation. By way of contrast, in any neoclassical model an act can be considered an act of exchange if it has an opportunity cost, which can be estimated in terms of forgone utility.

The Ricardian emphasis on technology reveals a further difference between the two concepts of exchange. In neoclassical theory, value is determined 'subjectively', as the result of a series of choices made under the influence of certain motives involving the attempt to maximize some quantity, usually utility or profit. But in Ricardian models no reference need ever be made to choices or to motives, and prices are determined without anything being maximized. The condition determining barter exchange values is that the system be able exactly to reproduce itself in the next production period, *given* the distribution between capital and labor of the surplus of output over necessary replacements. Clearly, 'final demand' plays no role in this, though it will be important in determining the physical composition of the surplus.

Since in a Ricardian model prices are not determined by maximization, the Ricardian concept of equilibrium also differs substantially from the neoclassical concept. A neoclassical system is in equilibrium when and only when every individual in the system is choosing those quantities from the alternatives available to them that they prefer to produce and consume, where 'preference' is interpreted as meaning, in some sense, maximizing. There are a number of different ways of expressing the idea underlying this definition of equilibrium, but however significant the modifications may seem for some purposes, all versions are based on the central ideas of choice among alternatives and maximization. By contrast, in a Ricardian (or any other) linear production model, this kind of 'choice' is not relevant, and equilibrium is defined in terms of technology and distribution, so that exchange equilibrium is a relation between a pattern of production and the pattern of inputs required to maintain the system at its current level of activity, which meets the additional constraint of distributing the surplus in the given proportions.

The important thing to see at this point is that the two concepts of exchange have different logical forms. 'Equilibrium in exchange' in one case means trading a set of outputs in such a way as to allocate them so that they can function as inputs; here exchange is an operation designed to eliminate the difference between the matrix of outputs and the matrix of inputs. In the other case, 'equilibrium in exchange' means that the set of quantities associated with the prices (or the two sets taken together) will maximize some index. These two notions have nothing in common.

Walrasian and Ricardian theories of value not only differ with respect to substitution but, because of their divergent treatments of technological interdependence and distribution, are obliged to interpret certain basic economic terms in distinct and incompatible ways. For example, by putting the direct conflict of interest between labor and capital in the foreground, a Ricardian theory can more easily examine the effects of growth on the labor market and thus on distribution. Even more important, because a Ricardian value theory permits the specific technology used to be displayed in detail, it is able to present a closer analysis of all questions concerning technical progress. No matter how disaggregated a concept of capital is desired, a Ricardian value theory can accommodate it; for the object of the theory is to determine the rate of profit and prices together, given relative shares (determined, for example, by the effects of growth on the supply and demand for labor), whereas the difficulty in the neoclassical approach arises in trying to determine relative shares along with prices and the rate of profit, given the quantities of capital. Hence, this latter theory can only work with a very simple concept of capital which is inappropriate for the study of growth.

In summary, we have tried to suggest, first, that some of the apparently intractable problems facing modern growth theory actually have no very close connection with growth, but arise instead from tensions within the value theory normally presumed to underlie growth models; and second, that if this value theory is replaced by a Ricardian one, these problems will either disappear or become more amenable.

References

ALLEN, R. G. D. (1960), *Mathematical Economics*, Macmillan, 2nd edn.

ATSUMI, H. (1960), 'Mr Kaldor's theory of income distribution', *Rev. econ. Stud.*, vol. 27, pp. 109–18.

DEBREU, G. (1959), *Theory of Value*, Wiley.

DOBB, M. H. (1960), *An Essay on Economic Growth and Planning*, Routledge & Kegan Paul.

GALE, D. (1960), *Theory of Linear Economic Models*, McGraw-Hill.

HICKS, J. R. (1965), *Capital and Growth*, Oxford University Press.

KALDOR, N. (1960), 'A model of economic growth', in *Essays on Economic Stability and Growth*, Duckworth, pp. 256–300.

KALDOR, N. (1961), 'Capital accumulation and economic growth', in F. A. Lutz and D. C. Hague (eds.), *Theory of Capital*, Macmillan, pp. 177–220.

KALDOR, N., and MIRRLEES, J. A. (1962), 'A new model of economic growth', *Rev. econ. Stud.*, vol. 29, pp. 174–90.

LEONTIEF, W. W. (1953), *Studies in the Structure of the American Economy*, Oxford University Press.

LEWIS, W. A. (1954), 'Economic development with unlimited supplies of labour', *Manchester School*, vol. 22, pp. 139–91.

LEWIS, W. A. (1955), *Theory of Economic Growth*, Allen & Unwin.

LITTLE, I. M. D. (1957), 'Classical economic growth', *Oxf. econ. Pap.*, vol. 2 (new series), pp. 152–77.

MATHUR, G. (1965), *Planning for Steady Growth*, Blackwell.

PASINETTI, L. L. (1962), 'Rate of profit and income distribution in relation to the rate of economic growth', *Rev. econ. Stud.*, vol. 29, pp. 267–79.

PASINETTI, L. L. (1963), *A Multi-Sectoral Model of Economic Growth*, Cambridge University Press.

QUANDT, R. E. (1958), *Microeconomic Theory*, McGraw-Hill.

ROBINSON, J. (1960), *Collected Economic Papers*, vol. 2, Blackwell.

ROBINSON, J. (1962), *Essays in the Theory of Economic Growth*, Macmillan.

SAMUELSON, P. A. (1957), 'Wages and interest: a modern dissection of Marxian economic models', *Amer. econ. Rev.*, vol. 47, pp. 884–912.

SAMUELSON, P. A. (1962), 'Parable and realism in capital theory: the surrogate production function', *Rev. econ. Stud.*, vol. 29, pp. 193–206.

SEN, A. K. (1968), *Choice of Technique*, Macmillan, 3rd edn.

SETON, F. (1957), 'The "transformation problem"', *Rev. econ. Stud.*, vol. 24, pp. 149–60.

SOLOW, R. M. (1963), *Capital Theory and the Rate of Return*, North-Holland Publishing Co.

SRAFFA, P. (ed.), with DOBB, M. H. (1951), *The Works and Correspondence of David Ricardo*, vol. 1, Cambridge University Press.

SRAFFA, P. (1960), *Production of Commodities by Means of Commodities. Prelude to a Critique of Economic Theory*, Cambridge University Press. [See Reading 4.]

WALRAS, L. (1954), *Elements of Pure Economics*, trans. W. Jaffe, Allen & Unwin.

WICKSELL, K. (1954), *Value, Capital and Rent*, trans. S. H. Frowein, Allen & Unwin.

Part Five
The Double-Switching and Capital-Reversing Debate

The phenomena of double-switching and capital-reversing were thoroughly explored in a series of papers that were published from 1965 to 1969, though the phenomena themselves had been identified by Sraffa in the mid-twenties (though not published until 1960) and Joan Robinson and Champernowne in the early fifties. The issues on which they bear are two: the concept of aggregate capital as used in the aggregate production function and the applicability of results obtained from simple neo-classical marginal productivity parables to heterogeneous capital models. While both sides of the debate seem to be in agreement as to *why* the phenomena arise, the extent of the ramifications for received economic theory is still not agreed upon. We reprint here Samuelson's paper on the surrogate production function (Reading 10) which is a key watershed on the way to the main debate, his excellent 'summing up' article (Reading 11) which explains clearly *why* the phenomena arise and which applications of the parables are affected, and two outstanding papers from the neo-Keynesian camp – Bhaduri's (Reading 12) which spells out a neo-Marxist interpretation of the implications of the results of the debate, and Pasinetti's (Reading 13) which re-examines Irving Fisher's contribution in the light of the debate and argues (as, too, does Garegnani, 1970) that the traditional demand-and-supply approach to distribution puzzles is vitiated by the new results. [Reading 13 and Garegnani (1970) are excellent examples of explicit spellings out of Sraffa's implied critique of marginalist theory.]

Reference

GAREGNANI, P. (1970), 'Heterogeneous capital, the production function and the theory of distribution', *Rev. econ. Stud.*, vol. 37, pp. 407–36.

10 P. A. Samuelson

Parable and Realism in Capital Theory:
The Surrogate Production Function[1]

P. A. Samuelson, 'Parable and realism in capital theory: the surrogate production function', *Review of Economic Studies*, vol. 39, 1962, pp. 193–206.

Introduction

Repeatedly in writings and lectures I have insisted that capital theory can be rigorously developed without using any Clark-like concept of aggregate 'capital', instead relying upon a complete analysis of a great variety of heterogeneous physical capital goods and processes through time. Such an analysis leans heavily on the tools of modern linear and more general programming and might, therefore, be called neo-neoclassical. It takes the view that if we are to understand the trends in how incomes are distributed among different kinds of labor and different kinds of property owners, both in the aggregate and in the detailed composition, then studies of changing technologies, human and natural resource availabilities, taste patterns and all the other matters of *micro*economics are likely to be very important.

This general viewpoint has been referred to, and not with complete admiration, as the 'MIT school'. And I do stand by it as the best tool for the description and understanding of economic reality, and for policy formulation and calculated guesses about the future.

At the same time in various places I have subjected to detailed exposition certain simplified models involving only a few factors of production. Because of a Gresham's Law that operates in economics, one's easier expositions get more readers than one's harder. And it is partly for this reason that such simple models or parables do, I think, have considerable heuristic value in giving

1. Dedicated to Joan Robinson on the occasion of her memorable 1961 visit to MIT. (Acknowledgement, non-incriminating, to the Ford Foundation for research finance is gratefully made.)

insights into the fundamentals of interest theory in all its complexities.

It is the case, I believe, that Robert Solow and I have pretty much the same general views in this matter, having arrived independently and together at the same general conclusions. But Solow, in the interest of empirical measurements and approximation, has been willing occasionally to drop his rigorous insistence upon a complex-heterogeneous-capital programming model; instead, by heroic abstraction, he has carried forward the seminal work of Paul H. Douglas on estimating a single production function for society and has had a tremendous influence on analysts of statistical trends in the important macro-aggregates of our economy. One might almost say that there are two Solows – the orthodox priest of the MIT school and the busman on a holiday who operates brilliantly and without inhibitions in the rough-and-ready realm of empirical heuristics. Just as red wine and white wine are both good, so are both Solows of vintage quality. But if I were forced to choose between red and white wine, I for one would reveal a preference for the red.

But must there always be a need for mutually exclusive choice? Cannot each in its place be useful? What I propose to do here is to show that a new concept, the 'surrogate production function', can provide *some* rationalization for the validity of the simple J. B. Clark parables which pretend there is a single thing called 'capital' that can be put into a single production function and along with labor will produce total output (of a homogeneous good or of some desired market-basket of goods). In so doing, I may also be providing some extenuations for Solow's holiday high spirits.

When I tried to explain all this in correspondence with my good friend Nicholas Kaldor (the chap who likes to talk about a 'stylized' – i.e. non-rigorous but suggestive – description of a modern economy), he replied with the amiable gibe: 'You are trying to pretend that J. B. Clark can be defended as "stylized" Samuelson.' That is much what I want to argue here. I shall use the new tools of the surrogate production function[2] and surrogate capital to show how we can sometimes predict exactly how certain quite complicated heterogeneous capital models will behave by

2. One might call this the 'as if' production function.

treating them *as if* they had come from a simple generating production function (even when we know they did not *really* come from such a function).

I must not overstate my case. There are many realistic capital models where many of the tricks developed here will not work: later I give instances.

Heterogeneous capitals model of the linear programming type

I begin with a concrete model in which there are a great variety of capital goods: call them alpha, beta,..., 999 or anything else, and think of each as cooperating with a fixed crew of workers and being as specific as you like to one kind of use. Assuming for simplicity that society produces only one kind of homogeneous final output, we can regard the use of each kind of physical good as a separate linear programming activity and can adhere to the most extreme assumption of fixed proportions (involving L-shaped isoquants of the Leontief-type). Constant-returns-to-scale is assumed throughout, but it is understood that concrete capital goods depreciate only gradually over time and that society cannot convert one kind of good into another except by the slow device of refusing to replace one kind and alternatively producing more of the other.

One need never speak of *the* production function, but rather should speak of a great number of separate production functions which correspond to each activity and which need have no smooth substitutability properties. All the technology of the economy could be summarized in a whole book of such production functions, each page giving the blueprint for a particular activity. Technological change can be handled easily by adding new options and blueprints to the book, but for simplicity I shall assume that technical knowledge does not change.

Finally it is enough to assume that there is but one 'primary' or non-producible factor of production, which we might as well call labor (or a dose of labor and land). All other inputs and outputs are producible by the technologies specified in the blue-prints.

Along with our returns assumptions we stipulate the perfect knowledge condition appropriate to a perfectly competitive market, one which lacks monopolistic or monopsonistic domination. Alternatively we can think of this as a completely planned state that organizes itself for Pareto-optimality by explicit or implicit use of Lerner–Lange pricing (equivalent to the shadow-price dual variables of a linear programming problem).

The fundamental factor-price frontier

Given the stage directions of our system it acts out its own scenario just as a logical system develops its own theorems once its axioms are specified.

A first simple question is this: what various stationary or steady states are possible? Upon detailed reflection, one will agree that the system can 'end up' in a great variety of states in which the real wage of labor and the interest rate per annum (or, what is the same thing with our stipulation of no uncertainty, the percentage rate of profit) are determined. Once they are determined, all equilibrium machine rentals, valuations, commodity prices and all the rest are uniquely determined (provided, as in the usual discussion of 'substitution theorems', we rule out the influence of the composition of demand on such joint products as wool and mutton or new taxi rides and old).

Figure 1 portrays the steady-state configurations of equilibrium real-wage and interest rate. At A, society has, so to speak, been able to afford such 'time-intensive' or 'mechanized' processes as to produce a high real wage for workers and a low rate of interest or profit return. At B, the rate of interest is so high that society can afford only to use such direct processes as yield a low real wage. There is always a trade-off between the wage and profit-level: in the absence of innovation both cannot go up; and whatever the pattern of innovation, both cannot go down, since a simultaneous declining rate of profit and an immiserization of the wage-earner would be arithmetically impossible in the stipulated technology. A good name for this fundamental trade-off relation would be the factor-price frontier. A number of writers (von Thünen, Robinson, Samuelson, Sraffa, etc.) have indicated the existence of such a frontier for various capital models, and I shall not here venture to discuss its properties in detail, save to say that it will have non-positive slope and (in the most general case) be of any curvature.

If two economies have each a different book of technical blueprints, they will have different frontiers. Thus, an effective technological change will shift the frontier north-eastward, permitting higher real-wage rates at the same profit rate, or higher profit rates at the same real wage, or higher rates of both. One could try to define a technological change as 'neutral' or otherwise in terms of the way it shifts this frontier, but I shall not stop to discuss that question.

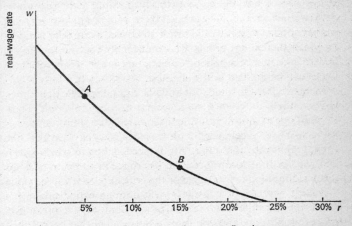

Figure 1 The factor-price frontier

Can two economies with different technologies (i.e. different sets of blueprints) have exactly the same frontier? Certainly it would be most unlikely for such a rare coincidence to happen; but it is not impossible. (Thus, imagine the planet Mars where there exist unicorns that do the work of horses, or where there are even more subtle background differences that yet end up with the same final wage–profit equilibria.)

In the singular case where two economies have exactly the same factor-price frontier, however they may be different in the background, we can treat them as equivalent in so far as predictions about their long-run interest- and wage-rate properties are concerned. And, what may be more useful, if two economies have approximately the same frontiers within a given range, we can use either one to predict the long-run properties of the other in that range.

A special model of heterogeneous physical capitals

All that has been said up until now is completely general, holding rigorously for any constant-returns-to-scale technology no matter how complicated are the technological processes and resulting book of blueprints. But now I want to consider a special subclass of realistic cases, to present certain valid results that hold rigorously for such models. Obviously, it would serve no purpose here to consider a model in which there were not diverse physical capital goods. And it would evade the issue to consider a model in which the capital goods were not highly specific to one use and to one combination of cooperating labor. None of these issues will be dodged in the slightest.

In particular, I assume that any one capital good, call it alpha, looks entirely different from a second beta capital good. Thus, think of one as a plow; another as a machine tool or loom, or as a much more 'mechanized' plow. No alchemist can turn one capital good into the other. Alpha needs labor to work with it in a fixed proportion: more than its critical proportion of labor will yield nothing extra; more of the critical proportion of alpha will itself, with labor constant, yield nothing extra; take away either input, while holding the other input at the previously proper proportion, and you lose *all* the product that has resulted from the combined dose of the two inputs. Just as alpha and labor can produce final output, it is assumed that they, too, can produce a flow of new alpha machines. I shall here assume that the same proportion of inputs is used in the consumption-goods and alpha-goods industries, with full warning that this is a drastically simplifying assumption whose limitations will be commented on later. Since alpha, like any other capital goods, will depreciate through time, we can reckon its net capital formation only after its physical depreciation has been made good or allowed for. To keep the alpha good homogeneous independently of age, one has to assume a force of mortality independent of age (or an exponential life table). This means that physical depreciation is always directly proportional to the physical stock of alpha, K_α: depreciation equals δ_α times K_α, where the average length of life of alpha is the reciprocal of the δ_α factor.[3]

3. In linear programming terminology, we have two activities: one uses a certain amount of L and K_α as inputs to produce a certain amount of

The same general assumptions are to hold for capital goods beta, gamma,..., etc. Each works with its peculiar proportion of labor, and can produce our market-basket flow of finished goods. Each can produce its own gross capital formation, and depending upon its peculiar length of life, we can reckon its physical depreciation and physical rate of net capital formation of the type $\dot{K}_\beta$. The present model, however, does not require any of beta to help in producing alpha, nor vice versa. Warning is given that this is a deliberate oversimplification of reality. What would the factor-price frontier look like if there were only the one physical capital, K_α? Figure 2(a) shows it as a straight line $M_\alpha N_\alpha$.

The horizontal intercept, M_α, gives that maximal profit rate which would be possible if labor were a redundant and free good. Thus, from our technical coefficient of the amount of alpha needed to produce a unit of itself, we can compute the fastest rate at which alpha can make itself grow. Call this, say, 40 per cent per annum. But if alpha has only a ten-year average life, we have to subtract 10 per cent for depreciation to get the maximum self-growth and profit rate of 30 per cent at M_α.

The vertical intercept, N_α, gives the highest productivity of labor on the supposition that the profit or interest rate is zero. The magnitude of this long-run real wage, $w = W/P$, is completely determined from the technical input coefficient alone: if less direct labor were needed to produce a unit of consumption and alpha output, w would rise; it would rise if, *ceteris paribus*, the machine became longer lived; and it would rise if less alpha were needed directly to produce consumption Q or the gross capital formation G_α.

Why is the frontier a straight line between these two intercepts? The answer is traced to our fixed-proportions postulate.[4]

---

final product; the second activity uses L and K_α in the same proportions to produce a certain number of units of new (gross) alpha capital goods G_α – and by convention we may choose as our unit for alpha capital goods just that amount which uses the same inputs as would the production of one unit of final consumption output. Needless to say, to produce one unit of *net* capital formation of alpha, $K_\alpha = dK_\alpha/dt$, requires additional inputs large enough to make good depreciation: i.e. $\dot{K}_\alpha = G_\alpha - \delta_\alpha K_\alpha$.

4. If more (less) alpha relative to labor were needed to produce itself than to produce consumption output, the frontier would be convex to the origin (concave to the origin).

With no substitutability possible, there can be no 'deepening of capital', and every stationary state produces exactly the same output related to the size of total labor employed. Hence, when labor's relative share of net product falls from all to one-half, its real wage must exactly halve; and the percentage rate of profit (or 'own-interest') will rise to half its maximum rate. Applying

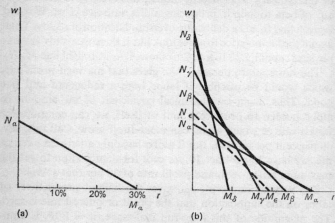

Figure 2 (a) The frontier for α. (b) The optimal frontier for $\alpha, \beta, \ldots$

the same reasoning to all other fractional division of shares, we end up with a perfectly straight line.

Figure 2(b) shows the various straight-line frontiers that would hold for physical capital goods, alpha, beta, gamma,..., etc. Each is characterized by its technologically derivable intercept coefficients of the N and M type. These are all calculated from the postulated book of blueprints specifying the model. Note that beta is a more 'roundabout, mechanized time-intensive' process than alpha. What do such terms mean? This, and no more than this: alpha will be used at very high interest or profit rates in preference to beta; but if the interest rate were lower, below 10 per cent, society would let alpha wear out and put all its resources into the gross capital formation of beta. Likewise gamma is more 'time intensive' than beta. And so it goes in the table and diagram. (Note too that process epsilon will never be used in a stationary state; once beta has been invented, it will never pay workers, capitalists or planners to start any new epsilon investments since epsilon is dominated by beta from the (a) wage, (b) profit and (c) technocratic productivity viewpoints.)

With all the different capital goods available, stationary equilibrium is possible only on the north-east frontier or 'envelope' of all the straight lines. Planners, electronic computers and arbitragers will be led, as if by a Visible Hand, to ensure that. The heavy curve in 2(b) shows the resulting factor-price frontier defined by the whole set of technical blueprints. This frontier consists of straight lines and corner points, which can initially be characterized as follows: on any straight-line segment, only the process corresponding to that line is being used. (Query: can you easily read off relative shares?)

At any corner point there is a blending of two adjacent processes, relative shares there characterizing each process separately. Geometrically, we can say that the corner has all the slopes between the limiting slopes of each separate process; each blending gives rise to one of these intermediate slopes, and from that slope we can infer the relative shares for society as a whole as an average of relative shares in the component processes.

The frontier and relative factor shares

If one believed the over-praised statement of Ricardo that 'Political Economy . . . should rather be called an inquiry into the laws which determine the division of the produce of industry amongst the classes who concur in its formation', the factor-price frontier would be among the most important concepts in this economic model. For, the frontier can (in the special diverse-goods model of the previous section) give us more information than merely what the wage and profit rates will be at any point. Improbable as it may first seem to be, it is a fact that the behavior of stationary equilibria *in the neighborhood* of a particular equilibrium point will completely determine the possible level(s) of relative factor shares in total output *at* that point itself. It is as if going from New York to its suburbs were necessary and sufficient to tell us the unseen properties of New York City itself.

Specifically, how do we infer the relative shares of wages and of property income at a point like A, when we know only the *rates* of wages and interest there? If A is at a point where the curve is smooth and cornerless, we need simply calculate its ordinary Marshallian elasticity, E, there: if E is unity, the wage bill and interest bill are each half of total net national product.

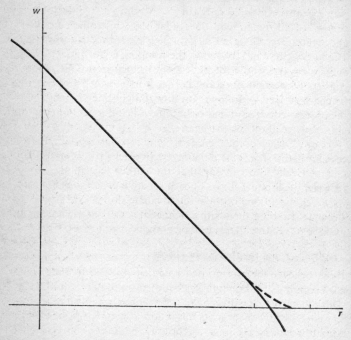

Figure 3 Double-log frontier

If E is inelastic and less than unity, labor gets less than half of the total product. If, as is more realistic for modern nations, the curve has an elasticity at A of around 3, then labor's share is three times that of property and labor gets three-fourths of the total.

Since elasticity rather than slope is crucial, it will obviously be useful to plot the frontier on double-log paper, as in Figure 3. No longer must it have the usual convexity-from-below property of Figure 2. On the depicted straight-line stretch, we have the elasticity of substitution equal to unity (much like the Cobb–Douglas case); above and below that range the double-log frontier is concave from below, indicating elasticity of substitution less than unity (which studies of different countries suggest may be the more realistic case). If the dotted alternative held, elasticity of substitution could be greater than unity and as the wage rate fell the relative share of labor could actually rise.

Our assumption of a finite number of heterogeneous physical capital goods makes it impossible that the frontier should be an iso-elastic curve of the type that would be implied by a single Cobb–Douglas production function of labor and a single homogeneous physical capital good of great plasticity of form and use. Actually, if there are a finite number of alternative capital goods and activity techniques, the factor-price frontier will have corners.[5] At such points, the elasticity coefficient is defined within a limited range of values (corresponding to all the slopes between the limiting slopes to the left and right of the point in question). At such corner points, a limited range of relative shares must be possible, depending upon the relative proportions of labor and non-labor inputs that can coexist there.

I shall not give here the mathematical proofs of all these assertions about elasticity and factor shares, and yet simple literary reasoning may at first be insufficient to convince the reader of the truth of what I have been saying. An interesting point developed in the next sections is that even in our discrete-activity fixed-coefficient model of heterogeneous physical capital goods, the factor prices (wage and interest rates) can still be given various long-run marginalism (i.e. partial derivative) interpretations. And all this without our ever having to pretend there is any quantitative aggregate of homogeneous 'capital' that itself truly produces anything.

The exact model of the Clark–Ramsey parable

Now let us forget our realistic book of blueprints. Instead suppose labor and a homogeneous capital jelly (*physical* not dollar jelly!) produce a flow of homogeneous net national product, which can consist of consumption goods or of net capital (i.e. jelly)

5. On double-log paper the frontier will consist of arches joining in cusps.

formation, the two being infinitely substitutable (in the long run, or possibly even in the short run) on a one-for-one basis. The resulting production function obeys constant-returns-to-scale and may have smooth substitutability and well-behaved marginal-productivity partial derivatives. Such a Ramsey model, if it held, could justify all of Solow's statistical manipulations with full rigor.

As is well known, labor's share is given by total labor times its marginal productivity. The marginal productivity of capital (jelly) tells us how much a unit of the stock of capital can add to its own rate of capital formation per unit time: the result is the (own) rate of profit or interest, a pure number per unit time like 0·06 or 0·18 per annum. It would even be 1·5 per annum if society could earn 150 per cent per year on its productive investments.

Since only factor-proportions count, Figure 4(a) shows the different real-wage and profit rates that would have to prevail at each level of capital–labor intensity in accordance with the law of diminishing returns. To get the factor-price frontier, we simply plot the magnitude of the upper curve against that of the lower, with the result shown in Figure 4(b).

Note how generally similar are the frontiers of Figure 2(b) and Figure 4(b), even though the former has been *rigorously* derived from a definitely *heterogeneous* capital-goods model and the latter from the neoclassical fairy tale. Indeed if we invent the right fairy tale, we can come as close as we like to duplicating the true blueprint reality in all its complexity. The approximating neoclassical production function is my new concept of the sur-rogate production function.

But what is the interpretation of the capital jelly J that all this presupposes? This can be called the surrogate (homogeneous) capital that gives exactly the same result as does the shifting collection of diverse physical capital goods in our more realistic model on pages 218–23. How can the quantity of surrogate capital J be computed at each stationary equilibrium situation in the Ramsey–Clark neoclassical model? Merely by calculating the slope of the factor-price frontier at each and every point and multiplying it by the easily measurable labor at that point. (See point 1 on page 226.)

There is still another way of calculating (or verifying) the magnitude of the surrogate capital that is to go into the surrogate production function that will predict all behavior. In any situation, there will be an observed market (or shadow) interest rate, and observed total output, and an observed labor share. The residual share of property, when capitalized at the observed interest or profit rate must, under our postulated absence of uncertainty, be equal exactly to the balance sheet value of heterogeneous capital goods, where each is evaluated at its well-determined equilibrium market price as established by spirited bidding of numerous suppliers and demanders. Call this observable national aggregate V and recall that, at the market rate of profit or interest, it yields the non-labor share. But the same is true of surrogate capital J. So, under our postulations, one can rigorously estimate J by

$$J \equiv V \equiv P_\alpha K_\alpha + P_\beta K_\beta + \dots,$$

where the equilibrium market (*numéraire*) prices of the heterogeneous physical capitals are weights that most definitely do change as the real-wage and interest rate are higher along the factor-price frontier.[6]

Conclusion

I trust the above shows that simple neoclassical capital models in a rigorous and specifiable sense can be regarded as the stylized version of a certain quasi-realistic MIT model of diverse heterogeneous capital goods' processes. But it is well to emphasize that a full-blown realistic MIT model cannot be so simply summarized.[7]

6. While I come to defend Solow, not criticize him, this shows he might better have used a current-weighted index number of capital (measured in terms of *numéraire* units) rather than the available fixed-weight indexes that purport to measure relevant real capital. The resulting bias ought to be roughly calculable.

7. I am grateful to Professor Piero A. Garegnani of Rome, formerly of Cambridge University and in 1961–2 a visiting Rockefeller Fellow at MIT, for saving me from asserting the false conjecture that my extreme assumption of equi-proportional inputs in the consumption and machine trades could be lightened and still leave one with many of the surrogate propositions. I hope he will publish his note showing why the surrogate case is so special. [See Garegnani, 1970 – *Eds.*]

Notes

1. Let Q = consumption goods plus net capital formation

$$= C + dJ/dt$$

$$= F(L, J) = L\,F\left(1, \frac{J}{L}\right) \equiv L\,F\left(\frac{J}{L}\right), \qquad 1$$

real wage $= w = \dfrac{\partial Q}{\partial L} = F\left(\dfrac{J}{L}\right) - \dfrac{J}{L}\,F'\left(\dfrac{J}{L}\right), \qquad 2$

$\qquad r$ = instantaneous interest (or profit) rate per annum

$$= \frac{\partial Q}{\partial J} = \frac{\partial (dJ/dt)}{\partial J} = F'\left(\frac{J}{L}\right). \qquad 3$$

Equations **2** and **3** are parametric equations for the frontier,[8] whose slope satisfies the basic duality relation

$$\frac{dw}{dr} = \frac{dw/d(J/L)}{dr/d(J/L)} = \frac{F' - F' - (J/L)F''}{F''} = -\frac{J}{L}.$$

Elasticity $= -\dfrac{w}{r}\dfrac{dr}{dw} \equiv \dfrac{wL}{rJ}$ = ratio of relative shares.

2. Suppose for some reason we pretended factor J were not directly observable to us. It could still be the case that all the intensive magnitudes Q/L, r, w would be uniquely inferable if any one of them were specified; and from the technical relation between any two of these, we could deduce the other relations and could also deduce the production function and any other relations that do involve J or any intensive ratios it can enter into.

8. Consider any homogeneous production function of the first degree, and involving any number of inputs $Q = Q(x_1, \ldots, x_n) \equiv m^{-1}Q(mx_1, \ldots, mx_n)$, $m > 0$. The usual returns assumptions are that $1 \leqslant Q(x_1, \ldots, x_n)$ defines a convex set; in the most 'regular', smooth case this means that the singular hessian matrix $(\partial^2 Q/\partial x_i\,\partial x_j)$ be negative semi-definite of rank $n-1$. We can easily define its factor-price frontier, by writing down the *minimum unit cost function*

$$c(w_1, \ldots, w_n) = \min_{\{x_i\}} \frac{\sum_1^n w_j x_j}{Q(x_1, \ldots, x_n)}.$$

This is a 'dual' function to Q, with the same homogeneity and convexity properties. For any number of factors, the convex-to-the-origin real-factor-price frontier is defined by $1 = c(w_1, \ldots, w_n)$, possessing the duality properties $\partial w_i/\partial w_j = -x_j/x_i$ and $-Ew_i/Ew_j = (w_j x_j)/(w_i x_i)$, relative factor shares.

Now the relations among w, r and Q/L that prevail for the quasi-realistic complete system of heterogeneous capital goods (pages 218–21) can – by extensions of modern linear and concave programming methods – be shown to have the same formal properties as does the parable system. (Note: this is not an approximation but a rigorous equivalence.) This perhaps justifies the surrogate production function as a useful summarizing device.

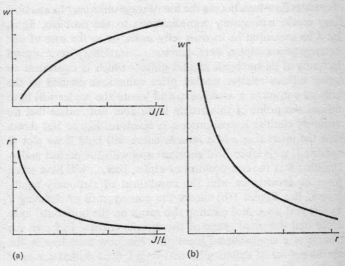

Figure 4 (a) Factor prices in relation to factor proportions.
(b) The surrogate frontier

3. If Q is not a single product or a fixed-composition dose of goods, relative price-ratios will generally change as the profit and real-wage rates change. This is the fatal flaw in a simple labor theory of value, as Ricardo's critics kept reminding him and as he himself realized. One would have thought he would cut his losses, but he persisted in thinking his theory could be defended as some kind of a useful approximation. I cut my losses and offer the surrogate function only as a dramatic model to show that mere *physical* heterogeneity need not lead to qualitatively new behavior patterns.

4. This surrogate case gives another example where a labor theory of value can help to make the analysis more complicated. Faced with a heterogeneous model in which there are terrible index-number problems involved in measuring any aggregate, some modern economists fall back in despair on wage units as a best approximation for measurement, including the measurement of some kind of an aggregate of capital itself. The present model, in which we know rigorously exactly where we are at each stage illustrates how treacherous the use of wage units may be and how they create *unnecessary* complications to the problem. Thus, let J be measured in its own jelly units, or in the case of our heterogeneous alpha, beta, gamma,... stationary state model in terms of its surrogate capital units – which is equivalent to using various relative market price valuations divided by the unit of output as a *numéraire*, and where the reader will have missed the point of this article if he does not realize that no viciously circular logical process is involved. Figure 5(a) shows that the usual shape of a returns curve will hold if we plot Q against J, with labor held constant and with the perfect understanding that the composition of alpha, beta,... will have taken form in consistence with the conditions of stationary equilibrium. But Figure 5(b) shows the consequence of deflating J by the real wage and plotting the result on the horizontal axis. Note that the usual shape of the returns curve – and even the notion of a single-valued function – has now been lost by the gratuitous act of deflating by real wages. (The dotted curves of the two figures show the same treacherous behavior of wage units in the simplest neoclassical case of the logically possible kind of versatile physical capital that is capable of being used with varying proportions of labor.)

5. Once relative commodity prices change, we lose our single real-wage rate and must define a different real-wage rate $(w/P_1, w/P_2,...)$ for each final good 1, 2,... with price of $P_1, P_2,....$ Each will be a function of the pure profit rate r defining its industry's frontier; but must each be a declining function?

At first one is tempted to ask: while raising the profit rate certainly must lower the real wage in terms of a good that has a longer-than-average period of production, can it not possibly raise the real wage of a very short-lived good?

The answer, in our model on pages 218–21, can be shown to be, no. Since every good involves some finite time in its production, raising the interest rate must lower the real wage expressed in terms of each and every good. Here is a brief sketch of a proof.

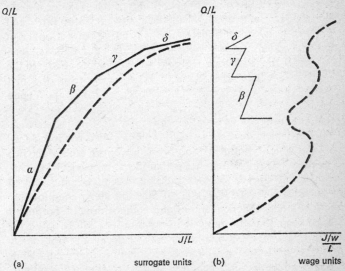

(a)   surrogate units   (b)   wage units

Figure 5 (a) The surrogate function. (b) The distortion from wage units

With no joint products, my 1960 generalized substitution theorem (in the Åkerman *Festschrift*) assures us that the price pattern at any profit rate is independent of final demand. And so for any one good we can always assume that it alone is produced – which brings us back to the already settled one-good case. *Q.E.D.*

6. The following analysis shows how to derive the factor-price frontiers in the general case when the proportions of inputs in various consumption- and capital-goods industries are not necessarily alike. For any possible process, such as alpha or gamma, let a_c and a_k represent the labor requirements per unit flow of consumption- and capital-goods output respectively; let b_c and b_k represent respectively the needed capital-goods inputs for the same purposes; and let δ represent the depreciation

factor as before. Then the following cost-of-production equations must hold.

$$P_k = a_k W + b_k(r+\delta)P_k$$
$$P_c = a_c W + b_c(r+\delta)P_k.$$

These can be easily solved to give P_c/P_k whenever the profit rate r is specified[9]; with r specified, the real-wage rates W/P_c and W/P_k can be also easily determined. Alternatively, if either of these real-wage rates is specified, we can solve the above equations to get the profit rate and all the other price-ratios. (In the special case where $P_k = P_c$, $a_c = a_k$, $b_c = b_k$, from the first equation alone we can get $W/P_c = \{1-b_k(r+\delta)\}/a_k$ and Figure 2(b).)

Note that the above equations are valid also in a neoclassical model in which there is a versatile homogeneous capital (call it K or J) which combines smoothly with labor in each of the two industries. The only difference is that the a and b coefficients are no longer a finite set of constants but instead become smooth functions of the ratio $(W/P_k)/(r+\delta)$. Since the above equations are intensive ones, independent of the composition of output, it will be clear that the same industry frontiers will be valid for states of *balanced* exponential growth or decay and not merely for stationary states in which no widening of capital-cum-labor is permitted. However, when the system is growing exponentially, a different over-all social capital–output ratio will hold at the same profit–wage point if the machine industry needs relatively less or more of machines than does the consumption industry. This shows that the slope and elasticity of any one frontier does *not* in the general case give relative factors and shares.[10]

9. In an unpublished paper, I have shown how such equations provide a powerful generalization of the factor-price equalization theorem. With appropriate a/b intensities and non-specialization, equalization by trade of goods prices will equalize the interest rate r and not merely the rentals of machines; of course, all this without any flows of investment funds at all!

10. If true joint-costs are present, the non-substitution theorem fails. There will then be no simple trade-off between r and w independent of the composition of demands for C and $\dot{J}$ and no real-wage/interest rate frontier curve definable. Example: the social transformation function $(C^2+\dot{j}^2)^{\frac{1}{2}} = (LJ)^{\frac{1}{2}}$ can yield as equilibrium profit-wage configurations *any* point in the two-dimensional quadrant of Figure 4 (b) that lies *beyond* a certain rectangular hyperbola, if only we make the composition of final demand for consumption and investment appropriate!

7. Can wage and profit rates be given a 'marginal productivity' interpretation in our realistic blueprint economy? Yes, as dual variables even though surrogate or other capital aggregates are eschewed. Thus, let

$$\ldots, r_{t-1}, w_{t-1}, r_t, w_t, \ldots,$$

represent equilibrium market prices corresponding to the following production-possibility schedule for society

$$T(\ldots, C_{t-1}, C_{t+1}, C_1, \ldots; \ldots) = 0,$$

where the dots beyond the final semi-colon refer to initial and terminal stocks of *all* physical capital goods. Then necessarily

$$(1+r_t) = -\frac{\partial C_{t+1}}{\partial C_t}$$

$$w_t = \frac{\partial C_t}{\partial L_t}.$$

If the market (or State) has the foresight to price correctly only for very short periods and if there are very few alternative activities and techniques, this transformation locus can have very sharp corners and the range of possible slopes or marginal productivities may be wide; hence the above equalities become non-narrow inequalities, which are then of limited predictive value.

8. Historical comments. The dual relation of note 1 is an easy extension of Wicksteed's 1896 exposition of homogeneous production functions, and will surprise no reader of the works on indirect or dual-utility functions by Hotelling, L. Court, R. Roy, Houthakker, Samuelson, and others over the last thirty years.

The frontier itself is implied in Joan Robinson's book on Marx and by von Thünen. Sraffa gives a version of it in his 1960 book, based upon researches of the earlier thirty-five years. Before my own article on Marx (1957), I know of no explicit reference to its properties. Relevant also are my earlier papers on Ricardo, factor-price equalization, simple and generalized substitution theorems, LeChatelier principles and the Legendre transformations of thermodynamic and general minimum systems.

The J. B. Clark parable was given rigorous form in Frank

Ramsey's 1928 production function. Solow, Tobin, Meade, Phelps, Uzawa, Swan and I have written extensively on related and generalized models. Joan Robinson has properly questioned the Clark model's realism and relevance, and Nicholas Kaldor is even more scathing in rejecting neoclassical production functions. Simple Harrod–Domar models are often interpretable in terms of a fixed-proportion homogeneous function.

Reference

GAREGNANI, P. (1970), 'Heterogeneous capital, the production function and the theory of distribution', *Rev. econ. Stud.*, vol. 37, pp. 407–36.

11 P. A. Samuelson

A Summing Up[1]

P. A. Samuelson, 'A summing up', *Quarterly Journal of Economics*,
vol. 80, 1966, pp. 568–83.

The phenomenon of switching back at a very low interest rate
to a set of techniques that had seemed viable only at a very high
interest rate involves more than esoteric technicalities. It shows
that the simple tale told by Jevons, Böhm-Bawerk, Wicksell and
other neoclassical writers – alleging that, as the interest rate
falls in consequence of abstention from present consumption in
favor of future, technology must become in some sense more
'roundabout', more 'mechanized' and 'more productive' –
cannot be universally valid.

The simplest Austrian and more general models

Figure 1 shows the simple picture of Böhm-Bawerk and von
Hayek, in which labor is applied *uniformly* for a shorter (or
longer) period of time and in consequence society gets a smaller
(or larger) output of consumption. When the structure of production is elongated, as in going from 1(a)'s short period of
production to 1(b)'s longer period and to 1(c)'s still longer period,
each unit of consumption good is produced with successively
less total labor – from $5+5 = 10$, down to $3+3+3 = 9$, down
to $2+2+2+2 = 8$ units of labor. In 1(a) the interest rate is
thought to be high in reflection of society's small stock of goods
in process. By accumulating more goods in process to fill the
longer-period pipeline of 1(b), society ends up with one-ninth
more steady-state consumption and with a lower interest rate.
By building up Böhm-Bawerk's 'subsistence fund' enough to

1. My thanks go to the Carnegie Corporation for providing me with a
reflective year in 1965–6 and to Felicity Skidmore for research assistance.
None of the other writers in the symposium has seen this summary, which
reflects my own appraisals only.

get into a 1(c) configuration, society enjoys still another increment of steady state consumption (arriving at nine-eighths of the 1(b) level or ten-eighths of the 1(a) level) and again with a still lower interest rate.

Readers of Böhm-Bawerk's *Positive Theory* or von Hayek's *Prices and Production* will not need Descartes' rule of signs to be convinced that 1(c) is more roundabout or mechanized than

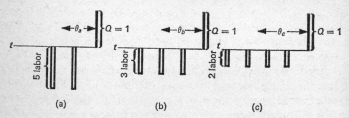

(a)   (b)   (c)

Figure 1 In the conventional Austrian model, labor is uniformly applied prior to production of final output. In going from 1(a) to 1(b) the average period of production, however measured, rises and reduces the total labor needed per unit of output. 1(c) is still more roundabout in the Austrian sense, and lowering of interest or profit rate leads unequivocally to lengthening of the period of production and to all the conventional features of the neoclassical capital-theory parables.

1(b) or 1(a), and that as the interest rate declines the competitive system can never go back to 1(a) (or any other Figure 1 state) once it has been left behind.[2]

But now look at Figure 2, which tells more simply the full story of the twenty-fifth and eighth degree polynomials of the Sraffa–Pasinetti example of reswitching. Is 2(a) more or less roundabout than 2(b)? Our eye looks at the time-shape of labor inputs and cannot say: are 7 units of labor invested for 2 time periods more or less roundabout than 6 units of labor invested for 1 period and 2 units invested for 3 periods of time?

There is no obvious answer. Of course, we can calculate

2. I have not appended to Figure 1 the familiar triangle of goods in process, obtainable from synchronized steady-state repetitions of each of these processes. 1(a)'s triangle would be visibly longer than 1(b)'s. However, when labor is not applied uniformly – as in Figure 2 – the structures are not simple triangles and a measure of length becomes more ambiguous.

Böhm-Bawerk's arithmetic-average-time-period of production,[3] but such a measure presupposes simple rather than compound interest and has no longer a presumptive claim on our attention. For what it is worth, 2(a) has a longer conventional period of production than 2(b). Yet at very high interest rates, i.e. more than 100 per cent per period, 2(a) will win out in the competitive market over 2(b). Lest you think 2(b) must therefore be more roundabout, be warned that when the interest rate drops below 50 per cent per period, 2(a) again drives out 2(b) and it continues to hold its own down to a zero interest rate.[4] (Admittedly, 100

3. In 1(a) this weighted-mean is given by

$$\theta = \frac{5 \text{ labor} \times 2 \text{ periods} + 5 \text{ labor} \times 1 \text{ period}}{5 \text{ labor} + 5 \text{ labor}} = 1\frac{1}{2} \text{ periods}$$

$$= \frac{\sum_{1}^{N} L_t \times t}{\sum_{1}^{N} L_t} \quad \text{in general}$$

$$= \frac{S}{\sum L_t}$$

where S is the subsistence fund, consisting of total goods in process (evaluated at their *labor* costs!) and $\sum L_t$ is total output (evaluated at labor costs).

For 1(b), $\theta = \dfrac{3 \times 3 \text{ periods} + 3 \times 2 \text{ periods} + 3 \times 1 \text{ periods}}{9 \text{ labor}} = 2 \text{ periods}$.

For 1(c), $\theta = 2\frac{1}{2}$ periods.

Generally, if labor is invested *uniformly* over $(1, 2, ..., N)$ periods,

$$\theta = \frac{1 + 2 + ... + N}{N} = \frac{N+1}{2} \text{ periods}.$$

Hence, in the simple Böhm-Bawerk triangular structure of production, θ and the range N move always in the same direction (as do all higher statistical moments). Böhm-Bawerk's θ in effect neglects compound interest in favor of simple interest, ignoring interest on the interest part of the value of all intermediate goods. For 2(a) and 2(b), we get respectively

$$\theta = \frac{2 \times 3 \text{ periods} + 0 + 6 \times 1 \text{ periods}}{8} = 1\frac{1}{2} \text{ periods}$$

$$\theta = \frac{0 + 7 \times 2 \text{ periods}}{7} = 2 \text{ periods}.$$

4. At a zero interest rate, the process with the lowest total labor requirement, $\sum L_t$, the zeroth statistical moment, will win out. For two processes with tied $\sum L_t$, Böhm-Bawerk's measurement of mean θ, or first moment, will be decisive at low interest rates: that with lower θ will be preferred, as can be determined from simple interest calculations alone. But, as Wicksell pointed out to Böhm-Bawerk, compound interest (involving higher powers of i) means that, in general, along with the mean we must also calculate the

per cent and 50 per cent are high rates, selected merely to keep the arithmetic simple. The reader can think of each period as a decade if he wants to pretend to be realistic.)

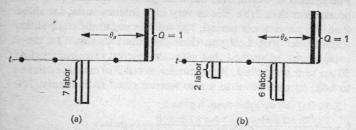

(a)   (b)

Figure 2 Comparing the time intensity of 2(a) and 2(b) is ambiguous: is 7 labor invested for two periods less or more roundabout than 2 labor for three periods and 6 for one period? At interest rate above 100 per cent per period, 2(a) will be used; at interest rate between 50 and 100 per cent, 2(b) will be used; but at interest below 50 per cent, the system reswitches back to 2(a)!

Why reswitching can occur

To help economic intuition, suppose champagne is the end product of both 2(a) and 2(b). In 2(a), 7 units of labor make 1 unit of brandy in one period. Then 1 brandy ferments by itself into 1 unit of champagne in one more period. In 2(b), 2 units of labor make 1 grapejuice in one period. In one further period 1 grapejuice ripens by itself into 1 wine. Then 6 units of labor shaking 1

---

variance, the skewness, kurtosis and all the higher moments of the time distribution of labor invested. Hicks (1946, pt 3, pt 4 and ch. 17 app.) gives a quite different definition of 'the average period of production', which allegedly *always* increases as the interest rate declines. As applied to 2(a) and 2(b), it would seem to say that 2(a) has a longer and longer average production period as interest drops steadily from 200 per cent to 100 per cent – even though technology has not changed at all! Actually, however, the Hicks definition cannot even be applied to the comparisons of 1(a), 1(b), 1(c) or 2(a), 2(b). For Hicks's definition must take into account the fact that, under perfect competition with free entry and constant-returns-to-scale, the prices of all final, intermediate and input goods will change with the interest rate until *net* present-discounted-values are again zero. Then *his* average is found to be always infinite! cf. Samuelson (1947, p. 188). Hicks (1965, ch. 13) is in agreement with the upshot of the present symposium.

unit of wine can in one more period produce 1 champagne. All champagne is interchangeable.

Now what happens at very high interests, above 100 per cent per period? Interest on interest on interest of the 2 units of labor invested for 3 periods in 2(b) becomes so colossal as to make the 2(b) way of producing champagne ridiculously dear. So, of course, 2(a) gets used at highest interest rates.

Now go to the other extreme. At zero interest, or negligible interest, only labor and wage cost matters. 2(a) takes only 7 units of labor in *all* the stages, as against 2(b)'s 8 units in all. So again, at very low interest rates, 2(a) wins out competitively.

Does 2(b) ever give lower cost of production of champagne? Yes. For any interest rate between 50 and 100 per cent, 2(b) turns out to be best. Let us verify that 2(a) and 2(b) are tied at the switching point $1+i = 1+1$ corresponding to 100 per cent interest per period. Suppose each unit of labor costs $W = \$1$. Then 1 brandy costs $7 wages + $7 interest = $14. And 1 champagne from 2(a) costs $14 brandy + $14 interest = $28. Now calculate the 2(b) cost. 1 grapejuice costs $2 wages + $2 interest = $4. 1 wine costs $4 grapejuice + $4 interest = $8. And 1 champagne costs ($8 wine + $6 wages) + $14 interest = $28, the same as in 2(a).

The reader can verify that 2(a) and 2(b) are again tied at $1+i = 1+0.5$, at $15.75 each. But now try an intermediate case, $1+i = 1+0.6$. Then brandy costs $7 (1·6) = $11.2. And champagne costs $11.2 (1·6) = $17.920 from 2(a). However, from 2(b) it costs only $17.792: namely, grapejuice costs $2 (1·6) = $3.2; wine costs $3.2 (1·6) = $5.12; and finally, champagne from 2(b) costs ($5.12 + $6) (1·6) = $17.792, seen to be the only economic result.[5]

5. The present example, like that of Pasinetti, represents a decomposable or reducible matrix. Thus, there are goods – like grapejuice or brandy – that do not require champagne as an input, directly or indirectly. Hence, the submatrices of the two processes are also decomposable. Furthermore, brandy of one process does not need grapejuice of the other as an input. Hence, the present example does not *itself* refute the Levhari theorem, which purported to apply to indecomposable or irreducible matrices only. However, the Levhari theorem is false, as the irreproachable counter-examples of Morishima, Sheshinski and Garegnani show. Moreover, each of these Pasinetti-type *sub*matrices can be made indecomposable by

Figure 3 summarizes the effect of interest rate changes on the relative costs of producing champagne by the two methods. At very high rates of i, 2(b) costs much more than 2(a). The cost ratio, C_B/C_A, falls as i falls, reaching unity at the switchpoint S_{ab} of Figure 3; it continues to fall until i is about 70 per cent per period, rising from this minimum as i falls farther. At the switchpoint, S_{ba}, again the cost ratio equals unity, continuing to rise to the eight-sevenths level of pure labor costs at $i = 0$.

Reswitching in a durable-machine model

The simplest possible example of reswitching has been demonstrated for an Austrian circulating-capital model. The same kind of arithmetic can be used to show that similar reswitching can occur in a durable-machine model.

Suppose we have two machines, each producible instantaneously by 1 unit of labor. Machine A yields 18 units of output 1 period later and 54 units of output 3 periods later. Machine B yields 63 units of output 2 periods later. Which is more durable? More capital intensive? At a zero rate of interest, the present discount value (PDV) of A exceeds that of B (since $18 + 54 > 63$). At an interest rate of 100 per cent per period, both turn out to have equal PDV and choice will be indifferent between them. At still higher interest rate, say 200 per cent per period, machine A will turn out to have the higher PDV. At interest rates between 50 and 100 per cent per period, machine B will turn out to be more profitable. But – and this is the essence of reswitching – below 50 per cent machine A will again have the preferable PDV.[6]

---

adding as a requirement for its first output at least a little of *its* final output. This would still leave a *total* system matrix, composed of two indecomposable submatrices, but *itself decomposable*. This decomposability can be got rid of by the following device: Let the production of first-stage brandy and of first-stage grapejuice each require, along with labor and a little end-good champagne requirements, a little of penultimate-stage wine *and* brandy. This would convert the Pasinetti–Sraffa model into an irreproachable indecomposable matrix, and provide a legitimate counterexample to the Levhari proposition.

6. Note that the numbers (7) and (6, 2) have been modified to (18, 54) and (63) so that the switching points will again be at $i = 0.5$ and $i = 1$. For the cautious reader, I append the following table of (i: PDV_A, PDV_B), drawn up on the assumption that output sells for $1 per unit (0: $72, $63;

In passing, I should mention that Irving Fisher's technique of calculating present discount values handles all cases, that of durable capital goods and the circulating-capital model of Böhm-Bawerk's *Positive Theory of Capital*. Moreover, Fisher's

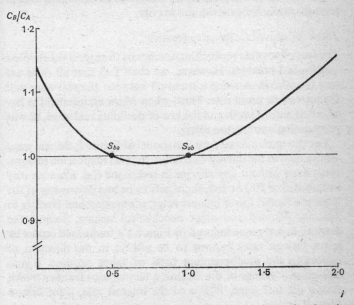

Figure 3 Reswitching back to 2(a) from 2(b) occurs because the plotted curve of relative cost fails to be one-directional. Between switch points, technique 2(b) is used: elsewhere 2(a) is used

tools of general equilibrium put Böhm-Bawerk's theory of interest on a rigorous basis for the first time, showing how Böhm-Bawerk's two subjective factors of time preference interact with his third factor of technical productivity to produce an equilibrium pattern of interest. It is ironical that Böhm-Bawerk should have rejected Fisher's analysis in rather churlish terms, in part because of his propensity to differentiate his product

0·5: $28, $28; 0·66: $22.464, $22.68; 1: $15.75, $15.75; 2: $8, $2.33). A sample calculation for $i = 0.5$ and $1/(1+i) = 0.66$ goes as follows:

$$\$18(0·66) + \$54(0·66)^3 = \$12 + \$16 = \$28 \text{ and } \$63(0·66)^2 = \$28.$$

from that of all other writers and in part because of the archaic nineteenth-century notion that a quasi-mathematical formulation fails to come to grips with the true essence and causality of an economic problem.

For the rest of this comment, I shall stick to circulating-capital models merely for expositional brevity.

The well-behaved factor-price frontier

The fact of possible reswitching teaches us to suspect the simplest neoclassical parables. However, we shall find that all cases are well behaved in showing a trade-off between the real wage and the interest or profit rate. Thus, when Marx enunciated the law of falling rate of profit and the law of declining real wage, he was proclaiming one law too many.

For the conventional Austrian model of Figure 1, the real wage always rises as the interest rate falls – for two reinforcing reasons. First, even without any change in technique (i.e. when we stay in case 1(a) or 1(b) or 1(c), there gets to be less *discounting* of the wage product at lower interest rates, a phenomenon familiar to Taussig, Wicksell and other neoclassical writers. Second, the changes in technique induced in Figure 1's traditional model by lower interest rates happen to be always in the direction of increasing the prediscounting total of labor product. Figure 4(a) gives a picture of the declining factor-price frontier, which relates the real wage, W/P, and the interest rate, i, for Böhm-Bawerk's case.

But now turn to the reswitching example of Figure 2. Can we still be sure that its factor-price frontier is a declining one? Assuredly there is less discounting of wage product at lower i. But it is no longer universally true that a lower i induces a change in technique which increases the prediscounting labor product. Figure 4(b) shows the factor-price frontier as the outer envelope of the light frontiers appropriate to each technique. The switch points are marked S_{ba} and S_{ab}, the latter being the point at which a lowering of i shifts us from 2(a)'s technique to 2(b)'s. Examine S_{ba}. There a lowering of i does increase W/P for both reasons – since 2(a) does give greater (gross) undiscounted wage product than 2(b), namely product of one-seventh rather than one-eighth. But when you examine S_{ab}, the lowering of interest rate from 101 per cent per period to 99 per cent is seen to induce a change from the 2(a) to 2(b) technique, thereby lowering prediscounting product to one-eighth from one-seventh!

Why can we be sure that in every case the envelope frontier slopes downward, which means that the improvement in real

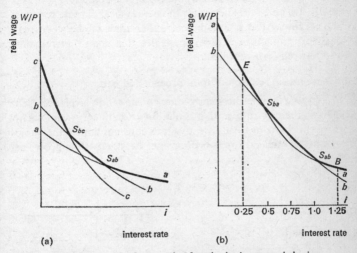

Figure 4 In every case the factor-price frontier is downward sloping, with real wage rising as interest rate drops. In the conventional Austrian case of Figure 1 there is both less discounting and an increase in prediscounting gross labor output. In Figure 2's reswitching example, only the first reason operates, being at first partially offset by 2(b)'s drop in prediscounting gross labor output

wage from less discounting always outweighs any 'perverse' disimprovement in gross product? This follows geometrically from the properties of a continuous outer envelope. Economically, it follows from the workings of ruthless competition. Under perfect competition, either workers can hire capital goods or capitalists hire workers. At a lower interest rate, or cost of capital, workers can always pay themselves a higher real wage even without changing techniques; so capitalists will have to match up. And ruthless competition will ensure that, at any given i and money wage, the price of the finished product will be at its minimum – thus ensuring the maximum W/L out on the declining envelope.

Figure 4 shows the real wage in terms of the final consumption good, champagne in our case. But the same declining frontier could be drawn for the real wage expressed in terms of any intermediate product – such as grapejuice, wine or brandy.

Both 4(a) and 4(b) show that the neoclassical parable remains valid as far as the factor-price frontier trade-off between real wage and profit rate is concerned. But that is all that remains valid regardless of reswitching.

Unconventional relation of total product and interest

Now let us examine the steady-state consumption levels for each different interest rate i. If population is stationary (and technology unchanging), this steady-state consumption is the same thing as real net national product per head. (If labor grows at

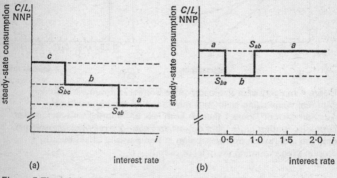

(a)   interest rate   (b)   interest rate

Figure 5 The left-hand Austrian model shows the conventional rise in steady-state *per capita* consumption as the interest rate falls, as a result of the alleged fact that roundaboutness is productive. But the reswitching example on the right illustrates that, at first, steady-state consumption may decline at lower interest rates, only agreeing ultimately with the diminishing returns tale of the neoclassical parable

the geometric rate of n per year, we could generalize our analysis by plotting *per capita* consumption against each different i rate, an easy task skipped here.)

In the nice Austrian case of the parable, Figure 5(a) shows that lowering interest always, if anything, raises net national product (NNP) and steady-state consumption. As we move from 1(a) to 1(b) to 1(c), the steps marked a, b, c in Figure 5(a) are shown as rising. At $i = 0$, we are in the Schumpeter–Ramsey Golden Rule state of Bliss, with maximum NNP.

But Figure 5(b) shows a reversal of direction of the steps as a result of Figure 2's reswitching. When i drops from 101 per cent per period to 99 per cent, NNP actually falls. Of course, diminishing returns asserts itself 'eventually', in that at zero interest rate we are in the Golden Rule state of Bliss. (But note that this maximum level of consumption was also reached for interest rates above 100 per cent. It is no longer literally true[7] to say, 'Society moves from high interest rates to low by sacrificing current consumption goods in return for more consumption later, but with each further dose of accumulation of capital goods resulting in a lower and lower social yield of incremental product.' Actually, society can go from B to E in Figure 4(b) without making any physical changes at all: a reduction of profit from a 125 per cent rate per period to a 25 per cent rate, merely lowers what a critic might call the 'degree of exploitation of labor' prevailing. In Figure 5(a) the apologist for capital and for thrift has a less difficult case to argue.

Unconventional capital–output ratios

Since the Second World War the literature on growth and development has brought the capital–output ratio into prominence. Before the war this concept was met frequently in the shape of the accelerator. And Böhm-Bawerk's average period of

7. The reversal of direction of the (i, NNP) relation was, I must confess, the single most surprising revelation from the reswitching discussion. I had thought this relation could not change its curvature if the underlying technology was convex, so that there had to be a concave, basic Fisher (intertemporal) production-possiblity frontier, of the form

$$0 = F(K_0; C_0, C_1, \ldots, C_T; K_T),$$

where K_0 is the vector of initial capital stocks, K_T the vector of terminal capital stocks and C_t the vector of consumption goods available at any time t. I had wrongly confused concavity of F with concavity of the (i, NNP) steady-state locus. Note that reswitching *reveals* this possible curvature phenomenon, but is not necessary for it. Later I correct another misconception revealed by reswitching.

production, θ, was actually a primitive capital–output ratio, namely that one which would prevail if the interest rate were zero and all goods could be priced at their wage costs alone: i.e. θ can be written as the ratio of Böhm-Bawerk's subsistence fund, S, to final output, where S and NNP are both reckoned in labor terms or wage costs alone.

More accurately, we can calculate for each interest rate i, the true market cost of each intermediate and final good inclusive of interest as well as wage costs, and can calculate the aggregate value of all capital goods. This can then be divided by the true market value of all final goods, to give the capital–output ratio.

Figure 6(a) shows that in the simple model of Böhm-Bawerk, von Hayek and other Austrians, the capital–output ratio does rise steadily as the interest rate falls. This duplicates the behavior

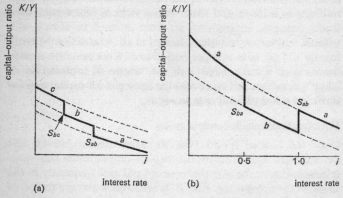

(a)   interest rate   (b)   interest rate

Figure 6 In the neoclassical case on the left, lowering the interest rate is expected to raise the capital–output ratio. However, the reswitching example of Figure 2 involves a fall in the capital–output ratio as i drops through the point S_{ab}, inducing a less rather than more capital-intensive technique

of the simplest J. B. Clark parable of a single homogeneous capital that, together with labor, produces aggregate output by a standard production function of Cobb–Douglas or more general neoclassical type.

But the reswitching model of Figure 2 is seen in Figure 6(b) to lead to a pattern of capital–output ratio that fails to move in one direction. Thus, at the switch point S_{ab}, lowering i a little induces a shift from 2(a) technique to 2(b), giving rise to a significantly lower capital–output ratio.

Such an unconventional behavior of the capital–output ratio is seen to be definitely possible. It can perhaps be understood in terms of so-called Wicksell and other effects. But no explanation is needed for that which is definitely possible: it demonstrates itself. Moreover, this phenomenon can be called 'perverse' only in the sense that the conventional parables did not prepare us for it.

Such perverse effects do have consequences. Thus, suppose you have a theory of life-cycle saving which, like Modigliani's, attaches significance to the wealth–income or capital–output ratio. Then the dynamic stability of some of your equilibria may be affected by the fact that the capital–output ratio drops as i drops. Similar stability and uniqueness problems may be raised for a Solow–Harrod growth model.

Nevertheless we must accept nature as she is. *In a general blueprint technology model of Joan Robinson and MIT type, it is quite possible to encounter switch points, like* S_{ab} *of Figure 6(b), in which lower profit rates are associated with lower steady-state capital–output ratios.*

Reverse capital deepening and denial of diminishing returns

We can use the contrasting models of Figure 1 and Figure 2 to demonstrate a startling possibility. In the conventional parable, people accumulate capital goods by sacrificing current consumption goods in return for more future consumption goods, with the interest rate depicting the trade-off or substitution ratio between such consumption goods.[8] So far so good. All this turns out to be essentially true in every case.

But, in the conventional model, successive sacrifices of consumption and accumulations of capital goods lead to lower and lower interest rates. This conventional neoclassical version of

8. In all cases, $1 + i_t = -\partial C_{t+1}/\partial C_t$ along the transformation function $T = 0$ of the previous footnote; if smoothness is not present, the above equality becomes an inequality $R \leqslant 1 + i_t \leqslant L$, where L and R are the left-hand and right-hand derivatives $-\partial C_{t+1}/\partial C_t$, which may diverge little or much depending upon the technology.

diminishing returns is spelled out at length in Samuelson (1964, pp. 595–6). Unfortunately, until reswitching had alerted me to the complexity of the process, I had not realized that the conventional account represents only one of two possible outcomes. When we are in the Figure 2 technology, the story can be reversed: after sacrificing present consumption and accumulating capital goods, the new steady-state equilibrium can represent a rise in interest rate![9]

There is perhaps no need for me to describe in detail how the traditional neoclassical model of Figure 1 goes from the high interest rates that make short-period 1(a) optimal to lower interest rates that make 1(b) optimal. Suffice it to assert that, in going from the steady-state of 1(a) (where say 90 labor produce $90/(5+5) = 9$ units of output or consumable NNP per period) to the more roundabout steady state of 1(b) (where the same 90 of labor produce $90/(3+3+3) = 10$ units of NNP), there must first be a net sacrifice of consumption to below the *status quo ex ante* rate of 9 per year.

In fact, Professor Solow (1967), has proved what at first glance appears to be a remarkable theorem, showing that the present discounted value of all the *net* gains in future consumptions resulting from a switch from a process like 1(a) to a process like 1(b) (net in the sense that all sacrifices of consumption must be taken into account, with their proper discount, as subtractions) will balance out to exactly zero, if the interest rate used in discounting is that of the switch point S_{ab} between process 1(a) and 1(b). In a bookkeeping sense, therefore, the Fisherian yield

9. This can happen whenever NNP rises with i, as in Figure 5(b). The change in curvature of the steady-state relation $NNP/L = C/L = f(i)$, when f'' becomes greater than zero, was wrongly thought by me to be ruled out by the fact that $\partial^2 C_{t+1}/\partial C_t^2$ – or its finite-difference equivalent – can never be positive in a convex technology. The last fact is correct, and it has important implications. But it does not imply diminishing returns to the *steady-state* relations of Figure 5. Teleologically speaking, the invisible hand of a competitive system cares nought what happens to NNP but only what happens to what I have called net net national product, which is that available to the primary factor labor alone, excluding the 'necessitous return' to capital (which can be regarded as an intermediate product – like horses and their fodder – producible or available within the system at constant costs once the i rate is specified).

of product received in terms of product sacrificed is precisely measured by the market rate of interest. In this sense the market rate measures the 'net productivity of capital' even in a model where there is no homogeneous capital good of the Meccano set or 'leets' type, and where there are no smoothly substitutable factors in the relevant production functions.

Upon further reflection, one realizes that Solow's result is indeed as much a bookkeeping as a technical relationship. For what else can happen in a system where the rate of interest and the total of wage cost is constant in every period, except that the value of consumption plus the value of net capital formation equals the level of factor income? As we shall see, Solow's result is merely an instance of this general accounting relationship, as applied to a constant-returns-to-scale technology in which residual monopoly profit is always zero because the competitive equalities must prevail.

I rush now to show what happens in the reswitching model of Figure 2 when we move from high interest rate, say 101 per cent per period, down to 100 per cent and subsequently to 99 per cent, thereby going from a steady-state equilibrium using the 2(a) technique to a new steady-state using the 2(b) technique. (Later the interested reader can perform for himself the reverse switch as we go down from 51 to 49 per cent, moving back from 2(b) equilibrium to 2(a) and this time duplicating the conventional consumption-sacrifice of the neoclassical parable.)

Table 1 shows us initially in equilibrium with the 2(a) technique. Up to time 2, all of society's labor (taken to be 56, the product of 7 and 8, to keep the arithmetic simple) is allocated to 2(a), with 8 (or 56/7) output emerging 2 periods later from this stage 2 allocation. After time period 6, the system has moved to a 2(b) equilibrium, producing only 7, or 56/(2+6), units of output or steady-state NNP. In between, society has been splashed with net consumption rather than having to sacrifice consumption: thus, in the transitional periods 3 through 6, the system generates $8+8+6+13 = 35$ units of champagne output which is definitely greater than $32 = 8+8+8+8$. Moreover, in agreement with Solow's theorem, and providing a trivial generalization of it, if we calculate the PDV of the 2(b) steady-state consumption stream, using the interest rate of 100 per cent characterizing the switch point S_{ab} and taking into account the transitional alteration of consumption, we must get the same PDV that the system would have had if it stayed permanently in 2(a).

Table 1 Transition from 2(a) to 2(b) Technique and Back Again

Labor	Time												
	1	2	3	4	5	6	7 ... 20	21	22	23	24	25
Stage 3	0	0	14	14	14	14	14 ... 14	0	0	0	0	0
Stage 2	56	56	42	42	0	0	0 ... 0	14	14	56	56	56
Stage 1	0	0	0	0	42	42	42 ... 42	42	42	0	0	0
Final output		8	8	6	6+7	7 ...	7	7	7	2+7	2	8

In the table the system is left in 2(b) equilibrium from period 7 to period 20. During this time we could imagine the interest rate dropping, suddenly or gradually, to 50 per cent from 100 per cent. Nothing real happens, except that the real wage goes up as a result of less discounting and also the price ratio of finished champagne rises relative to that of earlier-stage products. (Despite Ricardo and Marx, goods do not exchange in proportion to their total labor content, direct plus indirect.)

But now suppose that the system tries to accumulate capital from time 21 to 25. In going from 2(b)'s steady-state level of 7 to 2(a)'s steady-state level 8, the system must indeed sacrifice *consumption net*. Thus, $7+7+9+2 = 25$ is less than

$$7+7+7+7 = 28.^{10}$$

In summary, this section has shown that going to a lower interest rate may have to involve a *dis*accumulation of capital, and a surplus (rather than sacrifice) of current consumption, which is

10. And, at either switch interest rate ($i = 0·5$ of S_b or $i = 1$ of S_{ab}) there must be, at time 21, equality of PDV that would come from maintaining the old equilibrium forever after, with the PDV of the actual transition shown followed by perpetual 2(a) equilibrium. (Which i is then the true Solow net productivity of capital? Answer: either $i = 100$ per cent or $i = 50$ per cent will give the accountant's competitive identity of PDV, an instance of the multiplicity of Fisherian yield known ever since the 1930s.)

balanced by a subsequent perpetual reduction (rather than increase) of consumption as a result of the drop in interest rate. This anomalous behavior, which can happen even in models that do not admit of reswitching, might be called 'reverse capital deepening'. Whether it is empirically rare for this to happen is not an easy question to answer. My suspicion is that a modern mixed economy has so many alternative techniques that it can, so to speak, use time usefully, but will run out of new equally profitable uses and is likely to operate on a curve of 'diminishing[11] returns' (at least after non-constant-returns-to-scale opportunities have been exhausted). In any case, by the time one reaches a zero interest rate (or more generally the Golden Rule state where the interest and growth rates are equal), this kind of diminishing returns must have set in.[12]

Conclusion

Pathology illuminates healthy physiology. Pasinetti, Morishima, Bruno–Burmeister–Sheshinski, Garegnani merit our gratitude for demonstrating that reswitching is a logical possibility in any technology, indecomposable or decomposable. Reswitching, whatever its empirical likelihood, does alert us to several vital possibilities.

11. All my models involve constant-returns-to-scale, a fact not inconsistent with diminishing returns of consumption in terms of interest rate.

12. Suppose society maximizes a generalized Ramsey sum,

$$\sum_{0}^{\infty} \frac{U(C_t/L_t)}{(1+\rho)^t},$$

where ρ begins above $i = 1$. Then the system will have come into steady-state equilibrium using 2(a) as in the first and last part of Table 1. Now let ρ fall suddenly but permanently, say to $i = 0.55$. Then the system will ultimately come into the 2(b) equilibrium of the table's middle part. But suppose the initial drop in ρ has been from, say 1.1, down to 0.4, skipping completely intermediate values. Will the market interest rate drop gradually from $i = $ initial $\rho = 1.1$ to $i = $ new $\rho = 0.4$? The answer is: no. The system will come at once into the new equilibrium, which will be identical with the old labor allocation but with higher real wage and lower profit share. There is a moral here for a system that may not show literal reswitching: as it moves from high-i equilibrium to low-i equilibrium, it may not pass at all near to the equilibrium configurations on the factor-price frontier that correspond to intermediate interest rates! Dr Michael Bruno, visiting MIT and Harvard from Israel in 1965–6, has provided valuable analysis of similar optimal dynamic programs.

Lower interest rates may bring lower steady-state consumption and lower capital–output ratios, and the transition to such lower interest rate can involve denial of diminishing returns and entail reverse capital deepening in which current consumption is augmented rather than sacrificed.

There often turns out to be no unambiguous way of characterizing different processes as more 'capital intensive', more 'mechanized' more 'roundabout', except in the *ex post* tautological sense of being adopted at a lower interest rate and involving a higher real wage. Such a tautological labeling is shown, in the case of reswitching, to lead to inconsistent ranking between pairs of unchanged technologies, depending upon which interest rate happens to prevail in the market.

If all this causes headaches for those nostalgic for the old time parables of neoclassical writing, we must remind ourselves that scholars are not born to live an easy existence. We must respect, and appraise, the facts of life.

References

HICKS, J. R. (1946), *Value and Capital*, Oxford University Press, 2nd edn.

HICKS, J. R. (1965), *Capital and Growth*, Oxford University Press.

SAMUELSON, P. A. (1947), *Foundations of Economic Analysis*, Harvard University Press.

SAMUELSON, P. A. (1964), *Economics*, McGraw-Hill.

SOLOW, R. M. (1967), 'The interest rate and transition between techniques', in C. H. Feinstein (ed.) *Socialism, Capitalism and Economic Growth. Essays Presented to Maurice Dobb*, Cambridge University Press, pp. 30–39.

12 A. Bhaduri

On the Significance of Recent Controversies on Capital Theory: A Marxian View[1]

A. Bhaduri, 'On the significance of recent controversies on capital theory: a Marxian view', *Economic Journal*, vol. 79, 1969, pp. 532–9.

Recent controversies on capital theory between the Cambridge School and the so-called neo-classical school centre on the question of treating 'capital' as a 'factor of production' for a theory of distribution in a capitalist economy. It must be emphasized that questions like the measurement of 'capital' are, as such, not central to the controversy, but assume relevance in so far as they have a direct bearing on the theory of distribution. Since the rate of profit is a pure number per unit of time, distribution of income between 'profits' and 'wages' must reckon 'capital' in the same unit in which wages and income are measured. Consequently, a valuation problem arises unless by assumption 'capital' consists of the stock of the same commodity in which wages are paid, i.e. a one-commodity world. And once this valuation problem is faced, the foundations of a neo-classical parable in which the magnitude of 'capital' as a 'factor of production' is independent of the distribution of income become logically insecure. This is a classical problem in economic theory: Ricardo recognized that, even in his circulating-capital model, the pattern of relative prices corresponds to the ruling (uniform) rate of profit and, consequently, the valuation of commodities entering the production process as 'means of production' is not independent of that ruling rate of profit. Wicksell attacked the Austrian attempt to measure 'capital-intensity' in terms of the 'average period of production'. He realized that no such 'time-measure' of 'capital' was possible independent of the rate of profit. More recently, Piero Sraffa and Joan Robinson have produced logical arguments

1. I am indebted to Joan Robinson, Krishna Bharadwaj, Khaleeq Naqvi and Donald Harris for helpful comments and long discussions on the subject.

emphasizing the limitations of a neo-classical parable. Thus, the rate of profit may be *positively* correlated to the value of capital per man (i.e. the negative Wicksell effect) running counter to the neo-classical story, or what is still more disastrous for the neo-classical parable, the *same* technique of production may be competitive both at a relatively 'high' and a 'low' rate of profit, but dominated by a different technique for the interim values of the rate of profit (i.e. the reswitching of techniques).

Still, then, one may feel, and indeed it is often argued, that all this trouble arising from the valuation of 'capital' is no more than a usual index-number problem. Since ideal index-numbers are hard to find, one should let the matter rest at that and accept the simple-minded neo-classical parable as the *approximate* basis for a theory of distribution in a profit–wage economy. The present paper argues that under the obvious surface of an index-number problem deeper issues lie in connection with the valuation of 'capital'. It is better to face these issues and re-examine the teachings of conventional theory than to dodge them as mere index-number problems. In the view of the present writer, Marx's understanding of the role of 'capital' in the capitalist mode of production focuses attention on some of these central issues, which to the less sophisticated appear no more than yet another index-number problem.

In his famous introduction to *A Contribution to the Critique of Political Economy*, Marx drew an interesting analogy between *language* as a system of communication and the *social* organization of production. Like language, Marx claimed, economic production must be viewed in the context of a social organization: 'Production by isolated individuals outside a society ... is an absurdity as is the idea of development of language without individuals living together and talking to one another' (Marx, 1904, p. 268). Yet there are certain features common to languages of varying degrees of complexity – from the most 'primitive' to the more 'subtle' – which makes language as a *general* concept useful. The same is true of various types of economic organization geared to production. They also exhibit common features which lend themselves to abstraction in terms of general concepts. But the failure to recognize the major points of departure which differentiate one economic organization from another, is according to Marx, the basic source of confusion in political economy.[2] Marx's own distinction between the 'forces of production' and the 'relations of production' is relevant here. The former concept relates to man's relation to nature and technology while the latter corresponds to man's relation to man in a social organization of production. Each type of economic organization develops its own 'relations of production' or 'rules of the game', often sanctioned by law or religion. Marx insisted that concepts that are useful in political economy must take into account these 'rules of the game'. This methodological position gives rise to the notion of Marxian 'categories' by which abstract or general concepts are restricted to a specific set of 'rules of the game'. Economic theory, which ignores such 'rules of the game' and works in terms of general features only, runs the danger of being totally ahistorical in spirit.

Throughout his work, Marx maintained this methodological position in defining the notion of 'capital'. Taken out of a particular form of economic organization, the notion of 'capital' reduces to the idea of mere physical instruments of production or 'stored-up impersonal labour'. To use this notion of 'capital' holding in the abstract in the context of a particular economic organization, for example, the capitalistic mode of production, can be thoroughly misleading if it does not reflect the 'relations of production' which characterize a capitalist economy. Consequently, Marx emphasized that 'capital' in the context of the capitalistic rules of the game is also a *social relation* for commanding labour and generating surplus value. He categorically states: 'The means of production become capital only in so far as they have become separated from the labourer and confront labour as an independent power.'[3] In other words, means of production

2. Thus Marx (1904, p. 269) satirically writes: 'The failure to remember this one fact is the source of all wisdom of modern economists.'

3. Marx (1894, p. 396). Compare also, '. . . this brings to completion the fetishism peculiar to bourgeois Political Economy, the fetishism which metamorphoses the social, economic character impressed on things in the process of social production, into a natural character stemming from the material nature of those things. For instance, "instruments of labour are fixed capital" is a scholastic definition, which leads to contradictions and confusion . . . instruments of labour are fixed capital only if the process of

are *not* 'capital' unless owned by non-labourers. This emphasizes the relevant aspect of 'capital' for a theory of distribution: as a means for generating surplus value by exploiting live labour, capital is also a source of surplus value and income to the capitalists. Thus, 'capital' as a Marxian 'category' notion is: (a) an instrument of production – a pure physical object (belonging to the Marxian notion of 'forces of production'), and (b) a social ownership relation giving rise to capitalists' income (belonging to the Marxian notion of 'relations of production'). Taken out of the specific context of capitalistic mode of production, the last feature may disappear.

It must be granted that Marx himself was unable to indicate the *logical* implications of his understanding of the role of 'capital' for the formulation of a theory of distribution between profits and wages in a capitalistic economy. In the view of the present writer this is precisely what the recent controversies on capital theory do: they lay bare the *logical* weaknesses of treating 'capital' merely as an instrument of production in developing a theory of distribution in a capitalist economy.

The central consequence of treating 'capital' as a mere physical instrument of production results in the prevalent neo-classical methodology of treating 'production' and 'distribution' as two separable branches of inquiry. The conventional 'production function' is supposed to depict the pure production aspect of an economy and the profit-maximizing behaviour leading to marginal calculations gives a corresponding 'marginal productivity theory' of distribution. The single most important consequence of accepting the Marxian definition of 'capital', on the other hand, is to recognize the logical untenability of the separation between 'production' and 'distribution' in a general conceptual scheme. To this central theme of capital theory we turn in the next section and show its connection with the Marxian position on 'capital' in the last section.

The force of the argument that the separation between 'production' and 'distribution' is an artificial one can be analytically

production is really a capitalist process of production and the means of production are therefore really capital and possess economic definiteness, the social character of capital. . . . If not, they remain instruments of labour, without being fixed capital' (Marx, 1885, pp. 225–6).

demonstrated by starting with a definitional relation of the distribution of national income.[4]

Let Y = net national income measured in a homogeneous consumption good;

K = value of capital in terms of the same consumption good;[5]

L = number of employed workers;

r = the rate of profit, a pure number per unit of time; and

w = real-wage rate per worker per unit of time in terms of the consumption good.

Assuming that the net national income is distributed between profits and wages, we have a definitional relation,

$$Y = Kr + Lw. \qquad 1$$

Without any loss of generality we can normalize relation 1 by setting $L = 1$ and write in per worker measure

$$y = kr + w. \qquad 2$$

Since relation 2 is purely definitional in character, it should hold for all economies where net income is being distributed between profits and wages. Consequently, it should be compatible with any acceptable treatment of 'capital' in a theory of distribution including the 'marginal productivity theory'. Unfortunately this is not true in general. In order to see this, we may notionally compare two hypothetical economies – 'marginally' different in terms of output per head, y, value of capital per head, k, and their respective profit–wage configurations, r and w. This is obtained by totally differentiating relation 2, which gives

$$dy = r\, dk + k\, dr + dw. \qquad 3$$

It is clear that the 'marginal product of capital,' i.e. dy/dk, as derived from the definitional equation 3, *does not in general equal* the rate of profit.

Once this general point is realized, various *special* constructions can be erected which would restore the 'marginal productivity' relation by showing that the treatment of 'capital'

4. The following algebraic argument depends heavily on Bhaduri (1966).
5. This is value net of depreciation.

as a 'factor of production' is compatible with the definitional distribution relation **3** above. Two such noted attempts of recent years are due to Champernowne (1953–4) and Samuelson (1962). It is worth our while to examine the essence of their arguments briefly in order to realize their significance in relation to this central question of capital theory (i.e. the separation between 'production' and 'distribution').

Looking back at relation **3**, it is clear that the 'marginal productivity' relation will hold provided, by fluke or *by assumption*,

$$k \, dr + dw = 0 \qquad\qquad\qquad 4$$

which in turn implies

$$-\frac{dw}{dr} = k. \qquad\qquad\qquad 5$$

Equation **5** can be seen to be equivalent to Professor Samuelson's condition that the elasticity of the 'factor-price frontier' equals the distributive shares, when the factors are paid according to their marginal products in an economy with a homogeneous production function of degree one in labour and 'capital'. Garegnani (1970) has indicated how special this condition is. Since it fits in well with our algebraic formulation, I reproduce his diagram (see Figure 1).

In the figure the wage–profit frontier for a technique is represented by the curve AB, and the output per worker associated with that technique is represented by OA. At a profit–wage configuration given by point P on this frontier the value of capital per worker according to Samuelson's condition (i.e. condition **5**) corresponds to the slope of the tangent at P, i.e. $\tan \psi$. The value of capital following from the definitional relation **2**, on the other hand (i.e. $k = (y-w)/r, r > 0$ and, $y = w_{max} = OA$ at $r = 0$), is given by $\tan \varphi$, which is the slope of the line joining the points A and P. Thus, for *non-linear* wage–profit frontiers $\tan \psi$ and $\tan \varphi$ are not equal in general, and Professor Samuelson needs a *linear* relation between profit and wage to make these two values of capital per worker (i.e. $\tan \psi$ and $\tan \varphi$) equal. Unfortunately he achieves this by merely fixing his assumptions suitably, and this makes the 'surrogate capital' case a *special* model of very limited interest. The assumption which

Professor Samuelson makes to produce a straight-line frontier is the *uniform* 'capital–labour ratio' in all lines of production. In Marx's terminology this is equivalent to the assumption of *uniform* 'organic composition of capital' in all lines of production[6] – exactly the assumption which Marx himself made in the

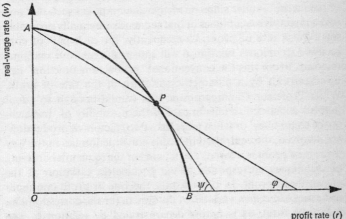

Figure 1

first two volumes of his *Capital* to avoid the famous 'transformation problem' that appears only in the third volume. Professor Samuelson rediscovered the importance of this assumption about a hundred years later!

A more imaginative attempt to restore the 'marginal productivity relation' is to be found in Professor Champernowne's 'Chain index of capital'. If we differentiate **2** for *given parametric values* of $r = \bar{r}$ and $w = \bar{w}$, then instead of the previous relation **3**, we obtain

$$dy = \bar{r} \, dk, \quad \text{i.e.} \frac{dy}{dk} = \bar{r}. \qquad\qquad 6$$

Economically, equation **6** compares two situations, both characterized by the *same given* profit–wage configuration $(\bar{r}, \bar{w})$. Consequently, equation **6** will continue to hold in the situation where

6. The 'direct' and 'indirect' labour component is valued at a *zero* rate of profit in accordance with the 'labour theory of value'.

two alternative methods of production are equally profitable at a *given* rate of profit so that the differences in the value of output per worker is exactly compensated for by the difference in the value of capital per worker to keep the *given* profit–wage configuration undisturbed.[7] This enables Professor Champernowne to arrange all the alternative methods of production in a 'chain' or 'sequence' (under some restrictive assumptions) such that any two consecutive techniques in that sequence are equally profitable for a *given* rate of profit. Consequently, for each pair of consecutive techniques relation 6 will satisfy the relevant marginal relation. From this the conventional 'production function' can be traced out by a parametric variation of the rate of profit. While Professor Champernowne was candid enough to admit that his construction fails in case of the possibility of 'reswitching of techniques' or when more than two 'factors of production' are involved, the central point in this construction lies in the way the rate of profit is treated. The 'chain' or the sequential ordering of techniques corresponds to the parametric variation of the *given* rate of profit. In other words, the rate of profit continues to be an *independent* variable of the system (or the corresponding real-wage rate), as is amply demonstrated by relation 6. The 'marginal productivity relation' in 6 does *not* give a theory of 'determination' of the rate of profit in any way, and this brings us back to the main current of the argument regarding the significance of treating 'capital' also as a social ownership relation.

For Marx this problem could be posed in a slightly different form. 'Capital' as a 'factor of production' is a total abstraction without any historical counterpart; it is not a Marxian 'category' belonging to a particular historical form of economic organization. In order to use this abstraction for a theory of distribution relevant to capitalist economies, one must also consider the social ownership aspect of 'capital' which allows for the exploitation of live labour and creation of surplus value for capitalists' income, corresponding to a *given* rate of exploitation. For an academic economist, Marx left open the question of how the rate

7. In recent jargon this is often described as a 'switch-point', when two techniques are equally profitable at some given profit-rate.

of exploitation is determined. He viewed it himself in terms of the balance of class-forces, and, significantly enough, did not try to provide a 'theory' of distribution. On a logical plane, however, once the rate of exploitation is given, the entire system of relative prices is determined under conditions of competitive equilibrium and the valuation of capital presents no problem in terms of any chosen *numéraire*. Whether to take the rate of exploitation as given from outside is essentially a matter of judgement for an academic economist. Alternatively, he could take the rate of profit or the real-wage rate as given.[8] But it must be recognized that the system of relative prices (which determines the value of the 'means of production' and, consequently, distribution) has a degree of freedom and becomes locked only when either the rate of exploitation or the rate of profit or the real-wage rate is taken as an independent datum. The rest follows as a matter of logic under the competitive assumption of equal rate of profit in all lines of production. The theory of distribution therefore continues to be a matter of *political* economy, simply because one has to form one's judgement regarding how this degree of freedom is closed through the functioning of capitalism. Marx's 'relations of production' reflecting the social-ownership aspect of 'capital' is unavoidable precisely here. But to pretend that we can still have a theory of distribution independent of such considerations is either a very *special* construction or faulty logic.

8. A large number of Cambridge growth models 'close' the system through a relation between the rate of profit and the rate of growth. See Kaldor (1957), Pasinetti (1962) and Robinson (1956).

In classical political economy the system was 'closed' through the 'iron-law of wages'. In Marx's writings there is also the notion of a long-run inflexible real-wage rate maintained through the 'reserve army' of labour continuously created through breakdown of 'pre-capitalistic modes of production' in the early stages of capitalism and through 'labour-saving innovations' at a later stage. It would appear that a *given* real-wage rate together with a *given* rate of exploitation overdetermines the system of equations for relative prices.

References

BHADURI, A. (1966), 'The concept of the marginal productivity of capital and the Wicksell effect', *Oxf. econ. Pap.*, vol. 18, pp. 284–8.

CHAMPERNOWNE, D. G. (1953–4), 'The production function and the theory of capital: a comment', *Rev. econ. Stud.*, vol. 21, pp. 112–35. [See Reading 2.]

GAREGNANI, P. (1970), 'Heterogeneous capital, the production function and the theory of distribution', *Rev. econ. Stud.*, vol. 37, pp. 407–36.

KALDOR, N. (1957), 'A model of economic growth', *Econ. J.*, vol. 67, pp. 591–624.

MARX, K. (1885), *Capital*, ed. F. Engels, vol. 2, Meissner, Hamburg.

MARX, K. (1894), *Theories of Surplus Value*, ed. K. Kantsky, 3 vols, Dietz, Stuttgart, 1910.

MARX, K. (1904), *A Contribution to the Critique of Political Economy*, trans. from 2nd German edn by N. I. Stone, Kerr.

PASINETTI, L. L. (1962), 'The rate of profit and income distribution in relation to the rate of economic growth', *Rev. econ. Stud.*, vol. 29, pp. 267–79.

ROBINSON, J. (1956), *The Accumulation of Capital*, Macmillan.

SAMUELSON, P. A. (1962), 'Parable and realism in capital theory: the surrogate production function', *Rev. econ. Stud.*, vol. 29, pp. 193–206. [See Reading 10.]

13 L. L. Pasinetti

Switches of Technique and the 'Rate of Return' in Capital Theory[1]

Excerpts from L. L. Pasinetti, 'Switches of technique and the "rate of return" in capital theory', *Economic Journal*, vol. 79, 1969, pp. 508–25, 529–31.

Whenever a new result emerges, in any theoretical field, it is natural to look back on traditional theory to verify whether, or to what extent, received notions may still be used or have to be abandoned. The outcome of the recent discussion on the problem of switches of technique[2] seems to have started a process of this kind for the analytical tools used in the theory of capital. In particular, one of these tools – Irving Fisher's notion of 'rate of return', which only a few years ago was revived and presented by Professor Solow (1963, p. 16) as 'the central concept in capital theory', has now come under discussion and has been defended by him with further arguments (Solow, 1967).

The occasion seems to be favourable for a reconsideration of Irving Fisher's notion. This is what is offered in the following pages.

Irving Fisher on the 'rate of return'

The notion of 'rate of return', as is well known, was originally introduced by Irving Fisher for the purpose of linking up his analysis of the rate of interest with marginal productivity theory.

In his book *The Rate of Interest* (1907), where the term 'rate of return' first appears,[3] Irving Fisher introduces his new concept

1. I should like to express my thanks to Mr Piero Sraffa, from whose patient and penetrating criticism I have benefited during the whole process of putting these notes together.
2. Sraffa (1960, ch. 12) and the Symposium in the *Quarterly Journal of Economics*, November 1966, with contributions by L. L. Pasinetti, D. Levhari, P. A. Samuelson, M. Morishima, M. Bruno, E. Burmeister, E. Sheshinski and P. Garegnani.
3. Irving Fisher seems to have developed the notion of rate of return mainly in response to criticism. This notion does not appear at all in his first basic theoretical work (1906). (We find there a 'rate of value return',

with the following example (1907, pp. 152–4). Suppose that a producer is faced with two alternative time streams of incomes, according to whether he goes into forestry or into farming:

| | *Annual value (in \$) of uses for:* | |
	Forestry	Farming
1st year	0	100
2nd year	210	100
Each subsequent year	100	100

A rate of interest exists at which the two options are equally profitable. As can easily be seen, this rate of interest is 10 per cent. In general, we may say that if option a is represented by a time stream $V_t^{(\alpha)}, V_{t+1}^{(\alpha)}, \ldots, V_{t+\tau}^{(\alpha)}$ and option β by another time stream $V_t^{(\beta)}, V_{t+1}^{(\beta)}, \ldots, V_{t+\theta}^{(\beta)}$, where the Vs are values (let us say \$), some of which are positive (incomes) and others negative (expenditures), there may be a rate of interest i which satisfies the equation

$$\sum_{k=0}^{\tau} (1+i)^{-k} V_{t+k}^{(\alpha)} = \sum_{k=0}^{\theta} (1+i)^{-k} V_{t+k}^{(\beta)}. \qquad \textbf{1}$$

Such a 'supposed rate of interest which will make equal the present values' (Fisher, 1907, pp. 152–4) Irving Fisher calls the 'rate of return on sacrifice' (pp. 153–4) or (as modified later) the 'rate of return over cost' (1930, p. 155).

Thus, the 'rate of return', according to this definition, is a rate of interest: that rate of interest at which two alternative production possibilities are equally profitable.

Irving Fisher then goes on to explain why he calls it the 'rate of return', and to do so he refers his argument to another nu-

which is yet another concept.) But that work was strongly criticized on the grounds that it neglected the productivity aspect of capital goods. And in his following theoretical work, Irving Fisher (1907) introduced the notion of 'rate of return'. As he explains: 'By means of it we are enabled to admit into our theory the elements of truth contained in some of the claims of the productivity theories, the cost theories and Böhm-Bawerk theory of the technique of production' (Fisher, 1907, p. 159). But criticism continued on the same ground, and Irving Fisher responded by elaborating the notion of rate of return still further. A whole chapter is devoted to it in the latest version of his theory (Fisher, 1930, ch. 7).

merical table. His explanation, for the purpose of later comparisons, may be more conveniently put in terms of the following example. Suppose that a farmer is producing each year a physical quantity X_α of a specific commodity. He can go on for ever with his farm as it is, and we may say that in this case he has chosen alternative α. Or else, suppose that he is offered the following opportunity (the result of which we may call alternative β): while keeping his going concern exactly as it is, he can increase production permanently to physical quantity X_β by simply undertaking an investment project for which he can pay with a certain quantity $(X_\alpha - \bar{X})$ of the commodity he produces, $\bar{X}$ representing the reduced saleable amount of the commodity in that year in which the investment project is undertaken. According to Irving Fisher, the ratio of the 'permanent increase' $(X_\beta - X_\alpha)$ in the income stream to the one-time 'cost' or 'sacrifice' $X_\alpha - \bar{X}$ of going over to alternative β, i.e.

$$\frac{X_\beta - X_\alpha}{X_\alpha - \bar{X}}, \qquad\qquad 2$$

represents the 'rate of return over cost'. The example has been stated on purpose in such a way as to make 2 a ratio of physical quantities; but in order to do so, we have had to take as given the prices at which physical quantity $(X_\alpha - \bar{X})$ is exchanged with the physical goods and services entailed by the investment project. With all prices taken as given, ratio 2 obviously provides a criterion for rational choice. It will be profitable or not profitable for the single producer to undertake the particular investment project which is considered according to whether 2 is greater or smaller than the current rate of interest (which we may take as indicating the prevailing rate of profit).

The reader may have noticed already that ratio 2 is not quite the same notion as that of the definition given before, although Irving Fisher does take it as if it were the same. Expression 1 defines that rate of interest at which two alternative time streams of values are equally profitable. Ratio 2, on the other hand, represents the rate of profit which is associated with an investment project that would make one method of production (which we have called α) change into another (which we have called β). This rate of profit may or may not coincide with the rate of profit at which the two methods are equally profitable. Actually, a positive rate of profit at which methods α and β are equally profitable might not even exist (think, for example, of a case in which β represents a newly invented technical improvement).

It will, therefore, be useful to keep these two notions distinct from each other. We shall refer to definition 1 and to definition 2 respectively as the first and the second Irving Fisher notion of rate of return.

But, of course, Irving Fisher is aiming at something further. In his following paragraph, by changing to another numerical example, he takes a further step,

the farmer may cultivate his farm with any degree of intensity; and for each particular degree of intensity he will have a different income-stream. He may, for instance, invest $100 worth of labor in the present, in order that in six months he may have a larger income than otherwise, by $200. If the rate of interest is 4 per cent (reckoned semi-annually) he would evidently prefer this option. . . . Another course would be to invest, not $100, but $200, in present cultivation. The extra $100 would add to his returns in a half year's time . . . let us say $150. . . . And so each successive choice, compared with its predecessor, shows a *law of decreasing returns for additional sacrifice*. Thus, if he invests, not $200, but $300, the third $100 thus sacrificed will add to his returns in six months, let us say $120 . . . in like manner he may sacrifice a fourth . . . a fifth . . . a sixth . . . a seventh $100 for $102. Thus far, each successive option is preferred to its predecessor. . . . The next option is to sacrifice an eighth $100 for an additional $101 in six months. Evidently . . . the farmer . . . will stop at the previous step, at which he gets 2 per cent return on the last sacrifice of $100. . . . We therefore reach the conclusion that where the options are indefinite in number, the option chosen, compared with a neighboring option with which it was in competition, yields a rate of return on sacrifice equal to the rate of interest. This rate of return . . . we shall call *the marginal rate of return on sacrifice* (Fisher, 1907, pp. 156–8).

At this point, Irving Fisher has arrived on the standard ground of marginal productivity theory, which is where he wanted to arrive. The words 'marginal rate of return' have here become another term for 'marginal product of capital'.

It thus appears that Irving Fisher does not regard the 'rate of return' as merely being a definition of a particular rate of profit. He is convinced that it represents something different, or rather something more, than the rate of profit, for the economic system as a whole: he is convinced that, when 'the options are indefinite in number', it is tending to the traditional notion of 'marginal product of capital', and therefore represents something which is not only independent, but actually a *determinant*, of the rate of profit (Fisher, 1930, p. 176).

It would not be fruitful, at this stage, to go into a detailed critical assessment of Irving Fisher's analysis which – although aimed at drawing conclusions for the economic system as a whole – is always carried out at the level of the single producer, where so many things, especially the price system, have to be taken as given. But we possess nowadays much more powerful analytical tools than those which Irving Fisher had at his disposal, and in the following pages we shall be able to analyse, directly with reference to a complete economic system, whether this theoretical framework of Irving Fisher's is consistent; and in any case whether either of his two notions of rate of return is of any help to the problem for which both of them have been invented, namely the problem of providing a general theory of the rate of profit.

A complete economic system

We shall consider an economic system (or economic systems) in which commodities are (singly or jointly) produced by labour and commodities at a constant technology supposed to be viable in the sense of permitting the production of a positive net product, besides the reproduction of all those commodities which are used up in the production process. The theoretical features of such an economic system have been extensively investigated in recent economic literature,[4] and there is no need to go into details here. We shall represent the net product (or net output) of any such economic system by a column vector of physical quantities Y and its capital goods, or means of production, by a column vector of physical quantities K. The labour force will be supposed to remain constant and the economic system itself will be supposed to be in a stationary state. Our analysis will therefore be concerned with stationary states or with transitions from one stationary state to another. The same analysis,

4. The single best reference is perhaps Sraffa (1960).

however, is easily and obviously extendable to steady growth states with increasing population.

An important feature of an economic system producing commodities by labour and commodities is, as is well known, that the distribution of its (physically specified) net product $\mathbf{Y}$ between wages and profits remains indeterminate. In other words, the price system remains open, in the sense that relative prices (which we shall denote by a row vector $\mathbf{p}$, whichever the commodity that is chosen as *numéraire*) are indeterminate, unless either one of the two distributive variables (the wage rate which we shall call w or the rate of profit which we shall call r) is fixed exogenously.

The problem which we shall undertake to examine is whether Irving Fisher's notions of rate of return can contribute in any way to a theory of the rate of profit, which would close the price system and thus explain the determination of the income distribution and the price structure.

An accounting expression

Irving Fisher's first definition of the rate of return, when referred to a complete economic system, may be investigated at once.

Let us consider two different economic systems, which we may call system α and system β, and let us suppose that they have exactly the same labour force, are both in a stationary state and use techniques which are the same except for at least one of their production processes.[5] The two net products, $\mathbf{Y}_\alpha$ and $\mathbf{Y}_\beta$ (we shall use α and β as subscripts to denote the system to which the corresponding variable refers), represent two indefinite streams in the future, which are unambiguously defined in physical terms. Capital goods $\mathbf{K}_\alpha$ and $\mathbf{K}_\beta$ are also unambiguously defined in physical terms. Each one of the two systems, taken by itself, can have any distribution of its net product between wages and profits. This means that in system α, in correspondence to *any* arbitrarily fixed wage rate, there is a rate of profit and a set of prices which make the discounted value of the indefinite future stream of profits equal to the value of capital goods. The same can be said of system β, although, even for the same wage rate,

5. In the whole of the present analysis comparisons will be made only between economic systems. Therefore the word *technique* will be used to mean the whole set of methods of production in operation in an economic system.

the rate of profit and prices in system β will in general be different from those in system α. (We shall consider, of course, only non-negative values of w and r, in the whole of the present analysis.)

It may, however, happen that if the wage rate were to be fixed at a particular level, in both systems, then, at that level of the wage rate, the rate of profit and the prices would also be the same in both systems. We shall call w^* such a particular wage rate, if it exists, and r^* and $\mathbf{p}^*$ respectively the rate of profit and the vector of prices which correspond to w^*. (w^*, r^* and $\mathbf{p}^*$ thus denote what has been called a 'switching point'.) At wage rate w^* the two systems are equally profitable, which means that their two streams of future profits, set against the values of their capital goods, satisfy equation 1 at $i = r^*$. Rate of profit r^* is what, in his first definition, Irving Fisher called the 'rate of return'.

It will be noticed that, given any two systems α and β, a wage rate w^* may not exist, which means that a rate of return in Irving Fisher's first sense may not exist at all. On the other hand, when a wage rate w^*, and thus a profit rate r^* and a price vector $\mathbf{p}^*$ corresponding to it, all exist, they may not be unique. There may be more than one wage rate at which the two systems are equally profitable (i.e. there may be more than one switching point).

We may now open a brief digression on rate of profit r^*. At prices $\mathbf{p}^*$, rate of profit r^* may be expressed as the ratio of total profits to the total value of capital goods in system α, or as the ratio of total profits to the total value of capital goods in system β, or as the ratio of the differences between the numerators and the denominators of these two ratios. These are all equivalent accounting expressions for r^*. The third has the property of containing elements pertaining to both systems, and in our case it may be expressed in yet another way. Since the labour force is the same in both systems, and thus also total wages are the same, the difference between the total profits of the two systems coincides with the difference between the two net products. The common rate of profit r^* can therefore also be expressed as

$$\frac{\mathbf{p}^*(\mathbf{Y}_\beta - \mathbf{Y}_\alpha)}{\mathbf{p}^*(\mathbf{K}_\beta - \mathbf{K}_\alpha)},\qquad 3$$

provided, of course, that $\mathbf{p}^*\mathbf{K}_\beta \neq \mathbf{p}^*\mathbf{K}_\alpha$.

We may now use accounting expression **3**, in this context, to represent Irving Fisher's first definition of the rate of return, since **3** is simply another way of expressing r^*.

But at this point we may ask: is this discussion relevant to the problem we are considering (that of finding an *explanation* of the rate of profit)? Clearly to call 'rate of return' that rate of profit at which two production possibilities are equally profitable is a definition; and this definition may be used no matter *which* explanation of the rate of profit is given. This simply means that, for the problem we are considering, this discussion is of no help at all. Expression **3** and for that matter definition **1** are compatible with any explanation, i.e. any theory, of the rate of profit.

Choice of techniques

But let us now consider Irving Fisher's second notion of rate of return.

We may begin by investigating a situation, for the economic system as a whole, which corresponds to the one considered in the first section for a single producer. We shall suppose that there exists an economic system, which we may call α, and that we want to consider whether a change-over to another configuration of the economic system, which we may call β, is or is not profitable. Such a change-over can be specified in physical terms. After ordering commodities in the same way in both systems, the physical differences between the two net products are expressed by vector $Y_\beta - Y_\alpha$, and the physical differences between the capital goods by vector $K_\beta - K_\alpha$. We shall suppose that the two net products have been chosen in such a way as to make Y_β and Y_α contain exactly the same physical quantities except for the first commodity, for which a larger physical quantity appears in Y_β than in Y_α. In other words, $Y_\beta - Y_\alpha$ is supposed to be a vector whose components are all zero except the first one, which is positive. Vector $K_\beta - K_\alpha$, however, will contain, in general, both positive components and negative components, the former representing the physical quantities which have to be added to the means of production and the latter representing the physical quantities of capital goods that become redundant. We shall represent the latter physical quantities –

those that become redundant – by vector $K_\alpha^{(w)}$, and we shall suppose (for simplicity, but without loss of generality) that they cannot be re-used in any way so that they would be entirely wasted if the change-over were to take place. In other words, out of the existing physical capital goods K_α, only physical quantities $K_\alpha - K_\alpha^{(w)}$ can become capital goods also in system β. Physical quantities $K_\alpha^{(w)}$, on the other hand, would be entirely wasted.

We have thus constructed our case in such a way as to be able to say unambiguously that, if the change-over were to take place, society as a whole would enjoy a permanent physical increase $Y_\beta - Y_\alpha$ in the net product, as against a once-for-all 'cost' represented by physical quantities $K_\beta - (K_\alpha - K_\alpha^{(w)})$, which would have to be added to the capital goods.

Permanent gain $Y_\beta - Y_\alpha$ and once-for-all 'cost' $K_\beta - K_\alpha + K_\alpha^{(w)}$ are defined in physical terms, but they represent heterogeneous commodities. Therefore, if we want to compute a single ratio among them to express the correspondent of Irving Fisher's ratio **2** for the economic system as a whole, we need a system of prices. But any system of prices depends on the distribution of the net product between wages and profits, i.e. it depends on the rate of profit, for whose determination (at least up to this point in our analysis) no criterion has emerged. This means that, in general, Irving Fisher's second notion of rate of return is not independent of the over-all rate of profit. Of course, this does not necessarily mean that it would be a useless concept. If we are prepared to accept a particular (arbitrary) way of fixing the over-all rate of profit and, moreover, if we are prepared to accept a convention on whether to use the prices of system α or the prices of system β let us call the chosen price system $p(r)$ (since in general $p_\beta \neq p_\alpha$ even for the same rate of profit), then Irving Fisher's second notion of rate of return, for the economic system as a whole, may be written as

$$\frac{p(r)(Y_\beta - Y_\alpha)}{p(r)(K_\beta - K_\alpha + K_\alpha^{(w)})}. \qquad 4$$

The problem is to specify the purpose for which this ratio can be used.

Incidentally, this formulation should make it clear by now why

Irving Fisher's second notion of rate of return should not be confused with his first – i.e. with accounting expression **3** – although particular cases may be hypothesized in which **4** comes to coincide with **3**. If $K_\alpha^{(w)}$ were to be equal to zero, if a rate of profit r^* existed and if prices were to be fixed exactly at $\mathbf{p}^*$, then **4** would also coincide with **3**. But ratio **4**, as such, clearly represents a much more general concept than accounting expression **3**. In particular, it is important to realize that, given any two techniques α and β, a ratio **4** can always be computed, i.e. always exists, while a rate of profit r^*, i.e. an accounting expression **3**, may or may not exist

But let us go back to the meaning of ratio **4**. This ratio, like ratio **2**, represents the rate of profit associated with the particular investment project which is considered (that investment project which would make the system change from α to β) when the over-all rate of profit is accepted as given. Comparison of **4** with this (predetermined) rate of profit obviously provides a criterion for rational choice between alternatives α and β. The change-over will be profitable or not profitable for the economic system as a whole (relatively to the over-all rate of profit which has been accepted as given) according as ratio **4** is greater or smaller than the (predetermined) rate of profit. The reader will realize that this procedure is nothing but one way (actually a complicated way) of expressing the problem of choice of techniques for the economic system as a whole.[6]

6. It consists in giving a quantitative expression to the rate of profit which is associated with the particular change that is considered, and then in comparing it with the over-all, predetermined, rate of profit which has been accepted as given. Of course, such a quantification – i.e. ratio **4** – will turn out to be different according to which predetermined rate of profit has been taken as given. This indeterminacy may or may not affect the choice between α and β. At least three categories of cases may be distinguished. There are cases in which ratio **4** is greater than the predetermined rate of profit no matter which (non-negative) predeterminate rate of profit is chosen. These are cases in which a rate of return in Irving Fisher's first sense does not even exist: technique β is unambiguously better than, i.e. completely dominates, technique α. There is then a whole series of other cases in which complications of various kinds may arise, owing to capital goods becoming redundant. And finally, there is a third category of cases in which – even without the complications of redundant capital goods – ratio **4** is greater than the (predetermined) rate of profit at some levels of the rate of profit

But does ratio **4** represent anything more than simply a device for presenting the problem of choice of techniques? This is clearly the relevant question for our purposes. A whole group of economists (marginalist capital theorists) have in fact seen in ratio **4** something more than a device for the problem of choice of techniques. They have seen in ratio **4** – Irving Fisher's second notion of rate of return – the technical foundation of a theory of the rate of profit itself. We are now in a position to investigate this claim carefully.

An abstract case

The basic ideas behind the claim just mentioned are expressed at their best by an abstract limiting case, constructed *ad hoc*, which it may be useful to examine in detail.

For our purposes, it will be convenient to present this abstract case within the theoretical framework of the previous pages. Thus, as in the preceding section, we may consider two economic systems, α and β, at such a composition of their net products as to make the difference $\mathbf{Y}_\beta - \mathbf{Y}_\alpha$ a vector whose components are all zero except for the first one – a positive component – referring to a commodity which we may call 'corn'. But now we add the crucial assumption that the corresponding physical capital goods $\mathbf{K}_\beta$ and $\mathbf{K}_\alpha$ happen to be such as to make $\mathbf{K}_\beta - \mathbf{K}_\alpha$ also a vector whose components are all zero except one, which is positive and which again happens to refer to 'corn'. This means that a change-over from system α to system β simply entails taking a certain physical quantity of corn from the net product of α and adding it to its means of production, while all existing capital goods remain as they are. For the two economic systems are supposed only to differ as to a physical quantity of corn in their net products, which we may call $y_\beta - y_\alpha > 0$; and as to a physical quantity, again of corn, in their capital goods, which (with explicit reference to a change-over from system α to system β) we may call $y_\alpha - \bar{y}$, where $\bar{y}$ is the (reduced) quantity of corn consumed in system α in that period in which the change-over takes place.

itself, and smaller at others. It is exclusively on this third category of cases, as will appear in the following pages, that marginalist-capital theorists have concentrated their analysis.

In these conditions, if we compute ratio 4, all prices cancel out completely both at the numerator and at the denominator, and 4 reduces to a ratio (let us call it R) of two physical quantities of corn, i.e. to

$$R = \frac{y_\beta - y_\alpha}{y_\alpha - \bar{y}}. \qquad 5$$

This is an expression which – unlike all expressions considered so far – is independent of prices and of the rate of profit.[7]

Owing to the way in which the case has been constructed, ratio R has the following relevant properties:

1. Any time that $r < R$, the technique which is more profitable is the one which entails a higher physical quantity of corn (as capital good) per man; and conversely, any time that $r > R$, the technique which is more profitable is the one that entails a lower quantity of corn per man.

2. If r happened to be exactly equal to R, the two techniques would be equally profitable. Thus R also represents rate of profit r^*. In fact, if we use accounting expression 3 to express r^*, we can see that in this case it comes to coincide with 5.

3. The difference $r - R$, which is the one that matters for any decision, is (since R is fixed) an increasing monotonic function of r. This means that there can only be one value of r (i.e. $r = R$) at which the two techniques are equally profitable. In other words, between the two techniques there can only be one switching point.

Thus, ratio R refers to a hypothetical world in which: (a) a rate of return in Irving Fisher's first sense always exists; (b) a rate of return in Irving Fisher's second sense can never give rise

7. It may be useful to point out the difference between ratio 5 and ratio 2. Ratio 5 is a genuine physical ratio: the net product (at the numerator) and the capital good (at the denominator) actually consist of the same physical commodity. Ratio 2, on the other hand, has been *expressed in terms of* the same physical commodity, but is not a physical ratio: the capital goods (represented by the denominator) are heterogeneous commodities which have required a system of prices in order to be expressed in terms of the commodity which appears at the numerator. In other words, ratio 2 necessarily implies a system of prices; ratio 5 does not.

to any ambiguity, since it emerges in physical terms; (c) the two notions of rate of return always coincide.

It is ratio R, with all the properties stated above, that represents the marginalists' ideal notion of a 'rate of return'. Once such a well-behaved rate of return has been obtained, its properties can easily be magnified by further assumptions.

Let us suppose that a further technique γ exists, and thus an economic system γ, whose net product and capital goods are the same as those of economic system β, except again for physical quantities of corn. The physical rate of return to a change-over from β to γ, let us call it R', would therefore also be a ratio of quantities of corn and would be lower than R – for, if it were higher, β would imply some waste of corn and comparisons would have been made directly between α and γ. Moreover, let us suppose the existence of a further technique δ with the same properties with respect to γ as γ has with respect to β and β has with respect to α. The physical rate of return of a change-over from γ to δ (let us call it R'') would be lower than R', and so forth. We can go on making assumptions of this type to the extent that we like. The interesting property is that all these techniques would be such that to order them according to the increasing quantity of corn they require as capital good (or according to the increasing quantity of corn they yield as net product) would be exactly the same as ordering them according to the decreasing physical rates of return in changing from any technique to the next.

The whole construction can be rendered even more elegant by supposing that the number of techniques, all of the same type, is not only very high but actually tends to infinity, in such a way as to make infinitesimally small the range of variation of the rate of profit within which any one technique is the most profitable one. In this way the switching points between techniques – although becoming infinite in number – all become irrelevant. For, at any rate of profit at which two techniques are equally profitable, there always exists a third technique which is more profitable than the former two. In the limit there always is one technique which becomes the most profitable one at any single point in the range of variation of the rate of profit. Any addition of corn to the means of production (no matter how small) always makes the system change directly from one technique to another without ever being at a switching point. Another interesting property is that, by the same process of tendency to the limit, ratio **5**, referred to any two neighbouring techniques, becomes a derivative (since both numerator and denominator become infinitesimally small): the derivative of corn as output with respect to corn as capital good.[8] This is exactly what marginalist capital theorists have called the 'marginal product' of corn used as a capital good.

The reader will realize at this point that the whole construction has come, after all, to take very familiar features. To say that, in the economic system considered, the net products and the capital goods entailed by any two neighbouring techniques are represented by vectors which are exactly the same, except for one component referring to the same commodity (corn) in both of them, is simply a device for presenting, in the language of linear algebra, the very familiar case of a hypothetical world in which there is only one relevant commodity, which can be used indifferently as a consumer good or as a capital good and which can be combined in any proportion with labour at decreasing physical rates of return to changing proportions.

8. All this can be expressed in terms of a diagram introduced by Professor Joan Robinson (1956). Let us suppose, to begin with, that only techniques a, β, γ, δ are known. Then, on Figure 1, the technical possibilities open to

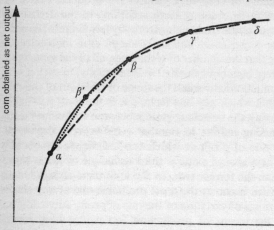

Figure 1

If such a hypothetical world existed it would clearly be a world in which a rate of profit on accumulated corn is inevitable *for technological reasons*. Given any existing physical stock of corn, any once-for-all addition of further corn would always mean by itself a higher permanent physical output of corn. In other words, any 'saving' of corn would always yield a physical rate of return, or rather a physical rate of profit, which would be the lower the higher the already existing stock of corn. This inverse monotonic relationship between physical rate of profit and existing stock of corn would permit an extension to the rate of profit of the marginal theory of prices (which, as is well known, interprets prices as indexes of scarcity). The smaller – i.e. the scarcer – the existing quantity of corn, the higher the physical rate of return (and of profit) to further savings.

As the reader will realize, the notion of rate of return, in this context, has been defined (without any ambiguity) according to Irving Fisher's second definition. Yet, in the discrete case, it always coincides with Irving Fisher's first definition; and, in the continuous case, it tends to the traditional notion of 'marginal product of capital'. This is clearly an ideal unifying framework:

---

the economy are represented by points α, β, γ, δ and by any linear combination of them – the broken straight segments $\alpha\beta$, $\beta\gamma$, $\gamma\delta$. Physical rates of return R, R', R'' are represented by the slopes of the same segments in the same order. Thus what is a switching point, on the scale of variation of the rate of profit, is represented on Figure 1 by a flat facet: the straight segment joining any two techniques.

We may now suppose that a further technique of the same type, called β', becomes known in between a and β. The former flat facet (switching point) $\alpha\beta$ becomes dominated by the two new flat facets (switching points) $\alpha\beta'$ and $\beta'\beta$, represented by the dotted segments on the diagram. And if we go on making assumptions of this type *ad infinitum*, then in between any two techniques – no matter how near to each other they may be – there always appears a third technique. All techniques crowd together, by becoming infinite, to form the smooth curve of the diagram. At this stage any movement along this curve, no matter how small, entails going *directly* from one technique to another. All flat facets (switching points) become irrelevant, and any segment joining any two neighbouring techniques tends, in the limit, to the tangent to the smooth curve, i.e. to the derivative of corn as net output with respect to corn as capital good.

any distinction has become unnecessary because the case has been constructed in such a way as to make any distinction unnecessary. It is in this unifying framework that the ideal notion of a physical rate of return becomes an ingredient of a marginal theory of the rate of profit.

The effects of an unobtrusive postulate

The infinite-techniques one-commodity case of the previous section only represents, of course, a hypothetical imaginary world of which no trace will ever be found in the real world in which we live. If it were to be taken by itself it would have no theoretical nor practical relevance whatever.

But abstract cases are always being constructed in economic theory when they can simplify the complexities of the real world while retaining the relevant features which are being investigated. In other words, abstract cases are indeed relevant when, and to the extent to which, they represent a simplified way of expressing the general case. This is precisely what the infinite-techniques one-commodity case has been believed to be. In other words, the belief has become widespread that, in general, an economic system in which commodities are produced by labour and capital goods behaves like the particular case of an infinite-techniques one-commodity world.

The origin of this belief can be traced back to an unobtrusive proposition which, for some time by now, has been adopted as a postulate, i.e. as a proposition that is so evident as not to need any discussion or justification. This proposition, which we shall call proposition 1, can be stated in the following way:

1. Any time that, at a wage rate w^*, two techniques α and β are equally profitable, the technique that becomes more profitable at a wage rate $w > w^*$ (or, which is the same, at a rate of profit $r < r^*$) is the technique which entails a higher value of capital goods per man.

The effects of this postulate are really striking. In order to make them emerge in their most elegant form, the postulate itself is usually supplemented with two further convenient assumptions, which we may call 2 and 3, namely:

2. It is always possible, for the economic system as a whole, to change over from any technique to another without any loss of

capital goods in the transition (call it the 'capital malleability assumption').

3. There exists a very high number of techniques, all of which may be ordered according to proposition 1.

The reader will notice, to begin with, that restrictions have been imposed. Proposition 1 does not say anything on the cases in which a rate of profit r^* does not exist. And assumption 2 ensures that no capital goods ever need be discarded. Thus ratio 4 on page 269 immediately becomes (let us call it ρ):[9]

$$\rho = \frac{\mathbf{p}(r)(\mathbf{Y}_\beta - \mathbf{Y}_\alpha)}{\mathbf{p}(r)(\mathbf{K}_\beta - \mathbf{K}_\beta)}. \qquad 6$$

It can now be seen that, if postulate 1 holds, ratio 6 possesses remarkable properties. Unlike R, ρ does contain prices $\mathbf{p}(r)$, and therefore is a function of r. However, owing to proposition 1, $\rho < r$ for any set of prices corresponding to $r > r^*$; and conversely, $\rho > r$ for any set of prices corresponding to $r < r^*$; while $\rho = r$ for that set of prices corresponding to $r = r^*$ (i.e. when r is put exactly equal to r^*, ρ also comes to represent Irving Fisher's first notion of rate of return). This simply means that, in the neighbourhood of r^*, ρ defined as above has all properties 1, 2 and 3 (see page 272). Unobtrusive postulate 1 plus restriction 2, in one stroke, have conferred upon ρ all the properties of a physical rate of return! Ratio ρ is not a physical rate of return, but – owing to proposition 1 – has all the properties of, and behaves exactly like, a physical rate of return. It is, as we may say, a 'surrogate' physical rate of return (or, for brevity, a 'surrogate' rate of return).

A whole series of consequences follows. At the switching points between any two techniques, the *direction of change* of all relevant magnitudes (i.e. value of capital goods, net output per man,

9. To be specific, the two mentioned restrictions imply that, with respect to ratio 4, ratio 6 has two strong limitations: it is supposed *not* to concern cases in which one technique dominates the other completely and it is supposed *not* to concern cases in which capital goods are specific to particular techniques. In other words, the first and second categories of cases specified in footnote 6 on pages 270–71 (which were trivially irrelevant in the one-commodity infinite-techniques case of the previous section) here are simply disregarded. Ratio 6 is supposed to concern exclusively the third category of cases of footnote 6.

rate of profit and wage rate) is exactly the same as in the artificial case of the previous section. Meanwhile, owing to the 'capital malleability assumption', no complication ever arises in re-using all existing capital goods; while the high-number-of-techniques assumption ensures the existence of many 'surrogate' rates of return, so as to make very small the relevant range of variation of each of them (i.e. the range within which each of them can move away from the neighbourhood of the corresponding r^*, where it has all the properties of a physical rate of return). But even this small indeterminacy can be eliminated altogether by assuming that the number of techniques is not only very high but tends to infinity. As the number of techniques is assumed to become infinitely large (and the magnitude of change in the rate of profit needed in order to go from any technique to the 'next' technique becomes infinitesimally small) then – owing to postulate 1 – the differences in the values of capital goods per man and in the outputs per man of any two neighbouring techniques become smaller and smaller. It is natural to think that, in the limit, values of capital goods per man and of output per man will tend to change continuously (owing to the continuous change of techniques), as the rate of profit continuously changes in the opposite direction. When this happens all switching points become irrelevant, as in the abstract case of the previous section. For, at any level of the rate of profit, there always is one technique which is the most profitable one. And at the same time any change in the rate of profit, no matter how small, always causes a change in the most profitable technique.

This is indeed a brilliant theoretical construction. The category of cases considered is restricted but sufficient to the purpose. Each technique, taken by itself, would be compatible with any rate of profit, but the point is that only one rate of profit makes it the most profitable technique. So that each technique remains in fact irrelevant (because dominated by other techniques) except at one single rate of profit, where it becomes the most profitable technique. A one-to-one correspondence is thereby established between each one of the infinite techniques and each one of the infinite (possible) rates of profit. And the relevant property is that this one-to-one correspondence is such as to put all techniques in a very definite order. As the rate of profit is consistently decreased, the techniques which successively become the most profitable ones are associated with higher and higher values of the capital goods per man (and with higher and higher net outputs per man). The desired relationship is thereby made to emerge: 'quantity of capital' and rate of profit are inversely related to each other! The basic idea for which the infinite-techniques one-commodity case had been constructed is thereby extended to being a general feature of any economic system.

It is clearly this brilliant construction (not the abstract case of an infinite-techniques one-commodity world[10]) which is theoretically relevant, since it aims at providing a *general* theory.[11] But it is precisely this theoretical construction that the recent results, emerging from the discussion on the reswitching of techniques, have opened up for challenge. To these results it will now be useful to turn.

Implications of the reswitching of techniques

The recent discussion on the switching of techniques, as is well known, has disproved the validity of proposition 1 of marginal capital theory. We know by now that lower rates of profit may be associated with higher or lower ratios of net output to the value of capital goods (and similarly with higher or lower net outputs per man, with higher or lower values of capital goods per man). And we know that this may happen as soon as, in the one-commodity infinite-techniques construction, we introduce such

10. Indeed, if the infinite-techniques one-commodity case were to be taken by itself, in isolation, any question of practical relevance would be out of discussion. Where could we ever find any two methods of production that differ only by that particular physical input which corresponds to the commodity which is being produced? It seems inevitable that, if method a, with respect to method β, requires more corn to produce more corn it will also require some extra labour or machines, if nothing else, to transport and handle the extra corn. The very first assumption behind that abstract case, by itself alone, thus seems to be a practical impossibility. Yet the case is so much more restrictive. Not just one but an infinite number of such peculiar alternative methods of production is supposed to exist, and most of all no other type of alternative method is supposed to be known, not only for corn but for all commodities.

11. This is in fact the theoretical framework that Professor Solow (1963) has used. The whole analysis of the book is open to the challenge of the new results.

a small change as simply that of one other possible method of production for a second commodity.[12] Very far from embodying the relevant features of the general case and from being a simplified way of expressing it, the one-commodity infinite-techniques construction is thereby revealed to be an entirely isolated case. As such, it can have no theoretical or practical relevance whatever. At the same time the whole traditional idea that lower and lower rates of profit are the natural and necessary consequence of further and further additions to 'capital' is revealed to be false.

The implications of these new results for the problems which we have been discussing are rather important, and can now be worked out explicitly. To begin with, it should be clear by now that the assumptions themselves which have been put around the unobtrusive postulate of marginal capital theory no longer fulfil their purposes. The first of those assumptions – the capital malleability assumption – besides being revealed as completely arbitrary (two techniques may well be as near as one likes on the scale of variation of the rate of profit and yet the physical capital goods they require may be completely different) now also appears as entirely useless. For, whether it is satisfied or not, it makes no difference to the result that, in a constant technology framework, there exists in general no inverse monotonic relationship between the rate of profit and the total value of capital goods per man.

The second of those assumptions – infinite number of techniques – even more clearly than the first, is now revealed to fall amiss. For vicinity of any two techniques on the scale of variation of the rate of profit does not imply closeness of the total values of their capital goods. It is therefore not true that, as the number of techniques becomes larger and larger, the differences in the values of capital goods per man and outputs per man of any two neighbouring techniques necessarily become smaller and smaller. These differences might well remain quite large, no matter how infinitesimally near to each other two techniques are on the range of variation of the rate of profit. In other words, continuity in the variation of techniques, as the rate of profit changes, does not imply continuity in the variation of values of capital goods per

12. See the Symposium mentioned in footnote 2 on page 261.

man and of net outputs per man. This in fact seems to be one of the most important results emerging from the reswitching of techniques discussion. It seems to reveal capital theory as a field unsuitable to the application of calculus and infinitesimal analysis, and thus of marginal analysis.

But the implications which we are most interested in are clearly those referring to the 'surrogate' rate of return. If proposition 1 is not true the difference $r - \rho(r)$ may become indifferently positive or negative at *any* level of the rate of profit; which means that it is not a monotonic function of the rate of profit. Ratio 6 thus loses immediately all the properties of a physical rate of return. Falsity of proposition 1 simply makes it impossible to construct any expression, for the economic system as a whole, that behaves like the physical rate of return of the infinite-technique one-commodity case. In other words, in general, a 'surrogate' rate of return does not exist.

What, of course, always does exist is ratio 4 – Irving Fisher's second notion of rate of return – since it can be computed any time that there are two alternative techniques. But this ratio, first of all, refers to a wider range of cases than those considered by marginal-productivity theorists, and, secondly, when narrowed down to these cases it has none of the properties of either a physical or a 'surrogate' rate of return. Strikingly in contrast with what happens to ratio 5, its numerator and denominator, when a *continuum* of techniques is considered, do not necessarily tend to become infinitesimally small.[13] In other words, in general,

13. This proposition holds *a fortiori* for the numerator and denominator of ratio 3. Another implication of these results is that also the applicability of Professor Joan Robinson's diagram considered in footnote 8 (page 274) remains limited to the infinite-techniques one-commodity case. In the general case if one decides to evaluate the capital goods of each technique at that price system at which each technique becomes relevant, one cannot represent all the capital goods simultaneously on the same axis, simply because each technique – even at the same rate of profit – entails its own particular price system. If, on the other hand, one decides to evaluate the capital goods of all techniques at the same set of prices so as to be able to represent them all on the same axis, one loses the main purpose of the diagram itself, as can easily be shown. First of all, the choice of the set of prices is arbitrary. There exists one particular set of prices (and therefore one set of values of the capital goods) for each particular rate of profit which is chosen. This difficulty was stressed by Professor Joan Robinson herself, who tried to overcome it by complicating the diagram and drawing

Irving Fisher's second notion of rate of return *does not* tend, in the limit, to what traditional theory has called the 'marginal product of capital'. Since the difference between ratio **4** and the over-all rate of profit can be any function of the rate of profit, no criterion can be obtained from it for determining the rate of profit itself.

Irving Fisher's second notion of 'rate of return': conclusions

We can go back at last to the point where we left our analysis on page 271. After finding that ratio **4** – Irving Fisher's second notion of rate of return – bears no relation to what traditional theory has called the 'marginal product of capital' we can now conclude our discussion.

As we have seen, ratio **4**, or for that matter ratio **2**, simply represents the rate of profit associated with the investment project which is necessary in order to go from a certain technique α to another technique β when all prices (and the over-all rate of profit entering these prices) are taken as given. Comparison of this particular rate of profit with the over-all (predetermined) rate of profit obviously provides a criterion for rational choice between techniques α and β. (This is the problem of choice of techniques.) We may, of course, continue to call such a particular rate of profit the 'rate of return', if we like. This corresponds, after all, to a widespread practice among investors, who do talk

---

a particular curve for each particular rate of profit. But there is a second and much more damaging complication. Whatever be the prices which are chosen, there is no reason to expect that the order in which the values of the capital goods of the various techniques will emerge, at the chosen prices, should be the same as the order in which the various techniques become relevant on the scale of variation of the rate of profit. This is tantamount to saying that the latter order (which it was the very purpose of the diagram to represent) simply cannot be shown on the diagram.

There does not seem to have been any awareness of this second complication in the economic literature. For example, Morishima (1964) did notice the first complication (as can be seen from his figs. 13 and 14 on pp. 126–7), but missed the second complication altogether. On his figs. 10, 11, 15 and 16 (ibid., pp. 124, 128 and 129) all capital goods are evaluated at a particular set of prices – in his case the prices of technique ε – and yet they are represented so as to form a nice convex curve in the same order in which they become relevant on the scale of variation of the rate of profit. There is clearly no reason why, in general, it should be so.

of the 'rate of return' or also of the 'internal rate of return' of an investment project to mean the rate of profit associated with this investment project when all prices are taken as given. But if that is all that we do, then we must realize that we are simply using the words 'rate of return' as alternative words for 'rate of profit'.

This is clearly not what the marginal productivity theorists had claimed. They thought they could build on ratio **4** what they have called 'the physical or technical or productivity side' (Fisher, 1930, p. 176) of a theory of the rate of profit itself. We must conclude that, for this purpose, Irving Fisher's second notion of rate of return, as his first, is of no help at all. [. . .][14]

Concluding remarks

The implications of the phenomenon of reswitching of techniques for marginal capital theory appear to be the more serious the deeper one goes in uncovering them and bringing them out into the open. The initial result of no general relationship between rate of profit and value of capital goods per man came to contradict the marginal-theory interpretation of the rate of profit as a selector of capital intensity, i.e. as an 'index of scarcity' of the 'quantity of capital'. Further investigation now reveals that another traditional notion, that of 'rate of return', is devoid of any autonomous theoretical content.

Of course, one can always attribute to the words 'rate of return' a meaning. For example, one can choose to use the words 'rate of return' as another term for 'rate of profit'. This has in fact been done in two different ways: by calling 'rate of return' that rate of profit at which two techniques are equally profitable, and by following the entrepreneurs' practice of calling 'rate of return' that rate of profit which is associated with a particular investment project, when all prices are taken as given. But if one does so, i.e. if one uses the words 'rate of return' as a synonym for 'rate of profit', one cannot obviously pretend to use the notion of rate of return to *explain* the rate of profit.

The idea which had been basic to marginal capital theory was

14. Section IX of the original article, 'Professor Solow's analysis', has been omitted as it is a digression, not absolutely necessary for the main argument [*Eds.*].

another and a deeper one. The idea was that, even at the simplest stage of a stationary economic system, there exists something – to be called the 'rate of return' – which can be defined autonomously and independently of the rate of profit; something which is higher or lower according to whether the existing 'quantity of capital' is lower or higher, and as such represents a general technical property of the existing 'quantity of capital'. Such a thing would justify and *explain* the rate of profit. It is this idea which has been shown to be an illusion; for, in general, such a thing does not exist.

Appendix: a peculiar use of the term 'marginal product of capital'

The reader may have noticed that formula 3 (page 267) is an expression which has emerged on many other occasions in the economic literature of the past twenty years, and he may wonder whether it has always been interpreted consistently. Unfortunately the answer is that expression 3 has often given rise to some confusion, which seems to have originated from the formal appearance of the expression itself. As the reader can see, formula 3 happens to exhibit differences of net products at the numerator and of total values of capital goods at the denominator. If one is not careful one can quite easily be misled into associating it with the traditional concept of 'marginal product of capital'.

The formal similarity has actually been enhanced by the fact that expression 3 has often been written in terms of infinitesimal quantities; which can always be done, since any ratio may be expressed in terms of infinitesimal quantities if one multiplies both numerator and denominator by a constant which tends to become infinitesimally small. The procedure has, in fact, been given the following interpretation.

Let us consider a multi-commodity multi-technique economic system in which there are constant-returns-to-scale and in which means of production are such that no capital good need ever be discarded in passing from one technique to another. Then we may consider a process of 'capital accumulation' that starts from a situation in which the economic system uses only technique a and leads to a situation in which it uses only technique β, through an infinite series of intermediate stages in which it uses different linear combinations of the two techniques. If we compare any two of these intermediate stages, and compute the ratio between the differences of the two net products and the differences of the two total values of capital goods, at those prices at which the two techniques are equally profitable, we obtain a ratio which is nothing but expression 3, with a proportionally smaller numerator and denominator. More precisely we obtain

$$\frac{\mathbf{p}^*[\{\gamma \mathbf{Y}_\alpha+(1-\gamma)\mathbf{Y}_\beta\}-\{(\gamma+\Delta\gamma)\mathbf{Y}_\alpha+(1-\gamma-\Delta\gamma)\mathbf{Y}_\beta\}]}{\mathbf{p}^*[\{\gamma \mathbf{K}_\alpha+(1-\gamma)\mathbf{K}_\beta\}-\{(\gamma+\Delta\gamma)\mathbf{K}_\alpha+(1-\gamma-\Delta\gamma)\mathbf{K}_\beta\}]}$$
$$\equiv \frac{\Delta\gamma\ \mathbf{p}^*(\mathbf{Y}_\beta-\mathbf{Y}_\alpha)}{\Delta\gamma\ \mathbf{p}^*(\mathbf{K}_\beta-\mathbf{K}_\alpha)} \equiv r^*, \quad 8$$

where γ is an arbitrary constant and $\Delta\gamma$ is an increment of such a constant ($1 \geqslant \gamma \geqslant 0$, and $1 \geqslant \gamma+\Delta\gamma \geqslant 0$).

As the reader can see, the procedure has amounted to multiplying both numerator and denominator of 3 by a constant $\Delta\gamma$. If we now make $\Delta\gamma$ as small as we like (i.e. if we make the two intermediate stages we compare nearer and nearer to each other) we can make numerator and denominator of 8 as small as we like. This means that we can thereby write expression 3 as a limiting ratio of infinitesimal quantities, i.e. as a derivative. It is this derivative which has often been mistaken for the traditional concept of 'marginal product of capital'.

But the previous discussion should now also help to dispel this confusion. To obtain a ratio of an infinitesimal quantity of net output to an infinitesimal quantity of the value of capital goods does not necessarily mean having obtained a 'marginal product of capital'. This traditional concept was conceived as a limiting ratio of differences of two net products and of two 'quantities of capital' corresponding to two *different* techniques, each of which would be the most profitable at a *different* rate of profit. The derivative obtained above, on the other hand, is a limiting ratio of differences between two combinations of *the same* techniques at *the same* rate of profit. Such a derivative is simply another way of writing rate of profit r^* and clearly is not the derivative which marginal productivity theory has called the 'marginal product of capital'.

Of course, here again one might cut short all discussion and choose to call ratio 8 'marginal product of capital'. This would be a rather peculiar way of using this term; yet one could always claim the right to choose one's own definitions. One would have, however, to be consistent. If one singles out ratio **8** and chooses to call it 'marginal product of capital' one cannot obviously pretend to use it as if it were the concept which traditional theory has called the marginal product of capital, since that concept was something different. Indeed, if the traditional concept had not been something different, marginal productivity theory itself would never have become a theory. For, as we have seen, ratio **3** and for that matter ratio **8** are expressions which are compatible with any theory of the rate of profit.

References

FISHER, I. (1906), *The Nature of Capital and Income*, Macmillan Co.

FISHER, I. (1907), *The Rate of Interest*, Macmillan Co.

FISHER, I. (1930), *The Theory of Interest*, Macmillan Co.

MORISHIMA, M. (1964), *Equilibrium Stability and Growth*, Oxford University Press.

ROBINSON, J. (1956), *The Accumulation of Capital*, Macmillan.

SOLOW, R. M. (1963), *Capital Theory and the Rate of Return*, North-Holland Publishing Co. [See Reading 6.]

SOLOW, R. M. (1967), 'The interest rate and transition between techniques', in C. H. Feinstein (ed.), *Socialism, Capitalism and Economic Growth. Essays Presented to Maurice Dobb*, Cambridge University Press, pp. 30–39.

SRAFFA, P. (1960), *Production of Commodities by Means of Commodities. Prelude to a Critique of Economic Theory*, Cambridge University Press. [See Reading 4.]

Part Six
The Rate of Profits in Capitalist Society

One of the avenues leading away from the critique of the marginalist approach to distribution questions is that which seeks an explanation for the rate of profits in terms of the saving propensities of the capitalist class and the rate of growth of the economy. As we have seen, Pasinetti's (1962) paper precipitated the most recent discussion of these issues and led to the formulation of what Samuelson and Modigliani (1966) dubbed the anti-Pasinetti theorem, whereby it is the *average* product of capital which is related to the rate of growth and the saving propensity of a particular class – in this instance, the workers. The value of the rate of profits is again linked to the characteristics of the production function. In formal terms, these issues concern the long-run steady-state equilibrium values of certain key concepts, *if* the steady state exists. Meade, beautifully and simply, has sorted out the issues in terms of one diagram and we reprint his taxonomic note as Reading 14. We also reprint as Reading 15 Kaldor's views on the issues as contained in his critique of the paper by Samuelson and Modigliani (1966). Kaldor comments on the wider issues of neo-neo-classical methodology and the neo-neo-classical approach to economic analysis and presents his own positive contribution, a neo-Pasinetti theorem, in which the analysis is reset in the world as we know it rather than being confined within the bounds of the necessary requirements for long-run, steady-state equilibrium. Nuti's paper (Reading 16) could fit equally well into a number of slots: Part Two, because it is a vintage, putty–clay model; Part Five, because it adds a new (and unexpected) result to the double-switching analysis, namely, that the FpF is not inevitably nor necessarily downward sloping for all of its length; Part Six, because it is concerned with the relationship between the rate of profits and the rate of growth; and Part Seven, because it analyses some aspects of optimal growth within both a capitalist and a socialist (two varieties) environment.

References

PASINETTI, L. L. (1962), 'Rate of profit and income distribution in relation to the rate of economic growth', *Rev. econ. Stud.*, vol. 29, pp. 267–79.

SAMUELSON, P. A., and MODIGLIANI, F. (1966), 'The Pasinetti paradox in neo-classical and more general models', *Rev. econ. Stud.*, vol. 33, pp. 269–301.

14 J. E. Meade

The Outcome of the Pasinetti-Process

J. E. Meade, 'The outcome of the Pasinetti-process: a note', *Economic Journal*, vol. 76, 1966, pp. 161–5.

This note is intended solely to elucidate the boundaries which separate the various possible outcomes of the Pasinetti-process. It is, I believe, uncontroversial, but may help to throw light on some of the points at issue.

Assume: capitalists who do no work and save S_p of their income and workers who save $S_w(S_w < S_p)$ of their income. The Pasinetti-process is concerned with the nature of the ultimate long-run steady-state equilibrium when the ratio of property owned by capitalists to property owned by workers has tended to its final value. The outcome may take any one of three forms:

1. No steady-state equilibrium exists.

2. The distribution of property settles at a value at which $P/K = g_n/S_p$, where P is total profits, K total capital and g_n the steady-state rate of growth (the case examined by Pasinetti, 1962).

3. The distribution of property tends to a value at which $Y/K = g_n/S_w$, where Y is total income (the case which I exemplified with a Cobb–Douglas production function: see Meade, 1963).

The present note is a piece of geometric taxonomy to show how the boundaries between cases 1, 2 and 3 depend upon the interplay of the parameters g_n, S_p and S_w; and the technical characteristics of the production function.

Measure as in Figure 1 the rate of profit P/K on the horizontal axis and the output–capital ratio Y/K on the vertical axis. Draw the line OA at 45° to the axes. We are concerned only with the space between the vertical axis and the line OA, since below the line OA, P/Y is >1, i.e. profits would absorb more than the whole national income. Let $OB = g_n/S_p$ and $OC = g_n/S_w$ and complete the rectangle $OCDEB$. Since $S_p > S_w$, the point D lies above OA.

The long-run steady-state values of Y/K and P/K, if they exist, must lie either on the line CD or on the line DE. This can be seen as follows:

1. Consider first any point to the right of BG. Then $S_p P/K > g_n$. The property of capitalists is growing more quickly than the steady-state growth value. If this continues, sooner or later total capital will be growing at a higher rate than g_n, which is incompatible with steady-state equilibrium.

2. Consider next any point above the line CF. Then $S_w Y/K > g_n$. But total capital must be growing at least as fast as $S_w Y/K$ (it will be growing faster than $S_w Y/K$ if any significant amount of income is going to capitalists). Therefore, once more a steady-state equilibrium is excluded because capital is growing at a higher rate than g_n.

3. Consider finally any point inside the area $OCDE$. Here both $S_p P/K < g_n$ and $S_w Y/K < g_n$. Since $S_p P/K < g_n$, capitalists' property will be growing at a rate lower than g_n. In this case, then,

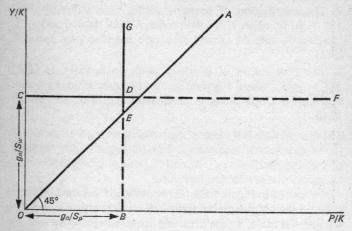

Figure 1

if a steady state exists the ratio of capitalists' to workers' property tends to zero; but if this were so, since $S_w Y/K < g_n$ capital would in fact be growing at a rate less than g_n, so that no steady state can exist.

On the line CD we have $S_w Y/K = g_n$ and $S_p P/K < g_n$. This is the case of the long-run steady state in which workers' capital comes to dominate capitalists' capital; and we have a long-run steady state with $Y/K = g_n/S_w$.

On the line DE we have $S_w Y/K < g_n$ and $S_p P/K = g_n$. This is the case (examined by Pasinetti, 1962) where the distribution of property adjusts itself between workers and capitalists until $P/K = g_n/S_p$.

We can now see how, given S_w, S_p and g_n, the production function will decide the outcome. The following are three illustrative cases.

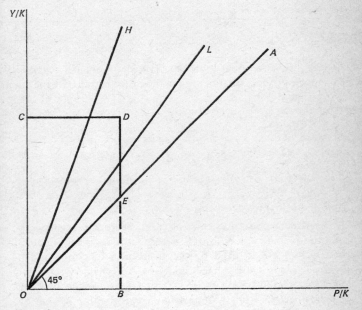

Figure 2

1. The Cobb–Douglas case of unitary elasticity of substitution between K and L (the amount of labour measured in efficiency units as expanded by Harrod-neutral technical progress). This

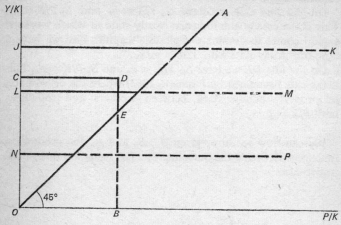

Figure 3

was the case examined in Meade (1963). In this case P/Y is fixed by the production function. In the case illustrated by the line OH in Figure 2 (where

$$\frac{P}{Y} < \frac{g_n/S_p}{g_n/S_w},$$

i.e. $S_w < (1-Q)S_p,$

where $1-Q$ is the proportion of income going to profits) we get the result $Y/K = g_n/S_w$. In the case of the line OL (where $S_w < (1-Q)S_p$) we get the result $P/K = g_n/S_p$.

2. The fixed technical coefficient case, where the elasticity of substitution between K and L is zero, is shown in Figure 3. In this case Y/K is fixed by the production function; and in Figure 3 three possible fixed values of Y/K (namely, ON, OL and OJ) are illustrated. With $Y/K = OL$ (since the line LM cuts the line DE) a steady-state solution exists with $P/K = g_n/S_p$. But with $Y/K = ON$ or OJ no steady state exists, since the lines

NP and JK cut neither CD nor DE. With fixed Y/K, therefore, no steady state exists if Y/K is $>BD$ or $<BE = OB$. In other words, with fixed Y/K, for a steady state to exist we must have $g_n/S_w > Y/K > g_n/S_p$ or $S_w < g_n K/Y < S_p$.

3. The fixed-rate-of-interest case, i.e. where the elasticity of

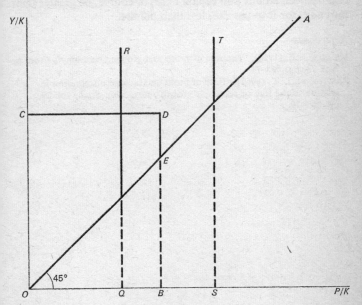

Figure 4

substitution between K and L is infinite and there are no diminishing returns to either factor. In this case P/K is fixed by the production function. In Figure 4 two possible values for a fixed P/K (namely OQ and OS are illustrated. With $P/K = OS$ (i.e. with $P/K > g_n/S_p$) no steady state can exist, since the line ST cuts neither CD nor DE. With $P/K = OQ$ (i.e. with $P/K < g_n/S_p$) a steady state exists with $Y/K = g_n/S_w$.

The ratio Y/K can find this predetermined value by a suitable adjustment of the ratio of K to L, and so of profits to wages, and so of capital to total income.

The above are, of course, only three particular examples of

production functions. The outcome with any production function can, however, be found by drawing on Figure 1 a line showing the technically given relationship between the rate of profit and the output–capital ratio and observing whether this line cuts *CD* or *DE* or neither. For the line to cut *CD*, the elasticity of substitution between labour and capital must, of course, be greater than zero and, for it to cut *DE*, less than infinite.

References

MEADE, J. E. (1963), 'The rate of profit in a growing economy', *Econ. J.*, vol. 73, pp. 665–74.

PASINETTI, L. L. (1962), 'Rate of profit and income distribution in relation to the rate of economic growth', *Rev. econ. Stud.*, vol. 29, pp. 267–79.

15 N. Kaldor

Marginal Productivity and Macroeconomic Theories of Distribution

N. Kaldor, 'Marginal productivity and the macro-economic theories of distribution', *Review of Economic Studies*, vol. 33, 1966, pp. 309–19.

Professors Samuelson and Modigliani (1966) have written a long critical essay on macroeconomic theories of distribution which demonstrates, not only the splendid analytical powers of the two authors, but also the intellectual sterility engendered by the methods of neo-classical economics. The assumption of profit maximization under conditions of universal perfect competition involves, as a logical step (given the postulate of substitute relationships between factors), the assumption of production functions which are linear-homogeneous and 'well behaved' (with isoquants asymptotic to the axes). In addition, it has also been found necessary to assume either that capital is completely 'malleable', or else that capital–labour intensities are identical in all industries in all circumstances – so that *real* capital can be uniquely measured in value (money) terms – and that there is no technical progress, except of the 'Harrod-neutral' type which falls like manna from Heaven. Given sufficient refinement of analysis no doubt many other such 'assumptions' may have to be added. (One obvious candidate which has not been incorporated yet in neo-classical models is the absence of 'Sraffa effects' – though it may be difficult to formulate the necessary conditions explicitly.) There is no room here for increasing returns, learning by doing, oligopolistic competition, uncertainty, obsolescence and other such troublesome things which mar the world as we know it. Markets operate in such a way that 'competition will *enforce* (their italics) *at all times* (my italics) equality of factor prices to factor marginal productivities' (p. 271) and even if marginal productivities did not exist (in the 'fixed coefficient case' on pp. 287–9) 'markets' would still operate in such a way as to punish immediately a factor in excess supply, be it capital or labour, with a zero price.

I would not wish to deny that these 'abstractions' are necessary to make the system logically consistent, given the basic assumptions concerning how markets behave and how entrepreneurs behave (profit maximization *combined with* universal perfect competition). But one must not fall into the error of supposing that assertions about reality can be derived from *a priori* assumptions. Whether well-behaved homogeneous-and-linear production functions exist or not is a question of fact. They cannot be presumed to exist as a consequence of some basic postulate, such as 'profit maximization under competitive conditions'. If adequate empirical observation *established* the existence of production functions of constant-returns-to-scale, if entrepreneurs can be *shown* to be confronted by infinitely elastic demand and supply curves, if the progress in technical knowledge could be *shown* to be of the kind which affected the productivity of all resources equally, and which proceeded at some autonomous rate in time, independently of entrepreneurial decisions concerning production and investment, the situation would be different. But all that we can tell from empirical observation is that output per unit of labour increases with the passage of time – to an extent that varies significantly between different industries and different countries – whilst output per unit of capital shows no systematic trend, upwards or downwards. We know that in a majority of cases, if not all, there is a positive association between the rate of increase of output-per-man and the rate of increase of output. But it is not possible to isolate the element of 'autonomous' technological change from elements which are induced by, or associated with, changes in output or in investment.

However, for Professors Samuelson and Modigliani, assumptions like homogeneous linear and 'well-behaved' production functions, or autonomous 'Harrod-neutral' technical change, are not meant, I suppose, to be descriptions of reality (though in many places they argue as if they were) – they are 'abstractions' which are intended merely as intermediate stages in the process of analysis. It is the hallmark of the neo-classical economist to believe that, however severe the abstractions from which he is forced to start, he will 'win through' by the end of the day – bit by bit, if he only carries the analysis far enough, the scaffolding can be removed, leaving the basic structure intact. In fact, these props are *never* removed; the removal of any one of a number of them – as for example, allowing for increasing returns or learning-by doing – is sufficient to cause the whole structure to collapse like a pack of cards.[1] It is high time that the brilliant minds of MIT were set to evolve a system of non-Euclidean economics which starts from a non-perfect, non-profit maximizing economy where such abstractions are initially unnecessary. (Of course the neo-classical purist would argue, again on *a priori* grounds, that in the long run the non-profit maximizers will fall by the wayside – profit maximization will emerge by a Darwinian process of selection. This *may* be true in a static world with perfect foresight, in which profits can *only* be made through the relentless pursuit of the principle of substitution. But in a world of imperfect foresight and changing technology, the Darwinian process may favour the successful innovator who operates on hunches rather than the *homo oeconomicus* of the more pedestrian type, the careful equator of marginal substitution ratios.)

These general observations will, I think, be helpful in appreciating the particular comments that follow.

Capitalists and workers

Samuelson and Modigliani assume that any macroeconomic theory which makes use of the notion of differences in savings propensities between profits and wages requires an identifiable class of hereditary barons – a class of capitalists 'with permanent membership' – distinguished by a high savings propensity and of a 'permanent' class of workers distinguished by a low savings propensity. I cannot, of course, speak for Dr Pasinetti, but as far as my own ideas are concerned, I have always regarded the high savings propensity out of profits as something which attaches to

1. This is occasionally admitted – cf. for example, Samuelson and Modigliani (1966, p. 271, fn. 2) which says that 'the assumption of constant returns-to-scale is essential both to Pasinetti's and our own analysis, for otherwise the concept of a Golden-Age steady state becomes self-contradictory'. If the specification of a 'Golden-Age steady state' includes perfect competition, profit maximization *et al.*, this is obviously true. But if by a 'Golden-Age steady state' no more is meant than a steady rate of growth with a constant rate of profit, the proposition is not true.

the nature of business income, and not to the wealth (or other peculiarities) of the individuals who own property. It is the enterprise, not the particular body of individuals owning it at any one time, which finds it necessary, in a dynamic world of increasing returns, to plough back a proportion of the profits earned as a kind of 'prior charge' on earnings in order to ensure the survival of the enterprise in the long run. This is because: (a) continued expansion cannot be ensured in an uncertain world, and in the long run, unless *some proportion* of the finance required for expansion comes from internal sources; (b) the competitive strength of any one enterprise, in a world of increasing returns, varies with the enterprise's share of the market – it declines with any decrease in that share and improves with an increasing share; hence (c) in a world of expanding markets, continued expansion (by the individual firm) is necessary merely to maintain the competitive strength of the enterprise. Hence the high savings propensity attaches to profits as such, not to capitalists as such.

In the early days of industrial capitalism when the ownership and management of businesses were united in the same person (as in the case of the early ironmasters of England or, in more recent times, of Henry Ford) a high propensity to plough back business profits inevitably entailed a high propensity to save out of individual income. The capitalists of the nineteenth century, as Keynes once said, 'were allowed to call the best part of the cake theirs, and were theoretically free to consume it, on the tacit underlying condition that they consumed very little of it in practice' (Keynes, 1919, p. 17). But nowadays businesses are to a large extent owned by rentier-capitalists (shareholders) whose personal savings propensity need bear no relation to the savings propensity of the enterprises which they own. They are free to consume, in addition to their dividend income, as much of their capital (or their capital gains) as they like; in so far as they do so, this goes to offset the net acquisition of business assets by the 'workers': it does *not* reduce, but on the contrary, enhances, the difference in savings propensities between business income and personal income. (For reasons explained in the Appendix (page 308), the shareholders' consumption out of capital gains cannot be treated as a reduction of s_c; it has exactly the same effect as a reduction of s_w, since it causes a reduction of the net savings of persons that is available to finance business investment.)

The 'anti-Pasinetti theorem'

The foregoing remarks are sufficient, I think, to refute the authors' contention that provided the savings propensity of workers is high enough, the 'capitalists' (distinguished by their high savings propensity) will be gradually eliminated so that, in a Golden-Age equilibrium, only one 'savings propensity' is left. For this purpose they consider a situation in which the basic 'Pasinetti inequality' (i.e. that the share of investment in total income is higher than the share of savings in wages, or in total personal income) does not hold as regards the 'equilibrium' level of investment. They then proceed to demonstrate that the 'capitalists' will be gradually 'squeezed out'. However, the end of it all is not a violent revolution, à la Marx, but the cosy world of Harrod, Domar and Solow, where there is only a single savings propensity applicable to the economy – where in other words, $sY = s_w Y$.

The simple answer to all this is that, if the basic Kaldor–Pasinetti inequality is not satisfied, no Keynesian macroeconomic distribution theory could survive for an instant, let alone in Golden-Age equilibrium. If the 'equilibrium' level of investment was less than the workers' savings, it is impossible to contemplate that investment should play the active role and savings the passive role; for if we postulated that investment decisions were autonomous, either the full employment assumption would break down, or profits would have to be negative; and in either case it is clearly inconceivable that profits should be determined by the need to generate sufficient savings to finance investment. Moreover if we assume that profits are determined quite independently of this relation – either by marginal productivities in the Wonderland of Perfect Competition, etc., or by, say, Kalecki's 'degree of monopoly' – we need further to assume a purely non-Keynesian system where there is necessarily just enough investment to finance full employment savings – where, in other words, savings *govern* investment, not the other way round.[2] It is easy to refute

2. On the subject of 'full employment' the two halves of the Samuelson–Modigliani paper take up wholly contradictory positions. In the first half it is automatically (and continually) ensured by the marginal productivity

Pasinetti by postulating conditions in which the Pasinetti model could not possibly work, and where, therefore, something else must take its place – whatever that something else may be. Professors Samuelson and Modigliani assume, as a matter of course, that it must be Walras. In disproving Pasinetti they conjure up a Walrasian world in all its purity – a world in which all savings get invested somehow, without disturbing full employment: because any excess of savings over its equilibrium level induces a corresponding excess of investment over its equilibrium level. It is a world in which excess savings in search of investment necessarily depress the rate of interest, r, to whatever level required to induce the necessary addition to investment, which means that, given a sufficient fall in r, a value of k/y can always be found (this is where 'well-behaved' production functions come in) to make $nk/y = s_w$.

The validity of the Pasinetti inequality, $s_w < I/Y$ – or, in the Samuelson–Modigliani way of looking at it, $s_w < \alpha(k)s_c$ – is a matter of fact, just as perfect competition, constant-returns-to-scale *et al.* are matters of fact. Empirical investigation can disprove the former, just as it can disprove the latter. The question is, does it, and if so, which?

A side glance to reality

There is just one occasion where the two authors find it necessary to discuss the realistic values of the variables in order to justify their concern with the 'anti-Pasinetti' case where 'capitalists' are saved out of existence by the 'workers'. It occurs in their footnote 1, p. 274, which is adduced in support of the statement that values of $P/Y = \alpha(k^*) = \frac{1}{4}$, $s_c = \frac{1}{5}$ and $s_w = 0.05$, which

equations. But in the second half, dealing with macroeconomic theories, they become highly sceptical of its ever occurring, and pour scorn on people like Marshall, Pigou or myself for suggesting that unemployment has been small or trendless. Compare, for example, the statement in Samuelson and Modigliani (1966, p. 277) that 'as long as the production function is well behaved, failure of (8) or even (7) to hold *cannot interfere* with full employment' (my italics) with their footnote 3, p. 294, which says that if you believe in a mechanism making for full employment: 'You can – as the Duke of Wellington once said – believe in anything.' Is there nothing, literally nothing, in a capitalist system which makes for full employment equilibrium – outside the cosy world of neo-classical theory?

(in their view) rule out the Pasinetti theorem, 'are econo-metrically reasonable for a mixed economy like the US, UK or Western Europe'.[3] In this demonstration however, they make no less than four slips:

1. The 'corporate savings propensity of $\frac{1}{3}$' relates to savings out of net profits, after capital consumption allowances. The share of corporate profits of $\frac{1}{4}$ relates to the share of *gross* profits in the gross national product (GNP). The empirical 'savings propen-sity' out of gross profits after tax is not $\frac{1}{3}$, but 0·7 for the United States and the United Kingdom, and somewhere around 0·8 for Germany and Japan. (From the point of view of the mechanics of a Keynesian model, it is *gross* savings out of *gross* profits, and *gross* investment, that are relevant, not *net* savings and *net* investment; indeed in a more realistic 'vintage' model it is not even possible to say *ab initio* what the latter are.)

2. The value $s_w = \frac{1}{12}$ is probably a realistic one for the net savings of wage and salary earners (i.e. net of dis-savings of retired wor-kers); it is not, however, an indication of the savings available for the acquisition of business capital or for lending to the business sector, since a large part of it goes to finance personal investment in consumer durables. The only consumer durable which is statis-tically relevant in this connection is residential housing (since furniture, cars, etc. are statistically reckoned in consumption, not in investment, in official national income accounts) and the latter must be deducted before the value of 's_w' relevant to the model can be estimated.

The net acquisition of financial assets by the personal sector – which is the measure of the personal saving available for lending

3. Incidentally, the very demonstration that these figures are inconsistent with the Pasinetti theorem is based on a piece of circular reasoning – it assumes what it intends to prove. For it supposes that the share of profits is determined by the technical coefficients of the production function, irrespec-tive of anything else, in particular the investment coefficient, I/Y, which is here supposed to be governed by the savings generated by a predetermined profits share, dictated by the production function – whereas the whole dis-pute between Keynesian and non-Keynesian theories is whether investment determines savings, or vice versa. (I admit that they do not quite go the whole hog and postulate a world under a full Cobb–Douglas dictatorship where the share of profit is a technologically given constant, irrespective of anything else.)

to other sectors – appears to be very much smaller, as the following estimates show:[4]

	Percentage of personal disposable income (average 1960 to 1965)	
	United Kingdom	United States
Personal saving	6·9	10·3
less investment in dwellings	−2·8	−4·7
less investment in fixed assets and stocks by unincorporated businesses	−1·8	−4·5
equals net acquisition of financial assets by the personal sector	2·3	1·1
of which		
increase in life assurance and pension funds	4·7	2·6
increase in other financial assets (net)	−2·4	−1·5

4. The figures are derived from the official national income accounts for the United States and the United Kingdom and are, as far as possible, on a comparable basis. The source of the figures for the United States is the *Survey of Current Business*, May 1966; for the United Kingdom, *Financial Statistics*, June 1966, and *Economic Trends*, April 1966.

Personal disposable income, as defined here, is reckoned before deducting capital consumption. Gross personal saving includes any capital transfers received *less* any capital transfers paid. For both countries independent estimates of identified acquisitions of financial assets *less* liabilities exceed the residual figures obtained from the official national income accounts; it is impossible to say how far the discrepancy is due to an underestimate of personal savings in the national accounts (and an overestimate of corporate etc. savings) and how far to under-recording of financial transactions between the personal sector and the others. For the US estimates based on identified financial transactions may be deduced from the May 1966 issue of the *Federal Reserve Bulletin*:

	Percentages of personal disposable income (average 1961–5)
Increase in life assurance and pensions funds	3·4
Increase in other financial assets	−0·5
Net acquisition of financial assets by personal sector	2·9

For both countries the figures of personal saving and of net acquisitions relate to the personal sector as a whole, including unincorporated enter-

In the United Kingdom personal saving as a percentage of personal disposable income appears to be lower than in the United States. But because investment in dwellings by the personal sector and investment by unincorporated businesses is relatively less important in the United Kingdom, net acquisition of financial assets appears to be somewhat higher.

Hence, whether we take the US or the UK figures, the value of s_w – in the only sense in which this is relevant to the Pasinetti theorem or the anti-Pasinetti theorem – is more like $\frac{1}{50}$ or $\frac{1}{100}$ than $\frac{1}{12}$.

3. In the above figures the 'increase in life assurance and pension funds' is probably a good indication of the net savings of wage and salary earners (after deduction of the savings that go to repay mortgages on houses), since these are so largely contractual in character. On the other hand, the net diminution in 'other financial assets' is probably a good measure of the net consumption of property-owners out of capital or capital gains. Since net spending in excess of dividend income involves a net sale of securities, which goes to offset at least a part of the net demand for securities originating from wage and salary earners' savings, it should be evident that spending out of capital gains is indistinguishable in its effects from a reduction in workers' savings. The fact that some of the capital gains are spent is thus in no sense a criticism of the 'realism of the strict Pasinetti assumptions'. There is nothing in the model which requires s_w to be positive – the model works just as well when it is negative, with the business sector being a net lender, not a net borrower, to the personal sector (cf. Appendix, pages 307–13). Despite the laborious attempt to 'generalize' the model to all kinds of cases – Pasinetti and anti-Pasinetti – Samuelson and Modigliani ignore the 'super-Pasinetti' case of $s_w < 0$ or the special 'arch-Pasinetti' case of $s_w = 0$.

4. With a 'realistic' value of s_w of, say, 0·01–0·03, and a 'realistic'

---

prises. Since the income of these enterprises is small in relation to total of personal income (14 to 15 per cent in the United States and 9 to 10 per cent in the United Kingdom), no great error can result from assuming that the saving (covering both capital consumption and other additions to reserves) of unincorporated enterprises is roughly balanced by their investment. (I am indebted to Mr L. S. Berman of the Central Statistical Office for these estimates.)

value of $s_c = 0.7$, one would have thought that the Kaldor–Pasinetti type of model is safe enough on empirical grounds – even allowing for 'Kuh–Meyer' effects, the validity of which is in any case highly questionable.[5] However, if one goes in for 'realism', surely one cannot ignore the existence of a third class, which is more likely to overspend its income than either 'workers' or 'capitalists', namely the Government. The 'net acquisition of financial assets by the personal sector' need not, in fact, finance business investment: it often goes to finance (probably only a part of) the net borrowing of the public sector. To find out whether 'the realistic value of the variables' threatens the Pasinetti model in an anti-Pasinetti direction, one should pose another question: how much of business investment is in fact financed out of personal savings? This information is found by looking at the net acquisition of financial assets of the (private) corporate sector; in the US this item has been positive for three out of the last six years, and in the UK it has been positive for five out of the six years (even after adjustment for net long-term investment abroad). In such years the corporate sector is a net lender to the rest of the economy, and not a net borrower. This comes to the same, from the point of view of the mechanics of the Keynesian-type distribution theory, as assuming a negative value of s_w; in its effects on profits it makes no difference whether the net dis-saving is due to the activities of the personal sector or of the Government.

The 'generalized' neo-classical theory

In section X of their paper Samuelson and Modigliani (1966) discover that their results do not, after all, depend on 'marginal

5. The correlation found by Kuh and Meyer between corporate savings and corporate investment does not in any way prove that corporate investment is confined by, or governed by, corporate savings: they may both reflect a common factor, the rate of return on capital employed. A company's retention ratio is clearly influenced by its long-run capital requirements: the *raison d'être* of the plough-back is to preserve a company's liquidity and thus to prevent its long-run expansion from being hampered by financial embarrassments. But there is always a 'liquidity cushion' (in Anglo-Saxon countries, often a pretty large cushion) between the current cash inflow of savings and the current cash outflow on capital expenditure; the purpose of retention is to protect the cushion, rather than to finance expenditure on a day-to-day basis.

productivity notions of the Clark–Wicksteed–Solow–Meade type'. *All* that they require is the postulate that the rate of profit, or interest, should be a single valued function φ of the capital–labour ratio K/L, with $\varphi' < 0$. No reason whatever is adduced to show why this assumption is any less restrictive than the whole bag of tricks specified in equations 1 and 2. The assumption of a functional relation between the rate of profit and the capital–labour ratio is *implied* in the assumption underlying equations 1 and 2; but without them it is purely arbitrary. Nor is any attempt made to support the validity (or plausibility) of such an assumption empirically. The K/L ratio, unlike the K/Y ratio, shows the widest of variations between the different countries – it is perhaps twenty times as high in the US as in India – whilst the rate of profit is often to be found to be higher in countries with a relatively high K/L ratio than with a low K/L ratio. (Of course they might have argued, in the manner of the Stanford inquiry, that in terms of 'corrected' labour units – corrected for Harrod-neutral differences in 'efficiency' – capital–labour ratios are everywhere the same!)

Fixed coefficients

Finally, they assert that macroeconomic distribution theories 'fare best' under the assumption of fixed coefficients 'for under variable coefficients one would have *no need* (my italics) for a genuinely alternative theory of distribution' – why search for something new when you have such a satisfying explanation already?

It is at this point that they should have taken another sideglance into reality and adduced some empirical evidence to show that the most important 'predictions' of the marginal productivity theory – diminishing productivity to labour in the short period, constant-returns-to-scale to both labour and capital in the long period – are valid, as a matter of fact. However they could not have done this, because:

1. All empirical studies concerning the short-period relationship between output and employment (at least in manufacturing activities) show the elasticity of the former with regard to changes in the latter to be greater, not less, than unity ('Okun's Law'

makes it 3) which implies, of course, that the short-period marginal product of labour exceeds the average product. Since profits are non-negative, the proposition that the price of each factor is 'at all times' equal to its marginal product cannot possibly hold. Another way of putting the same point is that in order to get diminishing short-period marginal productivity for labour (or increasing marginal labour cost), firms must operate plant near full (or maximum) capacity. Experience shows that even in times when production is limited by labour shortages, plant is not (normally) fully utilized.

2. All empirical studies concerning the relationship of productivity and production (again, for manufacturing activities) reveal the existence of (long-run) increasing returns, both on account of the economies of large-scale production, and of the subdivision of processes (and of industries) with an increase in the scale of activities. Again the proposition that factor prices are equal to their marginal products cannot hold, because the marginal products do not 'add up' to the total product.

However, the authors believe they have demonstrated (by *a priori* reasoning) that there is no room for anything other than marginal productivity if there are possibilities of factor substitution. Hence 'recognizing the empirical oddity of the postulate' they proceed to explore the case of fixed coefficients, and find that here at last the Kaldor–Pasinetti proposition has some 'definite meaning' as an explanation of relative shares. However, they hasten to add that 'whatever value the above model has as an exercise, its economic relevance is in our view very dubious' because an economic system of this kind would be subject to the wildest instability: if the capital–labour ratio wasn't exactly right, either profits would be zero or wages would be zero (according to whether capital were just a little too much or a little too little); and there is no guarantee that a system fluctuating between the extremes of zero profits and zero wages would tend to generate just the right amount of capital to be consistent with positive values for both.

But what kind of an 'economic system' are they 'observing'? Is it Ruritania, Solovia, Cloud-Cuckooland or the USA and other members of the Group of Ten? If 'excess' labour caused wages to fall to zero, how could there ever be unemployment – of the Keynesian or any other kind? And if 'excess' capital caused profits to fall to zero, how could there ever be profits, considering that the employment capacity of the prevailing capital equipment, in any advanced community, is always larger and often very considerably larger, than what is needed to secure full employment for the existing labour force? Indeed, how could capacity ever be underutilized and still earn a profit?

The whole antithesis that *either* marginal productivity 'must explain' pricing and distribution *or else* there must be fixed coefficients, is neo-classical circular reasoning carried *in extremis*. The proposition is true but only in the abstract Wonderland of Perfect Competition, profit maximization plus the etceteras specified at the beginning. Their appeal however to the need to reconcile 'the relatively smooth functioning of behaviour and of share imputation in *observed* economic systems' is an appeal, not to the Wonderland, but to the Real World. Can't they see that it is *possible* for a market economy to be 'competitive' without satisfying the neo-classical equations? Can't they imagine a world in which marginal productivities are *not* equal to factor prices, and are not in any definite relationship to factor prices – a world, for example, in which, with the approach of labour scarcity, the share of wages is falling, not rising, despite the fact that the marginal productivity of labour is constant or rising and capital (in the relevant sense) is redundant in relation to labour? Unless they make a more imaginative effort to reconcile their theoretical framework with the known facts of experience, their economic theory is bound to remain a barren exercise. One is reminded of what Clapham (1922, p. 561) wrote fifty years ago: 'I have a fear lest a theory of value which should prove permanently unable to state of what particular and individual values some of its more important conclusions were true might in the long run be neglected by mankind.'

Appendix: a neo-Pasinetti theorem[6]

Dr Pasinetti has shown that on certain conditions the rate of profit, in a true long-run Golden-Age equilibrium, will be independent of the rate of savings of 'workers', because the additional

6. I should like to acknowledge the benefits from discussion with F. H. Hahn, L. L. Pasinetti and J. A. Mirrlees.

consumption generated out of the workers' property income will offset their savings out of wage income. The difficulty with this proposition (apart from the fact that it is 'very long run') is that it assumes that workers spend the same fraction of their income, irrespective of whether it accrues to them as property income or wages. In a world where enterprises are organized as corporations, and property income takes the form of dividends, this would imply (as Professors Samuelson and Modigliani point out) overspending their dividend income by the exact fraction required to make their consumption equal to $(1 - s_w)P_w$, irrespective of the division of profits between corporate retentions and dividends.

Moreover, once we allow spending in excess of dividend income, there is no reason to confine such spending to workers. 'Capitalists' also spend some part of their capital gains (or even their capital, in the absence of such gains) and, as Professor Modigliani has reminded us, the limited length of human life must add to such temptations.

Hence at any time there must be capitalists (or shareholders) who overspend their current (dividend) income (and the same must be true of course of retired workers who consume over the years of retirement their accumulated savings), just as there are active workers who save a certain fraction of their income for retirement. Just as net saving out of income sets up a demand for securities, net dis-saving out of income (= net consumption out of capital or capital gains) sets up a supply of securities. There is also a net supply of new securities issued by the corporate sector. Since, in the securities' market prices will tend to a level at which the total (non-speculative) supply and demand for securities are equal, there must be some mechanism to ensure that the spending out of capital (or capital gains) just balances the savings out of income *less* any new securities issued by corporations.

Let us divide the community into wage and salary earners, W, who save (through the intermediaries of pension funds and insurance companies) some fraction of their income during their working life and consume it in retirement; so long as the population is rising and income per head is rising, the savings of the working population must exceed the dis-savings of the retired population by an amount which can be expressed as some fraction, s_w, of current wage-and-salary income. (I am assuming also that s_w is net of personal investment in consumer durables, i.e. in housing.)

Let us further suppose that the shareholders' net consumption out of capital (i.e. their consumption in excess of their dividend income) is some fraction, c, of their capital gains G.

And finally, let us suppose that corporations (having decided on retaining a fraction, s_c, of their profits) decide in addition to issue new securities equal to some fraction, i, ($|i| < 1$), of their current investment expenditure, gK (where $K =$ capital, $g =$ the growth rate).

Equilibrium in the securities market then requires that

$$s_w W = cG + igK.$$

For such an equilibrium to exist, at least one of these items must be responsive to changes in the market prices of securities. Such an item is cG, since G is nothing else than the change in the market value of securities. This varies not only with the rise in dividends and earnings per share, but also with the 'valuation ratio' v, i.e. the relation of the market value of shares to the capital employed by the corporations (or the 'book value' of assets). In other words, if the market value of securities is pN (where $N =$ number of shares, $p =$ price per share) and given a constant valuation ratio

$$G = N \Delta p = v \Delta K - p \Delta N \qquad 1$$

(i.e. the increase in the corporations' assets *multiplied* by the valuation ratio *less* the value of new securities issued). Since

$$\left. \begin{array}{r} \Delta K = gK, \\ p \Delta N = igK, \\ G = vgK - igK. \end{array} \right\} \qquad 2$$

Hence[7] $\quad s_w W - c(vgK - igK) = igK.$ $\qquad$ 3

There is in addition the savings = investment equation

$$s_w W - c(vgK - igK) + s_c P = gK. \qquad 4$$

7. We subsume in the definition of c a constant share of assets owned by shareholders, for reasons explained below.

Since $W = Y-P$, $P = \rho K$ (P = profits, ρ = the rate of profit), the above can be written

$$s_w Y - s_w \rho K - cvgK + cigK = igK \qquad \textbf{3a}$$

and $\quad s_w Y + (s_c - s_w)\rho K - cvgK + cigK = gK. \qquad \textbf{4a}$

After rearranging the terms and dividing through by gK we get

$$\frac{s_w}{g}\frac{Y}{K} - \frac{s_w \rho}{g} - cv + ci = i, \qquad \textbf{3b}$$

$$\frac{s_w}{g}\frac{Y}{K} + \frac{(s_c - s_w)\rho}{g} - cv + ci = 1. \qquad \textbf{4b}$$

Solving for v and ρ we get

$$v = \frac{1}{c}\left[\frac{s_w}{g}\frac{Y}{K} - \frac{s_w}{s_c}(1-i) - i(1-c)\right] \qquad \textbf{5}$$

and $\quad \rho = \dfrac{g(1-i)}{s_c}. \qquad \textbf{6}$

The interpretation of these equations is as follows. Given the savings coefficients and the capital-gains-consumption coefficient, there will be a certain valuation ratio which will secure just enough savings by the personal sector to take up the new securities issued by corporations. Hence the *net* savings of the personal sector (available for investment by the business sector) will depend, not only on the savings propensities of individuals, but on the policies of the corporations towards new issues. In the absence of new issues the level of security prices will be established at the point at which the purchases of securities by the savers will be just balanced by the sale of securities of the dis-savers, making the net savings of the personal sector zero. The issue of new securities by corporations will depress security prices (i.e. the valuation ratio) just enough to reduce the sale of securities by the dis-savers sufficiently to induce the net savings required to take up the new issues. If i were negative and the corporations were net *purchasers* of securities from the personal sector (which they could be through the redemption of past securities or purchasing shares from the personal sector for the acquisition of subsidiaries) the valuation ratio would be driven up to the point at which net personal savings would be negative to the extent necessary to match the sale of securities to the corporate sector.[8]

In a state of Golden-Age equilibrium (given a constant g and a constant K/Y, however determined), v will be constant, with a value that can be $\gtrless 1$, depending on the values of s_c, s_w, c and i. All that one can assert is that, given the Pasinetti inequality, $gK > s_w Y$, $v < 1$ when $c = 1 - s_w$, $i = 0$; with $i > 0$ this will be true *a fortiori*.[9]

The rate of profit in a Golden-Age equilibrium (as given by equation 6) will depend only on g, s_c and i, and will then be independent of the 'personal' savings propensities, s_w and c. In this way it is similar to the Pasinetti theorem in that the rate of profit will be independent of s_w (and also of c) but it is reached by a different route; it will hold in any steady growth state, and not only in a 'long-run' Golden Age; it does not postulate a class of hereditary capitalists with a special high-saving propensity. In

8. The above equations assume that savings out of dividends are zero; cG is intended as the net excess of shareholders' consumption over dividend income. It would be possible to assume that there is only a single savings propensity for the household sector which applies equally to wages, dividends and capital gains. If we denote this by s_k, equations 3 and 4 above become

$$s_c P + s_k \{W + (1 - s_c)P\} - (1 - s_k)gK(v - i) = gK$$

and $$s_k \{W + (1 - s_c)P\} - (1 - s_k)gK(v - i) = igK.$$

From this we obtain

$$\rho = \frac{g(1 - i)}{s_c}$$

as before, and

$$v = 1 - \frac{1 - s_k Y/gK}{1 - s_k}$$

in place of equation 5 above. This implies that $v < 1$, when $s_k Y < gK$ (since $Y > gK$, in all cases).

9. Assuming $g - s_w Y/K > 0$, it follows from 5 that $v < 1$ provided that

$$\frac{s_c - s_w}{cs_c}(1 - i) + i \leqslant 1. \qquad \textbf{a}$$

When $c = 1 - s_w$; **a** will hold if

$$\frac{s_c - s_w}{(1 - s_w)s_c} \leqslant 0$$

or $s_c - s_w \leqslant s_c - s_w s_c$. $\qquad \textbf{b}$

Since $s_c < 1$, **b** must hold.

the special case $i = 0$, it reduces to the simple Pasinetti formula, $\rho = g/s_c$.

The assumption that corporations issue securities which are a constant fraction, i, of their investment, irrespective of anything else (in particular, irrespective of v) is of course arbitrary. It is possible to conceive of numerous other assumptions to characterize the corporations' collective behaviour with regard to the issue of new securities. For example it would be possible to assume that the corporations' issue of new securities will depend on the *ex post* difference between their savings, $s_c P$, and their investment, gK, and that such *ex post* differences are only 'recognized' at the end of certain intervals of time (of the accounting periods); any intervening difference being met by a depletion (or accretion) of their cash reserves. In other words, they issue securities periodically, to make good any past depletion of their liquid reserves; in the converse case, they respond *ex post* to an accretion of cash reserves by redeeming securities (such as debenture issues or preference shares). Assuming that these accounting intervals are long enough, v and s will establish themselves at values corresponding to $i = 0$; this means that net personal savings will be zero, and the *ex post* difference between $s_c P$ and gK will be zero: *no* new securities will, in fact, be issued (or redeemed) because there will be no occasion to. This kind of behaviour will thus lead to the simple Pasinetti formula $\rho = g/s_c$.

Has this 'neo-Pasinetti theorem' any very-long-run 'Pasinetti' or 'anti-Pasinetti' solution? So far we have not taken any account of the change in the distribution of assets between 'workers' (i.e. pension funds) and 'capitalists' – indeed we assumed it to be constant. However, since the capitalists are *selling* shares (if $c > 0$) and the pension funds are buying them, one could suppose that the *share* of total assets in the hands of capitalists would diminish continually, whereas the share of assets in the hands of the workers' funds would increase continually until, at some distant day, the capitalists have no shares left; the pension funds and insurance companies would own them all!

But this view ignores that the ranks of the capitalist class are constantly renewed by the sons and daughters of the new Captains of Industry, replacing the grandsons and granddaughters of the older Captains who gradually dissipate their inheritance through living beyond their dividend income. It is reasonable to assume that the value of the shares of the newly formed and growing companies grows at a higher rate than the average, whilst those of older companies (which decline in relative importance) grow at a lower rate. This means that the rate of capital appreciation of the shares in the hands of the capitalist group as a whole, for the reasons given above, is greater than the rate of appreciation of the assets in the hands of pension funds, etc. Given the difference in the rates of appreciation of the two funds of securities – and this depends on the rate at which new corporations emerge and replace older ones – I think it can be shown that there will be, for any given constellation of the value of the parameters, a long-run equilibrium distribution of the assets between capitalists and pension funds which will remain constant. But it would require further investigation that goes beyond the limits of this Appendix to demonstrate this formally.

References

CLAPHAM, J. H. (1922), 'The empty boxes: a rejoinder', *Econ. J.*, vol. 32, pp. 305–14.

KEYNES, J. M. (1919), *The Economic Consequences of the Peace*, Macmillan.

SAMUELSON, P. A., and MODIGLIANI, F. (1966), 'The Pasinetti paradox in neo-classical and more general models', *Rev. econ. Stud.*, vol. 33, pp. 269–301.

16 D. M. Nuti

Capitalism, Socialism and Steady Growth[1]

Excerpts from D. M. Nuti, 'Capitalism, socialism and steady growth', *Economic Journal*, vol. 80, 1970, pp. 32–45, 48–54.

Introduction

The purpose of this paper is that of considering the choice of production techniques from the point of view of both the capitalist entrepreneur maximizing the present value of his firm's assets at a given interest rate and the socialist planner maximizing the consumption per head associated with the maintenance of a given growth rate.

A model of production is set up, in which output is made of a versatile consumption and production good, called *putty*, and of the *machines* which are made of putty and are necessary to assist labour in order to produce putty. It is assumed that technical choice is irreversible, i.e. that putty is moulded and baked into clay machines of given specifications which cannot be turned back into putty or into machines of different specifications. Also, their use is not affected by technical progress which improves the design of new machines but not the operation of those already constructed.

This framework, which Phelps (1963) first named 'putty-clay', has been widely used in recent economic literature (e.g. Bliss, 1968; Johansen, 1959; Kemp and Thanh, 1966; Salter, 1960; Solow, 1966; Solow, Tobin, von Weizsäcker and Yaari, 1966). This paper, however, differs from other putty–clay models in that it does *not* contain two customary assumptions, namely that:

1. Acknowledgements are due to Maurice Dobb, Piero Garegnani, Richard Goodwin, Malcolm MacCallum, Joan Robinson, Luigi Spaventa and Piero Sraffa for helpful comments and criticisms on an earlier draft of this paper. Responsibility for any error, needless to say, rests solely with the writer.

1. The process of transforming this versatile consumption-production good into durable machines is costless, i.e. no labour is needed to mould and bake putty into clay.

2. Putty is turned into clay machines instantaneously, so that there are no gestation lags of investment. Both assumptions, as we shall see, reduce significantly the scope of technical choice.

The first assumption, that the transformation of putty into clay is costless, is necessary to keep a putty–clay model in the realm of a one-commodity world. Only in this case can gross investment be measured simply by the amount of putty which is turned into clay in each period. If moulding and baking putty into clay requires labour the value of a new machine expressed in terms of putty depends on the interest rate (or the wage rate). *Gross* output will be made up of that part of putty which is actually devoted to consumption *plus* the output of machines; in addition to the sector producing putty, one needs as many other sectors as there are units of time – in the course of the gestation period of machines – during which labour is needed to process putty into machines. To measure *net* output a number of other sectors are needed, in addition to the putty-producing sector, equal to the number of time units into which the lifetime of a machine can be broken, from the beginning of its construction to the end of its lifetime, because each machine at each different stage of its construction or its operation is a different commodity. We can look at the production process either as joint production of putty and machines or as joint production of dated putty. In this system, as Professor Kaldor (1937, p. 159) once put it, 'the inputs of different dates jointly produce the outputs of different dates; and it is impossible to separate out the contribution to the output of different dates of the input of a single date'. Output per head – whether gross or net – associated with a given technique would then depend both on the rate of interest – determining the price of each machine in terms of putty – and the growth rate, determining the relative proportion of putty and machines of all kinds in total output. The assumption of the costless transformation of putty into clay and the use of *gross* measures evade this fundamental issue of capital theory.

The second assumption, of no gestation period of investment, which is also customary in putty–clay models, eliminates one of the possible dimensions of technical choice, namely the possibility of a trade-off between the length of the gestation period and the durability of fixed equipment.[2] Both assumptions, as we shall see, are relevant to the problem of 'reswitching' of techniques, i.e. the eligibility of the same technique at more than one level or range of the interest rate, with other techniques being eligible at intermediate levels.[3]

Neither assumption is made in this paper. A more flexible model will be used instead which takes into account the labour cost of investment and the gestation and durability of investment, and is designed to handle production techniques characterized by any possible time profile of output and inputs.

Within this framework conditions for reswitching of techniques are stated, and the problem is shown to be relevant both to the capitalist firm and the socialist planner. A version of the Golden Rule of Accumulation is stated, with a second-best proposition. It is shown that the relevance of the reswitching phenomenon is not affected by technical progress. Relative prices of machines and consumption goods are introduced, and the conditions for macroeconomic equilibrium are examined under both capitalism and socialism. In the context of the model the concept of capital is shown to be dispensable under socialism.

Assumptions

There is a versatile commodity, putty, which can be either consumed directly or turned into machines by an irreversible process requiring labour. Time is divided into periods of equal length. Putty is perishable and lasts for one period only, unless it is turned

2. Bhaduri (1968) has investigated this aspect of technical choice in a simple case. He finds that 'on economic grounds (other things being equal) one may expect a combination of shorter durability and shorter construction period to be more advantageous in a fast growing economy' (Bhaduri, 1968, p. 346). Here we shall treat gestation and durability more generally, as being only a partial aspect of technical choice – and not necessarily directly related – without the 'other things being equal' assumption.

3. This phenomenon was first noticed in the modern literature by Champernowne (1953–4), Robinson (1953–4) and Sraffa (1960), and has been widely debated in a series of papers in the *Quarterly Journal of Economics*, vol. 80, 1966. See also Harcourt (1969).

into clay. Clay machines last for more than one period; their durability depends on their shape, the amount and the time pattern of labour and putty which has gone into their making.

Putty is produced by labour and machines. Labour is homogeneous. The technical specifications of machines, i.e. the pattern of the time flow of inputs and outputs associated with them, differ and cannot be altered after their construction. A 'technique of production' is represented by a time flow of putty output, in which the putty to be moulded and baked into durable machines appears with the negative sign, and a time flow of labour inputs. The sequence of the time pattern of putty output is given by $\{a_i\}$, where $a_i \leqslant 0$ for $i = 0, 1, \ldots, k-1$ is the amount of putty which is needed initially to be handed over to the workers making machines during period i (the making of a machine can take more than one period; if one single period is needed, $k = 1$; if putty is being produced by labour only, then $k = 0$); $a_k > 0$, $a_i \geqslant 0$ for $i = k+1, \ldots, n$ is the putty which is produced thereafter, during each of the subsequent $n-k+1$ periods. We assume that

$$\sum_{i=0}^{n} a_i > 0,$$

i.e. total net putty output over the time of operation is strictly positive. The sequence of the time pattern of labour inputs required first to make machines, then to operate them to produce the flow of putty output, is given by $\{l_i\}$, where $l_0 > 0$ (because labour is always required to start the process), $l_i \geqslant 0$ for $i = 1, 2, \ldots, n$. We also assume that l_n and a_n are both positive. There are constant-returns-to-scale. The scale of a technique of production is taken so that $l_0 = 1$. Any convex combination of two techniques is also a technique, but the number of techniques which cannot be expressed as a convex combination of other techniques is finite. The length of k and n is not necessarily the same for all techniques. If a process does not have to be operated to the nth period, but can be stopped after a number of periods $m < n$, each length of operation of the same process is regarded as a separate process. We neglect 'inferior' techniques, i.e. such that they give an amount of output at some period lower than another technique, without having a higher output at some other period, and/or a lower labour input at the same or some other period.

We shall consider the full-employment growth of economies

with access to this kind of technology, under institutional conditions corresponding to textbook capitalism, centralized and decentralized socialism. In all systems production is organized in productive units called firms, by managers who are all equally efficient. In each period total labour supply is given, and growing at a steady rate λ, $\lambda > -1$. Labour is hired by firms at a real wage w per man per period, paid at the end of the period. Managers are homogeneous with the rest of the working force, and the input of their labour is included in the labour coefficients l_t. Economic systems differ in three respects: property relations, market conditions and criteria for technical choice.

Under centralized socialism physical productive assets belong to the State which appropriates whatever is produced in excess of the payment of wages. It is a monopsonist in the labour market and fixes the wage rate w, to which labour supply is inelastic. Firms are simply administrative units, managers are State officers who are ordered to use the technique chosen by the central planner and receive the necessary material inputs and wage fund (in excess of their current production of putty) free of charge as grants from the State.[4] Among the production techniques available, the central planner selects the technique maximizing the rate of consumption per head associated with the maintenance of full-employment steady growth.

Under decentralized socialism physical productive assets belong to State firms. Firms have access to a perfectly competitive labour market, and have infinite power of borrowing and lending putty from and to the State, at a rate of interest r fixed by the State. They have built their assets by borrowing from the State in the past, they appropriate current output and pay wages and interest out of it. Among the production techniques available, they select the technique maximizing the present value of their assets at the ruling interest rate.[5] The socialist planner will still

4. Central fixing of the wage rate, free investment funds granted from the State budget, central choice of production techniques, administrative orders to the managers of State firms: these are aspects typical of the pre-war Soviet planning system.

5. These characteristics can be found, for instance, in the Czechoslovak economy in 1967. According to the documents of the 1967 economic reforms, wage guidelines were fixed centrally, but managers could pay additional bonuses to workers, out of an enterprise fund made of retained

wish the technique maximizing consumption per head to be chosen, but the only way he can affect technical choice is by choosing the interest rate, r, which is the basis of the decisions of State managers.

Under capitalism, physical productive assets belong to individual capitalists, either directly or through shareholding. Firms have access to a perfectly competitive labour market and have infinite power of borrowing and lending putty at a rate of interest r. Capitalists appropriate the excess of output over what is needed to pay managers and workers the competitive wage, consume part of it and accumulate the rest. Among the production techniques available, the one which maximizes the present value of the assets of capitalists at the ruling interest rate is chosen.

Both under capitalism and decentralized socialism macroeconomic equilibrium requires that the production of putty in excess of current consumption requirements should be equal to the material input requirements in the construction of machines. The conditions for equilibrium will be examined in the next sections; we can imagine, provisionally, that the economy in question is connected with a perfect international capital market.

The 'wage-interest' frontier

We shall first consider the implications of the present-value maximization criterion for technical choice.

Suppose there is one technique only, and no technical progress. The present value of v starting a unit scale process, $\{a_i\}$, $\{l_i\}$, is given by

$$v = \sum_{i=0}^{n} (a_i - w l_i)(1+r)^{-i}. \qquad 1$$

Since the labour market is competitive, as long as v is positive workers will be successful in demanding higher wages from firms competing with each other trying to get hold of labour. Equilibrium in the labour market requires that

$$v = 0. \qquad 2$$

profits, subject to the payment of a tax on the wage fund, called 'stabilization' tax. See Czechoslovakia (1966). The present value criterion for investment choice was introduced in April 1967 by the State Commission for Technology (see Czechoslovakia, 1967; Nuti, 1970).

At each level of the interest rate there is, for a given technique, a maximum wage rate which firms, performing lending and borrowing operations, can afford to pay to workers and make no loss. This is given by the following equation, obtained from **1** and **2**:

$$w = \frac{\sum_{i=0}^{n} a_i(1+r)^{-i}}{\sum_{i=0}^{n} l_i(1+r)^{-i}}.$$

3

This we call the 'wage–interest frontier'. [. . .] The function has the following properties:

1. For $r = 0$,

$$w = \frac{\sum_{i=0}^{n} a_i}{\sum_{i=0}^{n} l_i} > 0.$$

2. There is only one value of r, r^*, for which $w(r) = 0$ because

$$\sum_{i=0}^{n} l_i(1+r)^{-i}$$

is always positive, and because there is only one inversion of sign in the coefficients of the polynomial at the numerator.[6]

From **1** and **2** it follows that $w(r) > 0$ for $0 \leqslant r < r^*$.

3. The sign of the first derivative of $w(r)$ is negative for $r = r^*$ but for $0 < r < r^*$ does not have to be negative throughout, and the graph of $w(r)$ may present 'bumps'. The maximum number of bumps may be shown to be given by the number of alternations of sign of

$$\frac{a_{i+1}}{l_{i+1}} - \frac{a_i}{l_i},$$

for $i = k, \ldots, n$. Bumps, therefore, might occur if output per man fluctuates from the kth period onwards, for instance, if machines require periodical repairs and spare parts are made out of current

6. The number of positive real roots of a real polynomial is equal to the number q of its variations of sign – after having suppressed all terms having zeros as coefficients – or is less than q by a positive even integer.

output (a_t could even become negative for some $i > k$ if repair requirements exceed current output, but we have assumed that this is never the case). The economic meaning of the bump is that, over some range of the rate of interest, a firm is a borrower in some periods and a lender in some other periods, and it gains from an increase of the interest rate as a lender more than it loses as a borrower, so that it is able to pay a higher wage rate if it can perform lending–borrowing operations at a higher interest rate. The presence of bumps, however, is not essential to the following argument.

4. The only cases in which the $w(r)$ function is a straight line are ones in which $l_0 = 0$. This will never be the case under our assumptions, because we always have $l_0 > 0$.

Possible graphs of equation 3 are given in Figure 1.

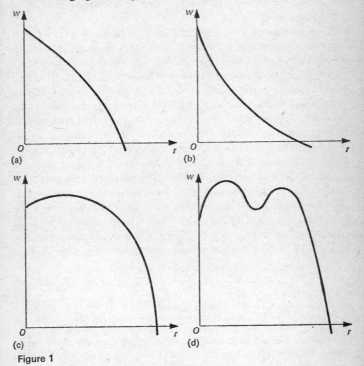

(a)

(b)

(c)

(d)

Figure 1

If a given process does not have to be operated to the nth period but can be stopped before at no additional expense we draw the wage–interest frontier for each length of operation T such that $k \leqslant T \leqslant n$, and superimpose them on the same diagram.[7] Some of them might be inferior. For instance, if output per man is constant after the machine is built, i.e. $a_i/l_i = \bar{a}$ for $i \geqslant k$, any length of operation $T < n$ will give a lower wage rate than $T = n$ at all values of the rate of interest. If, however, output per man varies over the operation of a machine it might happen that different lengths of operation will be best over different ranges of the interest rate. If the wage frontier has bumps this procedure will smooth the bumps out of the external boundary of the frontiers.[8] If different lengths of operation of a technique appear in the outer boundary of its wage frontiers the optimum economic lifetime of plant is shown to depend on the interest rate.

If we perform the same operation for all techniques of production available and superimpose all the $w = w(r)$ functions in the same diagram, we obtain a picture whose outer boundary gives the maximum wage rate which firms confronted with a given range of techniques can afford to pay, given the rate of interest at which they can undertake lending and borrowing operations. Throughout this paper by $w(r)$ we shall always indicate this outer boundary, which is illustrated in Figure 2.

It might be impossible to rank techniques of production so that each technique is associated with a single value or range of values of the interest rate. Reswitching of techniques might be observed in economies with access to the same technology and different values of the interest rate: the same technique might be in use at two different values of r, with another technique used at intermediate values of r. If there are two techniques, A and B, reswitching means that A affords the same wage rate as B at

7. Of course there is no point in considering $T < k$, because

$$\sum_{i=0}^{T} a_i \leqslant 0$$

for $T < k$, and at non-negative interest rates the wage would be negative.

8. Choosing the length of operation T might not always be possible, for instance, if putty is mined in open-cast mines requiring the replacement of topsoil with relatively large labour expenses towards the end of the operation of the process.

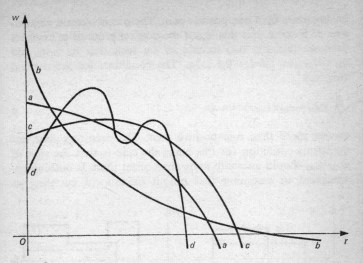

Figure 2

more than one level of the interest rate. Suppose technique A is given by (a_{Ai}, l_{Ai}), where

$$a_{Ai} \leqq 0 \quad \text{for } i = 0, 1, \ldots, k_A - 1$$
$$a_{Ai} \geqq 0 \quad \text{for } i = k_A, \ldots, n_A$$
$$l_{Ai} \geqq 0 \quad \text{for } i = 0, \ldots, n_A,$$

and technique B is given by (a_{Bi}, l_{Bi}), and $k_A \gtreqless k_B$, $n_A \gtreqless n_B$. Reswitching will occur if the equation

$$\frac{\sum\limits_{i=0}^{n_A} a_{Ai}(1+r)^{-i}}{\sum\limits_{i=0}^{n_A} l_{Ai}(1+r)^{-i}} - \frac{\sum\limits_{i=0}^{n_B} a_{Bi}(1+r)^{-i}}{\sum\limits_{i=0}^{n_B} l_{Bi}(1+r)^{-i}} = 0 \qquad 4$$

has more than one positive root. This condition can be rewritten as

$$\sum_{i=0}^{n_B} l_{Bi}(1+r)^{-i} \sum_{i=0}^{n_A} a_{Ai}(1+r)^{-i} - \sum_{i=0}^{n_A} l_{Ai}(1+r)^{-i} \sum_{i=0}^{n_B} a_{Bi}(1+r)^{-i}$$
$$= 0, \quad 5$$

having more than one positive root. There is no reason whatsoever to assume that this is not the case on grounds of realism. Suppose that the two techniques are such that $n_A = n_B$ and $l_{Ai} = l_{Bi}$ for all $i = 0,1,\ldots, n$. The condition for reswitching becomes

$$\sum_{i=0}^{n} (a_{Ai} - a_{Bi})(1+r)^{-i} = 0 \qquad\qquad 6$$

having more than one positive root. The necessary (but not sufficient) condition for this being the case is that the sign of $a_{Ai} - a_{Bi}$ should alternate more than once: there is nothing extravagant in assuming that output (investment counting as

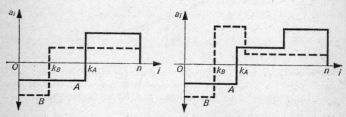

Figure 3

negative output) with one technique is higher in two periods and lower in an intermediate period, with respect to another technique, as in Figure 3.

The actual number of roots (and therefore of switching points) can be found by using Sturm's theorem.[9] When reswitching

9. Let $f(x)$ be a polynomial with real coefficients such that $f(x) = 0$ has no multiple roots. Construct the identities

$$c_0 f = q_1 f' - f_2, \qquad c_1 f' = q_2 f_2 - f_3,$$
$$c_2 f_2 = q_3 f_3 - f_4, \quad \ldots, \quad c_{k-2} f_{k-2} = q_{k-1} f_{k-1} - f_k,$$

where q_r/c_{r-1} is the quotient of the division f_{r-1}/f_r; f_k is a constant $\neq 0$, and each f_r is of degree one less than its predecessor. Let a and b be real numbers neither of which is a root of $f(x) = 0$, while $a < b$. Then the number of real roots between a and b of $f(x) = 0$ is the excess of the number of variations of sign in the chain

$$f(x), f'(x), f_2(x), \ldots, f_{k-1}(x), f_k$$

for $x = a$ over the number of their variations of sign for $x = b$. Terms which vanish are to be discarded before counting the variations of sign.

occurs, the available blueprints cannot be so ordered in a book that at a higher interest rate a higher numbered page contains the 'best' technique, unless the same blueprint can be inserted more than once. It should be noted that the actual number of reswitching points between the wage frontiers of two techniques is totally uninteresting: in a sense, we can say that the greater the number of reswitching points, the closer the two techniques can be considered to be and, therefore, the less important the fact of reswitching. A better measure, however loose, of the importance of reswitching can be given by the maximum difference between the wage rates afforded by the two techniques at the same rate of interest, because this is a measure of the maximum inefficiency which can result from a wrong choice of techniques (or otherwise some other statistics of the distribution of such differences, taken with the positive sign: $|w_A(r) - w_B(r)|$).

The 'consumption-growth' frontier

We shall now look at what determines, under the technical conditions already described, the level of consumption per head at different alternative steady growth rates, and its relation with the wage-interest frontier.

Suppose there is only one technique available, the number of projects (of unit scale) started in each period has been increasing at a constant rate g per period in the last n periods, and the amount of labour currently employed on projects just started is L_t. The number of projects started this period, therefore, is given by $L_t/l_0 = L_t$; the number of projects started during the period $t-1$ is equal to $L_t(1+g)^{-1}$, and in general the number of projects started at time $t-i$ is equal to $L_t(1+g)^{-i}$. A project started at time $t-i$ will require l_i units of labour and will be associated with a_i units of output (or $-a_i$ units of investment, if $i < k$). Current employment on projects started at time $t-i$, L_{t-i}, is, therefore, given by equation 7:

$$L_{t-i} = L_t(1+g)^{-i}l_i, \qquad i = 0,1,...,n \qquad 7$$

From this we can now determine total employment, N; total gross putty output, X; total putty needed as a material to make machines, J; and consumption, C. They are given by the following equations:

$$N_t = \sum_{i=0}^{n} l_i(1+g)^{-i} L_t, \qquad\qquad 8$$

$$X_t = \sum_{i=k}^{n} a_i(1+g)^{-i} L_t, \qquad\qquad 9$$

$$J_t = -\sum_{i=0}^{k-1} a_i(1+g)^{-i} L_t, \qquad\qquad 10$$

$$C_t = X_t - J_t = \sum_{i=0}^{n} a_i(1+g)^{-i} L_t. \qquad\qquad 11$$

From equations 8, 9 and 11 we can express gross putty output per head, $x = X/N$, and consumption per head $c = C/N$ as a function of the growth rate of investment:

$$x = \frac{\displaystyle\sum_{i=k}^{n} a_i(1+g)^{-i}}{\displaystyle\sum_{i=0}^{n} l_i(1+g)^{-i}}, \qquad\qquad 12$$

$$c = \frac{\displaystyle\sum_{i=0}^{n} a_i(1+g)^{-i}}{\displaystyle\sum_{i=0}^{n} l_i(1+g)^{-i}}. \qquad\qquad 13$$

Consumption and gross output of putty per head appear, therefore, to depend solely on the steady growth rate of investment which will be also the growth rate of the whole economy (as long as investment has been growing at that rate for the last n periods). At full employment (and without technical progress as we have assumed so far) the rate of growth in investment g will have to be equal to the rate of growth of employment λ. Equation 13, expressing consumption per head c as a function of the growth rate g of investment, $c = c(g)$ is exactly identical to equation 3, the wage-interest frontier, with g instead of r and c instead of w. All we have said in relation to equation 3 applies also to equation 13 which we shall call the 'consumption-growth' frontier because each of its points indicates the maximum consumption per head corresponding to a given steady growth rate, and vice versa, the growth rate (or rates, if there are 'bumps') achievable with a given level of consumption per head. This relation holds both in a socialist planned and in a capitalist economy, growing at a steady growth rate. If there is more than one technique, however, only under centrally planned socialism will the technical choice be determined with reference to the consumption per head maintainable at a given growth rate, whereas under capitalism and decentralized socialism maximization of present value, as we shall see, might lead to the choice of a different technique.

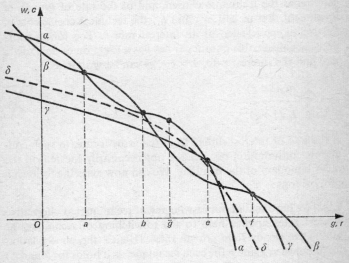

Figure 4

If we draw the graph of equation 13 for all techniques of production available, the outer boundary will give the maximum level of consumption per head which is consistent with each growth rate. The picture is represented in Figure 4, which looks exactly like Figure 2, so that we can measure w, c on the vertical axes and g, r on the horizontal axes. We can now draw the functions also for $g < 0$ and for $c(g) < 0$: negative growth rates – unlike negative interest rates – are economically quite plausible, and the properties of a steadily declining economy can be explored. Negative consumable output per head at some growth rate indicates how much steady external aid per head is needed, on top of subsistence real consumption per head, to maintain that growth rate.[10] However, in order to draw conclusions out of this framework, we need to know not only the outer boundary of the frontiers but also the whole network of frontiers and their interweaving. Under capitalism or decentralized socialism, where technical choice is based on the maximization of present-value criterion, consumable putty output per head, c, will be a function both of the interest rate which determines the technique chosen, and of the rate of growth of investment. Let us call $a_{i,r}$ and $l_{i,r}$ the technical coefficients of the technique selected at an interest rate r. The function expressing consumable output per head as a function of the growth rate and the interest rate, $c = c(r, g)$ can be written as

$$c = \frac{\sum_{i=0}^{n} a_{i,r}(1+g)^{-i}}{\sum_{i=0}^{n} l_{i,r}(1+g)^{-i}}.$$ 13'

If the rate of interest differs from the growth rate, in such conditions consumption per head is not necessarily located on the outer boundary of the frontiers. We can now state the following propositions:

1. All we have said about reswitching of techniques at alternative interest rates applies here to the reswitching of techniques at alternative steady state growth rates. (Hence, the same relation holds between T and g for each technique, as it holds for T and r.) If growth has been efficiently planned by socialist planners, one might find the same consumption-maximizing technique in two economies where investment grows at a different rate, and another technique in a third economy where investment grows at an intermediate rate.[11]

10. The maximum number of bumps in the function $c = c(g)$ for $c < 0$ is given by the number of alternations of sign of
$$\frac{a_{i+1}}{l_{i+1}} - \frac{a_i}{l_i} \quad \text{for } i < k.$$

11. If the consumption-growth frontier is increasing over a particular range of the growth rate the corresponding growth rates are in a sense inefficient, in that higher growth rates could have been attained, raising consumption per head instead of reducing it. The 'bump' in the frontier did not matter for the firm which had to take the interest rate as given, but matters for the planner to the extent to which he can control the rate of growth of labour supply through immigration and population policy.

2. If the criterion for technical choice is present-value maximization at a given interest rate, in a competitive labour market, we can state the following version of the Golden Rule:[12]

For a given growth rate of investment, a sufficient condition for consumption per head to be the highest consistent with such growth rate is that the rate of interest should be equal to the rate of growth of investment. If the number of techniques available is infinite, and there is no reswitching, and the switching points are dense, this is also a necessary condition.

From Figure 4 we can see that for any given value of g, say $\bar{g}$: (a) If $r = \bar{g}$, the technique (or techniques if there is a switch point at $\bar{g}$) chosen is that yielding the maximum consumption per head attainable at that growth rate. (b) Let us call the switching values of the rates of growth and interest a, b, e and f; if the consumption-maximizing technique switches at $g = b < \bar{g}$ and at $g = e > \bar{g}$, then as long as $b < r < e$ the present-value-maximizing technique and the consumption-maximizing technique will be the same (at $r = b$ or $r = e$ present value could be maximized by linear combinations of two techniques, but this would not necessarily maximize consumable output per head). (c) If there is reswitching the technique which maximizes consumable output per head at a rate of growth $\bar{g}$ might maximize present value also over some other range of r. In Figure 4, for instance, the technique maximizing consumable output at $\bar{g}$ is also chosen for $0 < r < a$ as well as $b < r < e$. This means that if $a < r < b$ firms can be induced to choose the consumption-maximizing technique either by increasing the interest rate, bringing it closer to $\bar{g}$, or by reducing it further and bringing it closer to zero. The difference between g and r, in other words, cannot be taken as a measure of inefficiency. (d) Suboptimality can take not only the form of the wrong plant but also of the wrong length of operation of the 'right' plant.

12. This is the mirror-image of von Neumann's statement about the conditions to obtain the maximum growth rate corresponding to a given level of consumption per head (see von Neumann, 1945–6). Several versions of this rule have appeared since: see Hahn and Matthews (1964). In the context of planned socialist growth the same rule is also stated by Dobb (1969, ch. 8).

3. We can also state the following 'second-best' proposition (whether or not reswitching occurs). If $r \neq \bar{g}$, consumption per head might be higher for values of r farther away from $\bar{g}$ than for values closer to $\bar{g}$, and if for some reason the ranges of r over which the (consumption-maximizing) technique is chosen are unattainable, there will be a range of values of r over which a 'second-best' technique will be chosen, yielding the second highest consumption per head at a rate of growth $\bar{g}$ *among the techniques forming the frontier*. In Figure 4 this is technique γ which would be chosen over the range $c < r < f$. It appears, however, that, at the rate of growth $\bar{g}$, γ is inferior to a technique δ which does not appear anywhere along the frontier and will never be chosen at any value of the interest rate. A typical case would be that of the steadily declining economy, where, if the rate of interest is not allowed to be negative, the consumption-maximizing technique will never be chosen by firms (unless that technique is also the best at positive growth and interest rates). If wages and prices, however, are expressed in money terms and are expected to change in time at a steady percentage rate p, the parameter relevant to technical choice would not be r, but $\{(1+r)/(1+p)\}-1$. Even if there are constraints on the values of r, this 'deflated' interest rate can be made equal to g, provided expectations can be generated of a steady percentage rate of price increase p such that

$$p = \frac{r-g}{1+g}. \qquad\qquad 14$$

The rule for obtaining optimal technical choice in conditions of steady-state growth would now become $r = p+(1+p)g$. [. . .]

Income and capital

So far we have discussed the problems of growth and technical choice without having to measure the value of 'machines' in terms of consumption goods (except that we have stipulated that the value of an investment option, i.e. of a machine not yet built, must be zero). If we want to measure 'income' according to international statistical conventions, however, the relative prices of machines of all ages in terms of consumption goods are needed, as the income produced in one period is a collection of heterogeneous objects, made of whatever happens to be in existence at the end of the period, *minus* whatever was in existence at the beginning of the period, *plus* what has been withdrawn from the productive system in the form of consumption.

Call v_j the value in terms of consumption goods (putty) of a machine used in a given process of a unit scale at the beginning of period j of its existence (or, more generally, the value at time t of having 'access to' a unit scale process started at time $t-j$). Suppose there is no technical progress, wages are paid at the end of the period, and either there is no money or prices are constant in time. The value of a machine is given by

$$v_j = \sum_{i=j}^{n} \{a_i - l_i\, w(r)\}(1+r)^{-i} \quad (j = 0,...,n).\qquad\textbf{15}$$

The value v of a piece of equipment embodying a given technique depends on its age j and the rate of interest r. We know that $v_0 = 0$ for the technique which is best at any given interest rate, by the very definition of $w(r)$ (see equation 3). For a given technique, however, the 'price' Wicksell effect dv_j/dr and the 'ageing' effect $\{v_{j+1}(r) - v_j(r)\}$ can in principle take either sign. When there are many techniques the level of the interest rate will determine *which* of the techniques is in use as well as the relative value of the different processes at each period of their operation.

From equation **7** we can obtain the number of machines of all ages in existence, so that the value of the capital stock of an economy will be given by

$$V_t = L_t \sum_{j=1}^{n} v_j(1+g)^{-j}\qquad\textbf{16}$$

which from **15** can also be written as

$$V_t = L_t \sum_{j=1}^{n} \sum_{i=j}^{n} \{a_{i,r} - l_{i,r}\, w(r)\}(1+r)^{-i}(1+g)^{-j}.\qquad\textbf{16'}$$

In steady growth, net investment I_t undertaken during period t is given by

$$I_t = gL_t \sum_{j=1}^{n} v_j(1+g)^{-j}\qquad\textbf{17}$$

which can also be written as

$$I_t = gL_t \sum_{j=1}^{n} \sum_{i=j}^{n} \{a_{i,r} - l_{i,r}\, w(r)\}(1+r)^{-i}(1+g)^{-j}.\qquad\textbf{17'}$$

Income produced during period t, $Y_t = C_t + I_t$ from **11** and **17'** can be written as

$$Y_t = L_t\left[\sum_{i=0}^{n} a_{i,r}(1+g)^{-i} + g\sum_{j=1}^{n}\sum_{i=j}^{n}\{a_{i,r} - l_{i,r}\,w(r)\}\times \right.$$
$$\left. \times (1+r)^{-i}(1+g)^{-j}\right]. \quad \textbf{18}$$

Income per head, $y = y(r, g)$, can be obtained from **18** and **8**:

$$y = \frac{\sum_{i=0}^{n} a_{i,r}(1+g)^{-i} + g\sum_{j=1}^{n}\sum_{i=j}^{n}\{a_{i,r} - l_{i,r}\,w(r)\}(1+r)^{-i}(1+g)^{-j}}{\sum_{i=0}^{n} l_{i,r}(1+g)^{-i}}.$$
$$\textbf{19}$$

The value of output per man in an economy with access to a given technology depends on the interest rate which determines the technique chosen (if many are available) and the relative prices of machines and consumption goods, and on the growth rate which determines the weight of each kind of commodity in output.

If there is only one technique we have that if $g = 0$, $y = c(0)$; if $r = 0$, $y = w(0) = c(0)$, so that we can say that $y(0, g) = y(r, 0)$. If the rate of interest is zero the value of output per man does not vary with the growth rate; if the growth rate is zero the value of output per man does not vary with the interest rate; and the value of output per man is the same in both cases.

If there are many techniques this is not necessarily the case. If $g = 0$, $y = c(r, 0)$; if $r = 0$, $y = w(0) = c(0, 0)$. If the interest rate is zero the value of output per head still does not vary with the growth rate; but if the growth rate is zero the value of output per head will vary with the interest rate, and the two will be the same only if r is in the range for which $c(r, 0) = w(0)$.

The value of 'capital per man' in the economy is given by **8** and **16'**:

$$\frac{V_t}{N_t} = \frac{\sum_{j=1}^{n}\sum_{i=j}^{n}\{a_{i,r} - l_{i,r}\,w(r)\}(1+r)^{-i}(1+g)^{-j}}{\sum_{i=0}^{n} l_{i,r}(1+g)^{-i}}. \quad \textbf{20}$$

As we saw on pages 319–25, unless one has *faith* that the nature of technology is such that reswitching of techniques does not occur, there is no reason to assume that each technique will be associated with a single value or range of values of the interest rate. But even if there is no reswitching, for a given growth rate the same *value* of capital per man can occur at more than a single level or range of the interest rate; or, conversely, for a given interest rate the same value of capital per man can occur at more than a single level or range of the growth rate (see Garegnani, 1970; Spaventa, 1968, 1970).

The concept of 'value of capital', therefore, does not add anything to the analysis of the problems of choice of production techniques for the capitalist firm and the socialist planner. The values associated with a given technique of production *depend on* the criterion and parameters of technical choice and, therefore, *cannot provide* themselves any criterion or parameters on which technical choice could be based.

The analysis of the notions of income and capital could be easily extended to the cases where there is technical progress, wages are paid at the beginning of the period and price level is not constant, but the nature of the problem would remain unchanged.

Macroeconomic equilibrium under socialism and capitalism

If we rule out international borrowing and lending, the maintenance of equilibrium growth requires that actual consumption per head should be equal to consumable output $c = c(r, g)$, whatever the actual relation between r and g. Equilibrium relations must, therefore, hold between growth rate, interest rate and saving propensities. This, however, poses different problems under socialist and capitalist conditions.

The socialist planner will provide a certain amount of collective consumption per head, $z > 0$; will collect the voluntary savings of workers who will save, say, a fraction s_w of their net wages; will collect a fraction b of workers' wages in taxes, or pay out a corresponding subsidy of $b < 0$. As long as the planner can choose b and z, he can ensure that the condition is satisfied

$$z + (1 - s_w)(1 - b)w(r) = c(r, g) \qquad 21$$

and obtain simultaneously equilibrium growth and the desired balance between private and collective consumption. This is true whether or not he sticks to the Golden Rule, whether he chooses the technique himself or instructs State managers to use the present-value maximization criterion. As long as equation 14 is satisfied, the excess of current putty output per head over c will be exactly equal to the amount required to maintain the rate of growth g, because this is exactly how we have defined c in equations 11 and 13. The interest rate workers get on their savings is presumably negligible, because the socialist planner does not want them to turn into *rentiers*, but even if they get the full rate, r, the planner can always adjust z and b to obtain 14. If $w > c$, out of what is collected by the planner from the workers in the form of savings and taxation, $(s_w + b - bs_w)w$, an amount $(w - c)$ per man employed will have to be lent each period to firms via the credit system. If $c > w$ the planner will use the excess of firms' repayments and interest payments over current loans to firms, equal to $c - w$ per man employed, to finance collective consumption or to subsidize wages. From one period to another, if $g \neq 0$, the stock of machines of all ages (in gestation, new, used) will grow (or decline) at a rate g, the machine-mix depending on g, but unless he has to comply with international statistical agreements, the planner does not have to assess the 'value' of the State's capital stock and its net change in time (net investment). All he might want to know is the sum of gross output which is due to come in the future from the stock of machines already existing in the economy. Let us call ρ the rate at which he discounts future output (this can be equal to zero, or to the interest rate he charges State firms, or it can take some other value). At the beginning of time t there are $L_t(1+g)^{-j}$ machines of age j in existence. The cumulative discounted putty output A_j of a machine of age j is given by

$$A_j = \sum_{i=j}^{n} a_i (1+\rho)^{-i}. \qquad 22$$

Total cumulative gross putty output A_t from the stock of machines already existing in the economy at the beginning of time t is, therefore, given by

$$A_t = \sum_{j=0}^{n} \sum_{i=j}^{n} a_i (1+\rho)^{-i} L_t (1+g)^{-i}. \qquad 23$$

He might want to calculate A_t excluding unfinished machines, in which case the sum is taken only for $j = k,..., n$. He has no reason to subtract wage costs from future putty output: if, however, he wants a measure of discounted future *surplus* of output over *necessary* labour inputs he will subtract the *subsistence wage* rather than $w(r)$. All these measurements have no interest for the managers of State firms. If they happen to exchange machines and putty with each other they will assess the value of a machine in the same way as a capitalist manager would (i.e. subtracting from future output the expected wage costs as in equation 15). Their measure, in turn, is of no interest for the planner: if they have followed his instructions of maximizing the present value of their assets, in a competitive labour market, the value of their assets assessed from their point of view is equal to their outstanding liabilities to the State. The planner knows this magnitude from his books, but it is a purely accounting notion of no operational significance from *his* point of view.

The planner is 'making profits' in the sense that if $g > 0$ production of machines in each period exceeds the replacement of machines which have come to the end of their physical life-time; if $g < 0$ he is only making a 'gross profit'. Since profits are only the measure of investment undertaken, and in this sense are 'reinvested' by definition, there is no need for measuring profits, i.e. the net change in time of the capital stock. Within the framework outlined in this paper, this is true even in a socialist economy where 'profits' are used as a source of bonus payments (to the managers and workers) and investment finance, because if all managers are equally efficient, profits in equilibrium should be maximum and equal to zero. If managers are not homogeneous and managerial abilities need material rewards to come forward, infra-marginal managers would secure quasi-rents to their firms. At the ruling interest rate they would be able to pay a wage higher than that offered by the marginal manager, but they will actually pay the same rate as he does. Given whatever limits the size of their undertakings, infra-marginal managers will obtain quasi-rents equal to the numbers of workers they employ times the difference between the wage rate they could afford to pay and the wage rate offered by the marginal manager. The value of their assets, again, would not have to be assessed to compute their 'profits'. Even under this form of decentralized socialism, which we could call 'managerial socialism' to stress the role of managers in the decision-making process and the enjoyment of profits, the socialist planner could still make sure that actual total consumption does not exceed nor fall short of the level consistent with the maintenance of full-employment growth. In addition to the usual instruments of economic policy (namely, the choice of the level of collective consumption and wage taxation of subsidizing), the planner could lay down rules about the share of profits retained by enterprises and the way they should be divided among managers and workers and between consumption and investment.

The problem of macroeconomic equilibrium and the role of profits and capital are, of course, entirely different in a capitalist economy. Whatever is produced in excess of what is needed to pay wages accrues to the capitalists in the form of profits; the evaluation of profits requires the evaluation of machines; capitalists might consume part of their profits; workers will get an interest rate on their savings comparable to that of capitalists. Unless there is State intervention, additional equilibrium relations will have to hold between saving propensities, output and consumption per head, rates of interest and growth. Let us suppose that all investment has to be financed out of profits, *either* because the workers' propensity to save is zero *or* managers of firms have the power to retain part of the profits and distribute the rest to shareholders, and both workers and shareholders have a zero propensity to save (so that s is equal to the retention ratio); *or* workers have a propensity to save $s_w > 0$, but this entitles them to control over a share of total profits equal, in steady state, to their share in current savings.[13] When this is the case we can write the equilibrium condition as

$$(1-s)\{y(r, g)-w(r)\} = c(r, g)-w(r), \qquad 24$$

13. The relation between growth rate, saving propensities, profit rate and distributive shares has been put forward by Kaldor (1956) and Robinson (1956); and generalized by Pasinetti (1962). Pasinetti has shown that if workers receive an interest payment on their savings equal to that of capitalists, under certain conditions the propensity to save of workers does not affect the determination of the profit rate and the distributive shares. This proposition has been further discussed by Samuelson and Modigliani, Kaldor, Robinson, and Pasinetti in the *Review of Economic Studies*, vol. 33, 1966.

where s is the propensity to save out of profits. Whenever $y > w$, the equilibrium value of s, s^*, corresponding to a given pair of values of r and g is given by

$$s^* = \frac{y(r, g) - c(r, g)}{y(r, g) - w(r)}. \qquad 25$$

Suppose a capitalist economy is organized according to the Golden Rule of Accumulation so that $r = g$: in this case $c = w$, and it follows from 25 that the only equilibrium value of the saving propensity of capitalists is unity. It follows that capitalist exploitation takes two forms: one is the capitalists' acquisition of consumption of goods through straightforward command over other people's labour; the other more subtle form of exploitation is the lower average level of consumption per head associated with a suboptimal technical choice, whenever consumption out of profit prevents the fulfilment of the Golden Rule. (It should be emphasized again, perhaps, that the Golden Rule yields optimal technical choice only in conditions of steady-state growth, if the criterion of optimality is taken to be the highest rate of steadily growing consumption per head; out of steady state or with a different optimality criterion the rule would not necessarily hold.)

Whenever the saving propensity of capitalists is less than unity, for each steady growth rate there will be one, or possibly many pairs of values of r and s^*. Given the constraint $1 \geqslant s \geqslant 0$, if w is a decreasing function of r we have $c(r, g) < w(r)$ for all $r < g$: for the constraint to be satisfied the growth rate must not exceed the interest rate.

In a capitalist as in a socialist economy, the notion of 'value of capital' is not necessary to determine technical choice. In a planned socialist economy the only relevant parameters are the consumption per head – and its behaviour in time if there is technical change or the economy is out of a steady state – and the growth rate of employment. The concept of 'value of capital', however, is indispensable to the political economy of capitalism because it performs two fundamental roles, one practical and one ideological.

At a practical level the evaluation of machines of different kinds and different ages in terms of ouput is needed to settle transactions among capitalist firms, to determine the value of the legal exclusive right to use machinery and the value of the pieces of paper embodying such rights. It is necessary to determine distribution of income not between the haves and the have-nots but among the haves.

The ideological role of 'the value of capital' is that of breaking the direct actual link between the *time pattern* of labour inputs and the *time pattern* of output in which any technology can be resolved, and establishing instead a relation between *current* output and *current* labour. To this purpose the *current* 'value of the capital stock' is needed; a mythical conceptual construction in which the past and the future of the economy are telescoped into the present. Attention is focused not on past labour but on the present value of the embodiment of past labour, and its current productiveness can be taken to provide a justification for the attribution of the surplus of current output over the wage bill to those who have appropriated the embodiment of past labour, thereby providing the current basis of future appropriation.

References

BHADURI, A. (1968), 'An aspect of project-selection: durability versus construction-period', *Econ. J.*, vol. 78, pp. 344–8.

BLISS, C. J. (1968), 'On putty–clay', *Rev. econ. Stud.*, vol. 35, pp. 105–32.

CHAMPERNOWNE, D. G. (1953–4), 'The production function and the theory of capital: a comment', *Rev. econ. Stud.*, vol. 21, pp. 112–35. [See Reading 2.]

CZECHOSLAVAKIA (1966), 'General guidelines for enterprise operation, valid from January 1, 1967', in *New Trends in the Czechoslovak Economy*, booklet 6.

CZECHOSLOVAKIA (1967), *Zásady hodnocení ekonomické efektivnosti investic* (Criteria for the assessment of economic effectiveness of investment), State Commission for Technology.

DOBB, M. H. (1969), *Welfare Economics and the Economics of Socialism*, Cambridge University Press.

GAREGNANI, P. (1970), 'Heterogeneous capital, the production function and the theory of distribution', *Rev. econ. Stud.*, vol. 37, pp. 407–36.

HAHN, F. H., and MATTHEWS, R. C. O. (1964), 'The theory of economic growth: a survey', *Econ. J.*, vol. 74, pp. 779–902.

HARCOURT, G. C. (1969), 'Some Cambridge controversies in the theory of capital', *J. econ. Lit.*, vol. 7, pp. 369–405.

JOHANSEN, L. (1959), 'Substitution versus fixed production coefficients in the theory of economic growth: a synthesis', *Econometrica*, vol. 27, pp. 157–76.

KALDOR, N. (1937), 'Annual survey of economic theory: the recent controversy on the theory of capital', *Econometrica*, vol. 5, pp. 201–33. Reprinted in N. Kaldor, *Essays on Value and Distribution*, Duckworth, 1960, pp. 153–91.

KALDOR, N. (1956), 'Alternative theories of distribution', *Rev. econ. Stud.*, vol. 23, pp. 83–100.

KEMP, M. C., and THANH, P. G. (1966), 'On a class of growth models', *Econometrica*, vol. 34, pp. 257–82.

NUTI, D. M. (1970), 'Investment reforms in Czechoslovakia', *Soviet Stud.*, vol. 21, pp. 360–70.

PASINETTI, L. L. (1962), 'Rate of profit and income distribution in relation to the rate of economic growth', *Rev. econ. Stud.*, vol. 29, pp. 267–79.

PHELPS, E. S. (1963), 'Substitution, fixed proportions, growth and distribution', *Int. econ. Rev.*, vol. 4, pp. 265–88.

ROBINSON, J. (1953–4), 'The production function and the theory of capital', *Rev. econ. Stud.*, vol. 21, pp. 81–106. [See Reading 1.]

ROBINSON, J. (1956), *The Accumulation of Capital*, Macmillan.

SALTER, W. E. G. (1960), *Productivity and Technical Change*, Cambridge University Press.

SOLOW, R. M. (1966), 'Substitution and fixed proportions in the theory of capital', *Rev. econ. Stud.*, vol. 29, pp. 207–18.

SOLOW, R. M., TOBIN, J., VON WEIZSÄCKER, C. C., and YAARI, M. (1966), 'Neoclassical growth with fixed factor proportions', *Rev. econ. Stud.*, vol. 33, pp. 79–115.

SPAVENTA, L. (1968), 'Realism without parables in capital theory', in CERUNA, *Recherches récentes sur la fonction de production*, Universitaire de Namur, pp. 15–45.

SPAVENTA, L. (1970), 'Rate of profit, rate of growth and capital intensity in a single production model', *Oxf. econ. Pap.*, vol. 22, pp. 129–47.

SRAFFA, P. (1960), *Production of Commodities by Means of Commodities. Prelude to a Critique of Economic Theory*, Cambridge University Press. [See Reading 4.]

VON NEUMANN, J. (1945–6), 'A model of general economic equilibrium', *Rev. econ. Stud.*, vol. 13, pp. 1–9.

Part Seven
Optimum Growth Theory

A defence of marginal productivity theory as applied to
capital requires a demonstration of the proposition that in a
steady state the marginal product of aggregate capital equals
the rate of interest. This proof is provided in Reading 17 for
the case where technology is described in terms of a finite
intertemporal production function. An outline of the history
of this latter concept and an account – from the neo-classical
point of view – of its meaning and application to steady-state
analysis is provided in Part II of the Introduction. One of the
steps in the application is the satisfaction of what are
essentially static efficiency conditions. A more general analysis
of efficiency in the context of capital accumulation is provided
by Dorfman, Samuelson and Solow in Reading 18 – a justly
celebrated piece of economic theory. The analysis uses a
sequential formulation of technology but the concept of
efficiency is still essentially static. The concept of an optimum
(consumption-maximizing) steady state introduces an aspect
of efficiency which has no counterpart in static conditions.
It is not a new concept – as explained on page 40 in the
Introduction, it has its roots in the work of Wicksell (1934) –
but it has received widespread discussion only in the last
decade.

Reference

WICKSELL, J. G. K. (1934), *Lectures on Political Economy*, trans.
  from 3rd edn by E. Classen, Routledge & Kegan Paul.

17 N. F. Laing

Trade, Growth and Distribution: A Study in the Theory of the Long Run[1]

Excerpt from N. F. Laing, *Trade, Growth and Distribution: A Study in the Theory of the Long Run*, 2nd edn 1969, University of Adelaide (privately published), pp. 87–9. 1st edn published in 1965.

Imagine a competitive barter economy in a stationary state in which the own rate of interest (the same for all commodities) always has been and is expected to be always at the level R. Technology is specified in the form of a relation between the primary inputs and the final outputs of a finite number of consecutive periods. (A technique of production is thus a cycle of primary inputs and final outputs.) The relation between the primary inputs and final outputs of the different periods over all techniques is assumed to be smooth, convex in inputs and concave in outputs and subject to constant-returns-to-scale. Consider the optimum technique at the rate of interest, R. With this technique the primary inputs have certain marginal intertemporal products. It will be shown that if capital is aggregated using the rate of interest, R, and the marginal intertemporal products of the optimum technique as prices, the marginal product of aggregate capital equals R when the optimum technique is employed and there is an infinitesimal change of technique. The proof is given, first, for the capital invested at any particular stage of the single input–output cycle of the optimum technique and then for the capital stock needed to maintain a set of the input–output cycles of the optimum technique so staggered as to give a constant flow of final output.

It is assumed for simplicity that there is a single type of primary input, I, and a single type of primary output, C. A suffix attached to I or C indicates the period in which it occurs. A marginal change in technique is described by the set of marginal increments in primary inputs (dI_t for $t = 0,\ldots, n$) and in final outputs

1. I wish to express my gratitude to G. C. Harcourt, my co-editor, and to Robert M. Solow for their help in revising this excerpt for publication here. The responsibility for the views expressed is solely my own.

(dC_t for $t = 0,\ldots, n$). The value of n, i.e. the duration of the technique, is determined by the choice of optimum technique; it covers all periods in which production either is, or has just ceased to be, efficient. (Production has become inefficient if the return on the first application of an input is less than that input's marginal return in the earlier periods. If the return on the first application equals that input's marginal return in earlier periods, so that production has just ceased to be efficient, that period must be included as one in which production might be increased by a marginal change in technique.)

The marginal increments which describe the change in technique must, because of the assumption of smoothness of the production function, satisfy the following equality:

$$\sum_{t=0}^{t=n} dI_t \, \frac{\partial C_m}{\partial I_t} = \sum_{t=0}^{t=n} dC_t \, \frac{\partial C_m}{\partial C_t}, \qquad 1$$

where m is a value of t in the range 0 to n. The partial derivatives in equation 1 are assumed now to be those of the optimum technique. If the partial derivatives are interpreted as market prices, equation 1 can be rearranged to show the change in capital invested at a particular stage, say, by the end of period $m-1$, for the given change in technique, as equal in value to the return on this extra investment. Thus:

$$\left(\sum_{t=0}^{t=m-1} dI_t \frac{\partial C_m}{\partial I_t} - \sum_{t=0}^{t=m-1} dC_t \frac{\partial C_m}{\partial C_t} \right)$$
$$= \left(\sum_{t=m}^{t=n} dC_t \frac{\partial C_m}{\partial C_t} - \sum_{t=m}^{t=n} dI_t \frac{\partial C_m}{\partial I_t} \right). \qquad 2$$

The left-hand side of equation 2 is the increment in investment at the end of period $m-1$ due to the change in technique and the right-hand side is the gross return (interest and principal) on it.[2] A more revealing form of equation 2 is obtained by valuing the increment in investment in terms of C_{m-1} and the return on it in terms of C_m. Since $(\partial C_m / \partial C_{m-1}) = (1+R)$, equation 2 becomes:

$$\left(\sum_{t=0}^{t=m-1} dI_t \frac{\partial C_{m-1}}{\partial I_t} - \sum_{t=0}^{t=m-1} dC_t \frac{\partial C_{m-1}}{\partial C_t} \right)(1+R)$$
$$= \left(\sum_{t=m}^{t=n} dC_t \frac{\partial C_m}{\partial C_t} - \sum_{t=m}^{t=n} dI_t \frac{\partial C_m}{\partial I_t} \right). \qquad 3$$

2. A result in this form was obtained by T. C. Koopmans in 1957. Details are given on page 37 in the Introduction.

Equation 3 implies that the net rate of return on the increment in investment at any stage of the optimum technique equals the market rate of interest, R. This is the first part of what we set out to prove and contains the essence of the matter.

Let us consider what the change in technique implies for the change in the total stock of capital needed in a stationary state. In any period there is an input–output cycle at each of the $(n+1)$ stages of the optimum technique, from the one beginning to the one ending in that period. For each of these input–output cycles an equation in the form of equation 3 can be written. In all the equations the period m, at the beginning of which invested capital is measured, is the same but the period in which the summations commence differs, ranging from $m-n$ to m. If the first terms in the summations on the right-hand side of equation 3 are separated out each equation can be written in the following form:

$$(\Delta K_{m-1,i})(1+R) = dC_{m,i} - dI_{m,i}\frac{\partial C_m}{\partial I_m} + \Delta K_{m,i}, \quad (i = 0,\dots, n) \quad 4$$

where K is the value of invested capital, its first suffix indicates the period in whose product the capital is valued and at the end of which the capital exists and i indicates the relevant input–output cycle. It should be noted that $\partial C_m/\partial I_m$ is the same for all the input–output cycles if, as we assume, only efficient techniques are used. Summing equations 4 over i we obtain:

$$(1+R) \sum^i \Delta K_{m-1,i} = \sum^i dC_{m,i} - \frac{\partial C_m}{\partial I_m} \sum^i dI_{m,i} + \sum^i \Delta K_{m,i}. \quad 5$$

But in a stationary state

$$\sum^i dI_{m,i} = 0$$

(total primary inputs are constant) and

$$\sum^i \Delta K_{m-1,i} = \sum^i \Delta K_{m,i}$$

(the stock of capital at the end of each period valued in the product of that period is constant). Equation 5 can therefore be written as:

$$R \sum^i \Delta K_{m-1,i} = \sum^i dC_{m,i},$$

i.e.
$$R = \frac{\sum^i dC_{m,i}}{\sum^i \Delta K_{m,i}}. \quad 6$$

This shows what we set out to prove because

$$\sum^i dC_{m,i}$$

is the increment in the total flow of final output in every period and

$$\sum^i \Delta K_{m,i}$$

is the increment in the stock of capital in every period.

There appears to be no difficulty in generalizing this result to cases in which there is more than one type of primary input and final output, and in which steady growth takes place.

We have already referred to Koopman's discovery of the essential part (equation 2) of the above argument. A very similar argument was used still earlier but in a different context by Champernowne. It can be found on pages 74–5 of Reading 2. Very similar, too, is Swan's defence of the 'neo-classical procedure' where he invokes the relation of short-run and long-run cost curves. See page 110, footnote 14, of Reading 3 and the passage in the text to which the footnote refers. Finally, mention should be made of the very closely related results of Solow (1967).

The significance of the result obtained in this note has seemed to the writer to be that it means that the equilibrium rate of interest, as determined by a steady-state analysis and on quite general assumptions about the nature of roundabout methods of production, *equals* the marginal product of capital. (This view is explained more fully in Part II of the Introduction.) But second thoughts have been made necessary by the criticism of Solow's results by Samuelson and Pasinetti. Samuelson (Reading 11, page 247) plays down their significance – 'as much a bookkeeping as a technical relationship'. Pasinetti criticizes Solow's results as being merely definitional.[3] The argument which has been presented in this note certainly starts from what is, on our assumption of the smoothness of the production function, an equality.

3. Unfortunately, it was impossible, for reasons of space, to reprint Pasinetti's criticism which occurs in section IX of the article from which Reading 13 is extracted. Essentially, it is an application to Solow's result of Pasinetti's argument as set out in footnote 9 on page 23 of the Introduction of this volume.

What this means is more than that the equilibrium rate of interest equals the marginal product of capital, although that is still true. It means that the equilibrium rate of interest *is* the marginal product of capital. That this is not an empty proposition follows from the fact that it is not true of non-optimum techniques. That it is an interesting addition to what we were already saying follows from the fact that it permits meaning to be created where none was obvious. We can now say, what we did not know before, that the *equilibrium* rate of interest is, by its nature, the marginal product of value capital.

Reference

SOLOW, R. M. (1967), 'The interest rate and transition between techniques', in C. H. Feinstein (ed.), *Socialism, Capitalism and Economic Growth. Essays Presented to Maurice Dobb*, Cambridge University Press, pp. 30–37.

18 R. Dorfman, P. A. Samuelson and R. M. Solow

Efficient Programmes of Capital Accumulation

Excerpt from R. Dorfman, P. A. Samuelson and R. M. Solow,
'Efficient programs of capital accumulation', in *Linear Programming
and Economic Analysis*, McGraw–Hill, 1958, pp. 309–25.

Introduction

The end result of the previous chapter [not included here] was
to supply us with the instantaneous technological transformation
locus (or production-efficiency locus):

$$T\{S_1(t), S_2(t); S_1(t+1)+C_1(t+1), S_2(t+1)+C_2(t+1)\} = 0. \qquad \mathbf{1}^{1}$$

Most of the time we shall want to use this locus in slightly different
form, after it has been solved for one of the net outputs, say,

$$S_2(t+1)+C_2(t+1) = F\{S_1(t+1)+C_1(t+1); S_1(t), S_2(t)\}. \qquad \mathbf{2}$$

These loci have the virtue of being able to include as special cases
almost any economic theorist's model of capital, for example,
the special point-input, point-output model of Jevons, the Böhm-
Bawerk triangular capital model, the various models involving
produced durable goods (Evans, Lange and others).

We know already that this instantaneous, one-period locus
requires many efficiency conditions to be satisfied in the background. It might naturally be thought that no more can be required in the way of production-efficiency conditions than that
the system be operating optimally at each and every instant of
time. Consumers or the market would then decide, via tastes
and time preference, how rapidly capital stocks are to grow to
increase future consumption possibilities at the expense of current consumption.

Such a view is short-sighted and incomplete. *It overlooks*

1. $S_n(t)$ is the stock of factor or commodity n at time t. $C_n(t)$ is the consumption of n at time t. In the function T the stocks of period t serve as
inputs in production and the stocks available as inputs in period $t+1$
together with the consumption of period $t+1$ are the outputs [*Eds.*].

important additional intertemporal production-efficiency conditions which have received little emphasis in the literature of economic theory. It is the task of this chapter to elucidate these multi-period requirements for optimality and to indicate some of the dual price and interest implications.

For this analysis we reverse the order of the previous chapter and study the smooth neoclassical production-possibility schedule first. Afterward comes the Leontief no-substitution model. This is to take advantage of the economist's familiarity with marginal-rate-of-substitution and own-rate-of-interest concepts. The Leontief case will then be clearer by analogy, and linear programming provides the needed analytical technique. Throughout this chapter we continue the previous convention of treating the graphically accessible case of two commodities and of counting time in discrete periods. The case of continuously flowing time can be handled by the more sophisticated methods of the calculus of variations in terms of n commodities and capital stocks, but we do not give this extension here.

Intertemporal efficiency conditions in the smooth case

The transformation function 2 can be thought of as derived from neoclassical production functions in which inputs are smoothly substitutable for each other, obeying the law of constant-returns-to-scale and the generalized law of smoothly diminishing returns as proportions are varied. It represents an efficiency frontier in the sense of giving the maximum obtainable $S_2(t+1)+C_2(t+1)$ for specified capital-stock availabilities $S_1(t)$ and $S_2(t)$ and specified carryover $S_1(t+1)+C_1(t+1)$. Because the underlying production functions have smooth marginal productivities, so will the transformation function F. Because we banish all scale effects, doubling all the variables in F will just double the left-hand side. F is a homogeneous function of the first degree.[2]

Intertemporal efficiency conditions

At any one point of time, F describes the best menu available to society. But life goes on. Whatever stocks $S_1(t+1)$ and $S_2(t+1)$ are retained will become the inputs to produce a menu for $t+2$.

2. This assumption could be lightened, but then the role of competitive market prices would become ticklish.

We must inquire whether extending the horizon in this way adds anything not already contained in our instantaneous efficiency locus. Imagine initial stocks $S_1(0)$, $S_2(0)$ to be given. Imagine consumption $C_1(1)$, $C_2(1)$ to be specified at whatever level tastes might have decreed. Then what maximum frontier or best menu of $S_1(2)+C_1(2)$, $S_2(2)+C_2(2)$ can we hope for at the end of two periods? We might just as well take $C_1(2)$, $C_2(2)$ as also specified and ask for the maximal frontier of capital stocks $S_1(2)$, $S_2(2)$ which we can bequeath to posterity. It is clear, or experiments will soon show, that there are numerous alternative time paths of development which do satisfy the instantaneous relations 2 at *each* period of time and which provide the same profile of consumption, but which wind up at the end of period 2 with different amounts of capital. One such path might easily end up with less of every capital stock than some other path. Obviously, we must regard such a time path as *inefficient, even though it satisfied 2 at $t = 0$ and $t = 1$.* The point is simply this: there are many efficient ways of providing $C_1(1)$ and $C_2(1)$, and each way leaves a different composition of capital stocks $S_1(1)$ and $S_2(1)$. Some of these capital stocks will be quite inappropriate for the subsequent provision of $C_1(2)$ and $C_2(2)$. We must select among the instantaneously efficient time paths only those whose final stocks cannot all be improved upon.

Figure 1(a) is familiar from the last chapter. For the initial endowment $S_1(0)$, $S_2(0)$ it shows how much is producible at time 1, over and above the prescribed consumption point R: $C_1(1)$, $C_2(1)$. Figure 1(b) shows the isoquant, or input aspect, of 2. To each point of outputs for period 2, such as S, there is a concave locus of *minimal* required inputs in the previous period, such as KL.

Now note that each and every point on the instantaneous efficiency frontier MN in Figure 1(a) will, after period 1's consumptions have been subtracted, be regarded as an initial input for the output of period 2. Hence every point such as a, b and c on MN generates in 1(c) a new and different instantaneous efficiency locus such as $M_a N_a$, $M_b N_b$, $M_c N_c$, etc. Intertemporal efficiency means that we want to get as north-east as possible in 1(c). Clearly, to get the most of both goods in this sense we must (and can) end up on the *envelope EF* of the separate loci $M_a N_a$,

M_b N_b, etc. The fact that perpetual one-period efficiency can be inefficient over longer periods can now be illustrated. If society wants commodities in period 2 in the proportions given by point S in 1(c), efficiency *requires* that the way station for $t = 1$ be

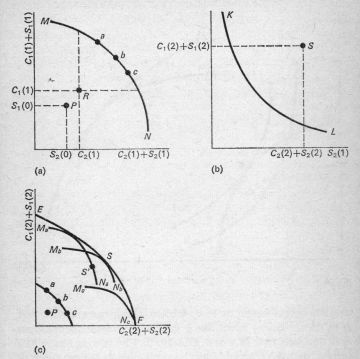

(a)

(b)

(c)

Figure 1

point b. A path to a, and thence to S', violates no one-period efficiency rule, but is inefficient compared with the path to b and S. Only paths leading to the envelope are efficient.

Anyone familiar with modern economic theory could guess the rule that leads to the efficiency envelope. He would suspect that marginal rates of substitution (MRS) must be proportional in some sense. And he would be right. We shall show presently that a necessary condition for intertemporal efficiency is the following: the MRS between any two goods regarded as outputs of the previous period must equal their MRS as inputs for the next period.

Graphically, this rule is shown by the tangency conditions in Figure 2. Point e is an efficient envelope point. Why? Because the

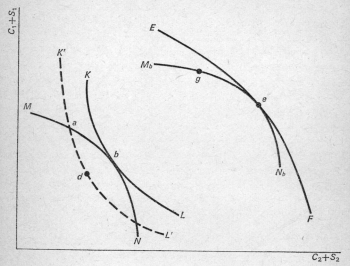

Figure 2

required-inputs isoquant to e, labeled KL, is tangential to MN at b. An inefficient point like g generates a requirements locus K'L' that intersects MN at a. Observe that by moving along MN from a toward b it would have been possible to achieve more of both stocks than at, say, d. But d can produce g. Hence g must be inefficient. This kind of production arbitrage through time is impossible if the MRS tangency conditions hold.

Analytic formulation

In terms of partial derivatives the proportionality rule can be written

$$\left[\frac{\partial S_2(1)}{\partial S_1(1)}\right]_{C_i(1) \text{ and } S_i(0) \text{ constant}} = \left[\frac{\partial S_2(1)}{\partial S_1(1)}\right]_{C_i(1) \text{ and } S_i(2) \text{ constant}}$$

or in terms of the derivatives of the transformation curve as

$$\frac{\partial F\{S_1(1)+C_1(1); S_1(0), S_2(0)\}}{\partial S_1(1)}$$
$$= -\frac{\partial F\{S_1(2)+C_1(2); S_1(1), S_2(1)\}/\partial S_1(1)}{\partial F\{S_1(2)+C_1(2); S_1(1), S_2(1)\}/\partial S_2(1)}. \quad 3$$

The left-hand side is the slope of MN, the right-hand side the slope of KL (Figure 2).

To derive this all-important marginal efficiency-envelope condition we have to maximize

$$S_2(2)+C_2(2) = F\{S_1(2)+C_1(2); S_1(1), S_2(1)\}$$

subject to prescribed $C_1(1)$, $C_2(1)$, $C_1(2)$, $C_2(2)$, $S_1(2)$, $S_1(0)$, $S_2(0)$ and

$$F\{S_1(1); S_1(0), S_2(0)\}-S_2(1)-C_2(1) = 0.$$

The variables in our problem are $S_1(1)$, $S_2(1)$ and $S_2(2)$. The last of these disappears because we can maximize F. We can also get rid of $S_2(1)$ by using the constraint. In abbreviated but unambiguous notation, we have to maximize

$$F\{S_1^2+C_1^2; S_1^1, F(S_1^1; S_1^0, S_2^0)-C_2^1\} = f(S_1^1)$$

since $S_1(1)$ is the only variable left. Hence all we have to do is differentiate with respect to S_1^1 and set $f'(S_1^1) = 0$. With a little calculation we get 3.[3]

We can strengthen our intuitive grasp of 3 by juggling it around to make it read

$$\frac{\partial F\{S_1(2)+C_1(2); S_1(1), S_2(1)\}}{\partial S_2(1)}$$
$$= -\frac{\partial F\{S_1(2)+C_1(2); S_1(1), S_2(1)\}/\partial S_1(1)}{\partial F\{S_1(1)+C_1(1); S_1(0), S_2(0)\}/\partial S_1(1)}. \quad 4$$

The left-hand side is $\partial S_2(2)/\partial S_2(1)$, a direct *own* rate of interest in terms of good 2. It shows how much more of good 2 we could dispose of over this period, had there been a little more of it in

---

3. The calculus-trained reader can work out the second-order convexity conditions that 3 determines a true maximum. We are assuming the maximum to be an interior one, so none of the non-decumulation, non-negativity conditions come into play.

the productive 'bank' in the previous period. The right-hand side is a little complicated. It tells us how much more of good 2 we could have in this period had we indirectly sacrificed some $S_2(1)$ to get more $S_1(1)$ (the denominator) and used the latter to produce more $S_2(2)$ (the numerator). The intertemporal efficiency condition 4 says that on the margin the direct and indirect processes must yield the same.

Many goods and many periods

Without going into detail it can simply be stated that the same envelope rule applies for any number of goods. Any pair of goods must satisfy the rule (as the reader can prove by holding all but two S constant and going through the previous reasoning). With three goods, this yields two independent conditions.[4] With n goods we select any one as *numéraire*, pair each of the other $n-1$ with it, and derive $n-1$ independent conditions, much like 3 or 4.

It is much more interesting and important to consider optimal programs extending over more than two future time periods. The two-good case will provide enough generality. Refer back to Figure 1(c). Starting with the initial stocks $S_1(0)$, $S_2(0)$ at P, and with all consumption points prescribed, we have the efficiency locus for $t = 1$, and the envelope frontier EF of goods that the system can have left at $t = 2$. Now what can $t = 3$ provide? Each point on EF in Figure 1(c) or Figure 2 can generate a new instantaneous efficiency locus in period 3, as shown by $R_f S_f$, $R_e S_e$, $R_g S_g$ in Figure 3(a). The best that society can arrange to do in this period is to reach the envelope $E'F'$, a sort of envelope-to-the-envelope.

The logic is the same for any future period. For $t = 4, 5, \ldots$, we wish to reach the maximal frontier compatible with technological possibilities, consumption profiles and initial conditions. Reflection shows that the solution to this problem is given by the succession of envelopes-to-envelopes-to-envelopes, etc. To see this it is enough to note that once we have found the maximal frontier for T periods of time, the frontier for $T+1$ periods must be the envelope of instantaneous efficiency loci starting from all points

4. There are three pairs that can be constructed from three goods. But if the rule holds for any two pairs, it must hold for the third.

of the T envelope. It can never pay to start from inside the *T* envelope, it is impossible to start from outside and this is the best that can be done from points on it. Figure 3(b) shows the proliferation of envelopes attainable at each subsequent period

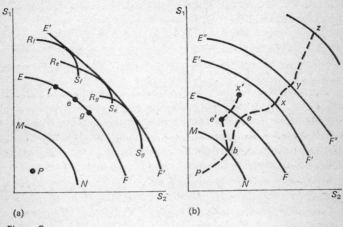

(a)   (b)

Figure 3

from the initial point P; it is understood that consumptions $C_i(1)$, $C_i(2)$,..., are specified. It will bear repeating that only paths which hop from envelope to envelope to envelope have any claim to efficiency. Once we are off the sequence of envelopes, a uniformly better point can be found, and hence a uniformly better future. Such an optimal path is *Pbexy ... z* in the diagram. *Pbe'x'* is inefficient.

The relationship between efficiency envelopes and efficient paths should be understood. The envelopes could be defined as the loci of successive terminal points on optimal paths. Conversely, optimal paths are those that go from envelope to envelope. Each optimal path crosses each efficiency envelope once and only once. Each point on an efficiency envelope lies on one optimal path (and only one, if we assume diminishing MRS).

Do we have to find new super-duper envelope rules to cover programs involving more than two periods? Fortunately not, and the above reasoning shows why. Our simple envelope rule 3 or 4 handles all cases! All we need do is replace 0, 1, 2 by t, $t+1$, $t+2$ and require the equation to hold for all t.

Formal analysis

The mathematical maximum problem involved is easily set down. We are given initial stocks $S_1(0) = S_1^0$, $S_2(0) = S_2^0$; consumptions $C_i(0) = C_i^0, C_i(1) = C_i^1,..., C_i(T) = C_i^T, i = 1, 2$; and one terminal stock $S_1(T) = S_1^T$. Subject to

$$F(S_1^t+C_1^t; S_1^{t-1}, S_2^{t-1})-C_2^t-S_2^t = 0 \quad (t = 1, 2,..., T),$$

maximize $\qquad S_2^T+C_2^T = F(S_1^T; S_1^{T-1}, S_2^{T-1}).$

The variables in this problem are the intermediate capital stocks S_1^1, S_1^2,..., S_1^{T-1}. The S_2^t could be eliminated by the instantaneous efficiency constraint, and the resulting function differentiated with respect to its remaining variables S_1^1, S_1^2,.... But this substitution procedure is lengthy, and here it is best to introduce Lagrange multipliers, one for each time period, and to write the new expression[5] as follows:

$$G = F(S_1^T+C_1^T; S_1^{T-1}, S_2^{T-1})+$$
$$+ \sum_{t=1}^{T-1} \lambda_t\{F(S_1^t+C_1^t; S_1^{t-1}, S_2^{t-1})-S_2^t-C_2^t\}$$
$$= F^T+ \sum \lambda_t[F^t-S_2^t-C_2^t].$$

Now differentiate with respect to S_1^t and S_2^t and set the derivatives equal to zero:

$$\frac{\partial G}{\partial S_1^t} = \lambda_t \frac{\partial F^t}{\partial S_1^t}+\lambda_{t+1} \frac{\partial F^{t+1}}{\partial S_1^t} = 0 \qquad (t = 1, 2,..., T-1)$$

$$\frac{\partial G}{\partial S_2^t} = -\lambda_t+\lambda_{t+1} \frac{\partial F^{t+1}}{\partial S_2^t} = 0 \qquad \lambda_T = 1, \text{ by convention.}$$

Hence, $\quad \lambda_t \frac{\partial F^t}{\partial S_1^t} = -\lambda_{t+1} \frac{\partial F^{t+1}}{\partial S_1^t}$

$$\lambda_t = \lambda_{t+1} \frac{\partial F^{t+1}}{\partial S_2^t},$$

and dividing one equation by the other we find

$$\frac{\partial F^t}{\partial S_1^t} = -\frac{\partial F^{t+1}/\partial S_1^t}{\partial F^{t+1}/\partial S_2^t}$$

5. Some readers may prefer to skip this paragraph and just look at the results.

or, written out in full, without abbreviation,

$$\frac{\partial F\{S_1(t)+C_1(t);\ S_1(t-1),\ S_2(t-1)\}}{\partial S_1(t)}$$
$$= -\frac{[\partial F\{S_1(t+1)+C_1(t+1);\ S_1(t),\ S_2(t)\}]/\partial S_1(t)}{[\partial F\{S_1(t+1)+C_1(t+1);\ S_1(t),\ S_2(t)\}]/\partial S_2(t)}$$
$$(t = 1, 2, ..., T). \quad \textbf{5}$$

Comparing this with **3**, we verify what was said above. The frontier for a T-period program is defined by the original two-period envelope condition **3**, repeated for each two-period stretch. The interpretation in terms of paths moving always from envelope to envelope has already been given.[6]

It is worth noting explicitly that **5**, together with the instantaneous locus itself,

$$S_2(t)+C_2(t) = F\{S_1(t)+C_1(t);\ S_1(t-1),\ S_2(t-1)\}$$
$$(t = 1, ..., T) \quad \textbf{2a}$$

provides a system of two *difference equations* for the unknown capital accumulation programs $S_1(t)$, $S_2(t)$. Equation **5** is of second order – it involves two lags; **2a** is of first order. Correspondingly there are three boundary conditions: $S_1(0)$, $S_2(0)$ and $S_1(T)$ are prescribed (as are the $C_i(t)$, which play the role of arbitrary functions). The dynamic efficiency equations are non-linear. We shall have to analyse them a bit more closely later.[7]

Own-rates of interest, flow prices and stock rents

We have already given a purely 'technocratic' interpretation of the efficiency conditions in terms of direct and indirect processes of production over time. It is natural to wonder whether a

6. The secondary conditions for a true maximum are too long-winded to be set down here. The calculus-trained reader should write them out for, say, $T = 3$, and interpret them in terms of generalized diminishing returns.

7. Instead of beginning with initial stocks as at P in Figure 3 and working outward to successive expanding envelopes, we could have begun with a prescribed terminal point $S_1(T)$, $S_2(T)$ and worked backward. First there is a locus of minimal requirements at $T-1$. Each point on this locus in turn generates a locus for $T-2$, and the inmost envelope of these loci gives the minimal requirements two periods earlier. An excellent exercise would be to carry through the formal analysis in terms of these ever-contracting requirement loci.

shadow-price formulation is possible, linking up intertemporal efficiency with competitive market behavior. Such is indeed the case.

Let the money price of a unit of commodity 1, delivered at time t, be $p_1(t)$ and that of the second commodity $p_2(t)$.[8] We also need the concept of the rent per period of each capital good S_i. Thus $r_1(t)$ is the rent, for the tth period, of the services of 1 unit of S_1, reckoned in money terms. Likewise $r_2(t)$ is the money rent per unit of stock S_2. These rents are *net* earnings over and above necessary maintenance and replacement expense.

Now consider r_1/p_1, the rent per period of 1 unit of S_1 divided by the price of 1 unit of S_1. This ratio is a pure number, or percentage, per unit time. If $r_1 = 2$ and $p_1 = 20$, then $r_1/p_1 = \frac{1}{10}$ and we may say that one period's use of S_1 costs $\frac{1}{10}$ unit of S_1. An owner of S_1 can consume one-tenth of his stock annually, and his rental earnings will just suffice to maintain his stock intact. In money terms he can consume $r_1(t)S_1(t)$. If he wishes to devote all his rents to investment in S_1, he can convert money rents of $r_1(t)S_1(t)$ into $\{r_1(t)S_1(t)\}/\{p_1(t)\}$ new units of S_1. Hence his capital stock will grow according to the rule

$$S_1(t+1) = S_1(t) + \frac{r_1(t)}{p_1(t)} S_1(t) = \left[1 + \frac{r_1(t)}{p_1(t)}\right] S_1(t). \qquad 6$$

From this formula it is clear that $r_1(t)/p_1(t)$ behaves like an interest rate; it is in fact the own-rate of interest per period of good S_1.[9]

The own-rates of different goods need not be equal in equilibrium. In fact, they must not all be equal if relative prices are changing. Any good whose relative price is rising will have a low own-rate; any good whose relative price is falling will have a high own-rate. The fundamental arithmetical relationship

8. Prices are quoted in money terms purely for convenience. There is no cash, and hence no liquidity problem, in our model economy. Money serves only as a unit of account. We could instead have chosen Commodity 1 as *numéraire* and set $p_1(t) \equiv 1$. Other commodity prices would then be expressed in terms of *numéraire*.

9. If S_1 were chosen as *numéraire*, so that $p_1 \equiv 1$, then the formula would reveal r_1 itself to be an own-rate. The *numéraire* own-rate is what we think of as *the* rate of interest, 'the rent of money'. Fisher, Wicksell, Marshall, Thornton, Sraffa, Keynes, Lerner and others have discussed own-rates.

between own-rates can be easily worked out. One dollar will buy $1/p_1(t)$ units of S_1. According to **6**, this will yield money rents of $r_1(t)/p_1(t)$ and the stock itself will have a sale value of $p_1(t+1)/p_1(t)$ in the next period. And the same applies to S_2. Under competition the net advantages of investing in the two stocks must be equal; hence,

$$\frac{r_1(t)}{p_1(t)}+\frac{p_1(t+1)}{p_1(t)} = \frac{r_2(t)}{p_2(t)}+\frac{p_2(t+1)}{p_2(t)} = r_0(t)+1. \qquad 7$$

The extreme-right-hand member shows what would happen to a *numéraire* good; that is, r_0 is essentially a money rate of interest. Equation **7** confirms that appreciating goods have low own-rates and depreciating goods have high own-rates. If the equivalence of **7** were not realized, an arbitrager could change from one kind of investment to another, thereby tending to make sure profits and also tending to wipe out the discrepancies. For example, if $r_1(t)/p_1(t)+p_1(t+1)/p_1(t)$ were to exceed $r_2(t)/p_2(t)+p_2(t+1)/p_2(t)$, it would clearly pay to convert cash and S_2 into S_1, to hold the S_1 (collecting rents) for one period, and then, if desired, to convert back to cash, or S_2. This would tend to increase $p_1(t)$, decrease $p_2(t)$ and restore the equality. Anyone will be content with a lower rent if he can be sure that his stock will be increasing relatively in value.

Competitive markets and dynamic efficiency

Now let us use what we know about competitive equilibrium to connect up these price relationships with technological characteristics. For stock rents we have the usual value-of-marginal-product equations and for commodity prices we have the usual MRS equations. Thus, $r_2(t)$ must equal the value (at next period's prices) of the marginal product of $S_2(t)$ in the production of $S_2(t+1)$.

$$r_2(t) = \left[\frac{\partial F\{S_1(t+1);\, S_1(t),\, S_2(t)\}}{\partial S_2(t)} - 1\right]p_2(t+1). \qquad 8$$

The -1 appears because we don't want to count the initial increment in $S_2(t)$ as part of its own marginal product. Using subscripts 1, 2 and 3 for partial derivatives with respect to the successive arguments, we can simplify the notation so that **8** becomes $r_2(t) = (F_3^{t+1}-1)p_2(t+1)$. Correspondingly, the net marginal product of $S_1(t)$ in producing $S_1(t+1)$ is $(-F_2^t/F_1^t)-1$, and we get

$$r_1(t) = \left(-\frac{F_2^{t+1}}{F_1^{t+1}}-1\right)p_1(t+1). \tag{8a}$$

Finally, the price ratio $p_1(t)/p_2(t)$ must under competition equal the MRS between $S_1(t)$ and $S_2(t)$ as outputs; hence,[10]

$$\frac{p_1(t)}{p_2(t)} = -F_1^t = \frac{\partial S_2(t)}{\partial S_1(t)}, \tag{8b}$$

$$\frac{p_1(t+1)}{p_2(t+1)} = -F_1^{t+1}. \tag{8c}$$

Equations **7** and **8a** to **c** are the competitive price and own-rate equilibrium conditions for a dynamic capital-accumulating system. We shall now show that *together they imply the purely 'technological' intertemporal efficiency conditions* **5**, which we deduced from entirely non-market considerations.

Insert **8** and **8a** in **7** to get

$$\left(-\frac{F_2^{t+1}}{F_1^{t+1}}-1\right)\frac{p_1(t+1)}{p_1(t)} + \frac{p_1(t+1)}{p_1(t)} = (F_3^{t+1}-1)\frac{p_2(t+1)}{p_2(t)} + \frac{p_2(t+1)}{p_2(t)}.$$

The last term on each side cancels off against the -1 in parentheses. In what is left, substitute for $p_1(t)$ and $p_1(t+1)$ from **8b** and **8c** and divide out common factors. What is left is

$$-\frac{F_2^{t+1}}{F_1^t} = F_3^{t+1}$$

or $$\frac{\partial F^t}{\partial S_1^t} = -\frac{\partial F^{t+1}/\partial S_1^t}{\partial F^{t+1}/\partial S_2^t}$$

which is nothing but **5**. This enables us to assert the following very important 'invisible-hand' principle.

10. The observant reader will remark that there are two more value-of-marginal-product equations that have not been written down: one for the use of $S_1(t)$ in producing $S_2(t+1)$ and one for the use of $S_2(t)$ in producing $S_1(t+1)$.
Exercise. Formulate these two equations and show that they follow from equations **8** to **8c** and so add no independent information. [Hint: the relevant marginal productivity of $S_1(t)$ is not $\partial F\{S_1(t+1); S_1(t), S_2(t)\}/\partial S_1(t)$, because a small increment of $S_1(t)$ will *ceteris paribus* increase $S_1(t+1)$; and this side effect on $S_2(t+1)$ must be canceled off. Hence $r_1(t) = (F_2^{t+1}-F_1^{t+1})p_2(t+1)$.]
Exercise. Using **8** and the calculations preceding **5**, interpret the Lagrangian multipliers λ_t.

If perfectly atomistic competitors cause resources to be channeled into consumption and investment programs so as (a) to maximize their current net profits or in any case to prevent net profits from becoming negative, and (b) to make it a matter of indifference how further increments of investment are scheduled, then an efficient program of capital accumulation will result.

This presumes no uncertainty so that *ex ante* expected prices or rates of change of prices -- which each competitor knows but cannot himself affect -- will correspond exactly to *ex post* observed prices. Under these strong assumptions of perfect certainty, where the *ex ante* future must agree with the *ex post* past, the whole future pattern of prices is knowable but each small competitor need know with certainty only the present instantaneous rate of change of prices.

A glance back at Figure 3(b) will reduce the relation of prices and intertemporal efficiency to familiar terms. An efficient capital program is one that hops from envelope to envelope, like *Pbexyz*. Now with each such efficient path we can associate exactly one profile of relative prices, that is to say, draw the successive tangent 'budget lines' to the envelopes at the successive points of the path. As usual the slopes of these tangent lines will give the relative prices corresponding to this particular path. There are various ways of verifying this. Perhaps the easiest is to recognize first that competitive current-profit maximization will necessarily equalize the price-ratio and the instantaneous MRS. This is the content of equation **8c**. But Figure 3(a) shows the basic envelope relationship according to which at each point of an efficient path its instantaneous transformation curve is tangential to (i.e. has the same slope as) the envelope. So the slope of the envelope will also come into equality with the price-ratio.

A geometrically obvious consequence of this is that along an efficient path, at each point of time the total value of capital stocks $p_1(t)S_1(t) + p_2(t)S_2(t)$ is at a maximum at the corresponding efficiency prices. In other words, if the whole history of future prices were to be announced initially, entrepreneurs would allocate resources in such a way as to maximize the current value of their assets at each point of time. But now we come to a subtle point. Not every time profile of relative prices can lead to consistent behavior in this way. In fact only price profiles which correspond to efficient paths will work. Any other price profile will lead to inconsistency of the following kind: a certain capital program will maximize, say, $V(t_0) = p_1(t_0)S_1(t_0) + p_2(t_0)S_2(t_0)$, for the given prices. But this program will involve $S_1(t_0-1)$, $S_2(t_0-1)$, and earlier capital stocks which do not maximize $V(t_0-1)$, etc., at the earlier given prices. In Figure 3(b), suppose that prices for $t = 3$ are announced which would maximize $V(3)$ at the point x. Then the corresponding capital program is $Pbex$. But if prices for $t = 2$ other than those determined by the slope at e were announced, then $V(2)$ and $V(3)$ could not *both* be maximized. This inconsistency does not arise if prices corresponding to an efficient path are announced. In this case entrepreneurial short-run and long-run maximization coincide.

But we have just finished proving that *under full competition only the consistent case can arise*. That is the meaning of the invisible-hand principle. The little-appreciated fact is that the arbitrage-induced own-rate relations 7 have this effect. They knit successive price-ratios together in such a way that only sequences leading to efficient programs can arise. Thus we needn't worry about arbitrarily announced time profiles of future prices. Under competitive assumptions only price ratios obeying 7 are eligible. Under such prices, long-run asset-value maximization and current-profit maximization coincide. Economic intuition should tell us this. In the example of the last paragraph, there is a clear differential between a program aimed at maximizing $V(3)$ by production and one aimed at first maximizing $V(2)$ by production and then by trade at current prices converting to capital stocks in proportions best suited to maximizing $V(3)$ in the next period. The function of competition is to wipe out such gaps, and no prices which permit them can endure.

The reader familiar with the theorems of modern welfare economics will not need to be reminded that competition guarantees only that *some* efficient capital program will be followed. There are infinitely many such time paths, fanning out from initial point P in Figures 3(a) and (b). One goes through each eligible[11]

11. If disinvestment is not allowed, only points on MN which are north-east of P are eligible, and a similar restriction must be made on EF, etc. Observe how this confines eligible paths to a sort of irregular cone emanating from P.

point of MN and continues on so that one path goes through each point of EF and $E'F'$, etc. A *particular* efficient program is picked out by the invisible hand only if one arbitrary bit of information is added, for example, the price-ratio at $t = 1$ (which picks out a point on MN and the corresponding path), or the price-ratio at some horizon date $t = T$ (which picks out the point of budget-line tangency on $E^{(T)}F^{(T)}$ and the path leading to it).

Mathematically, this arbitrariness reflects the fact that the difference equations of intertemporal efficiency, **2a** and **5**, were shown to be subject to three boundary conditions. Competition ensures that the equations will hold, and history provides two initial conditions. The remaining degree of freedom lets us pick out one more point through which the efficient path must pass.

The truly remarkable thing about the intertemporal invisible hand is that while it results in efficiency over long periods of time, it requires only the most myopic vision on the part of market participants. Just current prices and current rates of change need to be known, and at each moment long-run efficiency is preserved. But for society as a whole there is need for vision at a distance. If, for example, it is desired that at $t = T$ capital stocks should be in some given proportions $S_2(T)/S_1(T)$, only explicit calculation will show what prices $p_1(T)$, $p_2(T)$[12] need to be quoted in order that competition should lead a myopic market inevitably to the appropriate point on the envelope for $t = T$.

One interesting sidelight before we leave the subject of intertemporal pricing: consider any efficient capital program and its corresponding profile of prices and own-rates. *At every point of time the value of the capital stock at current efficiency prices, discounted back to the initial time, is a constant*, equal to the initial value. This law of conservation of discounted value of capital (or discounted net national product) reflects, as do the grand laws of conservation of energy of physics, the maximizing nature of the path.[13]

12. Or $p_1(1)$, $p_2(1)$.

13. The details of the proof are left to the reader who cares. It is to be shown that

$$\frac{p_1(t+1)S_1(t+1)+p_2(t+1)S_2(t+1)}{1+r_0(t)} = p_1(t)S_1(t)+p_2(t)S_2(t).$$

Here $r_0(t)$ is the 'money' rate of interest and can be substituted for in two

Maintainable consumption levels

Having deduced the relations that efficiency requires we are now in a position to investigate the behavior of efficient paths under special assumptions about consumption. We might consider (a) the case of zero net capital formation, with all the productive potential of the system going into consumption, or (b) the case of zero consumption (labor treated as just another stock) with all the productive potential going into capital accumulation, or (c) an intermediate case in which some fraction of available resources is used for current consumption and the remainder for net investment. Naturally, the more stringent the assumptions, the more we can say about the resulting paths. In this section we turn to the case a, in which capital is just being maintained intact.

By substituting $S_i(t+1) = S_i(t)$ into our transformation function **2a** we get

$$C_2(t+1) = F\{S_1(t) + C_1(t+1);\ S_1(t),\ S_2(t)\} - S_2(t). \qquad 9$$

This gives a whole frontier of possible consumption combinations that are obtainable from any given endowment of capital $S_1(t)$, $S_2(t)$. In fact equation **9** defines the consumption-possibility schedule of static economic theory. The capital stocks play the role of fixed non-augmentable resources. This consumption frontier is obtainable at the time t for which the capital stock is prescribed. But more than that, these consumption levels are steadily obtainable *from then on*. This is because of our assumption that capital is maintained intact, neither growing nor diminishing, so that this frontier repeats itself indefinitely.

Figure 4 shows the menu of different consumption bundles available for one particular stock of capital. Note the infinity of different consumption possibilities: the ones under the curve are clearly non-optimal.

In national-income statistics an attempt is made to give a single number which will characterize the consumption frontier. In real life where the number of commodities, however aggregated, greatly exceeds two, the national-income statistician is trying to

---

different ways from **7**. The rest is manipulation of **8** to **8c** and **5** and use of Euler's theorem on the homogeneous function F. It is simplest to assume all consumption to be zero.

use a single number – real national product – to summarize what is really a surface of $n-1$ dimensions, an $(n-1)$-fold infinity of different values.

So far we have been following Leontief in assuming that negative capital formation is physically impossible. The income statistician cannot make such a simplifying assumption; he knows

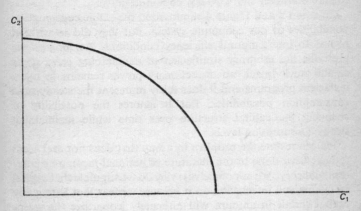

Figure 4

that economies can for a short time speed up their consumption levels at the expense of capital maintenance and replacement. Therefore he cannot accept any observed amounts of consumption and presume that they fairly reflect the economy's real national-product potential. He must make sure that the presupposition of 9 is realized, so that $S_i(t) = S_i(t+1)$; or, if this is not so, he must make appropriate allowances. Actually, in the simple case in which the flow of consumption is *addible* to the stock of capital, the statistician can work with the quantities $C_i(t+1)+S_i(t+1)$ or $C_i(t+1)+\Delta S_i$ and from them compute his measures of real product. All allowances for keeping capital intact will then have been made. His task would be somewhat more difficult, but our analytic task would not, if the transformation curve in 2 had been replaced by the more general and perhaps more realistic one:

$$S_2(t+1) = f\{S_1(t+1); C_1(t+1), C_2(t+1); S_1(t), S_2(t)\}.$$

All our previous analysis of efficiency would hold good except that now $\partial f/\partial C_i \neq \partial f/\partial S_i(t+1)$. However, note that up to now we have had no need of derivatives like $\partial f/\partial C_i$.

From now on we shall drop the assumption that net investment cannot be negative, but we shall retain the assumption that consumption and investment flows are additive and shall at most require that their sum $C_i + \Delta S_i$ be non-negative.

Equation 9 and Figure 4 summarized the stable consumption possibilities of our economic system. But they did so without regard to intertemporal efficiency conditions. As long as we prescribe the arbitrary straitjacket of maintaining *every single* capital stock intact, no discretionary power remains to reject inefficient programs and 9 does fairly represent the steady-state consumption possibilities. But it ignores the possibility of changing the capital structure over time while maintaining steady consumption levels.

We can restate the problem in a way that does not ever seem to have been done in the literature of national-income or pure-capital theory. We ask ourselves: why do we stipulate that capital be maintained intact? We do it because we fear that letting any capital shrink in amount will ultimately jeopardize the maintenance of current consumption levels. If we could be sure that current consumption could be indefinitely maintained, we would not care what specifically is happening to the various capital stocks.

Now it is easy to show that most of the consumption levels shown to be possible in equation 9 represent definitely inefficient capital programs maintained over time with zero net investment. If we pick at random one of the feasible consumption levels in Figure 4, someone else can show us how to get still more of every consumption good, forever.

For any given $\bar{S}_1$, $\bar{S}_2$ we can expect only one stationary consumption level to be efficient. For if we are to have $S_i(t) \equiv \bar{S}_i$ and $C_i(t) \equiv \bar{C}_i$, *and* our efficiency conditions 5 and 2 are to be satisfied, we must have

$$0 = F_2(\bar{S}_1 + \bar{C}_1; \bar{S}_1, \bar{S}_2) + F_1(\bar{S}_1 + \bar{C}_1; \bar{S}_1, \bar{S}_2)F_3(\bar{S}_1 + \bar{C}_1; \bar{S}_1, \bar{S}_2)$$
$$= F(\bar{S}_1 + \bar{C}_1; \bar{S}_1, \bar{S}_2) - \bar{S}_2 - \bar{C}_2. \qquad \textbf{10}$$

Here are two equations. If we take $\bar{S}_1$ and $\bar{S}_2$ as given, the law of diminishing returns assures us that we can solve these equations for one and only one set of consumptions $\bar{C}_1$, $\bar{C}_2$. Any other prescribed feasible consumption program must be inefficient.

Just what does inefficiency mean in this context? It means that (a) we can drop the assumption that each capital be maintained intact; (b) we can permit some stocks to increase and others to decrease; and (c) we can end up with a program that from now until kingdom come gives us more of every single consumption flow than the prescribed inefficient program.

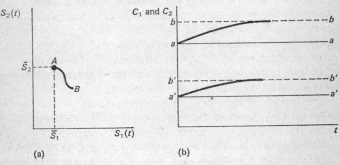

(a)   (b)

Figure 5

Figures 5(a) and (b) illustrate this. When $S_1(t) \equiv \bar{S}_1$ we stay at A in Figure 5(a) and enjoy steady consumption levels aa and $a'a'$ in Figure 5(b). By letting $\bar{S}_1$ increase and $\bar{S}_2$ decrease to B in Figure 5(a) we are able to enjoy the heavy-line consumption levels. Only the asymptotic levels bb and $b'b'$ corresponding to B are efficient levels satisfying 10. From A, some quite different consumption levels are efficient (although, when tastes are consulted, not necessarily *desirable*).

Any particular composition of capital stocks is appropriate for only one composition of steady consumption levels, namely, the consumption levels obtained by finding the efficient path with $\Delta S_i \equiv 0$, which gives 10, and then solving these equations for $\bar{C}_1$ and $\bar{C}_2$. If, as is overwhelmingly likely to be the case, the given initial capital structure is not appropriate for the particular desired steady-state consumption program, we can find the capital structure which is appropriate. All we have to do is solve equation 10 in reverse. By disinvesting in one stock and investing in the other, it will be possible simultaneously to improve consumption of both goods, preserving the desired proportion and over time to create a capital structure appropriate for the desired composition of consumption. As this is done, physical capital is not maintained intact, but the consumption potential to eternity is maintained and even improved.

In an efficient stationary state, defined by equation **10**, all the own-rates of interest are equal. (This follows from **10** in conjunction with equation **8** to **8c**.) In turn **7** or **8b** and **8c** then imply that relative prices are constant. If the economy is capable of capital growth in all its parts – and many economies dependent on exhaustible resources are not – the common own-rate of interest will be positive. Its numerical value will differ depending on the exact taste pattern for consumption flows. Though capable of growth, consumption is so large that the system is stationary. Consequently the earlier figures with expanding frontier envelopes are no longer appropriate. Consumption is here so great as to make the envelope be a single negatively inclined locus passing through the initial $\bar{S}_1$, $\bar{S}_2$ point.

Parenthetically we may remark that positive time preference in the Fisher or Böhm-Bawerk sense would have to be assumed if a maximizing individual or set of individuals is to come into such a stationary (efficient or inefficient) equilibrium.

Further Reading

General

A. Asimakopulos, 'A Robinsonian growth model in one-sector notation', *Austral. econ. Pap.*, vol. 8, 1969, pp. 41–58.

M. Blaug, *Economic Theory in Retrospect*, Heinemann, 2nd edn, 1968.

E. H. Carr, *What is History?*, Penguin, 1961.

A. Cockburn and R. Blackburn (eds.), *Student Power*, Penguin, 1969.

M. H. Dobb, *Political Economy and Capitalism*, Routledge & Kegan Paul, 1970.

R. Gårlund, *The Life of Knut Wicksell*, trans. N. Adler, Almqvist & Wiksell, 1958.

F. H. Hahn, 'Equilibrium dynamics with heterogeneous capital goods', *Q. J. Econ.*, vol. 80, 1966, pp. 633–46.

F. H. Hahn and R. C. O. Matthews, 'The theory of economic growth: a survey', *Econ. J.*, vol. 74, 1964, pp. 779–902.

G. C. Harcourt. 'G. C. Harcourt's reply to Nell', *J. econ. Lit.*, vol. 8, 1970, pp. 44–5.

G. C. Harcourt, *Some Cambridge Controversies in the Theory of Capital*, Cambridge University Press, in press.

J. R. Hicks, *Capital and Growth*, Clarendon Press, 1965.

R. F. Kahn, 'Exercises in the analysis of growth', *Oxf. econ. Pap.*, vol. 11, 1959, pp. 143–56.

N. Kaldor, *Essays on Value and Distribution*, Duckworth, 1960.

R. L. Meek, *Economics and Ideology and Other Essays. Studies in the Development of Economic Thought*, Chapman & Hall, 1967.

M. Morishima, *Theory of Economic Growth*, Clarendon Press, 1969.

E. H. Phelps Brown, *Pay and Profits*, Manchester University Press, 1968.

P. A. Riach, 'A framework for macro-distribution analysis', *Kyklos*, vol. 22, 1969, pp. 542–65.

J. Robinson, *Exercises in Economic Analysis*, Macmillan, 1960.

J. Robinson, *Essays in the Theory of Economic Growth*, Macmillan, 1962.

R. M. Solow, 'A contribution to the theory of economic growth', *Q. J. Econ.*, vol. 70, 1956, pp. 65–94.

G. J. Stigler, *Production and Distribution Theories*, Macmillan Co., 1941.

Vintage models and econometric applications of the concept of an aggregate production function

P. A. Diamond, 'Technical change and the measurement of capital and output', *Rev. econ. Stud.*, vol. 32, 1965, pp. 289–98.

F. M. Fisher, 'Embodied technical change and the existence of an aggregate capital stock', *Rev. econ. Stud.*, vol. 32, 1965, pp. 263–88.

G. C. Harcourt, 'Investment-decision criteria, capital-intensity and the choice of techniques', *Czech. econ. Pap.*, vol. 9, 1968, pp. 65–91. Reprinted in J. T. Dunlop and N. P. Federenko (eds.), *Planning and Markets. Modern Trends in Various Economic Systems*, McGraw-Hill, 1969, pp. 190–216.

B. S. Minhas, *An International Comparison of Factor Costs and Factor Use*, North-Holland Publishing Co., 1963.

W. E. G. Salter, 'Marginal labour and investment coefficients of Australian manufacturing industry' ,*Econ. Rec.*, vol. 38, 1962, pp. 137–56.

R. M. Solow, J. Tobin, C. C. von Weizsäcker and M. Yaari, 'Neoclassical growth with fixed factor proportions', *Rev. econ. Stud.*, vol. 33, 1966, pp. 79–115.

J. K. Whitaker, 'Vintage capital models and econometric production functions', *Rev. econ. Stud.*, vol. 33, 1966, pp. 1–18.

Prelude to a critique of (marginalist) economic theory

G. C. Harcourt and V. G. Massaro, 'Mr Sraffa's production of commodities', *Econ. Rec.*, vol. 40, 1964, pp. 442–54.

D. H. Robertson, 'Wage grumbles', in *Readings in the Theory of Income Distribution*, American Economic Association, 1949, pp. 221–36.

J. Robinson, 'Prelude to a critique of economic theory', *Oxf. econ. Pap.*, vol. 13, 1961, pp. 7–14. Reprinted in J. Robinson, *Collected Economic Papers*, vol. 3, Blackwell, 1965, pp. 7–14.

J. Robinson, 'A reconsideration of the theory of value', *New Left Rev.*, vol. 3, 1965, pp. 28–34. Reprinted in J. Robinson, *Collected Economic Papers*, vol. 3, Blackwell, 1965, pp. 173–81.

P. Sraffa, 'The laws of return under competitive conditions', *Econ. J.*, vol. 36, 1926, pp. 535–50.

The double-switching and capital-reversing debate

A. Bhaduri, 'The concept of the marginal productivity of capital and the Wicksell effect', *Oxf. econ. Pap.*, vol. 18, 1966, pp. 284–8.

M. Brown, 'Substitution-composition effects, capital intensity uniqueness and growth', *Econ. J.*, vol. 79, 1969, pp. 334–47.

M. Bruno, E. Burmeister and E. Sheshinski, 'Nature and implications of the reswitching of techniques', *Q. J. Econ.*, vol. 80, 1966, pp. 526–53.

M. Bruno, E. Burmeister and E. Sheshinski, 'The badly behaved production function: comment', *Q. J. Econ.*, vol. 82, 1968, pp. 524–5.

F. M. Fisher, 'The existence of aggregate production functions', *Econometrica*, vol. 37, 1969, pp. 553–77.

P. Garegnani, 'Switching of techniques', *Q. J. Econ.*, vol. 80, 1966, pp. 555–67.

D. Levhari and P. A. Samuelson, 'The nonswitching theorem is false', *Q. J. Econ.*, vol. 80, 1966, pp. 518–19.

M. Morishima, 'Refutation of the nonswitching theorem', *Q. J. Econ.*, vol. 80, 1966, pp. 520–25.

L. L. Pasinetti, 'Changes in the rate of profit and switches of techniques', *Q. J. Econ.*, vol. 80, 1966, pp. 503–17.

J. Robinson and K. A. Naqvi, 'The badly behaved production function', *Q. J. Econ.*, vol. 81, 1967, pp. 579–91.

L. Spaventa, 'Realism without parables in capital theory', in CERUNA, *Recherches récentes sur la fonction de production*, Universitaire de Namur, 1968, pp. 15–45.

The rate of profits in capitalist society

K. J. Arrow, 'The economic implications of learning by doing', *Rev. econ. Stud.*, vol. 29, 1962, pp. 155–73.

D. M. Bensusan-Butt, *On Economic Growth. An Essay in Pure Theory*, Clarendon Press, 1960.

M. Bruno, 'Fundamental duality relations in the pure theory of capital and growth', *Rev. econ. Stud.*, vol. 36, 1969, pp. 39–55.

D. G. Champernowne, 'A note on J. von Neumann's article on "A model of economic equilibrium"', *Rev. econ. Stud.*, vol. 13, 1945–6, pp. 10–18.

P. Davidson, 'The demand and supply of securities and economic growth and its implications for the Kaldor–Pasinetti versus Samuelson–Modigliani controversy', *Amer. econ. Rev., Pap. Proc.*, vol. 58, 1968, pp. 252–69.

J. Hirschleifer, 'A note on the Böhm-Bawerk/Wicksell theory of interest', *Rev. econ. Stud.*, vol. 34, 1967, pp. 191–9.

E. J. Nell, 'A note on the Cambridge controversies in capital theory', *J. econ. Lit.*, vol. 8, 1970, pp. 41–4.

L. L. Pasinetti, 'A comment on Professor Meade's "Rate of profit in a growing economy"', *Econ. J.*, vol. 74, 1964, pp. 488–9.

L. L. Pasinetti, 'The rate of profit in a growing economy: a reply', *Econ. J.*, vol. 76, 1966, pp. 158–60.

L. L. Pasinetti, 'New results in an old framework', *Rev. econ. Stud.*, vol. 33, 1966, pp. 303–6.

J. Robinson, 'Comment on Samuelson and Modigliani', *Rev. econ. Stud.*, vol. 33, 1966, pp. 307–8.

The Golden Rule

M. Allais, 'The influence of the capital–output ratio on real national income', *Econometrica*, vol. 30, 1962, pp. 700–728.

A. Asimakopulos, 'The biological interest rate and the social utility function', *Amer. econ. Rev.*, vol. 57, 1967, pp. 185–90.

J. Black, 'Technical progress and optimal savings', *Rev. econ. Stud.*, vol. 29, 1962, pp. 238–40.

D. G. Champernowne, 'Some implications of Golden Age conditions when savings equal profits', *Rev. econ. Stud.*, vol. 29, 1962, pp. 235–7.

J. Desrousseaux, 'Expansion stable et taux d'intérêt optimal', *Annales des Mines*, vol. 25, 1961, pp. 829–44.

R. Findlay, 'Optimal investment allocation between consumer goods and capital goods', *Econ. J.*, vol. 76, 1966, pp. 70–83.

S. Gomulka, 'Extensions of the Golden Rule of Research', *Rev. econ. Stud.*, vol. 37, 1970, pp. 73–94.

J. A. Hanson and P. A. Meher, 'The neo-classical theorem once again', *Amer. econ. Rev.*, vol. 57, 1967, pp. 869–78.

J. G. M. Hilhorst, 'Is a Golden Age attainable?', *Weltwirtschaftliches Archiv*, vol. 1C, 1967, pp. 11–22.

K. Inada, 'On stability of the Golden Rule path in the Hayekian production process case', *Rev. econ. Stud.*, vol. 35, 1968, pp. 335–45.

L. M. Koyck and M. J. Welvaars, 'Economic growth, marginal productivity and the rate of interest', in F. H. Hahn and F. P. Brechling (eds.), *The Theory of Interest Rates*, St Martin's Press, 1965.

N. F. Laing, 'A geometric analysis of some theorems on steady growth', *J. polit. Econ.*, vol. 72, 1964, pp. 476–82.

N. F. Laing, 'On optimal paths of steady growth in neo-classical models', *Austral. econ. Pap.*, vol. 7, 1968, pp. 54–68.

N. Liviatan and D. Levhari, 'The concept of the Golden Rule in the case of more than one consumption good', *Amer. econ. Rev.*, vol. 58, 1968, pp. 100–119.

A. L. Marty, 'The neo-classical theorem', *Amer. econ. Rev.*, vol. 54, 1964, pp. 1026–9.

J. E. Meade, *A Neo-Classical Theory of Economic Growth*, Allen & Unwin, 2nd edn 1961 (see especially pp. 110–13).

J. E. Meade, 'The effect of savings on consumption in a state of steady growth', *Rev. econ. Stud.*, vol. 29, 1962, pp. 227–34.

E. S. Phelps, 'The Golden Rule of Accumulation: a fable for growthmen', *Amer. econ. Rev.*, vol. 51, 1961, pp. 638–43.

E. S. Phelps, 'Second essay on the Golden Rule of Accumulation', *Amer. econ. Rev.*, vol. 55, 1965, pp. 793–814.

E. S. Phelps, 'Models of technical progress and the Golden Rule of Research', *Rev. econ. Stud.*, vol. 33, 1966, pp. 133–45.

J. Robinson, 'A neo-classical theorem', *Rev. econ. Stud.*, vol. 29, 1962, pp. 219–26.

J. Robinson, 'Comment', *Rev. econ. Stud.*, vol. 29, 1962, pp. 258–66.

P. A. Samuelson, 'Comment', *Rev. econ. Stud.*, vol. 29, 1962, pp. 251–4.

P. A. Samuelson, 'A catenary turnpike theorem involving consumption and the Golden Rule', *Amer. econ. Rev.*, vol. 55, 1965, pp. 486–96.

K. Sato, 'Neo-classical theorem and distribution of income and wealth', *Rev. econ. Stud.*, vol. 33, 1966, pp. 331–5.

R. M. Solow, 'Note on Uzawa's two-sector model of economic growth', *Rev. econ. Stud.*, vol. 29, 1961, pp. 48–50.

R. M. Solow, 'Comment', *Rev. econ. Stud.*, vol. 29, 1962, pp. 255–7.

T. W. Swan, 'Growth models of Golden Ages and production functions', in K. E. Berrill (ed.), *Economic Development with Special Reference to East Asia*, Macmillan, 1963, pp. 3–18.

C. C. von Weizsäcker, *Wachstum, zins und optimale investitionsquote*, Kylos Verlag, Basel, 1962.

C. C. von Weizsäcker, 'Lemmas for a theory of approximate optimal growth', *Rev. econ. Stud.*, vol. 34, 1967, pp. 143–51.

Acknowledgements

Acknowledgements are due to the following for permission to reproduce the Readings in this volume:

1 Joan Robinson
2 *Review of Economic Studies* and D. G. Champernowne
3 *Economic Record* and T. W. Swan
4 Cambridge University Press
5 *Review of Economics and Statistics* and K. J. Arrow, H. B. Chenery, B. S. Minhas and R. M. Solow
6 North-Holland Publishing Company
7 Joan Robinson
8 Asian New Age Publishers
9 University of Chicago Press
10 *Review of Economic Studies* and P. A. Samuelson
11 *Quarterly Journal of Economics* and P. A. Samuelson
12 *Economic Journal* and A. Bhaduri
13 *Economic Journal* and L. L. Pasinetti
14 *Economic Journal* and J. E. Meade
15 *Review of Economic Studies* and N. Kaldor
16 *Economic Journal* and D. M. Nuti
17 N. F. Laing
18 McGraw-Hill Book Company

Author Index

Subject Index